The Ether

"*The Ether* is a thrilling fictional adventure about a very real battle that is happening right now—the battle between good and evil. If this book had only been an imaginative, spiritual adventure story I would have still loved it, but it is so much more—it's a book about the fight to discover the strength and true purpose that lies within each of us."

Crystal McVea –author of *New York Times bestseller* *Waking up in Heaven*

The Ether

VERO RISING

BOOK ONE

LAURICE E. MOLINARI

Also by Laurice Elehwany Molinari

Screenplays
My Girl (Columbia Pictures)

The Brady Bunch Movie (Paramount Pictures)

The Amazing Panda Adventure (Warner Bros.)

Anastasia (Fox Animation Studios)

Bewitched (Columbia Pictures)

ZONDERKIDZ

The Ether
Copyright © 2014 by Laurice E. Molinari

This title is also available as a Zondervan ebook. Visit www.zondervan.com/ebooks.

Requests for information should be addressed to:

Zonderkidz, 3900 Sparks Drive, Grand Rapids, Michigan 49546

ISBN 978-0-310-73555-7

Editor: Kim Childress
Cover illustration: Randy Gallegos
Interior design: David Conn & Ben Fetterley

Printed in the United States of America

14 15 16 17 18 19 /DCI/ 20 19 18 17 16 15 14 13 12 11 10 9 8 7 6 5 4 3 2 1

For Naz, who taught me the power of words from a young age ... 'til we dine at the Bumbingba restaurant.

CONTENTS

1

❖

THE LEAP
OF FAITH

Vero Leland had been trying to fly ever since he was old enough to stand. His earliest memory was standing on the rail of his crib, perfectly balanced like an Olympic gymnast on a balance beam. He fully expected his mother to clap when she turned around and saw him. Vero remembers stretching out his arms, intending to fly into his mother's outstretched hands. But instead of clapping, she turned and let out a heartrending shriek. Startled, Vero hit the floor with a thud and cried hard as his mother cradled him.

But what Vero's mother, Nora, didn't realize was that Vero wasn't crying in pain. He was crying tears of frustration from failing to get airborne.

After the crib incident, Vero didn't stop trying to fly. Instead, he became quite the climber. He'd climb and throw himself off the kitchen table, his parents' bed, the piano, and pretty much anything with a few feet of air below it ... until the winter of his fourth year. That's when his flying attempts reached a new and dangerous high.

It happened late one afternoon when Dennis Leland, Vero's father, was standing on a ladder and stringing hundreds of Christmas lights across the front of their two-story suburban house. Dennis was very particular about his holiday light display. Each bulb needed to hang exactly two inches away from the next, and they all had to extend fully, to just beneath the gutter. Christmas displays were taken very seriously in their suburban neighborhood of Attleboro, Maryland.

The men who lived on Vero's block had an ongoing competition, and each December the holiday displays grew more and more elaborate. Front yards were cluttered with inflatable Santas, seven-foot tall snowmen, and animatronic reindeer. One dad even convinced his wife and young children to perform a live nativity each night, complete with a real donkey and goat. However, the goat was quickly sent back to the petting zoo after it ate the plastic sprinkler heads, causing impressive geysers that drenched his family and ruined the nativity.

It was a clear but chilly December day when Vero's father climbed down the ladder to test the magnificent light show. Wearing his one-piece brown coveralls and his checkered hat with earflaps, he rubbed his hands together and said, "This is it, Vero."

With great pomp and ceremony, Dennis dramatically picked up the plug of the extension cord ... all of his hard work was about to come to fruition. But when he finally took a deep breath and plugged the extension cord into the outlet, nothing happened. The lights failed to illuminate. Vero heard him use a word he'd never heard before, followed by, "I'm gonna have to check every stinkin' light bulb one at a time."

A few minutes later, Dennis grumbled miserably as he started to climb the ladder with some extra bulbs in hand.

Vero called down to his father and said, "It's okay, Daddy. I can help." While his dad had been inside the house getting some fresh bulbs, Vero had climbed the ladder and now stood proudly on the roof. Being small and nimble, Vero thought he could walk along the steep roof and check each one of the bulbs for his dad, saving him numerous trips up and down the ladder.

Vero could tell his dad was thrilled with the idea because Dennis was standing completely still on the ladder and looking at Vero with huge eyes. But when Vero caught sight of the surrounding neighborhood below, his penchant for flying took hold of him again.

"Daddy! I could fly from up here!" Vero shouted, grinning wildly.

"No, Vero! No!" his father shouted. "Don't move! I'm coming to get you!" He took two more steps up the ladder before his boot slipped, and he fell smack on his back. Luckily, a small bush broke his fall.

"Daddy, are you okay?"

Then piercing shrieks were heard as Vero's mother ran out of the house wearing an apron splattered with powdered sugar. Her cries alerted the curious neighbors.

Mr. Atwood from next door was the first one on the scene, since he was already outside admiring his "It's a Small World" display. He didn't notice Vero up on the roof at first.

"For Pete's sake," he said. "Calm down the both of you. It's probably just a bum light bulb." Then he glanced up and saw Vero peering down at them. "Holy cow!" he yelled. "That kid's crazy!"

When Mrs. Atwood arrived moments later, Mr. Atwood wagged his stubby finger in his wife's stunned face and said, "I told you that kid was off, but you never believed me! Remember that time I found him in our tree trying to jump off a branch that was as high as the house? I almost broke my neck climbing up after him!"

"Quiet, Albert! I'm calling 9 – 1 – 1!" Mrs. Atwood yelled, cell phone in hand.

"Maybe it's all a big stunt to draw attention to his Christmas display?" Mr. Atwood muttered to himself as he watched more and more neighbors gather. "I wouldn't put it past Leland."

Vero's father, meanwhile, had regained his footing and was attempting to climb the ladder once again.

"Yes, hurry!" Mrs. Atwood shouted into the phone. "The wind is gusting. It could knock the boy clear off the roof!"

Mrs. Atwood ended the call and then turned to help Vero's mother, who looked to be in a state of shock. She took off her coat and wrapped it around Nora's shoulders. "The dispatcher promised the fire truck would be here any minute."

"Vero, please don't move ... " his mother said weakly. Vero saw she had flour on her cheek, streaked with a teardrop.

"Don't cry, Mommy," Vero told her. "I know I can do it this time."

Vero's five-year-old sister, Clover, joined them outside.

She'd been baking cookies with her mother, and she had flour in her blonde hair and down the front of her shirt. She opened her arms wide and called up to her little brother, "Jump, Vero! I'll catch you!"

Nora quickly clasped a hand over her daughter's mouth.

By now Vero's father had reached the top of the ladder. He tried to grab his son, but Vero was beyond arm's reach; so he only managed to graze Vero's foot with his fingertips.

As Vero inched away from his dad, he became unsteady on his feet, and a collective gasp rippled over the gathering below. Yet somehow Vero regained his balance, and the watching crowd breathed a sigh of relief.

It was all too much for Vero's mother who fainted. Luckily she landed in the lap of the inflatable Mrs. Claus.

Mrs. Claus is cradling Mommy like a baby, Vero thought. And that's when a shiny red hook and ladder fire truck pulled around the corner with its siren blaring.

Vero felt absolutely wonderful. He smiled broadly and stretched his arms out wide, feeling the cold rush of the oncoming wind. It was exhilarating!

The fire truck's ladder swiftly extended, and a fireman stood in the enclosed basket, ready to carry Vero back to the safety of the ground below.

Vero watched as Mr. Atwood cautiously approached the fire captain now standing beside the hook and ladder. When the fire captain finished barking orders into his walkie-talkie, Mr. Atwood said, "Captain, when this is all over, would you mind helping me out next door? I really need a lift in your basket. You see, I've got this Santa that I'd like to stick upside down in my chimney so it looks like he's diving in headfirst."

Fire Captain Conrad looked at Mr. Atwood incredulously. "Absolutely not," he said. Then he turned to the crowd and shouted, "Clear the area! We're trying to save a life here!"

Vero saw Mrs. Atwood slap the back of Mr. Atwood's head as they moved away from the truck.

"Hi, Vero," the fireman in the basket said, as the basket stopped level with the roof's peak. "Climbing onto a roof is a first for you, isn't it? We've done this in trees before, but never on a roof—at least not with me."

Vero looked at the fireman and smiled in recognition.

"Hi, Fireman Bob," Vero said.

"It's okay, Vero. Don't be afraid. I'm gonna help you just like I did before," Fireman Bob said slowly, as he reached his arms toward Vero.

But Vero wasn't scared. He looked down and saw that his mother was slowly waking up in Mrs. Claus's inflatable arms. And just as Fireman Bob almost grabbed him, Vero took a deep breath, jumped backward off the roof peak, and disappeared behind the house!

The neighbors gasped. Vero's mother immediately passed out again.

After Vero leapt off the house, the wind whipped against his face, and he felt like a bird soaring through the sky! Free-falling felt as natural to him as breathing.

But Vero's flying ecstasy was short-lived. Some powerful force—something other than the hard ground—abruptly ended his peaceful flight. He felt a sudden tightening around his chest like a yo-yo being yanked backward on a string.

Vero suddenly found himself in the arms of a man who'd somehow caught him in midair.

"Vero," the man said, "that's enough with the flying."

Vero didn't recognize him as one of the neighbors. He was an older man with longish silver-white hair, a closely trimmed beard, and violet eyes. He wore jeans and a red puffy winter coat.

"I can't always be here to catch you," the man said. "I need you to promise me you'll stop."

"But I have to fly," Vero told him.

"In time," the stranger replied, and he gently lowered Vero to the ground. "Everything in its own time. But for now, I need you to promise me you won't try to fly again until you know it's the right time."

Vero looked hard at the man. There was something familiar and likeable about him, and Vero thought he could trust him. Yet at the same time, Vero knew the man meant what he said.

"Vero?"

Four-year-old Vero nodded. "Okay, Santa," he said, and he grabbed the man's beard with both hands.

"I'm not Santa Claus."

"But you're wearing a red coat ... "

The stranger chuckled and said, "I'm too thin to be Santa Claus." As they heard the frenzied crowd rushing toward the backyard from the front of the house, the man locked eyes with Vero and said, "I expect you to keep your word."

Vero nodded again.

"All right. Now, I'm sorry about this next part, but it has to look believable," the man told him. And with that, the man twisted Vero's left ankle.

Vero screamed in pain, "That hurt!"

"I'm letting you off easy. It's only a sprain. Protocol says I should break both of them."

The panicked crowd descended upon Vero who was now sitting on the ground holding his ankle.

"He's alive!" shouted the fire captain.

Vero's father picked him up and hugged him tightly, and his mother had awakened and was right beside him. Vero saw tears streaming down his father's face, and his mom had flour-streaked tear marks across both cheeks now. Vero felt bad for upsetting them.

Clover walked up and said, "He's okay. The man just twisted his ankle."

"What man?" her father asked.

"The one sitting in that tree," she pointed.

Everyone looked at the tree. There was no man in it.

Mr. Atwood shook his head and muttered, "She's just as crazy as her brother."

2

BIRDS OF FLIGHT

Vero gave up his attempts to fly, but not because his parents installed safety bars on all the upstairs windows. Vero stopped because he didn't want to break his promise to the man who'd caught him. However, staying grounded wasn't easy.

On the family's vacation to Maine last summer, they'd hiked along cliffs overlooking the ocean, and Vero had to fight the urge to throw himself off the precipice and soar over the magnificent deep blue water below. He quickly jumped back and hugged the rock walls, as sweat poured down his face.

"Vero, what's wrong?" his mom asked.

"I . . . I . . . guess it's the height," Vero said. He couldn't let her know the truth.

"Wimp," Clover said. "Do you need to be carried the rest of the way?"

"Clover ... " Nora said in her warning voice.

"Keep your eyes on your feet and don't look up," Vero's dad advised. "Follow the path that way, and you'll make it to the bottom just fine."

Vero put on a good show. He did as his father instructed, made it safely to their rented cottage, and then stretched out on the sofa.

His mom felt his forehead and said, "You're a little warm."

"I'm okay."

Ignoring him, she spread a cool wet washcloth across his forehead. "Lie here for a while," she said.

Vero did as his mother instructed. As a matter of fact, because the allure of the cliffs proved to be so strong, he stayed on the sofa for pretty much the whole vacation, just watching TV and playing video games.

"If I'd known you were going to spend our entire vacation sitting in this cottage, we could have saved the money and stayed home," Vero's dad said.

He's right, Vero thought. *Just not for the reason he imagines.*

Last year while on a field trip to a local amusement park, Vero's friends harassed him because he wanted to ride on the Twirly—the giant carousel swings that rise up from the ground and spin around and around.

"Come on, Vero! Let's go on the Cyclone!" his best friend Tack said.

They stood on the pavement between the two rides and

watched the Cyclone pass by overhead, spinning its screaming passengers upside down.

"I heard some kid puked on it earlier!" Tack said. "It's so
awesome!"

Vero watched the coaster spin away and said, "Nah, I
think I'll stay here. Come find me when you're done."

"I think it's lame, but whatever," Tack said. Then he
ran off in the direction of the Cyclone, with his running
shorts slipping down and his strawberry-blond hair sticking straight up. "Wait up!" Tack called to their buddy Nate
Hollingsworth.

Vero rode the Twirly thirty-seven times that day. The
attendant kept track and let Vero know what number he
was at. "I ain't never seen no kid ride it so many times," the
attendant said. His name was Gary. He and Vero became
friends that day.

"What can I say?" Vero said, shrugging. "I like to swing."

But the thing was, if he closed his eyes and spread out his
arms on that ride, the sensation of the wind rushing against
his face and ripping through his hair made him feel like he
was flying—if only for a few minutes. He didn't care what
anyone else said. And that was a good thing because Tack
made fun of him the whole ride home.

Though he tried to avoid it, tried to ignore it, Vero's obsession with flying got him in trouble even with his feet firmly
planted on the ground.

Vero was now banned from the local pet store. The Pet
Place had dogs, cats, reptiles, rodents, and birds for sale, and

a photo of Vero's face was stuck to every cash register with a big red line written through it. If an employee saw Vero, he was to kick him out of the store immediately.

The Pet Place problems began one day when Vero and his family were strolling the suburban strip mall, eating ice cream they'd just purchased from the parlor boasting forty-seven flavors. Vero walked past the Pet Place and was suddenly overcome with such an intense and overwhelming sensation of suffocation and sadness that he doubled over and clutched his chest in pain. He'd been lagging behind his family, so Clover and his parents didn't see him when he dropped his ice cream cone and walked through the open doors of the pet store.

As he approached the bird section of the store, he saw cage upon cage of birds—macaws, canaries, exotics, and plain old finches. Vero locked eyes with a blue and gold Macaw.

Help me.

Vero heard the voice as if the bird had spoken the words aloud. Vero knew what he had to do.

Slowly, he reached out his hand and unhinged the cage door. The Macaw bowed his head in gratitude and flew straight through the open doors of the pet store. Vero then opened the next cage, and the next, until all of the cage doors were standing wide open. At first, some of the larger birds blinked and hopped to their door, unsure of what to do next. But when Vero opened the finches' cage and dozens and dozens of birds flew out through the main doors, the larger birds finally followed—just as Vero's family walked inside the store to look for him.

Vero's parents and sister ducked and yelled as the birds escaped to freedom right above their heads. "What is this, a scene from *The Birds?*" Vero's father asked. The pet store was now pure pandemonium.

With each flying bird, Vero felt the weight on his chest grow lighter and lighter.

Vero cost his parents a pretty penny that day, as the store manager expected them to pay for the lost birds. Vero would be doing chores for more than a year before his debt was paid off, but Vero didn't care. He'd do it again in a heartbeat. But he was no longer allowed in the store.

The local paper ran a story on the incident; but when the reporter called the house, Vero's parents wouldn't let him comment.

Vero was also banned from playing any neighborhood games after dark—by the neighbor kids. One hot summer night, Angus Atwood—only child to the Atwood family and a year older than Vero—distributed the Atwood family's collection of canning jars to all of the neighbor kids for catching fireflies. But Vero refused to take one. And he also chased the fireflies away, making them nearly impossible to catch, although a few kids still caught some.

"What's wrong with you, Vero?" Clover asked, her green eyes flashing dangerously. She stomped off for home to tell on him.

After Clover left, Vero grabbed Angus's jar and threw it on the cement sidewalk, shattering it and sending shards of glass flying everywhere.

"What'd you do that for?" Angus shouted.

"How would *you* like to be trapped in a jar?" Vero shouted back.

"Who cares? They're just stupid bugs!"

The other kids opened their jars and let the fireflies escape after that, but Angus was determined. He caught a firefly in his hand and stuffed it in a jar. Angus then screwed the lid on tight and held the jar high above Vero's head.

Vero watched as the firefly desperately smashed its body against the glass, trying to escape its prison. Vero grew more distressed as the firefly's light began to dim. As Angus jumped up to catch another firefly, Vero charged him. He ran headfirst into Angus's stomach, knocking the wind out of him and the canning jar out of his hand.

The jar rolled down the sidewalk, and Vero chased after it, catching it just before it rolled into a storm drain. Then he unscrewed the lid and set the firefly free.

"My dad's right!" Angus yelled after him. "You're a lunatic!"

3

❖

LOUSY BIRTHDAY

"Hurry up and blow out the candles!" Clover said. "I'm missing my show."

"Quiet, Clover," Nora said, sliding the soccer ball themed birthday cake closer to Vero. "You only turn twelve once."

Vero looked at Clover with sad, steely gray eyes.

Clover knew she was being mean. She didn't like doing it, but she had to. Still, she mumbled, "Sorry."

Immediately, Vero's eyes brightened. His eyes were the first things people seemed to notice about him. Typically a vivid pale gray like the wintertime sky, they changed between shades of blue, green, and gray, depending on the surrounding lighting. When Clover was small, she'd told Vero that his eyes were just like the mood ring she'd won at the state fair.

Vero's hair was dark brown, and height-wise he usually got placed in the middle row in the class picture. He'd always been skinny, and it drove Clover crazy when one of her friends would lift Vero up and spin him around because he weighed hardly anything. Her best friend Vicki especially loved to flip him over her hip when practicing her Judo moves.

But as Clover watched Vero lean over his birthday candles that night, she noticed he was sitting taller in his chair. It also looked like he'd finally started putting on some weight. She wondered if Vicki would be able to lift him anymore.

In every way, Vero looked like a normal twelve-year-old boy. But Clover knew he wasn't normal.

"Make a wish," Nora said.

"I wish this party would end," Clover said.

"Knock it off, Clover," Dennis said.

Vero sighed. He and Clover used to be so close. What happened?

Even though they looked nothing alike and Clover was a year older than Vero, there was a time when Clover insisted they were twins. She had brilliant green eyes, which was how she got her name. She was tall and slender like their mom. Her hair was long and blonde, and she usually wore it in a ponytail under a baseball cap. She was very pretty, but she didn't act like she knew it.

Clover used to laugh at Vero's jokes. They used to play soccer on the same coed team. They even sat next to each other on the school bus, where Clover told Vero stories she'd made up. Vero loved her stories about monsters and other creatures. Clover had always insisted the creatures were real—that she had seen them. Her parents would just chuckle and tell her it was nothing more than her overactive imagination. Her mom had said maybe Clover would become a writer one day.

But now the stories had stopped because Clover and Vicki rode to school with Vicki's older sister Molly. At school Clover ignored Vero whenever they passed each other in the halls. And at home, Clover hardly talked to Vero.

"She's going through a phase," Nora explained. "Her hormones are going crazy. She'll come out of it, you'll see."

But Vero wasn't so sure. He couldn't explain it, but somehow he knew that if Clover didn't come back to her old self soon, she'd be lost forever.

Vero closed his eyes, made a wish to himself, and in one breath blew out all twelve candles. He heard his parents clapping; but when he opened his eyes, he realized his wish hadn't been granted because Clover stood up from the table and said, "I don't want any cake." Then she went upstairs to her room and shut the door.

His second official day as a twelve-year-old started out just as great as his birthday party. First, he woke up with his back hurting. Then the milk in Vero's Cheerios was two days past the expiration date and tasted like it. Vero ate the cereal anyway. He told his mom about his sore back over his spoiled breakfast.

"It's time for a new mattress," she said. "That's probably what it is."

"I should be the one who gets a new mattress," Clover chimed in. "After all, I'm the favorite."

"Not true," Vero shot back.

"Ask Dad."

"Dad, is Clover your favorite?"

"Mom and I don't play favorites," Dennis said from behind his newspaper. "You both irritate me equally."

Nora slapped Dennis's shoulder playfully. He put down the paper and stood up. "I've got to get to work," he said.

"You've got a Cheerio stuck to your sleeve," Nora said.

Vero smiled as he watched his mom wipe cereal off his dad's suit jacket. Vero loved to watch his parents. After fifteen years of marriage, they still liked each other. Even though she was forty, Nora still looked a lot like she did in their wedding photos. Her blonde hair was pulled back in a ponytail, and she was dressed for her morning run. If not for the faint laugh lines, she could pass for Clover's big sister. Dennis's dark hair had a bit of gray in it, and his laugh lines were a bit more prominent than Nora's.

"Have fun on your run. I'll go with you this weekend," Dennis said, and he leaned over and kissed Nora. Clover looked at Vero and pretended to stick her index finger down her throat. Vero smiled at her, his sore back forgotten for the moment.

That good feeling didn't last very long. On the bus ride to Attleboro Middle School, Vero sat on a third grader's brown-bag lunch. Unfortunately, Vero didn't realize it until they'd reached the school, so the kid's lunch was smushed. When the kid started crying, Vero gave him his own lunch. So not only did he spend the day hungry, but he also had to walk around school with a huge jelly stain on the back of his pants.

The day brightened a bit when Vero got to be lab partners with Davina Acker in science. Davina was new to the school. Her family had recently moved to the area, and Vero thought she was beautiful. She had long brown hair that perfectly framed her sparkling blue eyes, and she had a warm smile for everyone.

In an attempt to be a gentleman, Vero pulled out a stool for her to sit on at his lab table. Unfortunately, Danny Konrad walked past and purposely bumped Vero. So Vero accidentally pulled the stool out too far, and Davina fell hard on the cement floor.

"Smooth move," Tack said, shaking his head as he took a seat next to Nate at the table in front of Vero's.

Vero's face burned red with embarrassment as he scrambled to help Davina stand up. "I'm so sorry! I didn't mean to … Are you all right?" Vero stammered.

Davina got back on her feet while Vero collected her books.

"Yes," she answered, rubbing her backside. "But I might be sore later."

"I'm totally sorry. I only meant to … "

"I know. I'm only kidding," Davina said without any bitterness. "You were just trying to be nice."

Vero sighed with relief. Vero caught Danny's glare from across the room and quickly turned away. He definitely didn't want any trouble from Danny. Even though they were both in the sixth grade, Danny was Clover's age—he'd been held back in third grade.

Vero remembered when Clover had a crush on Danny back in second grade. She'd drawn a pink heart around his head in their class photo. She had said she loved the way his dimples showed up whenever he cracked a smile. Clover still talks to Danny sometimes, and she says he's only gotten better looking over time. But she no longer carries a torch for him.

Clover didn't say so, but Vero imagined the reason why she no longer crushed on Danny was because some of Danny's favorite pastimes included knocking cafeteria trays out of kids' hands—especially on creamed-corn days; hiding Nate's clothes while he showered after gym class and then pulling the fire alarm; he even filled a teacher's car with packing peanuts because he'd given Danny a D on his report card—though no one could prove it was him. Danny bragged about that one to all the kids, but no one would turn him in. Everyone kept their distance from Danny.

"Do you still want to be partners for lab today?" Vero asked Davina.

"Sure," Davina said, pulling out her notebook. "I wonder what today's lesson will be?"

Their science teacher was Mr. Woods, a man whose wardrobe broke every fashion rule. He wore stripes with plaids, white socks with black pants, and sandals with suits. But every lesson was exciting. The kids had learned that the crazier his outfit, the more interesting the class.

Mr. Woods entered the classroom wearing a multicolor plaid suit jacket with equally plaid pants. He was carrying a cage with a blanket draped over it.

"This is going to be a good class," Vero whispered to Davina.

"What's in the cage, Mr. Woods?" Danny shouted.

"One of the most magnificent creatures ever known to man." Mr. Woods motioned everyone to join him. "Come on, gather 'round." Vero and Davina walked to the front of the room for a better view. When everyone had found a spot around the cage, Mr. Woods whipped the blanket off with the finesse of a magician. Sleeping peacefully in the corner of the cage was an orange and yellow snake.

"Sweet!" Tack said. The rest of the class oohed and aahed. Everyone, that is, except Vero, who took a step away. He hated snakes. He hated everything about them. His shoulders suddenly throbbed painfully.

"This is a corn snake," Mr. Woods said as he opened the cage, waking the snake. He gingerly picked it up and held it between his outstretched hands. "It gets its name from Indian corn. The pattern on the snake's body resembles the pattern on the corn cob."

Vero took another step back.

"Don't be scared," Mr. Woods said. "The corn snake is nonvenomous and is actually rather docile. He's only aggressive when he coils his body around his prey, constricting it, so it can no longer breathe. You can take turns holding him."

He held the snake out to Missy Baker whose blonde hair was always green during the first few weeks of school because she spent all summer in the pool. Her greenish hair provided a nice contrast to the snake's orange and yellow body. The snake slithered up her arm and traveled onto Danny's arm as he stood next to her.

"Hey, I think he likes me," Danny said.

Nate picked up the snake. It coiled around his hand.

"Hey, Nate," Tack said. "That snake has your beady eyes."

"Very funny," Nate said.

"Snakes get a bad rep," Mr. Woods continued. "The corn snake is very tame and makes a great pet."

Vero didn't agree with him, but he kept his mouth shut. He wanted to get a good grade in the class.

Mr. Woods removed the snake from Nate's hand and said, "I want everyone to have a chance to hold him." He placed the four-foot snake on Davina's forearm. She giggled as the snake crawled up her shoulder and around her neck. Davina didn't even flinch. She was perfectly comfortable with the creature.

"See? He's very sweet. I've raised him since birth," Mr. Woods said.

As Mr. Woods was talking, the snake looked up from Davina's chest and seemed to stare at Vero. Vero held its gaze.

"Next person," Mr. Woods said. As he stepped forward to remove the snake from Davina's shoulders, Vero swore the snake flicked its tongue and smiled at him. Then it began to squeeze Davina's neck. Davina gasped for air, unable to speak. Mr. Woods desperately tried to pry the snake off of Davina, but it constricted tighter and tighter. And all the while it stared right at Vero.

Davina's face started turning blue. Kids were screaming. The classroom erupted into chaos.

"Someone get a knife!" Mr. Woods shouted.

Vero knew a knife could accidentally cut Davina. Suddenly, a cold resolve consumed Vero, and it was unlike anything he'd ever experienced. Vero stepped forward, grabbed the snake behind its head, and pinched—hard! The snake let out a violent hiss, but Vero continued to crush the snake's head in his hand until it finally loosened its hold on Davina.

Then Vero furiously unraveled the reptile from around her neck and hurled it against the wall with such force that the snake slumped to the ground, unmoving.

Missy Baker was crying and shaking and rubbing her arm where the snake had been slithering only moments earlier.

Nate was leaning against Mr. Woods's desk, looking like he might throw up. Tack was balancing on top of a lab stool as if he'd seen a mouse scurry across the floor. And the rest of the class was staring at Vero like he was an alien who'd just stepped out of his spaceship. But the danger was past.

Mr. Woods crouched next to Davina who was sitting on the floor, coughing and holding her neck.

"I'm so sorry," Mr. Woods whispered. His face looked ashen. "I ... I had no idea ... "

She could have died. She almost died. Despite his courageous performance a moment ago, Vero's hands were shaking as he bent down until he was face-to-face with Davina. He was dimly aware of the rest of the class crowding behind him.

"Are you okay?" Vero asked.

Davina nodded. "I think so," she said, her voice scratchy. She smiled and took Vero's hand.

Suddenly Danny was there too, and he frowned at Vero. He reached down for Davina's other hand, and together they pulled her to her feet.

Davina smiled and said to Vero, "I'd say this more than makes up for you pulling my stool out from under me."

Mr. Woods picked up the limp snake and said, "Davina, I want you to go to the nurse's office, so she can take a look at your neck." His voice had regained its usual tone, but Vero saw his hands shake as he finished putting the snake's lifeless body back in its cage. "Missy, please walk with Davina. I'll meet you there in a few minutes."

As Vero watched Davina leave, Tack walked up behind him and whispered, "Dude, there's got to be an easier way to impress girls."

4

❖

BABY DOE

Everyone credited Vero's heroic defeat of the snake to "hysterical strength" brought on by an adrenaline rush. Vero had heard stories of people getting super-human strength in times of trouble, like a mom who lifted a car off her child, and a woman who swam across a raging river while dragging her unconscious husband to the shore. So Vero accepted the explanation.

After the excitement over the snake incident had passed, life in the Leland house settled back into a state of normalcy. They lived in Attleboro, Maryland, a suburb outside of Washington, DC, in a development that had been farms and orchards twenty years ago. Those original properties were torn down to make way for Vero's neighborhood, a planned development filled with nearly identical homes. The homes were so similar, in fact, that if a resident walked into his neighbor's house, he never needed to ask for directions to the powder room because it was in the same exact place as in his own home. More than once neighborhood kids had gotten confused and entered the wrong house after playing outside. The Lelands lived in a very *normal* neighborhood, and they lived very *normal* lives.

Nora drove a minivan and took her turn in the neighborhood carpool, driving kids to the weekly soccer games and Saturday afternoon movies. She'd been a nurse before becoming a stay-at-home mom, so she was the go-to mom whenever someone needed help bandaging a banged-up knee or bringing down a high fever. And she never refused anyone. Vero felt lucky to have her as his mother—most days.

Dennis worked as an analyst at the World Bank. He sat in an office all day and analyzed applications for international loans. The World Bank lent money to underdeveloped countries so they could build bridges or schools or clean up pollution. Vero's dad studied the requests, researched them from every angle, and made recommendations. His reports carried a lot of weight.

Dennis drove a government car, a generic-looking black vehicle that got traded in every three years. The kids were never allowed to eat in his car because candy wrappers or leaky juice boxes on the floor of a government car would be unpatriotic.

The Lelands took camping trips and beach vacations and mall outings, hosted birthday parties, attended school plays, supported various sports teams, played late-night pajama Twister games, and just about every typical family thing one could imagine. The family was so normal, in fact, that some psychologists might suggest that Vero's mom was overcompensating—trying to hide the fact the Vero was anything *but* normal.

Vero came into Nora's life one fateful night when she was working in the ER. A horrendous storm system had wreaked havoc across the area, as vicious winds knocked telephone poles onto cars and houses, the torrential rains flooded low-lying areas, and power outages occurred across the region. It was her regular night shift, and the ER was overrun with victims of the storm. Shortly after she arrived at work, an elderly man was wheeled in on a gurney.

"A metal sign broke loose and sliced open his head!" the paramedic yelled. "Vitals are not good!"

The man was unconscious and had lost a lot of blood. Nora assisted the doctor as he tried to save the old man, but the heart monitor announced that he had flatlined. All of their efforts to revive him were unsuccessful. The doctor declared the man deceased and moved on to help another storm victim. Nora was with the deceased man when an aide walked into the room.

"I'm here to take him down to the morgue," the aide said, and he draped a sheet over the body.

"Wait, please," Nora said.

As she pulled the sheet away from the man's face and tenderly closed his eyelids, the elderly man's hand suddenly grabbed her wrist! The aide screamed and jumped away from the gurney, sending a tray full of medical supplies crashing to the floor.

The dead man did not release his grip. He opened his eyes and mouth, letting out an unearthly moan. And through the moan, Nora heard him say, "Name the baby Vero. Raise him as your own."

Having heard the loud crash and the aide's shrieks, the

doctor rushed back into the room and saw the dead man clutching Nora's wrist.

He checked the old man's heartbeat to make sure they hadn't made a mistake. They hadn't. He was truly deceased. There was no sign of life coming from the old ticker. The doctor pried the man's fingers from Nora's wrist.

Oddly enough, Nora wasn't nearly as upset as she should have been. She should have been screaming her head off just like the aide. But it had happened so fast, she didn't have time to comprehend it all.

"It's common for a body to jerk or have involuntary movements as rigor mortis sets in," the doctor said.

"I've never seen *that* happen before!" the aide shouted. "And I heard the guy moan! Explain that!"

"Bodies can moan as gasses escape," the doctor answered calmly.

"It was more than a moan, Doctor," Nora said. Then she turned to the aide and asked, "Did you hear what he said?" She was putting together her thoughts, which didn't make much sense.

"No, I did not! I most definitely did not. It was just a moan!" the aide yelled.

"He said something about a—" Nora began, but the aide cut her off.

"They don't pay me enough to put up with this! I quit! I'm out of here!" And the aide stormed out of the hospital for good.

Nora took one last look at the elderly man and pulled the sheet back over him. As she walked to the nurse's station, she began to question whether or not the old man had said anything. Her mind had to be playing tricks on her.

So when she reached her desk and saw an infant lying on her chair, she wasn't sure the baby was real. That is, until the chair began to cry. Then Nora knew she'd better not sit on it.

All of the other nurses had been helping patients, so no one saw the baby arrive. The security cameras hadn't picked up a single image of Vero being dropped off. One moment he wasn't there, and the next he was.

Pediatricians on call that night gave the baby a complete physical from head to toe. He was perfectly healthy and rather cute. The hospital's social worker granted temporary custody to Nora until the child's parents could be located, or until a judge determined a permanent home for him.

"We'll just call him Baby Doe," the social worker said as she filled out the paperwork.

"His name is Vero," Nora told her.

"Vero?" the social worker asked. "Where'd you get that one?"

Nora grabbed the pen from the woman's hand and met her eyes with an unwavering gaze. She said, "I found him, and his name is Vero."

Seeing the conviction in her eyes, the social worker took back her pen and wrote VERO on the forms.

Nora loved Vero from the first moment she held him. The two bonded even before they left the hospital that night. As Nora stepped outside the hospital doors, she noticed it was oddly calm outside. The storm was now a memory. Clover was only a year old at the time, so Nora strapped Vero into

Clover's car seat before setting out for the all-night grocery store. Vero would need diapers and baby formula.

The store was completely empty except for a young man standing behind the cash register. He wore headphones and listened to music on his iPod to pass the time. After all, it was 5:30 in the morning, and the sun was not yet up. Nora read the labels on the various kinds of formula while baby Vero slept in the built-in baby seat on the shopping cart.

Out of the corner of her eye, Nora saw a figure, a man dressed in a long black trench coat that resembled a hooded robe. The hood was pulled far over his head, obscuring his face. When the man began to knock diapers off the shelves as he approached her, that little thing called intuition kicked in. Nora picked up Vero and sprinted down the aisle.

She turned back toward the entrance. Nora screamed at the cashier who was banging imaginary drums to some song on his iPod. He couldn't hear her, and she couldn't leave through the front of the store without running smack into her pursuer.

The huge double doors to the storage room caught her attention. She plowed through them. The storage room was filled with rows of shelves that were stocked to the ceiling with wooden pallets filled with all different sorts of foods and goods. Nora ducked behind a massive crate containing boxes of cereal, and silently prayed that Vero wouldn't make a sound. She peered around the corner of the crate and saw that the man in black was now surveying the warehouse.

He's abnormally tall, Nora thought.

It seemed like a stroke of good luck when the man went down another aisle. She exhaled with relief until ketchup bottles, soup cans, and products of all kinds started flying off the highest shelves in every direction and crashed to the floor. Vero began crying. Nora held him tightly to her chest and stepped out into the open. The man saw them.

"Stay away from me!" Nora shouted.

The man let out a chilling laugh as he slowly approached her. With her back against the locked loading-dock gate, Nora had nowhere to turn. The hooded man had cornered her like a trapped animal.

Instinctively she knew he was after Vero, and this man wouldn't hesitate to take her life in order to get what he wanted. "Please," Nora begged. "Don't hurt the baby!"

But her pleas fell on deaf ears as the dark figure loomed toward her. He reached out his hand to grab her, his face still hidden by his hood. Nora clutched Vero with all her might. She would die protecting him. She would die without seeing the face of her killer.

"God help me!" Nora shouted. "Please help us!"

Suddenly, the massive metal gate behind her blasted away with an immense *BOOM!* A blinding white light filled the room, and the figure instantly recoiled with a howl of intense agony. The light blinded Nora as well, so she didn't see the hooded man vanish. She also didn't see the baby in her arms staring directly into the brilliant light, smiling serenely. He wasn't even blinking.

"Are you okay, lady?" the deliveryman asked Nora as he pushed the metal gate open.

Nora was standing by the loading dock, still clutching Vero to her chest, and feeling totally bewildered. The radiant light was gone. It had been replaced with the regular morning sun that now streamed throughout the warehouse, coaxing Nora back to her senses.

"Yes, I think so," Nora said meekly.

The deliveryman's bright violet eyes and friendly smile helped put her at ease.

"He looks just like you," he said with a nod toward Vero. "But you should probably be getting him home to bed, no?"

"I don't understand ... there was a man in black chasing us ... and then you ... "

"I didn't see anyone," he said. "I just got here for my morning shift and found you standing there when I opened the warehouse door. But when I was driving in to work, I heard we had a decent-sized earthquake this morning. Unusual for DC, but not unheard of. Crazy times, huh? First that storm last night, and now an earthquake."

The deliveryman surveyed the damage as food and other goods were strewn all over the warehouse floor.

"I pity the poor sap who has to clean up this place," he said, shaking his head. But then he looked directly at Nora, his violet eyes piercing her own. "Really, you should be getting that boy home now."

"Y-y-yes," Nora said. "Home." She was stunned, confused. *What had just happened?*

"Can I help you to your car?" the deliveryman asked with a smile.

Nora blinked and came back to herself. "No, thank you. I'll get my groceries, and then I'll head home. Thank you again."

"No problem, ma'am."

Right before she went through the double doors and

reentered the main grocery store, she looked back at the man and said, "I didn't catch your name ... "

But he was outside unloading boxes from a produce truck.

No one besides Nora had seen the man in black. Nora didn't dare tell a soul what she'd experienced that night—not even her husband. She knew if she did, any judge would label her crazy, and she'd never be allowed to adopt the baby. So it was her secret to keep.

Weeks later, a judge formally permitted Nora and Dennis to adopt the baby, and he became Vero Leland.

As for Vero, he grew up knowing he'd been adopted. Nora told him that his biological parents had dropped him off at a hospital because they couldn't provide for him. And then Nora and Dennis became his parents, and Clover became his sister. There was never a need to question anything.

5

BACKSEAT DRIVER

Vero was smart in school. Good grades came easily to
him. He barely had to study, and yet he got all As on
his report cards. Mrs. Cleary, his language arts teacher, was
most impressed with his reading and writing—especially
his essays. She assigned him the more difficult books to read.
At the Lelands' parent-teacher conference, Mrs. Cleary presented Vero's essay on Milton's *Paradise Lost*.

"This poem is usually assigned in the twelfth grade, but
I wanted to see if Vero could handle it," Mrs. Cleary began.
"*Paradise Lost* tells the story of the fall of the angel Lucifer
and his descent into hell. Of how he turned against God,
was cast out of heaven, and spread his ills into the garden
of Eden, persuading Eve to take a bite from the forbidden
fruit."

"Yes, I remember reading that in college," Vero's dad said.

Vero sighed and rolled his eyes at the pride in his dad's voice. Vero looked at the clock, willing it to go faster.

Mrs. Cleary continued, "It's the original story of good versus evil. God was good. Lucifer was evil. There's no debating that. However, readers of the poem often debate Eve's sin. Some feel anger toward the very first woman because all of mankind was forced to live with the consequences of her choice. On the other hand, some feel sympathy for her. Eve was deceived, tricked by the serpent, and at a time when deception was unheard of. They feel she was simply a pawn in the great war between heaven and hell. I expected Vero to take one of these two viewpoints in his essay."

Nora squirmed in her seat. Vero thought she looked uncomfortable. He wished Mrs. Cleary would hurry up and get to the point.

"But Vero saw Eve's sin from a completely unexpected angle," Mrs. Cleary said. She began reading Vero's essay aloud, and Vero felt his cheeks burning. "It was the archangel Uriel's job to protect the garden of Eden. Uriel was the one who failed to prevent Lucifer from gaining access to the garden in the first place. Man's fall was actually the result of Uriel's poor job performance. If an archangel, a heavenly being, could be deceived by the serpent, then poor Eve never stood a chance. A human, especially one only recently created, could never be a match for the master of deception. So the archangel should have been aware of Eve's vulnerability and stayed extra vigilant."

Mrs. Cleary handed the paper to Vero's father. "Brilliant," she said.

Dennis beamed with pride. His entire face lit up. But

Nora didn't have the same reaction. She actually looked a bit sick.

"Vero's insight is far beyond that of his peers. It's a joy to read his papers. How did you ever come up with your idea?" Mrs. Cleary asked Vero.

"I don't know," Vero shrugged. "It just made sense to me."

"And he's modest too," Mrs. Cleary said, admiringly.

Nora suddenly stood up and declared, "He copied it off the Internet!"

Everyone else looked taken aback.

"No, I didn't ... " Vero said. "I swear."

"Mrs. Cleary, please give him the F he deserves," Nora said.

"Nora, don't you think you're overreacting?" Dennis said.

"Enough!" Nora shouted with a ferocity that silenced them all. "There's no way Vero could have such knowledge of these things! He may have fooled you, Mrs. Cleary, but not me. I'm done with this conversation!"

Nora pulled Vero out of his chair by his upper arm and dragged him out of the classroom. But not before Vero saw Mrs. Cleary turn to his dad with a bewildered expression on her face.

Dennis shrugged and said, "I'm sorry, but my wife has a hard time hearing that Vero is anything but normal."

"You just gotta stop getting such good grades," Tack said to Vero as they were changing clothes in the boys' locker room the next day.

"You sound like my mom," Vero said.

"Your mom doesn't want you getting good grades?" Tack asked, wide-eyed.

"Yeah, yesterday at my parent-teacher conference, she accused me of stealing an essay off the Internet. And no matter how much I tell her I didn't do it, she won't believe me. She won't even go there," Vero said. "It's like she wants me to dumb myself down. It's weird."

"Did you steal it?"

"No!" Vero shouted.

"Okay, chill ... but I think she's on to something. Getting good grades the way you do, everyone's gonna think you're a dork. It was okay being a super-genius when we were little, but now girls like jocks."

"Whatever you say, Tack." Vero snorted as he watched Tack shove an entire Hostess Ding Dong into his mouth.

"Whaa?" Tack asked, with a mouth full of chocolate. After he'd swallowed, he said, "I need the energy to run the hurdles."

Vero shook his head as Tack adjusted his extra-large sweatpants. Up until last summer, Tack had always been the pudgy kid. And he and Vero had been best friends since preschool.

It all started one afternoon during naptime when Tack accidentally rolled on top of a sleeping Vero. The preschool teachers panicked when they did a head count and couldn't find little Vero anywhere. They searched the classroom closets, bathrooms, and even inside the school's piano, but Vero was nowhere to be found. They immediately feared the worst: Vero had wandered off the schoolyard.

When Tack woke up and complained that his mat was lumpy, the teachers found Vero squashed underneath him.

Vero was perfectly fine; but from that day on, Tack had to sleep in a corner away from the other kids. And then he and Vero became inseparable.

They grew up sharing each other's lunches—with Tack typically eating the lion's share. They raced across the monkey bars, played with Tonka trucks in the sandbox, and spent hours on the seesaw. Tack would sit on his end with such force that Vero went flying into the air—which Vero loved, of course.

When Vero had a difficult time learning how to swim, Tack swam with him for hours to help Vero stay afloat. When Tack got sick and missed days of school, Vero brought his homework to him. (Although Tack didn't always appreciate that gesture.) When Tack's dog Pork Chop ran away from home, Vero posted flyers and searched the whole neighborhood until Tack's beloved English bulldog was finally found.

As they grew older, Vero remained much smaller than average, and Tack was the complete opposite. So whenever the other kids would tease Vero for any reason, Tack would stand behind him, pounding his right fist into his left palm. That usually sent the bullies running.

Standing next to his best friend, Vero appeared short but gangly, with long arms and legs. Vero's mother was constantly trying to fatten him up with protein shakes, while Tack's mother began padlocking the refrigerator between meals.

But during the past summer, both Vero and Tack had grown significantly. No one would call Tack fat anymore, maybe just big boned—although they wouldn't dare say *that* to his face either.

Tack's real name was Thaddeus Kozlowski. He got his nickname "Tack" from his older sister Martha. When their parents first brought Tack home from the hospital, Martha took one look at her little brother and declared he was as short and fat as a thumbtack. And it stuck. Since that moment, Thaddeus was called Tack.

Over the years Martha has tried changing her story, saying the reason for his nickname is because his brain is the size of a tack. But that simply wasn't true. It requires real intelligence to come up with new excuses for why you didn't do your homework, or how the latest zombie video game was beneficial for your hand-eye coordination. All of these things needed a certain amount of smarts, which Tack possessed in excess. But as his math teacher, Mrs. Grommet, told his parents, "His intelligence is utterly misguided."

As bad as Tack's grades were, Marty, Tack's father, was more disappointed that Tack would not be carrying on the family tradition. All of the Kozlowski men were dowsers. And after having three daughters, Tack's dad was thrilled when Tack finally came along because the dowsing gift was passed down through the male genes. But so far Tack hadn't shown any abilities in this area.

Dowsers have an innate ability to locate water, minerals, and oil underground. Using a Y-shaped rod or twig, Marty would explore an area, and the dowsing rod would twitch when it was over the target. A really gifted dowser didn't even need a rod or twig. Tack's Great-Great-Uncle Morris had never used any tools for his dowsing back in Poland. He just felt it in his bones. Tack, on the other hand, had shown no aptitude for the gift.

For years Marty took his son to the beach every summer

so Tack could practice finding metal under the sand. The only time Tack ever found anything happened two summers ago when he stepped on a melted Hershey's Kiss. Hardly impressive.

In years past, a dowser could make a good living finding wells for homes and such. But with modern technology and geologists, dowsers weren't in high demand any longer. While dowsing could be lucrative from time to time, the income wasn't enough to support a growing family. So Marty owned a hardware store in Attleboro, K & Sons Hardware, which he'd inherited from Tack's grandfather. And Tack helped out in the store from time to time.

Tack shut his locker door and locked the padlock (purchased from the family hardware store).

"Why are you running hurdles?" Vero asked. "I thought you wanted to do shot put?"

"That was before I grew taller," Tack said. "When I go over those hurdles, it'll be spectacular. Everyone on that track is gonna eat my dust."

Vero checked his laces.

"Why don't you run in the lane next to me?" Tack asked. "Maybe you'll pick up some pointers."

"Maybe," Vero said.

Minutes later, the boys were warming up for gym class during second period. As he stretched, Vero could see his breath in the air. It was unusually cold for an early spring day. The gray sky made it feel like snow might even be on the way.

There were eight lanes drawn on the track, each with ten hurdles set up at eight-meter intervals. A pit formed in Vero's stomach and he felt nervous for his friend. Tack had never run hurdles before.

"Are you sure you want to do this?" Vero asked.

"Why? Afraid I'm gonna beat you?" Tack replied with a smirk.

"Fine!" Vero said. "You wanna race? It's on!"

"Bring it!"

"Get on your starting blocks!" Coach Randy yelled.

Tack and Vero chose to run in lanes four and five, and boys from gym class filled the other six lanes. Coach Randy stood on the outside of the track while the runners lined up at their starting blocks. A cold wind suddenly blew through, catching everyone off guard. Coach Randy grabbed the top of his ball cap to keep it from flying off his head. He was never seen without his ball cap. Kids joked that his cap was guarded more securely than the Crown Jewels of England.

Vero turned his head to the left and glanced at Tack.

Tack mouthed, "You're going down."

Vero ignored his friend's taunt and faced forward again. Out of the corner of his eye, he saw Davina standing off to his right on the sideline. Their eyes met, and Vero's stomach flipped. He quickly returned his gaze to the ground in front of him and tried to focus on his feet.

"Runners, on your marks!" Coach Randy shouted. "Get set ... "

The starting gun shot into the air.

The runners took off. Vero and his classmates sprinted down the oval track toward their hurdles. It was a close start. Vero and Tack kept pace with the other sprinters, and everyone was neck and neck. Tack cleared the first hurdle with surprising ease. He looked over his shoulder and smiled smugly at Vero.

Seconds later, Vero reached the first hurdle in his lane. He began to leap, but what happened next sent a hush over his classmates. Vero didn't clear just the first hurdle — he cleared the second one too! He soared over *both* hurdles in one bound! Everyone was astonished. Coach Randy's mouth dropped open. And Vero was as surprised as everyone else. When his feet came back to earth, Vero continued running.

Now Tack looked ahead and saw that Vero had somehow passed him. As he came to the next hurdle, Tack watched as Vero cleared the third and fourth hurdles in a single leap! Tack was so surprised that he lost his concentration while he was still in midair and landed smack on top of the hurdle — it hit him right in his unmentionables!

Tack doubled over in pain and rolled into the next lane, which caused that runner to fall, which then created a domino effect. Runner after runner tripped over their hurdles and then each other until no one was left standing. That is, no one except Vero who crossed the finish line in first place. As he looked back and saw the mass of injured runners and hurdles lying on the track, Vero didn't feel as good about his victory.

The rest of the gym class students were agape.

And Coach Randy did a little victory dance. "State Championship, here we come!" he shouted.

"You should have *told* me you could jump like that," Tack said to Vero. He was now lying down in Nurse Kunkel's office with an ice pack across his unmentionables. "That was such an unfair advantage."

"I'm sorry," Vero said. "I didn't know I could do that."

"You can tell me the truth. I'll still be your friend," Tack said.

"What?"

"You're secretly taking ballet, aren't you? That move you did out there ... I've seen girls in my sister's ballet class do that one. But they can't do it nearly as good as you can. I think it's called a 'granny jet' or something."

"It's a *grande jeté*," Vero said in a flawless French accent.

"So you *have* been taking ballet!"

"No, I haven't!" Vero insisted. "I swear! I know what a *grande jeté* is because my family goes to see *The Nutcracker* every Christmas."

"*The Nutcracker*. Very funny," Tack said. "Well then, where did you learn to jump like that?"

"I don't know," Vero said. "It's not like I practice doing it or anything."

"The hurdles, the snake ... you've been acting weird lately," Tack said. "And it's like you're getting smarter. You're reading all of these big books, and you seem to understand them so easily when I can't even pronounce their titles!"

Vero couldn't disagree. And he didn't mention that his desire to fly had returned with a vengeance, and his back hurt all the time. But it was true: Vero *was* feeling different, and it was getting more and more difficult to hide these changes from people.

As Nurse Kunkel handed Tack a fresh icepack, she asked Vero, "Have you been checked for scoliosis?"

"What's that?" Vero asked.

"Curvature of the spine. From the way you're hunching over, I'd say you might want to have a doctor examine you. Has your back been hurting lately?"

Vero nodded and said, "My parents said it's probably because my old bed is so lumpy. They're gonna buy me a new mattress."

"Bend over and let me take a look," she commanded.

Vero flashed Tack an uneasy glance. He'd only come to the nurse's office to help Tack.

"Come on, hurry up," Nurse Kunkel said in her no-nonsense way.

So Vero bent over at the waist, letting his arms dangle in front of him as Nurse Kunkel had instructed. He tried not to shiver as she ran her cold hands underneath his T-shirt and along his spine. From his upside-down vantage point, Vero could see the nurse's enormous white orthopedic shoes behind him. But what he couldn't see was the look on Nurse Kunkel's face when she saw his protruding shoulder blades. Startled, she jerked her hands away, staggered back, and fell onto the cot where Tack was lying—and landed right on top of Tack.

Tack let out a high-pitched "Help!"

Nurse Kunkel immediately tried to stand up. But she was a large woman, so it wasn't easy. She was the exact opposite of one of those inflated punching-bag clowns, where no matter how hard they're punched, they bounce back up. In this case Nurse Kunkel couldn't lift herself off the cot. In her many attempts to get back on her feet, she steamrolled all over Tack, left and then right, but still couldn't prop herself up. Finally, she just rolled off the cot and fell onto the floor with a loud thud followed by silence.

Vero exchanged nervous looks with Tack.

"Is she dead?" Tack whispered.

"Of course I'm not dead, you idiot!" the nurse shouted from the floor. "Now help me up!"

Vero and Tack each grabbed one of Nurse Kunkel's hands and somehow hoisted her to her feet.

On any given day, the buttons on the front of her nurse's uniform were stretched to capacity, and they were known to occasionally shoot off her dress like bullets. There was a rumor that a button nearly took out a kid's eye when Nurse Kunkel leaned over to take his temperature. As Nurse Kunkel pulled herself and her uniform back together, Vero and Tack noticed that this latest incident had cost her three buttons.

"Thank you. I'm fine," she snapped, attempting to smooth her wiry hair. Face flushed, she turned to Vero and said, "You've got something worse than scoliosis. No wonder your back's killing you."

"What? What's wrong with me?" Vero asked.

"Kyphosis," she said.

Vero had no idea what Nurse Kunkel was saying.

"Hunchback syndrome," she continued. "It's one of the worse cases I've seen."

The nurse gave Vero's back another look, and Tack made sure he wasn't behind her this time.

"Hmmm ... when you stand up, I can't see it. That's very strange," she said. "Nevertheless, here ... " She quickly scribbled something onto a pad of paper, ripped off the page, and shoved it into Vero's hand. "Give this to your parents. *Tonight*. You don't need a new mattress. You need to see a doctor ASAP."

Vero reluctantly put the note in his back pocket. Tack looked at him with a worried expression on his face. Vero

knew exactly what Tack was thinking—just another weird
thing to add to the list.

Word of Vero's hurdle-jumping exhibition spread like wild-
fire throughout the school. Kids and teachers gossiped about
him in the hallways, locker rooms, and cafeteria. Coach
Randy begged Vero to join the school's track-and-field team,
but Vero refused. He was afraid to draw any more attention
to himself.

Later that day, school was dismissed early due to an
unexpected snowstorm that started right after gym class, for
which Vero was extremely grateful. He'd silently prayed for
a huge snowfall so he wouldn't have to go back to school for
a few days—or even weeks.

As students boarded the school buses for the ride home,
Tack, who was still recovering from his hurdle mishap, was
lying across one whole bus seat. So Vero had to look for
another place to park himself. The bus was overcrowded
with kids whose parents normally would have picked them
up but were now unable to leave work early or couldn't drive
in the bad weather. Even Clover was on the bus. She wasn't
allowed to ride with Vicki's older sister in any kind of treacherous weather.

When Vero reached the next-to-last row of bus seats,
he spotted his sister sitting with Vicki. He could possibly
squeeze in with them, but Clover shot him a most unwel-
coming look and then turned her face toward the window. It
was a clear sign that she wasn't happy with all the recent talk

about him in school, and she wasn't going to make room for him in her bus seat.

His only option was to head back to the front of the bus and sit directly behind the driver.

After checking the snow chains on the tires of the bus, the driver got on and started the engine. He then stood up and faced his passengers.

"Listen up!" the driver said. "It's starting to come down hard out there, so no messing around. Everyone stays in their seats and keeps quiet. Got it?"

No one answered.

"Got it?" he repeated.

"Yes, Mr. Harmon," the kids answered in unison.

Mr. Harmon was actually Wayne Harmon, a baby-faced nineteen-year-old who was not much older than the students. He got the bus driver job right out of high school because his uncle owned the bus company. And even though he'd gone to school with some of the kids on his route, Wayne insisted they address him as "Mr. Harmon."

The bus slowly pulled away from the curb. As Vero sat by himself, he glanced behind him at the other kids. They were busy texting, laughing, or swapping food from their leftover lunches. Vero was beginning to feel more and more isolated. He felt as if he were watching the scene on the bus through an invisible divider, like that piece of plastic that separates the backseat of a taxicab from the front.

Vero was sitting on the bus, he could feel the wheels vibrating on the road beneath him, yet somehow he felt as if he were elsewhere.

Vero turned back around and stared out the windshield. The snow was coming down hard. He'd always loved the snow. There was something so peaceful about it. He'd learned in Mr. Woods's class that no two snowflakes are alike, and it seemed so impossible. Of all the snowflakes that have fallen throughout the history of the planet, how could that be? But the scientists stood by their claim—the intricate ice crystals were full of endless possibilities.

Mesmerized by the falling snow and the swish-swish rhythm of the windshield wipers, Vero's enchantment was suddenly broken when an oncoming car crossed into the bus's lane. The car's driver wrestled to gain control of the steering wheel, but the car still careened toward them with no chance of stopping in these icy conditions.

Vero noticed another man in the car was leaning over the backseat. He appeared to be fighting the driver for control of the steering wheel. The falling snow obscured Vero's vision, but the face of the man in the backseat appeared distorted, unreal, with exaggerated facial features—a large snout-like nose and a massive forehead made his eyes appear sunken. As the car got closer, Vero saw what looked like a gruesome burn scar etched across his face. And his eyes! *Were his eyes glowing red?*

Vero jumped to his feet, pointing and shouting about the approaching car. Everyone on the bus grew silent. Vero felt Clover's eyes on him from the back of the bus. Somehow—he didn't know how—he could feel her hostility toward him.

"What's your brother doing?" Vicki elbowed Clover.

Clover sunk lower in the seat.

"He's headed straight toward us!" Vero shouted again.

"Sit down!" Mr. Harmon shouted back.

The car continued to slide closer and closer to the bus.

And now it was close enough for Vero to see the rage glowing from the monstrous red eyes of the backseat driver.

"Don't you see it?" Vero's voice was edged with panic, but Mr. Harmon seemed oblivious. "I said, sit down!"

A head-on collision was imminent. "Look!" Instinctively, Vero reached over Mr. Harmon's shoulder and yanked the steering wheel—just like the man in the backseat of the car was doing.

Suddenly, the entire windshield flashed white. A feeling of tranquility seized Vero, and somehow he knew they were safe. Then the whiteout disappeared, replaced by the steadily falling snow. Mr. Harmon brought the bus to a screeching halt at a stop sign. He opened the bus door, stood up, and pointed to the open door.

"Get out! You can walk home from here!"

"But I just saved your life! I saved *everybody's* lives! He was gonna drive his car right into us! See? That car over there!" Vero pointed to the car in the opposite lane, which was now stopped at the stop sign on the other side of the intersection.

"That car swerved over the center line for less than a second!" Mr. Harmon shot back. "It wasn't a big deal. You were the one who was going to cause an accident! It's bad enough that I'm driving in a complete whiteout. I don't need you yanking the steering wheel away from me!"

"But ... you didn't see ...?"

"Get off my bus! Now! Or I'll have some of the football players escort you off."

Mr. Harmon grabbed Vero's backpack and threw it out into the snow. Vero knew he wasn't going to win this fight, so he walked down the steps and into the snowstorm. The car that he'd been certain was going to hit them just moments before, accelerated cautiously through the intersection. As it drove past him, Vero saw the driver casually talking on his cell phone. There was no sign of the misshapen man in the backseat.

As the bus pulled away from the stop sign, Tack and Clover watched Vero through their bus windows with mortified expressions on their faces. Angus pointed at Vero, shook his head, and laughed. Vero knew exactly what Angus was thinking: *Wait 'til my dad hears about this!*

6

THE SNOW ANGEL

That night in his dream, Vero walked down a dark alley in a large, unknown city. Despite the recent rain, the alley was dirty and dingy. Vero stepped in puddles that had nowhere to drain. A light flickered on and off over a doorway. Large hairy rats climbed into an open dumpster in search of a meal. A yellow mutt with wiry fur hobbled over to Vero and knelt down, allowing Vero to stroke his head. Vero noticed the dog was missing his back left leg.

Suddenly, the dog's ears perked up, and Vero heard the faint sound of distant music. Vero scanned the upper apartment windows but saw nothing. Nor was anyone standing on the metal fire escapes above him. The dog got up, sniffed the air, and started walking farther down the dark alley. He looked back at Vero and barked, prompting him to follow.

Vero walked deeper into the eerie darkness, growing

more and more apprehensive. He wanted to turn back but felt compelled to find the source of the music. In spite of the eerie blackness surrounding him, Vero noticed a vast number of stars in the sky overhead, and their glimmering lights comforted him despite the deep shadows of the alleyway.

Vero's three-legged guide turned a corner, and Vero lost him. He called out to the dog, but it had disappeared. Boxes and garbage lined the street ahead and stood in haphazard piles in dim corners, leaning against decrepit brick walls covered with spray-painted symbols. The music was louder here. Vero tentatively jostled the piles of boxes in turn, eliminating each as the possible source of the enthralling music.

When Vero moved a big box out of his way, he saw Clover sitting on the sidewalk with her back against a brick wall. He gasped at the sight of her. Her clothes were torn and dirty. She seemed to be out of breath, and her hair was wet with sweat.

Despite her appearance, Clover smiled at Vero. Instantly she transformed into the old Clover—the sister who'd been his closest companion. His confidante. The sister he loved. Yet this version of his sister was older. She had aged. Clover reached out her hand, and Vero helped her up.

Still the music persisted. Clover motioned for Vero to follow her, and as they walked on, the music grew louder and became more distinct. Vero could make out the sounds of a lyre and a flute. An exquisite voice sang, and Vero was charmed by its melody. Vero thought of the irresistible sirens of Greek mythology that lured unsuspecting sailors to their deaths, powerless to resist the bewitching songs. He, too, felt captivated by the music, drawn to it.

Vero and Clover turned a corner and came upon a crowd

of people crammed into a tiny alley, their faces were hidden as they stood gazing upon something. He felt compelled to get a glimpse of it as well. The source of the music.

Clutching Clover's hand, Vero made his way through the throng of onlookers. He tapped a man's shoulder so he would let them pass, but when the man turned and was no longer obscured in shadow, Vero saw that he had the face of a lion. But Vero didn't feel threatened, just curious — curious enough to pause his search for the source of the music, which was definitely coming from whatever object all of these people were staring at.

The man turned his head toward Clover, and his face transformed into that of an ox, then an eagle, and finally a human, with striking violet eyes and a peaceful, welcoming expression. It reminded Vero of a program on his laptop where he and Tack once took Clover and Vicki's school photos and morphed them into animals.

"Who are you?" Vero asked, but before the man could answer, Vero's alarm clock woke him up.

Unlike the Clover in Vero's dream, the real-life Clover was in a foul mood that morning.

"He's ruining my life!" she shouted across the breakfast table to her parents.

Vero stared at his sister, trying to catch a glimpse of the old Clover who was nowhere to be found. And now after he'd spent some time with the old Clover in his dream, Vero realized he missed her even more. He felt a deep ache combined with an almost overwhelming disappointment.

"What!" Clover barked, when she noticed Vero was staring at her. "It's true!"

"If I didn't grab that steering wheel, we would have had been in a head-on collision," he explained again.

"Every single person on that bus — including me — said that car was never any threat," Clover said. "I was mortified!"

Dennis and Nora exchanged glances.

"It doesn't make any sense," Dennis said.

"I know what I saw," Vero said firmly.

But Vero held back some information, like that second driver in the backseat. Vero knew that if he were to divulge that information, they'd lock him up for good in the nearest loony bin.

"Come on, Clover. Aren't you exaggerating just a bit?" Nora said in a slightly accusatory tone.

"No!" Clover snapped. "You always accuse me of having an overactive imagination. But not this time! He's off! He needs help!"

Clover glared at Vero, wishing she could get inside his head. Sure, she'd probably never live this one down, and she may forever be known as Crazy Vero's Big Sister. But she knew Vero was hiding something.

"Vero, the principal called and said you'll need to meet with a counselor before he'll allow you back on the school bus," Nora said gently.

Vero saw the pain in his mother's face, and he felt guilty for having caused it. He nodded, hoping his compliance would take a little of that pain away.

"Okay, that's that," Nora said, fighting back tears. "Now, since today is a snow day and there's no school, we'll make it a cleaning day."

"Oh great," Clover groaned.

For once, Vero didn't mind wiping down kitchen counters, mopping hardwood floors, or even scrubbing toilets. He was grateful for the distraction. His mind needed a rest, and at least he wasn't at school.

His first job was to clean out the toy closet. As Vero pulled out his old Hot Wheels cars and Legos, he accidentally stepped on the World War II Corsair model airplane he'd built with his dad. As he picked up the broken airplane and ran his fingers over it, he was surprised that he wasn't more upset. Vero had a fleeting thought that the crushed model was just a relic of childhood. *Strange.*

"Vero!" Clover called from downstairs. "Mom said you're supposed to collect all of the laundry and put it in the washing machine!"

Vero placed the remains of the model airplane on a shelf. He couldn't bring himself to throw it away.

Vero grabbed the laundry bag off the washing machine and went from bedroom to bedroom looking for stray socks. He hesitated at Clover's bedroom door. She no longer allowed Vero access to her room, but gathering laundry was an exception.

Lucky me, Vero thought.

Clover's room looked the same as he remembered it. Posters of pop idols and boy bands hung on the walls. The lava lamp she'd received from their grandmother sat on Clover's nightstand, forming new blobs of purple bubbles. Her stuffed animals were scattered across the window seat, looking very much neglected. He looked at her ceiling fan and saw that little bits of dried toilet paper still covered the multicolored blades.

He remembered a day he'd spent with a ten-year-old Clover—three years ago now. It had been raining for days, they'd been cooped up inside, and they were bored out of their minds. Of course, this was when Vero was still allowed in Clover's room, so they'd been hanging out and trying to think of something to do.

"I just thought of a cool game," Clover said. She disappeared for a minute and returned with two straws and a roll of toilet paper. She handed Vero a straw and said, "Quick, turn on the ceiling fan."

Vero pressed the remote, and the blades began to spin.

"Now take some toilet paper and wet it." Clover handed him a roll of toilet paper.

Following Clover's lead, Vero ripped off a tiny piece and chewed it.

"We're gonna make spitballs and shoot 'em at the fan. You've got to lie on your back and hit the moving target to get any points. The red blade is five points, the blue is three, and the others are one point each."

"Cool," Vero said, and he and Clover spent the rest of that rainy afternoon shooting spitballs at the fan.

Vero smiled at the memory as he emptied Clover's hamper into the laundry bag. He looked on the floor of her closet for any stray items. Then he got down on all fours and searched under the bed. As he reached for a white T-shirt, something caught his eye. Clover's dream journal. Vero hadn't seen that in a long time.

Ever since she was little, Clover had kept the journal by her bed and would quickly jot down what she remembered about her dreams right when she woke up.

Vero couldn't help himself. The temptation to read it was

too strong. He sat on the bed and opened the book. Turning to a random page, he read about a dream in which a boy on the football team kissed Clover. Vero rolled his eyes. He then flipped to another page and read how a different boy on the soccer team kissed Clover. In the next dream, Clover got voted "most popular girl" by her class. Vero began to think these weren't dreams, but rather wishes. He tossed the notebook aside, bored.

The journal hit the side of her nightstand and landed open on the carpet. Vero bent to close the book and shove it back under her bed, but then he saw a sketch that made him pause. There, on the open page of Clover's journal, was a drawing of the same creature from his dream — the one with the four distinct faces of the man, the ox, the lion, and the eagle! Vero was stunned. It couldn't be possible, but there it was, drawn in Clover's style. Then he looked at the entry date. It was last night — the same night as his dream! *How could that be possible?* Somehow he and Clover had shared the same dream.

"You'd better not be in my bedroom!" Clover yelled from the hallway.

Vero quickly shut the diary and threw it under the bed just as Clover walked into the room.

"I'm getting the laundry," Vero stammered.

"Well you got it, now get lost."

Vero stood for a moment just staring at her. He didn't move.

"Clover ... "

"What?" she snapped.

Vero wanted so badly to ask his sister about her drawing, her dream. He needed her to confide in him once again. But he couldn't bring himself to ask. He picked up the laundry bag and headed for the door.

"Um, nothing . . . "

As Vero left his sister's room, Clover slammed the door shut behind him. His parents' bedroom door was shut when he walked past, but Vero could still hear their voices through the closed door. He paused to listen.

Mom: "I thought I could do it, but I can't. I won't send him to a psychiatrist!"

Dad: "The school didn't give us a choice in the matter."

Mom: "Then I'll homeschool him."

Dad: "And take him away from his friends? Nora, he's seeing things that aren't there. And when he was little, he was always trying to throw himself off of high places. I love him just as much as you do, but we need to find out what's going on with him."

Vero's heart sank. *Am I mental?* First Tack and Clover, and now his parents thought he was crazy. So the reckless car heading toward the school bus—was that just a hallucination? And the drawing in Clover's diary—was that also imagined?

Because he'd been adopted, Vero had often wondered about his biological parents. Now an image of a man and woman wearing straightjackets came to mind. Vero dropped the laundry bag, raced down the stairs and straight out the back door. He needed to get away from it all.

Vero ran into the backyard, trying to clear his head. His life was spinning out of control. Tears burned the corners of his eyes, and he fought to catch his breath. Twelve-year-old boys shouldn't cry. He was too old for this, but he couldn't stop the tears from leaking out of his eyes.

What's wrong with me? Am I crazy? He thought of the creature he'd seen in that car. Was he completely losing it?

He looked up at the low-hanging clouds as fresh snow started falling in big, fat flakes. The sight of the snow calmed him for a moment. He took in some deep breaths, and then slowly he became aware of the cold and realized he wasn't wearing a coat or boots. He'd been so distraught when he first came outside that he hadn't even noticed the frigid weather.

Looking around, he saw that the day's snowfall had turned everything completely white. The snow had interrupted daily life in the suburbs, and out here, at this moment, the stillness triumphed. The world felt eternally quiet.

Vero collapsed onto his back and stared up at the cold sky, as if it might hold some answers for him. He remembered his rooftop adventure all those Christmases ago, the feeling of standing on the roof, the certainty that he could jump into the crisp, clear sky and soar. And what about the man who had caught him? Did Vero imagine him as well?

Vero forced that notion away and thought of winter days long ago, when he and Clover played in the snow for hours and made snow angels across the lawn. Vero smiled to himself and then swept his arms and legs back and forth, like he and Clover used to do. The repetitive motion soothed him.

The longer Vero swept his limbs, the more tranquility embraced him. He closed his eyes, and his old urge to fly came back so powerfully that Vero fell into a trance. For the first time in a long time, the pain in his back was gone and a content smile spread across his face.

Vero had no idea how long he stayed there in the white stillness. Time seemed to stop, until, "*Squaaak!*"

A black raven flew overhead. *Was that a tail hanging from its backside?* Vero was suddenly very aware of the wet, cold snow.

"*Gawwk!*" the raven cawed again.

Were its eyes glowing red? Vero pushed himself up from the snow, and the raven flew away. Vero's body now felt heavy. He stood up and gazed down at his depression in the snow, his snow angel, with a mix of awe and fear. The wings were at least six feet long, with feathery details that Michelangelo himself could have painstakingly fashioned! Yet Vero had absolutely no recollection of making them.

Mental. He dashed into the garage, grabbed a shovel, and frantically dumped shovelful after shovelful of snow over his splendid angel. Ruining it felt like a sin, but he couldn't have anyone seeing this. He could only imagine what the Atwoods would say if they happened to peer over their fence and see it.

When he finished hiding the evidence, Vero leaned against the shovel to catch his breath. Then he looked up at Clover's window just in time to see her face disappear behind her curtains.

7

THE FALL

"Now, Vero, can you describe what you saw on the bus that day?" the stout, frizzy-haired counselor asked.

Vero sat on a sofa across from Dr. Weiss, who put her stubby legs up on her chair and proceeded to sit cross-legged. She picked up a yellow legal pad and a pen from the coffee table. Her brightly colored walls with murals of rainbows, stars, and cute furry animals were trying their best to relax him. But for Vero, no matter how many Skittles or M&Ms she offered him, Dr. Weiss was still a psychiatrist who had the power to lock him away in a nuthouse.

"Just take your time and tell me everything that happened."

Vero hesitated. He knew he had to be careful about his choice of words because so much depended on it.

"We got out of school early because of the snow ... " he began.

"Do you like snow, Vero?" she interrupted. "I love it. I always have."

"I like it except for when I have to shovel the driveway," Vero said.

Dr. Weiss laughed. "Good point."

"I got on the bus and sat behind the driver," Vero continued.

"Do kids pick on you? Is that why you sat behind the driver?" Dr. Weiss asked.

"No, I don't usually sit there. There just weren't any other seats open because of the snow," Vero fought to keep his voice civil.

But being a psychiatrist, Dr. Weiss seemed to notice the annoyance in his voice, and she instantly backed off. "Okay," she said, sitting back in her chair. "Then what happened?"

"We were driving, and the snow started hitting the windshield really hard. That's when I saw the other car coming into our lane."

Vero paused. *Should I continue?*

Dr. Weiss scribbled some notes across her legal pad. "And?"

"That's it," Vero said, deciding that he'd better stop there.

"I think you're not telling me everything."

Vero shook his head. He wasn't going to give her any more.

Dr. Weiss picked up the phone on the coffee table and spoke into it. "Could you bring Sprite in here?"

Before she'd replaced the receiver, the office door opened and a female Jack Russell terrier puppy bounded into the room. Sprite ran to Vero and immediately began tugging on his shoelaces. Vero laughed, picked her up, and held her on his lap. Sprite began licking his face.

"Isn't she cute?" Dr. Weiss asked as she reached over to pet the dog's head. "She's such a good girl." And that's when Dr. Weiss went in for the kill. "Vero, in order for me to help you, I need to know what you saw on that bus."

The puppy made him feel more at ease, and Vero dropped his guard. "The driver of the car was wrestling for control of the steering wheel. He was trying to yank it away from the scary guy ... "

But Dr. Weiss didn't hear the words *scary guy* because at that very moment, an ambulance sped past the window with its siren blaring.

"What? What did you say?" Dr. Weiss asked.

The surprise of the siren startled Vero and Sprite. The puppy jumped off his lap, and the moment was over.

"Who was the driver wrestling with?" she asked.

Vero knew that lying was wrong, but he couldn't tell her the truth. It was kind of like when Great-Aunt Sophie's hair-dresser burned a huge bald spot on the top of Sophie's head. When she asked Vero if she still looked pretty, he told her yes. It was a lie, of course. But the way Vero saw it, to tell the truth in that instance would just be mean.

Now with his sanity being questioned, Vero decided this was another time when he would need to stretch the truth. "I said he was wrestling with the steering wheel." Then Vero looked at the floor and managed to produce some real tears to make his story more convincing. "The car slid a little bit into our lane. Just like everyone said. I made the whole story up."

She handed him a tissue. "Why, Vero? Why did you do that?"

"Everyone was being mean to me. I had a bad day at school, and Tack, he's my best friend, he was mad at me and wouldn't let me sit with him on the bus. And then my sister ignored me. I was mad at both of them. So when the car slid across the center line, I thought that if I pretended to save everyone, then Tack and Clover would think I'd saved their lives and be nice to me again."

Dr. Weiss handed Vero another tissue, gave his forearm an encouraging squeeze, looked him square in the eyes, and said, "That was excellent sharing, Vero." Then she winked at Sprite and said, "And *you're* getting a steak bone tonight."

Vero glanced at the clock. It was exactly 11:30 a.m. Right now the kids in his class would be headed to the cafeteria for lunch. It was a bright, clear day, so they'd probably go outside and pelt each other with snowballs after they finished eating. He, however, was stuck sitting in the waiting room while his parents met with Dr. Weiss.

The receptionist was out for lunch. Vero had already leafed through all of the magazines, so he walked over to the aquarium and watched the fish swim back and forth, back and forth, over and over again. He envied the simplicity of their existence. Their entire lives were limited to the space within those four glass walls. Every day it was always the same—no surprises. The fish knew exactly what to expect—something Vero deeply craved.

Vero decided to use the restroom. He picked up the bathroom key from the receptionist's desk. The key was attached to a Rubik's Cube by a little chain, so no one could put it in his pocket and accidentally take off with it. Vero walked out of the waiting room and down the hallway to the men's room.

The doors on all three stalls were closed, so Vero bent down and looked for feet underneath. Empty.

A minute later, Vero was washing his hands in the sink when a rattling sound came from one of the stalls. Startled, he splashed water on himself.

"Ah man ... " he said aloud. He turned around, but the restroom was still empty. His heartbeat picked up a beat. But then he noticed an exposed heating unit overhead, just like the one in Tack's house.

That was it, Vero thought. The heater in Tack's house was ancient and made the same sound when it was running.

Vero looked down and saw that the front of his pants were wet. "Great," he said. "Now it looks like I peed my pants." He could just imagine the worried glances that would fly between his mom and dad and Dr. Weiss. *Maybe he's worse than we thought.* He searched for some paper towels, but there was only an electric hand dryer. He turned the drying nozzle so it pointed toward the floor and tried to contort his body underneath it. He was about to press the On button when a loud banging started from inside the end stall. Vero whipped around, his chest tight with fear, and his wet pants forgotten.

"Who's there?" Vero asked, but he knew no one had come into the restroom.

No reply.

Get out! Something inside urged him. *Now!*

Vero turned to run out, but he slipped on the wet floor and fell — hard. With his head pressed to the concrete floor, he now had a clear view under the bathroom stalls. This time he saw two sets of feet that hadn't been there before — and they weren't human!

Am I hallucinating? Do I need to be locked up in a loony bin?

What he saw were two sets of ugly, claw-like feet that resembled talons. He'd just hit his head on the floor, so could he be unconscious? Dreaming? Then the stall doors opened, and Vero saw the rest of the creatures who were attached to the clawed feet. He was in trouble.

They were covered in scales and fur and sharp claws for their hands and feet, a tiny slit for a mouth, and where there should have been a nose was only a flat space. But the worst part of their appearance was their eyes — or, actually, *eye*. Each creature had a single eye.

One of them turned its hideous head, and Vero saw that the eye went clear through, so it could see backward and forward at the same time!

Vero jumped up and sprinted for the door. Both creatures got down on all fours and bounded after him. Vero grabbed the door handle. A vague image of his mother flew through his mind, and he heard her say, "Use a paper towel whenever you leave a public bathroom, so you don't pick up more germs."

Sorry, Mom.

He needed to get out of there now! But before he could leave the room, a sharp pain ripped through his leg. One of the creatures had clawed him and was attempting to pull him back. Not waiting to see what would happen next, Vero kicked the creature as hard as he could in its grizzly face and dashed into the hallway.

He meant to run back to Dr. Weiss's office, but he sprinted the wrong way down the hall. He ran as fast as he could. He knew he needed to get outside, but he'd never been inside this building before. He ran straight into a dead end. He quickly turned around and, to his horror, saw the two creatures blocking him in, taunting him, and slowly, methodically approaching him from the other end of the hallway.

Vero stood frozen with terror.

Suddenly, they leapt toward him. Their bodies were turned backward as they flew the length of the hallway—the bloodshot eye in the back of each creature's head guiding them.

Please help me.

From the corner of his eye, Vero saw an emergency exit door, and he pushed through it mere milliseconds before the creatures were upon him.

Vero dashed up a staircase, winning some distance as the creatures struggled to open the door with their claws. But they soon followed, screeching in rage.

As Vero ran, he realized he was jumping whole staircases in a single bound—just like when he'd run the hurdles. He was so light on his feet that he quickly found himself at the top of the emergency staircase and bounded onto the roof of the office building. Though he had just cleared nine stories in a blink, Vero felt no need to catch his breath. He rapidly scanned the roof, looking for some way to escape. He was trapped.

The creatures appeared on the roof. Feeling no need to rush since Vero had nowhere to go, they steadily approached him, smiling evil, hideous smiles.

And that smile stretched their slitlike mouths clear across their faces, revealing rows of sharp, yellow fangs. When Vero glimpsed those fangs, he knew he couldn't win.

"What do you want?" Vero asked desperately.

The creatures' loud replies contained no words, only strange clicking and hissing sounds.

Vero slowly backed away until he was almost standing at the edge of the roof, and still the creatures pressed him. Then his foot got caught on a metal pipe that was part of the air conditioning system, and for a single moment, Vero balanced on the edge. But he was too far gone.

As he plunged off the side of the building, he flailed his arms wildly and somehow managed to catch hold of a ledge with his right hand. Then he swung his left hand up and dangled there, breathing heavily, nine stories above the concrete sidewalk below.

His whole life, Vero had believed he could fly. And he'd fearlessly jumped off of anything he could climb. But now, Vero wanted to cling to that edge with all his might. He closed his eyes against the dizziness.

Help me! Please!

From the rooftop above him, Vero heard an ear-piercing shriek, then the sound of metal clanging on metal, like the sound of clashing swords.

As Vero squinted into the sunlight above, the horrid face of one of the beasts appeared over the edge. Vero's heart pounded as he dangled from the ledge and looked into the eye of the beast. He saw the decaying, putrid teeth, and a drop of saliva fell from its gnarled tongue onto Vero's cheek, burning it like acid. But Vero did not let go. He could hear a scuffle on the roof above and beyond his line of sight.

The creature snarled viciously and opened its mouth, preparing to attack. But suddenly its head jerked back violently and out of Vero's view. Then a shrill wail sent a chill straight through him, and it was followed by an enormous thud. Vero felt himself slipping. He closed his eyes, preparing to fall, when a man's head peered out over the ledge.

"Grab my hand!" the man shouted.

The man stretched his hand toward Vero. Vero hesitated. Could this be one of the creatures in disguise? But his violet eyes looked familiar.

"Take it if you want to save your life! They're going to come right back!"

At this point Vero realized he didn't have much of a choice. So in an act of complete blind faith, Vero removed his right hand from the ledge and reached up to grab the man's hand. The man smiled warmly, and Vero felt relief— until the man abruptly withdrew his hand.

That day, Vero Leland fell nine stories and hit the pavement with a bone-crushing thud. He was dead.

8

❖

HOME

Tack once told Vero a joke.

"What's the last thing that goes through a bug's mind when it hits the windshield?"

Vero shrugged, not knowing.

"His butt!" Tack laughed.

A lot of things went through Vero's mind before he hit the pavement. Thoughts flew through his mind in flashes, in fractions of seconds, in completely random segments:

He wondered how much pain he would feel when his body broke into pieces.

He thought of his last birthday and realized there would never be another soccer ball cake or thirteenth birthday.

He thought of the bathroom key attached to the Rubik's cube. What had happened to it during his struggle with those creatures?

His last thought was of his mother and the heartbreaking look on her face when she was given the news of his death.

Then blackness.

"Come on, get up," Vero heard the voice and felt someone nudge his shoulder. He opened his eyes, and a face gradually came into focus.

"You!" Vero cried. "You tricked me!" It was the man from the ledge.

"Now before you jump to conclusions," the man said, "there are two sides to every story."

"Not in this case," Vero argued. He sat up and touched his chest, his shoulders, his head. "You let me fall!"

"If you'll recall, I said to take my hand if you want to live, and now here you are."

"What the . . . ?" Vero found no blood, nor cuts or bruises. His bones appeared to be intact. "Am I dead?"

"Well," the man answered. "That's not an easy question to answer."

"I fell from up there." Vero pointed to the top of the building.

Vero was more confused than ever, but one thing became very clear to him — he knew the man standing before him. He recognized the tightly cropped silver beard, which was the same color as his shoulder-length hair, the strong jawline, and those bright violet eyes.

"You caught me when I jumped off the roof that Christmas."

The man nodded. "See? I said you could trust me."

"You twisted my ankle!" Vero said. "And now you dropped me off a nine-story building! Who are you? And what's going on?" Vero jumped up and began pacing frantically, still checking his arms, his head, his ankles.

"I didn't have a choice, Vero. I had to make it look real. I couldn't have them find out who you are."

Vero froze. "Who am I?" he asked. He gazed into the man's eyes trying to decipher something, anything that might explain how he was still walking and talking instead of being road pizza.

"Not now. We've got to get out of here."

The man held his hand.

"I'm not falling for that again."

"Look, Vero, it seems you and I got off on the wrong foot ... no pun intended," he began. "But you need to —"

"You just killed me! That's a bit worse than getting off on the wrong foot!" Vero yelled. "And now you won't even tell me if I'm dead or not!"

"Do you see those two creatures anywhere? The ones who were about to rip off your head?"

Vero looked around. The creatures were nowhere in sight.

"Yeah, you can thank me for that," the man answered. "Now come with me."

Vero shook his head and backed away from the stranger. He ran to the front of the building where just an hour before he'd arrived with his mom and dad to see Dr. Weiss. Vero pulled on the door handle, but no matter how hard he tugged, the door wouldn't open. He kicked the door.

"Open!" he screamed. Then he kicked the door again.

"You're wasting my time," the man said.

Vero didn't care. He ran the length of the building to Dr. Weiss's window, where he could see his parents deeply engrossed in conversation with the doctor, talking about him.

"Mom! Dad!" Vero screamed and wildly flailed his arms, but not one of them so much as glanced Vero's way.

The man followed Vero and watched him pound on the glass. "They can't see you," he said.

"Then I *am* dead." The awareness was brutal.

The man placed his hand on Vero's shoulder. "Now will you come with me?"

Vero looked at the man, at his outstretched hand, and Vero grabbed hold of it.

The buildings, the trees, cars and people, everything before Vero's eyes melted away in a flash and was replaced by a lush green field that had no end. Effervescent wildflowers dotted the fields with colors so bright that Vero wished he had his sunglasses. Instead, he shaded his eyes with his hand and tried to take it all in.

In the distance Vero saw clusters of magnificent trees with leaves that closely matched the colors of the brilliant wildflowers. Red wasn't just red, and blue wasn't just blue. It was as if someone had taken a rainbow and wrung it through their hands, pouring the colors out upon the earth. The sky above was a blue so deep that it was nearly violet, and he felt warmth emanating from it, yet he saw no sun. It was as if he was being embraced by the sky. And the longer Vero stood there, the more he felt like this place wasn't so foreign after all. He felt comfortable with his surroundings, a sense of belonging.

"Is this heaven?"

"No."

"But if I'm dead, there are only two places you can go." A real fear overtook his thoughts. "So if it's not heaven, then is it . . . ?"

"It's the Ether."

"That's what I'm asking. Either what?"

"Not either. *Ether*. E-t-h-e-r." The man spelled it out. "The upper air. It has existed since the beginning. It's what ancient Greek philosophers described as that which is not known or understood but is essential to life. The Ether cannot be tested or proven in a lab, yet it is all around us."

The man looked at Vero with a steadfast gaze, his violet eyes intense. "You know this place, Vero. Close your eyes and let it wash over you. It's calling to you."

Vero closed his eyes and took several deep breaths. The man picked a wildflower and placed it in Vero's hand. As Vero opened his eyes and looked at the flower, he instantly understood the complexity of its nature and its simple beauty all at once, as if he could see right through it.

Vero felt as if he were seeing things clearly for the first time in his life. He looked at his surroundings. The trees, the grass, the sky, it all beckoned to him.

"Where are you, Vero?"

Vero didn't hesitate.

"Home."

"It's been a long time since you were here," the man said.

"I guess. I don't remember much," Vero replied.

"True knowledge unfolds in its own sweet time, and we don't want to overload you all at once."

Suddenly, a rustling in the tall grass caught Vero's attention, and he saw gazelles calmly grazing next to a pair of lions a few feet away. A male and female monkey happily swung from tree branch to tree branch. Two hippos sunned themselves along the banks of a mighty river. Vero gazed across the scene before him. Animals of all kinds roamed in every direction.

"Why are there two of all the animals?" Vero asked.

"You've gone to Sunday school, so you should know the answer," the man replied.

"You mean these are the actual animals ...?"

The man nodded.

"But they get along with each other."

"When they lived in such tight quarters on the ark, they learned to get along if they were to survive ... a lesson humans have yet to learn."

Without warning, the male lion bounded out from under a tree and darted over to Vero. Vero froze. His legs wouldn't move. As the lion approached, Vero protectively covered his face with his arms. But then, the ferocious lion fell to his feet, bowing his head to Vero. Vero's eyes went wide with disbelief.

"He's friendly," the man encouraged him.

Vero hesitantly stretched out his hand and stroked the lion's head. The lion rubbed his body against Vero like a cat.

Suddenly, the light above began to swirl into the shape of a circle, growing bigger and bigger. It spun so wide, it looked as if the sky had opened up. The swirling lights began to take form. They were angels, thousands and thousands of angelic beings flying at high speed.

Vero's mouth dropped open at the sight of the grandiose creatures with colossal wings. He felt their strength and power. He longed to join them, to be in their company.

Vero fell to the ground. He felt as if someone had punched him hard in the back, followed by overwhelming relief. He rose to his feet and stood, magnificent alabaster wings jutting out between his shoulders. The sky closed up, and the angelic beings disappeared from sight. Vero turned to the man.

"Am I ...?" Vero began.

The man quickly cut him off.

"Yes, Vero. You are a guardian angel."

9

***

THE ETHER
AND BACK

As Vero sat on the ground, his wings smoothly retracted inside his back with a slight popping sensation, almost like when Vero cracked his knuckles.

"Did I just do that?" Vero asked.

The man nodded.

"Where did my wings go?"

"They're hidden once again until you learn to handle them better. It takes time. But soon you'll be able to control them as easily as you move your arm."

With his left hand, Vero reached around and felt his back.

"My shirt's not ripped!"

"It mends itself each time."

"Are you a guardian angel too?" Vero asked the man.

The man shook his head and sat down next to Vero.

"I'm an archangel ... Uriel." He looked at Vero expectantly, one eyebrow raised over his violet eyes and a slight grin on his face.

Uriel? Then it dawned on Vero, and he blushed guiltily.

"Yes, your paper on *Paradise Lost.* You pinned the whole expulsion from the garden on me."

"Well, I meant ... uh, I didn't mean you were like drinking on the job or anything like that ... "

"Gee thanks," Uriel's words dripped with sarcasm. "It's not so easy recognizing the Wicked One. He's the master of deception."

His words rattled Vero back to the memory of the two frightening creatures that had chased him earlier.

"So who was chasing me?"

"Those were two of the Wicked One's minions. He sent them after you."

"But why me?"

"Because you're good. The Wicked One hates anything good. He wants to destroy all that is good."

"But now that I'm dead, he can't come after me, right?"

"Yes, he can," Uriel said. "And you're not really dead."

"But I fell from a nine-story building!" Vero protested. Vero thought of his mom and dad back on earth, probably wondering and worrying over where he was. Then Vero thought of Clover, her face in the bedroom window, the rainy days spent indoors, her mortified look as the bus drove off without him. The thought of Clover all on her own brought a well of emotions bubbling to the surface until Vero felt tears forming in his eyes. Vero held his face in his hands, embarrassed.

Uriel knelt before Vero and removed his hands from

his face. Vero lifted his head and met Uriel's gaze. His face seemed softer.

"Vero, you are made of the Spirit. And nothing of the Spirit can ever die."

Uriel stood beside Vero as he stroked the lion's head; his eyes were fixed on the puffy clouds above. Vero watched as they molded into the shape of a lion. Then just as quickly, they changed into a single cloud that resembled Clover's face. The clouds then shaped themselves into a huge question mark. Uriel chuckled when he saw the perplexed look on Vero's face.

"Uriel, how . . . ?"

"You're doing that with your thoughts," he explained.

"I was thinking it was so cool that I was petting a lion. But then I wished Clover could also pet him, and then I wondered how the clouds knew what I was thinking. Everything here is amazing. How can this not be heaven?"

Uriel chuckled. "You obviously haven't seen heaven."

"Seriously?" Vero must have looked as astonished as he felt because Uriel laughed again. "Don't get me wrong. These parts of the Ether are wonderful; but Vero, this is our battleground. The Ether is where we fight our spiritual battles."

"I don't understand," Vero said.

"The Ether is the spiritual realm that surrounds the earth. Lucifer and his evil followers also dwell here. They do everything in their power to destroy man, or at least what's good about man, and we do everything in our power to stop them."

"So where's your sword? Don't angels have swords?" Vero asked.

"Only when needed." Uriel began walking across the field. Vero followed.

"But guardian angels protect people, right?"

"Yes," Uriel replied.

"Is that what I'll be doing from now on?"

Vero watched as a flock of angels flew overhead.

"You will be trained first," Uriel explained. "You won't become a full guardian until you have completed your training. Then, once your training is complete, you will choose your destiny."

"I thought *this* was my destiny?"

"An angel is who you are. However, your destiny will be determined by the decisions you make."

"But ... "

"Vero, you were created with the gift of free will." Uriel stopped walking, grabbed Vero's shoulders, and looked very intently into his eyes. "At some point, we all have to choose between the light or the darkness."

"But I'm an angel, and angels are always good."

Uriel dropped his hands from Vero's shoulders. "Lucifer was once the most glorious of angels and loved by God. But when he fell, one-third of the angel ranks went with him. One-third chose to live outside the Light."

Vero pondered what Uriel said. The idea of the angels falling into darkness terrified him. What if that was his destiny? Would he really need to make that choice?

"Don't be frightened," Uriel said, placing his hand over Vero's heart. "A pure heart will never lead you astray."

Uriel removed his hand. "Now it's time for you to go back."

Vero raised his eyebrows, "Back where?"

"To earth, of course."

"I'm not staying here?"

"You will return for your training," Uriel said. "But for now, you are to go back to your family. Don't you miss them?"

Suddenly, a wave of homesickness swept over Vero. He looked to Uriel, crestfallen, "I know I was adopted, but I guess now my mom and dad really *aren't* my family anymore — "

"Your family is the people you love," Uriel cut him off.

"Do I have angel parents?" Vero asked.

"No, angels don't have children. Just as God is everyone's Father, so it is the same for us."

"But what if I no longer fit in down on earth?"

"Why wouldn't you?"

Vero spread his arms wide and said, "Because after all of this, do you think I can just sit down with my family and have a normal dinner? Should I ask Clover to pass me the milk and add, 'Oh, and by the way, I just happen to be a guardian angel'? Is that what you expect me to do?"

"Don't ever tell *anyone*," Uriel said sternly. "I stopped you once already in the psychiatrist's office. I sent that ambulance when you were about to mention the malture in the car."

"You did that?" The psychiatrist's office seemed like another lifetime ago.

Uriel nodded, "We can never appear to humans in our angelic form unless God allows us."

"What's a malture?"

"Maltures are Satan's creations — the evil fiends that tempt humans."

"How could Lucifer create anything?" Vero asked.

"Well, he can't create anything good. These maltures are an extension of his own evil and hatred. They have no souls."

Vero thought about the bus that day and what he'd witnessed. "That guy in the backseat of that car—he was a malture, wasn't he? One of them was trying to crash that car into the bus!"

Uriel nodded. "Yes, he was. I saw him too. And you did well, Vero . . . you have all the right instincts."

Vero smiled for what felt like the first time in a long time. *I'm not crazy,* he thought.

"You instinctively protected and saved those kids—exactly what a guardian angel is supposed to do."

Suddenly Uriel's eyes took on a faraway look. He was seeing something else.

What is it? Vero wondered.

Uriel turned to Vero. "I have to go," he said. "One of your fellow guardian angels is slacking off on the job and about to cause a ten-car pileup on a bridge."

"But I have a million more questions!" Vero protested.

"Just recall the last normal thing you were doing before all of this happened, and then I'll be in touch!"

Colossal wings shot out from Uriel's back. Uriel's wings were more elaborate than the other angels' wings, with outer feathers adorned in gold. A golden glow embraced Uriel as his wings created a gust of wind, knocking Vero to the ground.

"Don't worry, Vero, we'll be watching you."

Then the wind stopped blowing, the glow disappeared, and Uriel was gone.

Vero stood and looked out over the animals grazing in the lush fields. He closed his eyes and turned his face up to the sky, feeling the warmth of the light upon him. He wondered whether he would ever return to the Ether. Would he wake up in the morning and realize it had all been nothing but a dream?

Vero tried to remember where he'd been before the craziness began. He pictured his mother and father sitting in Dr. Weiss's office; but when he opened his eyes, he was still standing in the Ether. He closed his eyes once more and saw himself falling from the rooftop. He felt something wet on his cheek and opened his eyes. The lion was licking his face like a faithful dog. Vero stroked his mane.

"I have to go," he told the lion. "Hopefully, I'll see you again."

Vero gave it one last shot. This time when he closed his eyes, he saw himself standing in the men's room holding the Rubik's Cube attached to the key. When he opened his eyes, he stood before the stall doors and the sinks. Fear gripped him as he remembered the hideous maltures. But when Vero looked under the stall doors, there was nothing there — no hooked claws. He surveyed the bathroom and saw no sign of his previous struggle. Everything was in order, including himself — no bruises, cuts, or scrapes. Even his ripped pant leg from where the malture had clawed him was now perfectly mended.

Vero walked out of the bathroom and down the hallway. He opened Dr. Weiss's office door. The waiting room was still empty — except for the fish swimming around in their protected little world. He returned the Rubik's Cube key to the receptionist's desk and collapsed in a chair, completely exhausted. He glanced at the clock and saw the big hand click to 11:31. No time had passed since he'd been to the Ether! *How could that be?*

He heard his parents' voices inside Dr. Weiss's office.

They were on their way out. And they had no clue that while they'd been discussing his mental state, Vero had been attacked by two maltures, fallen off a roof, died, gone to the Ether, discovered he was a guardian angel, and returned to earth good as new.

As his parents opened the door, sweat trickled down Vero's forehead. Would they suspect anything?

His mom walked out and glanced at Vero with an odd expression on her face. Vero felt his heart drop into his stomach. *She knew!*

But then she smiled warmly and said, "Vero, tie your shoelaces before you trip."

"I was thinking we could go get some burgers for lunch," his dad announced.

Seeing his parents standing there wearing their sensible shoes and winter parkas, their ordinariness deeply moved Vero, and he realized that ordinary was something he would never be again. He hugged both his parents, afraid to let them go. He feared that if he did, he'd be letting go of the only life he'd ever known.

"It's okay, Vero," his dad reassured him. "You're going to be all right."

But his words were of little comfort. Vero's father had no idea that the boy he embraced wasn't even human. And he certainly wouldn't be able to protect his son from those maltures, should they ever return. All of it terrified him, but what scared Vero most of all was a question — would his parents still love him if they knew the truth?

Dr. Weiss walked into the waiting room with Sprite nipping at her heels.

"Hey now, don't take it so hard," Vero's dad said as he ended the hug. "Dr. Weiss says you'll be fine."

"We're happy you told the whole truth," Dr. Weiss said, patting Vero's back.

Vero caught his mother's gaze. Her worried expression told him she knew there was more to the story.

10

THE BULLIES

After his return from the Ether, Vero didn't want to be around anyone. He was still trying to make sense of everything that had happened there, so he told his parents he didn't feel well. They let him stay home from school the next day. And the next. And even the next. He also kept his distance from Clover—who probably didn't even realize he was doing it—and he avoided Tack as well, except for a few online rounds of golf on the latest edition of *The PGA Tour*.

Vero watched TV and played video games to dull his senses, but they proved to be only momentary distractions because his thoughts would always stray back to the Ether.

The Ether had been beyond glorious. It was so amazing, in fact, that it was now difficult for him to be confined inside a two-story house. He knew the walls of the house no longer defined his home—his true home was the infinite space of the Ether.

His parents loved him so much and had given him a wonderful home all these years, but he was beginning to feel like one of those birds in a cage at the pet store. The word *confused* couldn't even begin to cover it. Vero was a mess. He eventually retreated to the privacy of his bedroom and spent most of the day lying on his bed and staring at the ceiling.

His dad assumed he was upset and embarrassed by the bus incident. Being a nurse, his mom knew he had no fever or sore throat. She worried there was something else going on with him. But after a week of seclusion, both parents agreed he should return to school.

School now felt like an exercise in futility. Vero knew he would learn more in five minutes with Uriel than all his teachers could teach him during an entire year of school. To make matters worse, Coach Randy continued to hound Vero about joining the track team. But he refused. With the bus incident still fresh in everyone's minds, Vero didn't want to draw any more attention to himself.

Most kids avoided him, staying as far away as possible. When Vero walked down the hallway, it was like Moses parting a Red Sea of students. One day poor Nate scurried past him so fast that he wasn't watching where he was going and smashed his head on the open door of a metal locker.

When Vero tried to help him up, Nate stuttered, "No ... no ... I'm ... uh ... all good."

"It's awesome that you have that kind of power," Tack told Vero during lunch period.

Vero and Tack were sitting at a table in the cafeteria with noticeably empty space all around them. Vero glanced around the room and met eyes with Danny, who then moved both his fists like he was grabbing a car steering wheel. His friends, Blake and Duff, laughed and pointed at Vero.

Blake and Duff were big for their ages. They looked more like high school seniors than eighth graders, scruffy beards and all. Lately they seemed to follow Danny everywhere. But Vero rarely had to deal with them because Tack was usually at his side. No one wanted to mess with Tack who was equally big for his age, minus the beard.

Vero turned back to Tack. "You wanna trade places?"

"In a heartbeat," Tack answered. "That's *real* power when everyone is afraid of you."

Vero gave him a look.

"Okay, well, at least you're not being shoved into garbage cans or getting wedgies in the locker room anymore."

"Thanks," Vero said. "That makes me feel so much better."

As Danny continued to mock Vero from across the cafeteria, his elbow accidentally knocked over his drink. Water spilled all over the table and onto Blake's lap. He jumped up and headed for the restroom to get cleaned up. Duff followed him out the door, but not before sending Danny a menacing look over his shoulder.

"See? It's Karma," Tack said. "Danny made fun of you and look what happened!"

Davina quickly swooped in with some napkins to help clean up the mess. With her trademark smile, she picked Danny's cup off the floor and handed it to him. But her hand lingered near his for a split second too long, at least in Vero's opinion.

"Thanks," Danny said. His face lit up when Davina sat next to him.

Across the cafeteria, Vero watched with a jealous eye as

Davina and Danny spent the rest of the lunch hour talking and laughing.

"Some Karma," Vero muttered to himself.

By the end of the day, Vero was more than ready to leave school. Even though he was officially allowed back on the bus, his dad thought it might be better if he waited a few more days. So the buses all left without him. But by four o'clock, his father still hadn't arrived.

It was bitter cold outside, so Vero was waiting in the lobby, incessantly looking out the window for his dad's car, while constantly sidestepping the janitor's mop. It would be so great if he could just use his wings and fly home. It was totally unfair of Uriel to send him back to earth and expect him to act like nothing had ever happened.

"Forget this," Vero said. He shoved the door to the school open and trudged outside. The wintry air swept across his face and instantly invigorated him. He felt powerful. With a fierce determination, Vero walked around the side of the brick building. Scanning the area to make sure he was alone, he placed the palms of his hands against the wall of the school to brace himself. He knew the force of his wings could knock him to the ground. Vero closed his eyes tight, mustered up all his strength, and willed his wings to appear.

Nothing happened.

"Come on!" he shouted.

So he tried even harder and with a fiercer resolve. Sweat dripped down his face despite the frigid air. Still no wings.

He let out a yowl of frustration and banged his fist against the bricks.

"Hey, nut job! What did that wall ever do to you?" Danny yelled from behind him.

Could this get any better?

Vero turned around and saw Danny and his two buddies, Duff and Blake, standing there. All three of them were smiling darkly.

"Hey, wacko! He asked you a question!" Duff called.

Vero didn't respond. He started walking back toward the school entrance. He *did not* want to deal with these guys right now. But before he'd taken but a few steps, Blake grabbed Vero's shoulder and spun him around.

"It's rude to walk away when someone's talking to you. Didn't your mother teach you any manners?"

"Look, I'm just waiting for my ride."

"Well, I don't think they're coming," Danny said, looking around. "Even Mommy and Daddy don't care about you."

Vero felt his blood pressure rising. "No!" he shouted back. "Everybody knows that's *your* parents!"

A dark look passed over Danny's face, and Vero knew his words had stung. For a brief instant, Vero felt bad for Danny.

"Get him!" Blake said to Danny.

"Don't let him get away with that!" Duff shouted.

Before Vero could make a run for it, Danny's fist cut him hard across the jaw.

Vero staggered backward into Duff, who caught Vero and shoved him back toward Danny, who then hit him again — this time in the nose. Blood trickled down Vero's face. Duff and Blake laughed.

"I don't think he's learned his lesson yet," Blake said.

Danny seemed to hesitate, but Vero was done with this abuse. He was a guardian angel! A powerful being to whom lions bowed down! Vero made a fist and was about to strike Danny with his full strength when an unseen force prevented his arm from moving.

What? Not fair!

Danny took advantage of Vero's hesitation and slugged him hard in the gut. Vero doubled over and fell to the ground, cutting his forehead on the corner of a cement flowerbed.

"Bull's-eye!" Duff shrieked as he high-fived Blake.

Vero curled up on the ground, winded and in pain.

The bully crew walked on by, and as Duff passed him, he turned and spit on Vero.

What was that? For a split second, Duff's unusually blue eyes seemed to flash red!

Then a drop of blood dripped from the gash in his forehead.

No, Vero thought. *It was just my own blood blurring my vision.*

11

FAILED FLIGHT

The last thing Vero wanted was to attract more attention, so he didn't tell anyone about his encounter with Blake, Duff, and Danny—but especially not Tack. Tack would either (a) retaliate, or (b) make Vero retaliate. Neither one was an option. Vero still couldn't wrap his mind around what had happened when he'd tried to hit Danny, or what he thought he'd seen afterward ...

Not going there.

Instead, he worked hard to regain anonymity. His life became quiet and monotonous. Vero's basic routine consisted of going to school, going home, going to his bedroom, going to dinner, and going back to his bedroom. Yet his mind was consumed with thoughts of the Ether.

When will I see Uriel again? Had it really happened?

Eventually Vero broke his routine and went to a movie with Tack one Saturday morning.

"Wasn't it awesome when that meteor hit the dam and the water flooded everything?" Tack asked as they walked out of the theater and into the lobby.

"Yeah," Vero answered, completely disinterested.

"Or when that second meteor hit the desert and created that sandstorm?"

"Yeah, great," Vero said halfheartedly.

The truth was, all Vero could think about was the Ether.

"That movie's got Oscar written all over it!" Tack said as he pressed the Down elevator button. "Oh man, look!"

Vero turned around and saw a group of girls exiting the same theater. They were giggling about something. Were they laughing at him? Then Vero noticed one of the girls was Davina.

Tack licked the palm of his hand and tried to smooth down the double cowlick that made his hair protrude at the back of his head.

"How do I look?" Tack asked as the girls approached.

Vero didn't answer. He was too preoccupied with the sight of Davina. She'd been one of the few bright spots of being back on earth.

"Is my hair sticking up?" Tack asked.

With their backs to the elevator doors, Tack and Vero watched the girls pass by. They heard the chime and *whoosh* of the elevator doors opening.

"Dude, did you hear me?" Tack asked, giving Vero's shoulder a shove. "Can't you at least acknowledge me or something?"

Taken by surprise, Vero stumbled backward through the

open elevator doors—except there was no elevator floor to catch him!

When Vero opened his eyes, he was lying under a tree with delicious-looking apples, oranges, lemons, peaches, and pears hanging from its branches. He breathed in the magnificent aroma of the fruit, and he experienced instant peace.

Vero was back in the Ether.

As he was lying on his back, just marveling at the different fruits all sprouting from one tree, he felt a foot nudge his side. He quickly sat up and saw a girl with a slight build towering over him. She looked to be about his age. And she was pretty. Her skin was olive, her eyes were bright, and she had curly auburn hair—the fiery color of autumn leaves.

"You can eat some of those, if you want," she told him, absentmindedly twirling a curl around one of her fingers. "None of the trees are off-limits here."

The girl picked a peach off the tree and handed it to Vero. It was the size of a soccer ball, and Vero had to hold it with both hands.

"I don't know whether to dribble it or eat it," Vero said.

Then, right before his eyes, a tiny bud blossomed in the exact spot where the girl had picked the giant peach. It quickly grew in size until it matched the one Vero held. Vero looked at the new peach in complete astonishment.

"Pretty cool, huh?" the girl said. "Go ahead, try it!"

Vero looked at the peach and then back at the girl suspiciously. "Who are you?"

"My name's Ada. Ada Brickner."

"Good. Before I bit into this thing, I just wanted to make sure your name isn't Eve." Vero took a bite, and peach juice dripped down his hands. It was so fresh, so perfectly ripe, it tasted unlike anything he'd ever eaten. Until that moment his favorite food had been pizza, but no more. And the peach did more than fill his stomach—it felt as if it had nourished his entire body.

"Let's go. They're waiting for us," Ada said.

"Who's waiting for us?"

"The others."

"Oh, *the others*. That clears up everything. I'd better not keep *them* waiting."

Ada didn't respond. She turned and briskly walked away.

Vero quickly followed, still holding the massive peach in his hands.

"Why didn't Uriel greet me?" he called after her.

"There are more important things he's gotta do than welcome you," she shot back over her shoulder. "I know you're new to the Ether, but the first rule you need to learn is to leave your ego back on earth."

"So are you a guardian angel too?" Vero asked as he caught up to her.

"Yes. This is my third training session. I'm from a large city, East Coast."

"What? Are "the others" more guardian angels? Am I training with a group?"

Before Ada could answer, her wings sprouted from her back, and she took off in flight, leaving Vero standing alone on the side of the steep mountain.

"Hey! Come back here!" Vero shouted.

Ada didn't look back as she flew out of sight.

Vero willed his wings to appear, but nothing happened. He wearily walked along the side of the cliff, carrying the weight of his frustrations on his shoulders. Ada could command her wings with a single thought, but he wasn't able to do that. He couldn't help but wonder how a girl could have the power, but he didn't.

He wasn't sure where he was supposed to go, and he was hoping for some sort of sign to guide him. Looking out over the horizon, he saw nothing but endless white. There was no sign of Ada anywhere.

Suddenly, Vero heard a voice say, "Jump."

Vero spun around and nearly dropped the enormous peach. But no one was there. "Who said that?" Vero yelled. His eyes searched for the source.

"Jump," the voice repeated. It wasn't a frightening voice. It sounded firm but somehow trustworthy.

Vero peered over the edge of the cliff. Clouds hung in the air below him, preventing him from seeing the bottom. If he were to throw himself off the side of the mountain, he'd have no idea where he'd land. Yet the clouds beckoned to him.

Somewhere deep inside, Vero felt the clouds would protect him.

"Jump," the voice enticed him again.

If my falls from the rooftop and down the elevator shaft didn't destroy me, Vero reasoned, *then neither should a fall from a cliff in the Ether.*

He stood with his back straight, feeling full of confidence. While still holding the peach in his hands, Vero ran full speed toward the edge of the cliff and jumped into the unknown.

Vero was exhilarated as the crisp air held him. He felt a tug on his back as his wings quickly sprouted. Finally, he was truly flying! It was a feeling of pure freedom as he soared the skies. He'd never felt happier.

The clouds began to dispel, and Vero glimpsed the land far below. Instantly he became aware of the fact that his actions defied logic. Doubt spread through him with the swiftness of a deadly virus. Soon, Vero succumbed to uncertainty, and then the sky simply dropped him. Vero hit the side of the mountain hard.

The colossal peach flew out of his hands on impact. Vero tumbled head over heels down an incline that seemed to go on forever, and then he finally came to an abrupt stop with one last "Ooomph!"

He was unhurt but dazed. And when he looked up, he was surprised to see other kids sitting on the grass in a forest glade, staring at him with what seemed to be looks of disapproval. His face flushed hot, and then, as if his fall wasn't humiliating enough, the immense peach finished its descent and landed on Vero's head, splattering juice down the sides of his face.

Ada laughed.

"See what happens when you doubt?" Uriel asked, standing over him.

With his right hand, Vero felt his back.

"Don't bother," Uriel said. "Your wings are gone."

Disappointment swept over Vero. He overheard Ada whispering to a slight boy with ears that stuck out from his head and glasses that were too big for his face.

"Are you *sure* this is the guy?" she asked in a low voice.

Vero watched as the boy nodded.

"He doesn't seem so special," she said.

What did that mean? How did these other guardian angels know about him? Vero had so many questions, but somehow he knew Uriel wouldn't be forthcoming with any answers.

Uriel went around the group and introduced each angel in turn. Vero had already met Ada. The slight kid with the huge glasses was named Pax. Kane was a dark-haired boy who was built like a linebacker. X was a tall boy with a classic, angular face, chiseled nose, and high cheekbones. His light brown skin was flawless, and his chest and broad shoulders seemed exceedingly well developed for someone whom Vero thought couldn't be much older than himself.

Vero noticed how Ada shot an admiring glance at X during his introduction.

"Stop drooling," Kane said quietly, nudging Ada in her side and giving a slight nod toward X.

Ada flashed him an angry glance, then caught Vero looking at her and turned away — but not before Vero saw her blush.

"This is Vero. He comes to us from suburban America," Uriel told the group. "And obviously he's going to need some flying lessons."

Vero hung his head in embarrassment.

"I'll help him fly," X said as he stood up. "Kane can help too." X reached his hand down and pulled Kane to his feet.

For some reason Kane was less intimidating to Vero, probably because he was about the same height. But where Vero's body hadn't filled out yet, Kane exuded strength.

"Thank you," Uriel said.

"Should we go with them?" Ada asked Uriel.

"No, you and Pax have prayers to answer."

"Come on, let's get you airborne," X said to Vero. "We can start with that small mountain."

Vero followed X's gaze to the mountain looming behind them. He felt his heart skip a beat. There was nothing small about it.

12

❖

THE PRAYER GRID

Vero swallowed hard as he stood at the base of the mountain. It was a long way to the top. Kane and X began to climb. Vero, determined to keep up with them, followed.

"Is your name really X?" Vero asked, stepping over a large rock.

"It's Xavier. X for short."

"Where do you guys come from?"

"Large city, Europe," X answered.

"Island in the Indian Ocean," Kane said.

"So how come I can understand you? I mean, don't we speak different languages?"

"We do when we're on earth," X said. "But in the Ether we can all understand one another. The more advanced angels can communicate by thought. They don't even have to open their mouths."

"That way, words can never distort," Kane explained.

"They can read my mind?" Vero asked.

"Yeah, but it's no big deal unless you've got something to hide," X told him.

Vero thought about that for a moment and felt a twinge of guilt. Not all of his thoughts were good. He often wished Clover's friend Vicki, who constantly teased him for being so skinny, would wake up one morning with a face full of pimples. He also hoped some bigger guys would beat up Danny so he'd know what it felt like to be bullied. And he wished Clover, his own sister, could feel the meanness she regularly inflicted upon him.

"Of all of us, Pax is the only one who can read minds," X said. "But even he can do it only sometimes."

"As we advance more toward our spiritual selves, we'll get better at it," Kane added.

X stopped climbing and turned to Vero. "Try it again."

Vero was so caught up in his thoughts that he hadn't realized they'd reached the top. It was just like when he'd climbed nine stories when the maltures were chasing him, and he'd hardly broken a sweat. It wasn't until Vero looked over the edge that he began sweating.

"It's pretty far down. I really don't feel like falling again."

"You have to believe you can do it," Kane told Vero. "That's the secret to flying."

"It's a matter of trust," X chimed in. "When a mother bird throws her baby bird out of the nest for the first time, it has no idea how to fly. It's never done it before, but it trusts its instincts."

"But a baby bird has wings! Birds are supposed to fly!" Vero shot back.

"Well, so are you," Kane said.

Vero's mind flashed to when he was younger. He saw himself standing on the pitch of his roof, totally fearless. Back then he'd wanted so badly to fly. But now eight years later, having been in a human body and suppressing the urge to fly for so long, he'd forgotten his true nature.

"We'll catch you if you fall," X said.

Vero remained hesitant. It wasn't that he was afraid of flying; he was scared he wouldn't be able to do it. What if he couldn't? What if he failed completely? Would they make fun of him?

"Sometime today ... " Kane said.

But Vero didn't move.

"Maybe that mother bird is on to something ..." X said.

In one swift motion, Kane and X pushed Vero off the cliff. Vero fell into the sky, screaming, while Kane and X laughed and waved. Vero became angry. Really angry. He was sick and tired of people shoving him off buildings, down elevator shafts, and now off a cliff! He did *not* want to face-plant into the soil again.

As the ground quickly approached, Vero's anger turned into resolve. His thoughts raced. *I can do this. I CAN do this!* And suddenly, he knew he could. Vero's wings shot out of his back and took his body gracefully upward.

"Ride the wind!" Kane yelled to him.

Vero felt utterly lighthearted and invigorated. And for his trust, he was rewarded with panoramic views of the glorious world below. He saw crystal clear lakes hugged by fertile mountains. Fields of golden wheat swayed in the breeze. Herds of animals roamed over the open hills. The scene before him was far more beautiful than anything Vero had ever seen on earth.

Vero turned his head and saw X and Kane flying on either side of him.

"Sorry about the push, but you needed it," Kane said.

Vero recalled his fear when he'd learned to ride his bike without training wheels. Vero made his father promise to hold on to the back of the bike seat until Vero said he could let go. After two hours of clutching the bike, his father became frustrated and let go. Vero pedaled another ten minutes on his own before he realized his father was sitting on the front porch drinking a cool glass of iced tea. He hadn't even been mad at his father for breaking his promise.

Vero's anger at Kane and X was gone. "Ha!" Vero cried.

"Ya-hooo!" X hollered, and the three of them soared together.

Vero trailed them but quickly became distracted by the sound of rushing water. He looked down and saw not one, but three majestic waterfalls flowing into one another.

The three waterfalls were equidistant from each other and formed a perfect triangle. The water from each fell into a collective tranquil pool below. Vero lagged behind Kane and X; he felt drawn to the falls. He longed to have the water wash over him, and not just because he wanted to get the sticky peach juice out of his hair. No, he wanted to drink the water and let it cleanse his entire body.

Vero flew faster toward the falls. He was no longer shaky with the new wings. He grew excited with anticipation. The closer he got to the water, the more he felt as if his heart would leap out of his chest. It was almost within his grasp when he slammed up against what felt like an invisible glass barrier.

He suddenly remembered Tack's joke about the bug and the windshield. The impact caused him to lose his ability to fly, and he hurtled toward the ground. Kane and X flew to his side and caught him in midair. Vero regained control of himself, and Kane and X released him back to the wind.

"I told you to follow us," Kane said.

"Well, you could have warned me. What *was* that? Some kind of force field?" Vero asked.

"I guess," X said. "Not just anyone is allowed to drink those waters. You have to be invited."

Vero rubbed his head. It hurt. And exercising his wings depleted a great deal of his energy. He was wiped out.

"Can we take a break?" Vero asked.

"Down there—in the clearing!" Kane shouted.

X and Kane landed gracefully in a wide-open spot ringed by trees, which overlooked the valley below. Vero tried to imitate their landing technique, but he hit the ground with a loud thud.

"You have to flap hard and get your feet in front of you before you land," X said.

"Once again, thanks for the timely heads-up." Vero rolled back to a sitting position. He felt a slight push between his shoulder blades, and then his wings vanished.

"Why do they disappear?" Vero asked.

"Because we're not flying. But they'll come back when you need them," Kane said. "You'll also build up stamina for flying. The first couple of times really drain you."

"How long have you guys been coming to the Ether?" Vero asked.

"We started together. This is our fourth time," X answered.

"Do your earth families know you're guardian angels?"

Both men shook their heads no.

"Sometimes it cracks me up ... like the other day, my little sister's kite got stuck in a tree. I climbed the tree to get the kite, but my dad's practically having a heart attack because he thinks I'm gonna fall out of the tree and kill myself." Kane laughed. "He'd definitely have a heart attack if he could see me flying."

"I feel bad for my mother," X said. "Back on earth, I'm in a wheelchair. But Mom takes really good care of me. She has to feed me when my arms spasm, and I can't even hold a fork. Lots of times I hear her crying in her bedroom. It breaks my heart that she can't follow me here to the Ether and see me whole and know that I'm all right."

Vero thought of his own mother. It would be such a relief to tell her he was an angel, just so she wouldn't worry anymore.

"Then why do they do it this way?" Vero asked. "Why do we grow up with human families who have no idea who we really are? Isn't that sort of mean?"

"Our mission is to protect and guard humans, so we need to live among them. We need to understand their world," Kane said. "At least that's what Uriel says."

"But we live among humans for only a short time — until we finish angel training," X added.

"When is that?" Vero asked.

"I guess when we know everything we're supposed to know."

"Angels know everything, so won't that take forever?" Vero asked.

"First of all, only God knows everything," X said. "There's a ton of stuff that even the archangels don't know.

But once we have all the knowledge we're supposed to get, we leave our earthly lives for good."

"How long does that take?" Vero asked, picturing his own family.

"It's different for everyone, but most leave before they turn eighteen in earth years," X explained.

"What do you mean? I won't be with my family ever again after that?" Vero asked.

Kane and X exchanged glances.

"Yeah," Kane said. "They'll believe you died. Right now we can go back and forth between the two realms, and no one knows. But when you become a full-fledged angel, your body will stay on earth. They'll think you're dead and have a funeral for you. The whole thing."

Vero's head sunk to his chest. The thought of his parents having to bury him made him feel sick. He could visualize his mother sitting in the front pew of their church, weeping inconsolably while his father stoically held her. Even Clover would mourn his passing. Deep down, he knew his sister still loved him.

"But that's not fair," Vero protested.

"That's the way it is," Kane said.

"But Vero," X began, his voice sympathetic, "the hope is that one day, many years from now, you will all be together again."

Vero understood what X was telling him, but it still bothered him to know that his family would suffer.

Kane stood up. "Come on, we have to go," he said.

Vero and X stood up as well. Kane's wings opened and then X's. Vero touched his back. He couldn't feel any wings.

"My wings?" he questioned, pointing to his back.

"You might need to take a running start until you get it down," X said.

Vero backed up a ways and then sprinted toward the edge of the bluff. He boldly leaped off and instantly became airborne. Soon he was streaking like a beam of light across the Ether.

Vero, Kane, and X flew into an area that resembled an ancient Roman coliseum, but rather than being made of stone, this structure was made out of crystals. The walls were transparent, and thousands of angels of every age sat in the bleachers. The angels were looking down at what would be the arena's field, only it wasn't a green playing field. It was a massive grid full of lights in every possible color — brilliant, vivid colors that reminded him of the Lite-Brite he and Clover used to play with.

Suddenly a burst of light shot up from the grid, and an angel caught it and flew off with it. This happened again and again, continuously, as angels caught bullets of light and then flew away.

Vero hovered close to Kane and X. "What is this?" he asked.

"A prayer grid," Kane said, leading them to three empty seats. "Uriel wanted us to show it to you."

They flew to the seats and sat down. This time, Vero's landing was adequate, if not graceful. Vero watched with fascination as the bright beams shot up like geysers into the waiting hands of the receivers.

"What are they doing?" Vero asked.

"Catching prayers," an older voice said.

Vero turned and saw an angel smiling at him with the same violet eyes as Uriel's. His long hair was pulled back in a ponytail, and his round face was friendly. Vero felt immediately at ease with him.

"Welcome back, Vero," the angel said. "It's been awhile. I'm Raphael."

Vero stuck out his hand to shake Raphael's.

"Oh, I don't do that," he laughed.

Raphael then grabbed Vero and hugged him, totally catching him off guard. He squeezed Vero so tight that Vero was momentarily winded. Raphael squashed Vero a few more times and then mercifully let him go with a playful slap on the back. But the pat was hard enough that it made Vero cough.

"You're looking good, Vero. Earth has been kind to you."

"You're the archangel Raphael?" Vero choked out.

"I don't like to be so formal. I'm just Raphael. We all got such a big kick out of your book report ... everyone except Uriel, of course. You nailed him good!"

Vero couldn't help laughing; Raphael was easy to like.

Suddenly, a bright ray of light sped toward Vero, and without thinking, Vero reached up and grabbed it.

Astonished, Vero looked at the beam that was now illuminating his palm. He had no idea how he'd caught it. It was as if his hand had a mind of its own.

"Let's go." Raphael stood, suddenly serious, and grabbed Vero's arm. They flew off together, and in a flash they were sitting on a bench on a busy city sidewalk. Vero watched yellow cabs zip past them as they tried to speed through red lights. Impatient drivers laid on their horns. People crisscrossed sidewalks and streets in haste. Storefronts with elaborate window displays tempted pedestrians. Bike messengers weaved in and out of traffic. Horses pulled tourists in carriages.

"Are we in New York?" Vero asked.

Raphael pointed to a crowd of people walking past.

"They're in New York. You're not," Raphael said.

Vero was confused. How could he be sitting on a bench in the middle of the city, yet not be there?

A rather plump woman pulling a small cart filled with groceries approached the bench. She was breathing heavily when she parked her cart and sat down on Vero.

"Hey! I'm sitting here!"

Raphael chuckled. "Let me help you out."

Raphael kicked the woman's shopping cart so it rolled a few feet away from her. She leaned forward to retrieve it.

"Quick! Now!" Raphael shouted.

Vero saw his chance and jumped up and away from the woman before she could sit on him again. He looked back at the woman, studying her.

"She can't see us, can she?"

"Not at all."

"I knew she sat on me, but I didn't feel a thing," Vero said. "We're still in the Ether, aren't we?"

"Yes. And if you want proof, just close your eyes."

Vero hesitated.

"Come on, shut them tight," Raphael commanded.

Vero closed his eyes.

"Concentrate hard. Pray to see beyond the limited scope of human eyes."

Vero clamped his eyes even tighter. He tried to block out

the sounds and commotion of the busy city, but it wasn't easy. His mind wandered. He grew frustrated and opened his eyes again. Nothing had changed.

"I can't do it!"

Raphael stood before him, his playful disposition now gone. He bent down in front of Vero to block out any distractions. Vero could see a fervent conviction in Raphael's eyes as he lowered Vero's eyelids with his thumbs.

"The truth is there, and you must open your eyes and heart to it," Raphael said, coaxing him in a calm, yet resolute voice.

Vero concentrated as hard as he could. He cleared his mind of the world around him. One by one, the distractions of the city fell away. He had a single thought, and that was truth. The need to know the truth consumed him.

Raphael removed his thumbs, and Vero opened his eyes. The sight before him knocked him back against the bench. Everywhere he looked in this bustling city, there were angels—thousands of them—radiant noble angels protecting and assisting humans in their everyday endeavors.

Vero watched as an angel caught an elderly man in his arms, saving the man from a nasty spill after he failed to see an uneven sidewalk.

As a group of schoolchildren crossed a busy intersection, massive angels stood with their arms locked shoulder to shoulder, forming a solid line to prevent any cars or buses from breaking through.

Men and women wearing business suits walked into buildings through revolving glass doors, and the angels kept step with them.

As a little boy climbed a tree, an angel followed him on

the branch below, his arms stretched out to catch the boy if he should fall.

A homeless man wearing threadbare clothes lay on the sidewalk napping, and an angel cushioned his head while stroking his hair.

Two deliverymen unloaded their rig, and angels stood in the back of the truck, holding up several crates to keep them from collapsing.

A woman opened her purse to pull out a tissue, and an angel quickly spread his sheltering wings around her, preventing a devious-looking man from seeing the loose dollar bills in her purse.

Angels attended to every single person no matter how mundane the task. And the humans went about their business, never suspecting a thing.

But it wasn't only people that the angels protected. Godzilla-sized angels, taller than skyscrapers, stood around soaring buildings and kept guard at every corner. Other angels stood knee-deep in a river supporting a bridge span.

Vero was overcome with emotion. The immense outpouring of love these angels held for the humans caused tears to well up in his eyes.

Raphael placed an arm around Vero's shoulders as a mother pushed a stroller past them. Her baby girl, only six months old, sat smiling at the brightly colored mobile hanging above her. As the mother stopped in front of Vero, the baby reached out her arms and tried to grab him. At first Vero thought it was just a random act. But when the baby made eye contact with him and held his gaze, he suddenly felt exposed.

He turned to Raphael and said, "I thought people couldn't see us."

"That's true for most. But babies need to be gently eased into this world. Angels offer comfort during their transition. By the time she's a year old, she'll no longer be able to see you."

In her excitement, the baby giggled and stretched her arms toward Vero. It was the most innocent of gestures, and Vero was powerless to resist. He smiled and held out his hand, and the little girl took it in hers.

To the mother it looked as though her baby was grabbing for the mobile.

13

A CAB IN RUSH HOUR

Vero walked with Raphael down the busy city street, dodging throngs of people and their angels, trying to make sense of it all. Some angels acknowledged them, but most stayed focused on the humans entrusted to their care. Vero's mind flashed back to the snake incident in his science class.

"There's no such thing as hysterical strength, is there?" Vero asked.

"Nope. It's us," Raphael told him. "Now we'd better see what prayer you caught."

Vero abruptly stopped walking. He was completely caught off guard.

"I forgot about it," he said, feeling ashamed. Vero looked down at his hand. The ray of light was gone. "I must have dropped it."

Raphael laughed. "Do you think a prayer is like water that drips through your fingers?"

Vero didn't know what to think.

"Prayers are precious to God," Raphael explained. "None are ever lost."

Raphael took Vero's hand in his and turned it palm up. Vero's eyes went wide when a hologram of a woman appeared in his hand. She looked to be about thirty-five years old and wore a business suit. She had an anxious look on her face as she desperately waved her hand in the air. Vero felt her anxiety.

"She's in trouble," Vero said.

"Get closer," Raphael said softly.

Vero leaned into the image of the woman. He put his ear close to her mouth, and he heard her desperate plea.

"Please, Lord, let me get a cab," the woman said.

Vero jumped back upon hearing her request.

"A cab! A crummy cab is her prayer request?"

"By the time a prayer shoots up from the prayer grid, God has already decided to grant it," Raphael told Vero firmly. "It's your job to carry it out without question."

Raphael gave Vero an intimidating look that left no room for discussion.

Vero knew he had no choice. Somehow he had to flag down a taxi for the woman. It didn't seem like some Herculean task except for the fact that out of the thousands of cab drivers in New York, not a single one could see or hear him. Vero balled his hand into a fist, and the hologram of the woman vanished.

"How can I help her? Even if I stand right in front of a cab and scream at the top of my lungs, it'll just drive right through me. And besides, aren't we too late anyway? She must have asked for that cab awhile ago."

"We're not bound by time," Raphael said. "Look. There she is."

Raphael nodded his head toward a woman standing on the edge of the sidewalk.

She was waving her arms at passing cabs. Seconds ago, Vero held her in his hand, and now she was standing right before his eyes. It was amazing and freaky at the same time.

"The key is to make it happen so it appears seamless to humans—like nothing out of the ordinary. Go on now. Get her that cab."

Vero hesitated. Raphael smiled and gave him a gentle push toward the woman.

Vero approached tentatively, trying to buy some time while he figured out what to do. Unfortunately, nothing came to mind, so Vero wildly waved his arms like a mad man at every passing cab. Raphael chuckled and shook his head. As Vero jumped around, he failed to look behind him and bumped into someone, knocking him to the pavement.

"Hey! You knocked off my glasses!"

Vero turned and saw a familiar young angel sitting on the sidewalk behind him.

"Pax?"

"You're going to make me fail my mission," Pax said, as he put on his glasses.

Pax made a comical sight with his oversized glasses and his extra-large ears, but then Vero remembered Ada's comment to Pax about Vero: *He doesn't seem so special.* Was Vero somehow different from the others? More importantly, was he a disappointment?

"You need to move," Pax said.

Vero quickly stepped out of the way.

"Sorry," Vero said. "What are you doing anyway?"

"I need to keep this parking space open for the right person." Pax got up and stood between two parked vehicles on the side of the street. In font of Pax was a big SUV, and behind him was a delivery van. There was about four feet of space between the back of the SUV and the front of the van. Vero noticed that although those two vehicles were parked so close to each other, there was also three or four yards of clearance in front of the SUV and behind the van. Had those drivers parked better, there would be plenty of room for a car to fit between them.

Vero looked at the spot Pax had called a parking space. Even a motorcycle couldn't fit there!

"That's not happening," Vero informed him.

A sporty little red convertible slowed down as its driver eyeballed the space. Pax stood his ground in the spot, stared at the driver, and whispered, "Go away. It's too small. There's nothing here for you." The driver then quickly sped up, realizing she'd never squeeze her car into that tiny spot.

"See?" Vero announced. "I think you need to find a new space."

A gray nondescript four-door sedan crossed through the intersection and was headed their way. Pax sprang into action when he saw the car.

"Here he comes!" he shouted.

Vero watched as the sedan slowed down while the driver scanned the area, hopeful for a parking space. Vero felt bad for Pax because he was certain he was failing his mission.

He wondered what happened when guardian angels failed their tasks?

But to his astonishment, Vero watched as the scrawny angel placed his hands on the SUV's rear bumper and pushed it ahead four feet. He then turned and pushed on the van's front bumper with his super strength, moving it back far enough to create a parking space for the sedan. The van and SUV had rolled only a few feet, so the humans passing by on the sidewalk never detected a thing. They were too wrapped up in their own lives to notice the supernatural goings-on.

The gray car backed into the space. And then the driver got out, threw a few coins into the meter, and looked at his watch. "Thank God," he said and hurried off.

"How did you do that?" Vero asked.

Pax held his head high, proud of his accomplishment, "It's nothing you can't do."

"How old are you?" Vero asked.

"Ten."

Pax saw the look of disbelief on Vero's face.

"Yes, I'm small for my age," Pax said.

"I didn't say anything," Vero said.

"But you were going to."

Vero heard his prayer assignment try to hail another cab. "Can you teach me how to do that?" Vero asked desperately. "Please?"

Pax glanced over at Raphael, who was standing on the curb observing them.

Raphael nodded.

"Okay. Let's find a cab," Pax said.

Impressed by their nonverbal exchange, Vero asked, "Can you read my thoughts too?"

"Only sometimes," Pax said. "The first thing we need to do is find an empty cab."

Then Pax stepped off the curb and walked directly into oncoming traffic. Vero was impressed with Pax's confidence. Vero hesitated, afraid to leave the safety of the sidewalk.

Pax yelled to him, "Come on! They can't run you over! Remember, you're still in the Ether!"

The Ether was a difficult concept for Vero to embrace, and especially as an eighteen-wheeler headed straight for him. Pax wasted no time and stuck his head right up next to the windows of cabs and peered inside. He quickly moved from cab to cab. Vero waited for a taxi to stop at a light and then looked into the backseat for passengers. But they all seemed to be filled—businessmen and women on their way home, a woman who was already late to catch a plane at the airport, a man with two small children who were fighting over a piece of gum.

Vero didn't realize the light had changed from red to green. Panic gripped him when the traffic accelerated, and the next thing he knew he was being run through by trucks, cars, vans, and even bikes. So many vehicles struck him, he lost count. But not a single one of them hurt him. All Vero felt was a whooshing of wind through his body.

"I got one!" Pax yelled.

Vero saw Pax waving to him a block south of where he stood. Pax jumped into the backseat of a cab and motioned for Vero to follow. Vero ran over, but he was too slow. The cab pulled up to the curb to pick up a man wearing a business suit and holding a leather briefcase.

"Don't let him in!" Pax shouted to Vero. "You've got to stop him!"

Pax quickly locked the backseat door while the businessman tried to open it. The man tapped the window and motioned for the taxi driver to unlock the door. The driver released the unlock button, but Pax kept his index finger on the lock. The businessman tugged at the door again, but it still wouldn't open.

"The thing must be stuck," the driver said. Then he unfastened his seat belt and stepped out of the cab to examine the lock. Pax panicked.

"Hurry up! Get rid of him!" he said to Vero.

"How? I can't do anything!" Vero said. "Cars just drive right through me!"

"When we're answering prayers, we get incredible strength and can manipulate matter," Pax said. "You have the ability!"

As the driver jimmied the lock, Pax continued to hold the button down, completely frustrating the driver. Vero hesitantly pressed his index finger on the metal clasp of the man's briefcase, but it wouldn't unfasten. His finger went right through it.

"Don't be so wimpy!" Pax said. "If you *will* it, it *will* happen!"

Meanwhile, the businessman gave up and opened the front passenger door. "I'll just sit up here," he said to the driver.

"You're gonna lose the cab!" Pax yelled at Vero.

Realizing it was now or never, Vero pressed down hard on the briefcase latch. Instantly, the lid sprang open, and the man's papers flew out and were quickly snatched by the wind.

"I did it!" Vero yelled triumphantly.

The businessman ran off, chasing his papers.

"That was harsh ruining his papers," Pax said to Vero through the open cab window.

"It was all I could think of," Vero said. "You told me to hurry up."

The driver got behind the wheel, and the cab started to take off, leaving Vero standing on the curb.

"Hey! Get in here!" Pax shouted.

Vero sprinted after the taxicab.

Pax stuck his head out the window, cheering him on. "Come on! You're an angel! We move faster than New York City cabs!"

Raphael stood on the curb watching as Vero chased after the yellow cab. When a man jaywalked across the street, the cab slowed for a moment and Vero caught up to it.

"Help me get in!" he called to Pax.

Vero dove headfirst through the open backseat window. But before he could get all the way inside, the cab sped up again, so now his legs were sticking out in traffic. The cab changed lanes. A cement truck traveling in the opposite direction clipped Vero's right foot. Finally, Pax pulled Vero into the cab.

"Thanks."

"Your petitioner is up ahead," Pax said. "But there are three other people flagging down cabs, so we need to be sure the driver picks her."

"How do we do that?"

"Plant suggestions in his mind. You're allowed to influence him, but you can't direct him."

Vero was puzzled. What did that mean — influence but not direct?

"Whisper in his ear, tell him to notice that lady in the brown suit. But you can't go any further than that."

Vero looked at the man's ear. He was an older man with hair sprouting from his earlobes. The thought of whispering into his ear wasn't too appealing.

"Isn't there some other way?" he asked Pax.

"Not that I can think of."

Seeing no other option, Vero resigned himself to the task. He leaned forward. There wasn't a divider separating the front seat from the backseat, so Vero put his mouth close to the man's ear. It was worse than he'd expected. Not only had stray hairs sprouted, but also yellow crusty wax lined the outside of the man's ear canal. Vero nearly gagged, but he managed to get out the words, "Look at the lady in the brown suit." He quickly sat back.

"There. Done," he said to Pax.

Vero sat tall in the seat feeling proud of himself. Mission accomplished. But then, to his dismay, a huge moving van pulled up in the right lane and tried to pass the cab.

"Oh no!"

Vero knew the moving van would block the cab driver's view of the woman, and he became alarmed. Suddenly, he felt a tingle run through his body, giving him confidence. Was this the extra strength Pax spoke about? Vero impulsively reached over the front seat and yanked the steering wheel to make a hard right.

"You're not allowed to do that!" Pax yelled.

The cab swerved in front of the moving van. The van slammed on its brakes. Pax gripped the seat in front of him, bracing for an accident. Vero glanced behind him and saw Raphael pulling back on the rear bumper of the moving van. The van safely skidded to a stop. Pax and Vero caught their breath.

The driver of the moving van shouted a fair amount of swear words at the cab driver who looked totally bewildered. He had no idea what possessed him to cut in front of the moving van.

Raphael shot Vero a disappointed look. Vero felt humiliated. As the moving van drove off, the cab driver glanced over at the sidewalk and saw the woman in the brown suit standing on the curb under some construction scaffolding. The woman dashed over to the taxi and climbed in the back.

"Fifty-fourth and Lex, please," she told the driver breathlessly.

Vero and Pax climbed out the open window, and the cab drove on down the avenue.

"I hope wherever she's going it was worth the effort," Vero said to Pax as they watched the cab blend into the sea of yellow taxis. "It amazes me that God would bother with cab rides and parking spaces."

"You're famous!" Kane shouted at Vero as he walked across the green field of the Ether.

Vero saw Kane and the other young angels walking toward him.

"No one screws up that badly on their first prayer attempt. To save one person, you almost took out two!" Kane laughed.

Vero blushed. He knew he'd messed up big time. But he was also angry about having been thrown into the situation without any guidance. He'd only just learned a few weeks ago that he was a guardian angel. No one had explained any of the rules to him. How could he be expected to know what to do? Vero felt ripped off.

When he thought he was just a regular kid, his main responsibility was to keep his room clean. Now he was expected to save lives! It was incomprehensible! The enormity of it weighed heavily upon him.

"He's only messing with you," X said to Vero.

"No, he's right. I don't know what I'm doing. I just wish someone would explain everything to me."

"It's on a need-to-know basis here. They give out knowledge one tiny morsel at a time."

"Why?"

"Because they have to make sure you're ready for it. If you're not able to understand it, lies and deceptions can seep in. It goes all the way back to the garden of Eden," X said. "Adam and Eve wanted to know everything all at once, so they ate from the forbidden tree of knowledge. Look what happened to them."

"Yeah, but there are still some things I need to know now, like how do I defend myself if the maltures attack again?"

Every head turned in Vero's direction.

"What?" he asked.

"You were attacked on earth?" X asked.

"But we're supposed to be protected from the maltures when we're there," Pax added, sounding a bit fearful.

"Uriel had to defend me or else they would have gotten me," Vero said.

"What did they look like?" Ada asked in an awed whisper.

"They were covered with fur and scales. They had rows

of sharp yellow fangs. And each one had a single eye that went all the way through the head."

Ada gasped.

"But the scariest thing was . . . you could feel hatred and rage coming out of them. Like that hated and rage made up their very essence."

Everyone was silent for a moment.

"Has anyone else been attacked by them?" Vero asked the group.

"None of us," X said.

It was hard to imagine X in a wheelchair on earth. With his striking dark features and his strong build, Vero couldn't imagine him looking frail. Yet at that moment when X talked about the maltures, Vero definitely saw fear in his eyes.

14

THE TRACK
STAR

Vero heard beautiful music as he and Uriel walked through a meadow of waist-high wildflowers. Their petals swayed with the soothing rhythm. As the melody grew louder, soon the flowers' stalks also followed the beat. They were dancing! But the sight of dancing flowers brought him no enjoyment.

Sensing Vero's thoughts, Uriel said, "Have faith, Vero. The answers will come in time."

"Why haven't the others ever seen a malture?" Vero asked.

Uriel stopped walking, turned and placed both hands on Vero's shoulders, and looking Vero squarely in the eyes, said, "Do not be afraid, Vero. You are far greater and stronger than you know."

"But they attacked me!"

Uriel considered. He stared hard into Vero's eyes, making

sure he had his total attention. "The opposite of faith is not doubt. The opposite of faith is fear."

Vero contemplated Uriel's words as they resumed walking.

"When I first came to the Ether, I told you I was home. How did I know that?" Vero asked. "Have I been here before?"

"All living things spend time in the Ether before it's their earth time."

"So why didn't I remember the Ether when I was on earth?" Vero asked.

"You do as a baby, but gradually the memory fades."

"But why?" Vero asked.

"Because you must rediscover it, and return of your own free will. The knowledge of the goodness of the Ether exists in every living thing."

"But the Ether isn't heaven?"

"It's the middle ground between heaven and the lake of fire," Uriel said.

"Lake of fire?"

"Where darkness reigns."

"But everything I've seen in the Ether is wonderful," Vero said.

"You've seen but only a small part of the Ether."

Vero looked to Uriel. "What do you mean?"

"Lucifer's demons and maltures are also here in the Ether, and they would love nothing more than to dig their claws into a young angel like yourself."

Vero felt his stomach churn. "Am I special? I heard the other angels talking."

"We are all special to God," Uriel said sharply, and Vero

knew not to probe any further. "It's time for you to go back. You've learned enough for your second training."

"But wait! I still have tons of questions!"

"You feel like you haven't learned enough, but I disagree." Uriel motioned with his hand for Vero to explain what he's learned.

"I learned to fly better. I met some of the other angels. I now know what a prayer grid is—"

"I could have told you all of that," Uriel interrupted. "But what did you learn about *yourself*?"

Vero paused and looked down for a moment, then said, "I learned there's so much about myself that I don't know . . . but I want to."

Uriel slowly nodded, "Well said. And by the way, your petitioner got the job."

Vero gave him a curious look.

"The prayer you answered. The cab driver got her to the interview in time."

"Really?"

Uriel nodded.

"Uriel, one last thing . . . when I was flying past the three waterfalls, why couldn't I get close to them? Some sort of invisible force stopped me."

"That, Vero, is for another day."

Uriel smiled and then wrapped his wings around himself and disappeared.

Vero looked down at the dancing flowers. They finally brought a smile to his face.

"Mom would love to see this," he said to no one, allowing the soft petals to caress his fingers.

His mom adored flowers. It was always so easy to buy

presents for her birthday or Mother's Day. Flowers of every kind delighted her. He wished that someday his mother could stand where he now stood and dance with the wildflowers.

Vero realized he missed his mother. The last time he'd seen her, she was dropping off Tack and him at the movie theater.

The next thing Vero knew, an elbow jabbed him in the ribs causing him to stumble backward into a closed elevator door.

Vero opened his eyes in time to see a group of preteen girls headed his way.

"Dude, is my hair sticking up?" Tack was unsuccessfully attempting to flatten his protruding tuft of strawberry-blond hair.

Vero grabbed the wall to support himself. It took a few moments to regain his balance. He didn't remember the transition back to earth being so jarring.

"What's wrong with you?" Tack asked.

"Just relax!" Vero hissed.

How could Tack be so concerned about something as trivial as his hair with all that was going on around him? But then Vero reminded himself that for Tack, nothing had changed. He hadn't just been shown a completely new vision of the universe. At the moment, the most important thing in the world for Tack was that group of girls who were walking toward them.

"Since when does Davina hang out with Hollow Legs and Monkey Arms?" Tack whispered to Vero, but not nearly as quietly as he'd intended.

"Hey, Vero. Hey, Tack," Davina said.

"We heard what you called us, Tack," Sasha Wyburn said.

Sasha had earned her nickname because she could eat more than anyone else in the school—even Tack—yet she remained thin as a rail. So the other kids assumed the food must be stored in her long legs.

"Yeah, Tack," Amanda Farkas chimed in. "And I *don't* have monkey arms."

Amanda got her nickname because of her gangly arms. She was the go-to girl whenever a teacher needed a light bulb changed or something retrieved off a high shelf.

Amanda gave Vero a once-over as he clung to the wall, still trying to adjust, "What's wrong? You look like you're going to be sick."

Sasha eyed Vero, "Yeah, he does. It's probably because he just got a look at Tack's awful hair."

Tack shot Vero a silent plea for help, but Vero was too disoriented to respond.

"Let's go," Amanda said to Sasha, and they walked away. Davina lagged behind.

"Vero, you okay?" She seemed genuinely concerned.

"Yeah, probably put too much butter on the popcorn."

"What did you think of the movie?"

Her question caught Vero off guard. He'd totally forgotten about the movie, so he said the first thing that came to mind.

"It was great. I'd see it again."

"Really? I saw that movie last weekend, and there's no way I could ever sit through it again. I thought it was so impossible," Davina said. "I couldn't wait for it to end."

Vero felt like an idiot. *Why'd I say that?* He could feel the heat building in his face.

Then Danny appeared around the corner and locked eyes with Vero.

Perfect, Vero thought. *Would Danny try to start something here? In front of Davina?*

Davina smiled at Danny and turned to leave with him.

Vero felt a twist in his gut far worse than anything Danny could ever dish out. Davina had come to the movies *with Danny?* Vero found himself wishing Danny *would* try to insult him, trip him, put him in a headlock, even punch him in the face. Anything would have been easier to take than seeing Davina smile at Danny that way.

"Danny's brother is waiting for us," Davina said to Vero. "See you."

As they walked off, Danny glanced back at Vero with a smirk.

"She's too good for him," Tack said. "Get this ... Nate said he saw Danny out at that new house they're building on Fairburn. He was shattering the windows with a slingshot."

"Serious?"

"So don't worry. He's gonna wind up in juvie hall. Then you'll get your chance with Davina."

Vero watched Danny and Davina turn the corner with a concerned look on his face.

Clover waved her hand up and down in front of Vero's face, trying to get his attention during dinner. Vero finally saw her hand and snapped out of his thoughts.

"What?" he said.

"Pass the salt."

As Vero handed the saltshaker to his sister, Clover stared at him from across the kitchen table. She knew something was different about him. Ever since she was little, Clover had shared a connection with Vero. It was so strong that she'd been convinced they were twins. No matter how many times her mom and dad explained that Vero was adopted and that she was a year older, Clover still insisted. And as they'd gotten older, Clover felt their connection had only grown stronger. So Clover knew something was happening to her brother.

Besides the hurdle jumping and the bus incident, something was different ... something life changing.

She desperately wanted to know what was happening, but she was afraid to ask.

Because whatever it was also affected her.

Clover had secrets too—secrets that kept her awake at night. Even though Vero hadn't done anything she could name, she secretly blamed her brother for what she was going through. And she punished him for it—unfairly, she knew. But she blamed him anyway.

"You're quiet tonight," Nora said to Vero as she placed a basket of dinner rolls on the table. "You feel all right?"

"It's his heart," Clover said. "It's broken because Davina Acker went to the movies with Danny Konrad."

"I don't care about them!" Vero shot back.

"Really? Tack said you were practically crying the whole way home," Clover said with a smile.

"Who's Danny Konrad?" Dennis asked with a mouth full of mashed potatoes.

"He's a mean jerk," Vero said.

"Watch your mouth," Dennis scolded him.

"Danny used to be in Clover's class. But a few years ago, he was held back. Now he's in Vero's class," Nora said. She passed the green beans to Dennis. "You might remember the Konrads. We met them at Clover's kindergarten roundup. The teacher said Danny wasn't ready for kindergarten, but his mother and father insisted the school accept him. I remember wondering what the big deal was about waiting another year, and I really felt like they just wanted him out of the house. They're divorced now."

"I think Danny and Davina make a cute couple," Clover said. She knew she was hurting Vero's feelings. Why did she feel the desire to goad him?

Vero stood up abruptly, knocking his chair to the floor. "What's your problem?" he shouted in Clover's face. "What did I ever do to you?"

Clover felt a twinge of guilt. She wanted to apologize, but then she thought of Vero's snow angel and the otherworldly raven with its fiery eyes and rat's tail, and she felt scared. And she was angry about feeling scared. She narrowed her eyes and glared at Vero.

"Vero!" Dennis said sharply. "Pick up your chair and sit down."

Vero picked up the chair, but he didn't sit down. "I'm done," he said. He bunched up his napkin and threw it at Clover before leaving the room. "You'll miss me when I'm gone!" he shouted.

Clover noticed her mom watching Vero as he walked away. *Was she scared too?*

After dinner, Vero retreated to his bedroom and stared at the ceiling, wishing it would cave in and crush him. Or maybe

Mr. Atwood would miss his driveway and plow his SUV through Vero's bedroom window.

Davina and Danny. Davina with Danny. The more Vero thought about it, the less he understood.

Vero longed to go back to the Ether. He desperately wanted to get away from Clover and the idea of Davina being with Danny. But no catastrophe befell him. It was a quiet night, broken only by the sounds of his parents' muffled conversations about Vero.

Suddenly his bedroom door flew open, and Clover walked in.

Vero shot up. "What are you doing here?" he asked. "I'm surprised you even remember where my room is."

Clover ignored his comment and asked, "What did you mean by 'when I'm gone'?"

Vero wanted so badly to tell her the truth, to tell her their time together would be coming to an end soon, maybe even before he got his driver's license. He didn't want to spend his remaining time on earth fighting with Clover.

But he couldn't tell her. It was the rule. If he tried, Uriel would send a fire truck or set off a smoke alarm—just like he did in Dr. Weiss's office. So Vero shrugged and said, "Nothing. I didn't mean anything by it."

Clover studied him. She knew he was lying, but they no longer told each other their secrets. It had become too dangerous. Clover feared her secrets would land her on the shrink's couch next to Vero. Silence was the one thing they both shared.

"Okay, fine," Clover said, and she turned to leave.

"Clover, wait!"

She spun around, keeping her hand on the doorknob.

Now that she was looking at him, now that he had her attention, Vero wasn't sure what to say.

"Um ... " *Where to start?*

"What?" Clover demanded.

"Do you remember when I was four and I fell off the roof and twisted my ankle?"

Vero could tell his question disturbed her. He saw her hands start to shake. But now that he'd started, he couldn't stop. "Do you remember the man ... the man in the tree?"

His eyes begged for an answer, for something, anything. All she had to do was give him a nod, whisper yes. Clover locked eyes with her brother, staring him down. It was a silent showdown, and it was her move.

"No," she said. "I don't know what you're talking about." Then she walked out of the room and slammed the door behind her.

Silence had never sounded so loud to Vero.

Bright and early on Monday morning, Vero and Tack marched into Coach Randy's office and signed up for the track team.

"You're going to put this school on the map," Coach said. "We've lost every single track meet since I've been here, but now that's about to change. And Tack, I think the shot put is definitely a better choice for you than the hurdles."

"Me too. I'm pretty good at it. I've been practicing in our backyard."

"Keep it up," Coach Randy said.

"I can't anymore."

Vero and the Coach looked at Tack.

"I accidentally threw the ball through Mrs. Carlotti's window next door. Broke the glass. And her cat was sunning itself on the windowsill ... "

"Did you kill it?" Vero asked, wide-eyed.

"No, but it beaned him good. Ever since then, the cat keeps head-butting the walls."

"Do everyone a favor and stay away from the javelin toss," Coach said.

Vero's first track meet was against the crosstown rival, Lexington Junior High. The bleachers filled quickly with rowdy students, anxious parents, and the occasional miserable sibling who resented giving up a whole Saturday for a stupid track meet. They watched the oval-shaped field below as athletes stretched on the grass. As Vero and Tack were walking along the track, Coach Randy caught Vero's eye and gave him a double thumbs-up. Vero nodded back.

"And here we are ... our first track meet," Tack said between bites of his chocolate protein bar. "Still glad you changed your mind?"

Vero looked across the track and saw Danny sitting in the middle of the field, stretching.

"I guess we'll find out," Vero said, never taking his eyes off Danny.

"I'm glad I decided to go back to shot put," Tack said. "I figured, why not?" Tack messily shoved the rest of the protein bar into his mouth. After he'd finally swallowed, he said, "Plus, I realized I shouldn't deny my fans any longer."

Normally this remark would have gotten a rise out of Vero, but he was too intent on watching Danny scan the bleachers. *He's probably looking for Davina,* Vero thought, and his insides burned.

When Danny spotted Davina, he gave her a smile and slight wave, but then he continued searching the stands—until he caught Vero staring at him. Danny held Vero's gaze, refusing to turn away. But he didn't look like his normal, malicious self. Did he look disappointed? Nervous? Danny finally looked away first. *You should be nervous,* Vero thought.

"Runners for the boys' 400 meter to your starting positions," the announcer called.

Danny walked to the starting line.

Vero followed.

"Please don't embarrass me," Clover said to her parents as they found their seats in the stands. "It's bad enough I'm giving up my Saturday for this."

"Hush, Clover," Nora said while she adjusted the camera's strap around her neck. "You should be rooting for your brother. This is the first sport he's really gotten into."

"And we are … " Dennis shouted in Clover's face while waving a large, yellow foam hand, " … number one!"

The foam finger accidentally grazed the head of a father from the rival school, knocking his sunglasses from his face. Dennis quickly threw the finger into Clover's lap as the man turned around and gave the hairy eyeball.

"Sorry, she's overly excited for her brother," Dennis said.

Clover threw the foam hand back at her father, then slumped down and pulled her hoodie up over her ball cap. "Vero's played soccer and baseball," Clover said. "So what's the big deal now?"

"He never scored a goal in soccer or ever got on base," Dennis said. "But he was always lightning fast. I should have known back then that track-and-field was his calling."

Clover stood up.

"Where are you going?" Dennis asked. "As fun as this is, I'm gonna go sit with my friends."

"Stay here with us. We're Vero's cheering section," Dennis said.

Clover rolled her eyes and sat back down, "Mom, please stop him ... "

But Nora wasn't paying attention to Clover. She watched eagerly as Vero positioned his feet on the starting blocks. She was as excited as her husband was, but for different reasons. After the school bus incident, Nora had been desperate to get some normalcy back into their lives. If Vero played sports, then he'd be just like all the other boys. He'd fit right in. And if he performed well, then maybe people would simply come to know Vero as the track star and forget about the whole bus incident. And then maybe Nora would be able to move beyond it and stop lying awake at night, worrying. Maybe she could convince herself that the man who chased them in the grocery store all those years ago never existed.

Bang!

The official shot the starter's gun, and the runners took off. Danny took the lead by a few paces. The crowd cheered him on. Vero lagged behind in fourth place. As Danny raced ahead of him, stretching his lead, Vero glanced into the bleachers and saw Davina cheering her little heart out. *But who is she cheering for?*

Jealousy seized Vero, and before he knew it, he was gaining on the other runners. The crowd jumped to its feet as Vero flew by the two runners in second and third place and then caught up to Danny. The two ran neck and neck. As Vero saw the perspiration streaming down Danny's face, he realized that he was barely sweating.

The scene suddenly seemed surreal, like Vero was observing it as a spectator, seeing things in slow motion as Danny pushed himself harder than he ever had in his life.

And then Vero smiled smugly and left Danny in the dust, crossing the finish line a full two paces ahead of him.

The crowd erupted into cheers as Attleboro Middle took first and second place in the boys' 400 meter dash. Without thinking, Coach Randy whipped off his ball cap and threw it high into the air in celebration, revealing his bald head for all to see.

Vero saw Tack elbow Nate and say, "Look! Coach is bald!"

Vero looked up into the stands. His dad was on his feet, waving his foam hand proudly. Vero's mom was taking picture after picture, capturing the moment. Clover's mouth was ajar. But when her dad started whistling loudly, she inched her way to the next bench down and tried to disappear farther inside her hoodie.

Then Vero saw Blake and Duff in the stands, applauding and high-fiving each other. *Why are they celebrating Danny's defeat? Nice friends.*

Vero turned and saw Danny hunched over, still trying to catch his breath. Oddly, he suddenly felt bad for the guy. He considered confronting Blake and Duff, but then he saw

Davina walk over and place a hand on Danny's shoulder as she handed him a water bottle. Vero changed his mind.

Vero went on to win the high jump and the long jump events. His long jump even set a new school record. Soon it was time for the 80 meter hurdles. By now, it was Vero's day, and he was expected to win this event. The story of how he jumped two hurdles in a single bound had been exaggerated to four hurdles. And after watching him break the school's long jump record, the crowd totally believed the rumor.

"Good luck—not that you need it," Tack said as he shook Vero's hand. "The shot put is next, so I won't be able to watch you run."

"Good luck to you too," Vero said. "Try not to hit any cats."

As Tack walked over to the shot put ring, Vero took his place in the lane next to Danny. They got into position on their starting blocks, and Danny glanced over at Vero. His menacing look was meant to intimidate, but it didn't work. After the starter's gun went off, Vero dashed ahead of everyone. As he approached the first hurdle, Vero cleared it with no problem. The crowd's exhilaration spurred Vero on, and as the next hurdle got closer, he decided to leap over it and the next one in a single jump. Vero sprung into the air. A hush fell over the crowd as he hung in midair between the two hurdles ... when suddenly ... from out of nowhere ... an errant shot put ball smashed into Vero's skull. He crumpled to the ground.

The crowd gasped as Tack looked on in horror.

15

C.A.N.D.L.E.

"Yeah, you deserved that."

Vero felt the back of his head. No lump yet. He found himself sitting on the thick green grass of the Ether. It took a few seconds before he realized Uriel was standing over him wearing a scowl.

"What's the point in humiliating Danny like that? Your job is to safeguard people, not make them feel like dirt!"

Vero understood, but he didn't care. He was sick of Danny. "He's the one that deserves it!" Vero said. "He beats me up at school!"

"We saw that. I'm the one who held your fist back so you couldn't hit him."

That explained why Vero couldn't punch Danny that day.

" 'Turn the other cheek' isn't some cute catch phrase. It's a way of life for an angel," Uriel said.

Vero leaned forward and put his head in his hands. Could he do this?

Uriel sighed heavily and sat down in the grass next to Vero. "Track is one of the few *good* things Danny has in his life," he said softly.

"Not quite," Vero muttered.

Uriel knew exactly who Vero was talking about.

"Vero, it can never be. You know what you are and what will happen when you complete your training."

It was a hard truth to swallow, but Vero nodded. As much as he loved the Ether, though, it didn't diminish his love for the earth and its people — especially certain people.

"Come on," Uriel told him. "Take my hand. It's a much faster way to travel."

Vero grabbed Uriel's hand, and the next thing he knew, his feet were landing on rocky soil. Vero and Uriel now stood before an ancient Greco-Roman style temple. But it wasn't exactly like the temples Vero had seen illustrated in history books because this one wasn't in ruins.

Vast rows of columns, brightly adorned in soft pastel colors, lined the rectangular structure. They held up a perfectly arched dome roof. The stark white dome matched the equally stark white walls. The temple's design was simple and elegant.

Vero felt small and inconsequential as he walked up the glossy marble steps. The massive stone doors swung open as if they were expecting Vero. The entrance hall did not disappoint. It was the size of several football fields. Vero spun around and saw that the temple was many floors high. Each level had massive balconies that overlooked where he stood. The inside walls of the temple appeared to be made of gold mixed with diamonds — a gold that sparkled with crystal clarity to its core. The dome ceiling was quite high, yet Vero's eye could make out the intricate colorful tile patterns laid into the top. Vero's mouth hung open in awe. Uriel smiled as he watched Vero's reaction.

"It's my favorite architectural style," Uriel said.

"Greco-Roman," Vero said.

"Ha! Hardly. The Greeks and Romans got all of their ideas from us."

"What do you mean?" Vero asked.

"This temple was here long before the Greek civilization existed. See, one of the jobs of an angel is to inspire humans. So when those future Greek architects were sitting around in mud huts, we thought we'd help them out a bit. I believe it was Raphael who gave them a vision of this place."

"How?"

"Mainly through dreams."

Vero was curious. He wanted to know everything there was to know about the angel's role. There was so much to learn, and he was growing impatient.

"Entering dreams is one of the toughest tasks for an angel, but you'll learn soon enough," Uriel said.

The soothing sound of wind chimes echoed through the temple.

"What's that?" Vero asked.

"First period bell."

"Much nicer than the bell at my school," Vero said.

Hordes of kids suddenly streamed out onto the balconies and down the steps. Some looked as young as six or seven; others were Vero's age and older. Though none of them had their wings extended, Vero suspected they were all angels.

"What is this? Angel school?" Vero asked.

"Yes, it's all part of your training. You are now standing

in the Cathedral of Angels for Novice Development, Learning and Edification. Or C.A.N.D.L.E. for short. You will be one of the fledglings."

Vero smiled. "I get it . . . a fledgling is a young bird that's just gotten its wings."

"Correct."

"So all of these fledglings will be assigned a person to watch over, right?" Vero asked as he watched the angels walk across the marble floors to the different classrooms.

"Yes."

"Well then, who watches over that person until we're able to?"

"The Holders. They're an experienced group of guardian angels who fulfill your duties until you're ready . . . unless, of course, the soul hasn't yet been born on earth."

As Vero took in the hustle and bustle of the temple, someone bumped into him hard, knocking him to the ground. He looked up to see a female angel about his age. She was tall and athletic with short brown hair shot through with blonde streaks. She had three small hoop earrings in each of her ears. And with her faded jeans, chunky boots, and forceful attitude, she looked every bit the way he imagined a fierce warrior angel would look. Vero reckoned she was not a person to be messed with. She walked away without so much as a 'Sorry.'

"I thought angels were supposed to be nice to each other," Vero said.

Uriel watched the retreating figure of the rude angel and shook his head. "Sure. But it doesn't always work out that way."

Vero and Uriel walked through the temple until they reached a small open courtyard under a bright sky. A few angels sat on benches surrounded by meticulously manicured shrubs. A fringe of mature, leafy trees ringed the courtyard.

"This is your classroom," Uriel said.

"Really?" Vero asked, turning in a slow circle and scanning his surroundings.

"Students learn faster in a natural, relaxing environment."

Recalling his stuffy, crowded classrooms on earth, where he'd been forced to sit in a straight-backed chair for hours, Vero said, "Can you give my principal a vision of this place?"

Uriel chuckled. "I'll see what I can do."

Vero recognized the other fledglings. Ada was sitting next to Pax on the bench, his glasses slightly askew. X was lying on a bench with his dark face turned up toward the sun. Kane sat on the ground, leaning comfortably against a small tree. Uriel waved his arm toward the others. "And these are your classmates, Vero, whom I think you already know."

The other angels looked over at Vero. He nodded, acknowledging them.

Suddenly an angel flew into the courtyard with the velocity of a comet breaking through the atmosphere. As the angel slowed to a stop, he relaxed his wings and shook his head, trying to regain his equilibrium after his rapid flight.

The angel wore a light blue iridescent cloak that went down to his ankles. He had an angular face with a distinctly bent nose and a white goatee, and his short white hair looked wild and untamed. This angel was much bigger than Uriel, and more muscular; yet they shared the same violet-colored eyes. When the mighty angel regained his bearings, he turned and looked at Uriel with an intense gaze. Vero could tell by their expressions that the two were conversing mentally about something serious. Vero wished he'd learned how to tap into his inner angelic ESP. And just as that thought crossed Vero's mind, the impressive angel's gaze landed squarely on Vero.

Were they talking about me?

Pax's head quickly turned in Vero's direction. Had Pax tapped into their conversation?

Uriel then bowed his head to the angel and turned to the class. "For those of you who don't know him, this is the archangel Raziel. He will be instructing you today."

Raziel nodded to the group.

"Before I leave, remember this — trust the voice inside each of you, for it is Truth itself. We call it *Vox Dei*. That's Latin for 'God's voice.'"

As Vero reflected on Uriel's words, Uriel unfurled his wings and disappeared in a blur.

"Gather 'round," Raziel said abruptly, motioning toward benches arranged near a podium sitting on the grass. "Come on, come on."

X sat up, and Kane took a seat on a bench. But Raziel's intense scrutiny had made Vero uneasy, so he hesitated a moment.

Raziel noticed Vero's reluctance. "Do you want a separate invitation?"

Vero felt his face burn. "Sorry, I was just, uh, looking for a seat." He quickly sat next to Ada. Here it was his first official day of lessons, and he was already on the teacher's bad side.

Raziel seems to be a bit more high-strung than Uriel. No sooner had Vero thought this then Raziel silenced his thoughts with a glare. Vero shrunk down in his seat.

Raziel peered at the fledglings. "I am Raziel. I will be your teacher in basic angelic knowledge and understanding.

I expect your full attention at all times because it is my job to provide you with a complete grasp of who you are and what is expected of you. Should I fail in my attempt to educate you, it would be a great loss not only to you, but also to the heavens."

"What do you mean?" Pax asked.

"Not all angels make the cut."

The fledglings exchanged worried looks.

"Should you fail in the training process, then you automatically forfeit becoming a guardian. It's over."

"But what happens if we fail?" Ada asked. "I thought we'd die on earth only when our training is completed."

"Yes, that is true. But your training is 'completed' in two ways ... pass or fail. Should you fail your training, you will not be allowed back into your human body. To those on earth, you will appear to have died as per your most recent transition to the Ether, and your body will be buried. You will never become a guardian, and you will be assigned to the choir of angels."

"Is that a bad thing?" Kane asked.

"Of course not. Singing praises to the Almighty is a noble and joyous calling. But you'd better love to sing." Raziel paused a moment before continuing, "As you train, you will be judged according to your bravery, strength, character, combat skills, compassion, and, most importantly, your faith. Each of you has a crown waiting for you in heaven. Every time you do well, a jewel will be added to it."

"So the goal is to fill up the crown?" Ada asked.

"The goal is to get as many jewels as you can," Raziel answered.

"So are we in competition with each other?" X asked, a bit confused.

Raziel looked around at the group. "Don't think of it as competition, but rather as pushing each other to excel, to reach his or her full potential. Only the best can be guardians." For a moment, his expression seemed to soften. "This might be one of the hardest concepts for young angels to understand," he said. "I myself have struggled with this."

Vero mulled that over. He thought about the Navy flight school his father had attended. Since his childhood, Vero's dad had desperately wanted to become a Navy pilot. After college, he'd been accepted into Navy flight school, and he trained with a group of guys who all became close buddies. But even though they all trained together, only the best of the best would become pilots. So ultimately, the guys were competing with one another.

During flight school, for each maneuver mastered, his dad received an "attaboy" that went on his record. Though he received a decent number of attaboys, some of the other guys received more. His dad washed out of flight school, and the Navy assigned him to the job of supply clerk. His childhood dream to fly for the Navy went unfulfilled. After his father's tour with the Navy ended, he traded in that desk job for another desk job at the World Bank.

It had always bothered Vero that his father had been so close to getting his "wings" but had ended up sitting behind a desk.

"There are a lot of misconceptions about angels," Raziel continued. "First of all, we don't walk around with halos over our heads. Second, very few of us play the harp. Third, we don't lounge around on the clouds eating marshmallows all day. We are warriors—the fiercest of all warriors—because the enemy is always ready to strike, and the Fallen won't go easy on us. Your enemy prowls around like a roaring lion looking for someone to devour, so you will need to learn to defend yourself." Raziel's eyes rested on Vero. "Because we won't always be there to save you."

Vero's spirits dropped. Was Raziel angry with him because Uriel had to save him from the maltures on the roof? Does Raziel doubt he has what it takes to become a guardian?

"Vero, tell me some of the tasks that guardian angels perform," Raziel said.

"Uh, we protect humans ..." He thought of the prayer grid. "We answer prayers once God gives the okay. We're messengers. We try to influence humans ..."

"Mainly through ...?"

"Dreams," Ada jumped in. "We enter dreams to deliver messages."

"Good. Someone else?"

"We interpret visions," X offered. "We carry out God's commands, whether it be destroying entire cities or helping a person with a flat tire. We also assist humans at their death, helping them cross over."

An unfamiliar voice shouted from behind them, "We slay demons!"

Everyone turned to see that a new girl had entered the courtyard. It was the angel who'd rudely bumped into Vero inside the temple.

She sat under a tree.

"So nice of you to make it, Greer. Wouldn't you rather join us over here?" Raziel asked. The voice was polite, but the command was apparent.

"No. Not really."

Vero looked at Ada with raised eyebrows, awaiting

Raziel's response. Vero was sure that Raziel wouldn't let her get away with it. His eyes scanned the outdoor classroom, trying to figure out ways Raziel could punish her. But there was no corner to stand in or chalkboard to clean or even sheets of paper for writing essays.

Raziel silently stared at Greer for a moment, then said, "All right, let's continue."

Vero's forehead creased. *That's it?* Raziel had humiliated him in front of the whole class! He opened his mouth to protest, but Ada kicked Vero's leg and shook her head. Raziel's eyes flitted to Vero, then back to Greer. "Yes, you are correct. Slaying demons is another role of guardians. Our enemies' influence over humans can be strong. And often, slaying the demon is the only way to save them."

Kane raised his hand. "When do we learn that? When do we get our swords?"

"When you're deemed to be ready. And then Michael will instruct you," Raziel answered.

Vero's eyes lit up when he heard the name Michael. He knew about Michael from Sunday school — the archangel leader, a fierce warrior who cast Lucifer and his fallen angels out of heaven and banished them into darkness. From his studies at school, Vero knew about the Renaissance painter Raphael and his painting of Michael standing courageously with his mighty sword drawn, crushing the head of the fallen Satan.

In the Bible it was prophesied that Michael would slay the dragon and defeat Satan's army in the end times. Excitement rose in Vero's chest knowing that at some point in his training he would actually meet Michael. Would he be worthy to be in Michael's presence?

"And I'm not good enough for you?"

Vero snapped out of his thoughts to see Raziel standing over him, piercing him with a scornful look.

"Are you bored in my class?" Raziel asked.

Raziel can read my thoughts! Did Vero's admiration of Michael offend Raziel? Had Vero hurt his feelings? He suddenly felt totally exposed.

"I'm not worthy enough to hold your attention?"

What's Raziel's deal? Vero was beginning to realize he didn't like Raziel much, but then he immediately regretted the thought. The narrowing of Raziel's eyes confirmed it... he was reading Vero's mind.

"I'm not bored," Vero quickly said. Then he deliberately thought, *I'm happy to be here.*

"Then it will do you good to keep your mind focused on the lesson," Raziel said.

Vero heard Greer snicker. He looked over at her, and she flashed him a smug smile. Vero turned his head back to the lesson, not wanting to incur any more of Raziel's wrath.

"All of the mentioned tasks of the angels are correct. But the one that you failed to bring up is probably the most important. The one which must be obeyed before all others."

The young angels leaned forward eagerly — except for Greer who idly plucked blades of grass from the ground.

"The most important task for all angels to master is learning to accept God's will over your own," Raziel said. "Accepting God's will above your own is the ultimate expression of faith and love. It is also one of the hardest of our tasks. And why is that?"

Raziel looked out over the class. No one raised a hand,

but Greer stopped pulling grass blades and focused her eyes on Raziel.

"Because it involves trials and tribulations, pain and suffering," Raziel said solemnly. "It will require you to deny yourself for the sake of others or for the greater good. It will not be easy. At times, your heart will shatter when you witness man's injustice and cruelty to one another—especially when all you can do is sit back and watch. You are powerless to stop it because you trust in the will of God."

Vero's mind drifted back to the track meet. He thought about how he'd failed to deny himself for the greater good, about how he'd humiliated Danny in order to impress Davina. He'd been cruel. Then Vero recalled the giant angels he'd seen guarding the skyscrapers in New York City. They stood with their swords drawn protectively around tall buildings. He could only imagine their grief when they had to step aside, lower their swords, and allow two airplanes to crash into the tallest high-rises in the city on that fateful day in September many years ago. Their hearts must have shattered into a million tiny pieces. The pain would have been unbearable. Yes, accepting God's will would not always be easy.

The group was silent for a few moments as Raziel's grave words and the enormity of what was expected of them sunk in. Before Greer dropped her head and resumed picking at the grass, Vero caught a look of trepidation on her face. He noticed her fingernails were bitten down to the skin. Perhaps she wasn't so tough after all.

"How can you tell if something is the will of God?" Kane asked. "I mean, how will we know?"

"First of all, you have to be open to it. Next, you free your mind of any hateful thoughts. It helps to put your right hand over your heart and spread your fingers like this ... " Raziel demonstrated the gesture for them. "And then ... just listen. On earth the humans call it *intuition*. Here, it's *Vox Dei*—a sixth sense, an inkling as to what you should be doing. It is the voice of God working in your heart, directing you in times of question. But you must be open to that direction. You must be willing to listen."

Raziel's face grew even more sober.

"But not all messages come from God. The great deceiver can gain access to your minds in moments of doubt and weakness. If you give him any sort of opportunity, he'll seize the moment and hold great influence over you. His maltures will poison your minds." Raziel looked at each of them in turn to drive home his point.

"So for your lesson today, you're going to put listening to God's voice into practice, letting it guide you."

Raziel spread his wings. He flapped them in a graceful manner and began to rise into the air.

"Follow close behind."

The fledglings rose and released their wings. It felt good to stretch them. Vero admired the ease with which Raziel ascended into the current, like sails on a sailboat, flapping in unison with the wind. Vero was still awkward with his own flying skills. He didn't want to give Raziel any new opportunity to criticize him, so he prayed he could keep pace. As he fluttered his wings, Vero instantly felt lighter on his feet. Up until this point, he'd needed a good jump off a cliff to get airborne. He rose into the air, but only hovered. He watched as Raziel and the others were getting farther away from him. A feeling of dread overtook him because he was going to flunk his first real lesson. Without warning, Vero felt a forceful tug on his back. Someone was pulling him up by the back of his shirt collar! As he rose higher into the air, Vero cocked his head and saw Greer dragging him along.

"Humiliating, isn't it? Having a girl save you?" Greer snickered before she dropped him into the air.

It was, Vero thought, but he dared not admit it out loud. Then he felt his face turn bright red, betraying him.

Raziel and the class flew over an area of the Ether that Vero had never seen before. It wasn't the plush, green landscape he'd come to love. Rather, it looked brown and devoid of any sort of life. From Vero's vantage point, the ground looked like desert — barren and rocky. Uriel had warned him that not all parts of the Ether were wonderful; looking below, he now believed him. Even the brilliant light that normally lit up the sky seemed to dim. Vero hoped they were just flying through this area because he really didn't want to sightsee down there. But then Raziel beat his wings a little less furiously, and Vero knew they weren't just passing through.

As he landed, Vero saw the area was much worse than what he'd glimpsed from above. The sandy ground teemed with jagged rocks so sharp that Vero could feel them through his shoes. He experienced pain with every step.

Suddenly, he was overcome with thirst. His mouth felt unbelievably dry. He'd do anything for a cool glass of water. But looking out over the barren land without even so much as a cactus in sight, the hope of finding refreshment seemed impossible. Vero glanced at the other fledglings and could tell they were equally miserable. X grabbed his stomach as dehydration overtook him. Ada stuck out her tongue, panting. All of them looked dazed and confused. All except for Greer. She seemed to be alert as she took in her surroundings. It was as if she was immune to the harsh world around her.

"Here's where I leave you," Raziel told the group. "This is your first official test."

"We can't survive out here!" Vero protested.

Vero knew he was showing weakness, but he was terrified of being left there. He was certain he'd quickly die of thirst—or worse.

Raziel placed his hands on Vero's shoulders. "Do what I told you," he said calmly. "Do not be afraid. Trust your heart. Erase doubt from your mind and let God guide you out of here."

Raziel stepped back, curled up inside his tremendous wings, and said to the group, "Do not follow me." Then he disappeared, flashing like a falling star across the darkening sky.

Vero looked around at the others. They were on their own in this forsaken land.

Uriel was standing in the green fields of the Ether when a sudden wind appeared, bringing Raziel with it. Uriel nodded to his fellow archangel, acknowledging him.

What do you think of him? Uriel asked through his thoughts.

I see nothing special about him, Raziel answered. *He can't even fly well.*

The Almighty hasn't given us any clear signs, but I suspect enough, Uriel said.

If he is the one, then we must keep his identity hidden from the Wicked One for as long as possible, Raziel said.

And even then, it may not be enough time, Uriel said with great sadness in his eyes.

16

❖

BEHEMOTH

I'm out of here," Kane said as he surveyed the vast desert.

"Raziel said not to follow him," Ada protested.

"I don't care."

Kane flapped his wings, determined to leave, but he couldn't get airborne. The more he flapped, all he managed to do was stir up sand and dust, creating a sandstorm. Particles of sand flew into the eyes and mouths of the others, making their already grim situation worse.

"Knock it off!" X shouted.

"Stop!" Vero said, covering his eyes with his arm.

But Kane grew more and more desperate, fanning his wings feverishly and making the sandstorm unbearable. Ada fell to the ground under the force of the gale winds and covered her head to protect herself. The others struggled to stay on their feet. Greer grabbed Kane's left wing and wouldn't let go.

Through his obscured vision, Vero watched as she pulled

Kane's other wing and tackled him to the stony ground. While holding him down, she rubbed his face into the dirt until he came to his senses. Vero marveled at Greer's incredible strength.

Kane's wings began to weaken and eventually stopped flapping. Greer released him and stood up.

"Way to stay cool under pressure," Greer said.

Kane sprang to his feet, spewing dirt from his mouth. Vero couldn't help smiling. Needing Greer to help him fly had made him feel inadequate. But now, seeing how easily she'd wrangled the well-muscled Kane to the ground, Vero felt a little better.

"Some force out there is clipping our wings," Greer announced. "Obviously, we can't fly out of here, as Kane just demonstrated."

Kane glared at Greer so intensely that it made Vero feel uncomfortable. Kane's look told Vero that Kane wasn't the type to let bygones be bygones, though Greer seemed oblivious to Kane's evil eye.

"So what are we going to do?" Pax asked.

"We're going to do what we were told to do. Close your eyes and listen for guidance," Greer said.

"It's kind of hard to concentrate when you're dying for a drink," Ada said.

"Whatever we're going to do, we'd better do it quick!" X shouted as he pointed to the sky.

All heads turned upward to see a flock of enormous condors circling above. They were massive! Three times the size of any birds that Vero had seen on earth.

And even from a distance, Vero could see they had a

ravenous look in their eyes. They began circling the fledglings, around and around, never breaking formation.

"Now we've got a ticking clock," Pax said.

"I can't do this!" Ada cried.

"Close your eyes and block out everything else," Greer said.

"It's not that easy!" Pax shouted.

"Of course not," Greer replied in a calm voice. "But it's your only shot at getting out of here."

Suddenly one of the massive birds nosedived right for them. X quickly picked up a rock, and with the skill of a quarterback, nailed the swooping bird right in the head.

"Eat that!" X shouted.

The bird flapped around in midair, briefly disoriented, and then rejoined the others, still circling above.

Greer turned to Ada and said, "Grab my arm."

The moment Ada latched onto Greer, Ada visibly relaxed.

Vero closed his eyes, which was rather unpleasant due to the sand particles that were now scratching his eyeballs. He desperately tried to ignore his fear and the strange, consuming thirst. He thought of his mother and wished she were with him, and then he decided to focus on her.

Vero pictured his mom sitting on the edge of his bed like she did when he was sick with a fever. She smoothed his hair, dipped a washcloth into a bowl of cold water on his nightstand, and dabbed his forehead. Thinking of its coolness and his mother's comforting presence eased Vero's discomfort momentarily. With his eyes tightly shut, Vero began walking as the image of his mother gently smiling at him guided him and reassured him that he'd be all right. He forged blindly ahead.

Again, his mother finished wringing out the washcloth and tenderly placed it back on Vero's forehead. This time he could actually feel the cold against his skin. Vero opened his eyes and discovered he was standing before a cold stone wall. He stepped back and saw an arched stone doorway. He did not see any of the other angels around. Desperate to flee the desolate scene behind him, Vero walked through the doorway.

Once inside, he instantly felt better. It was much cooler inside the lofty rock walls. Passageways greeted him in every direction. Vero counted three different paths to travel, but he had no idea which one to take. Vero felt a tap on his shoulder and quickly spun around to see X and Pax.

"Where are the others?" Vero asked.

"Don't know," X said. He was bent over with his hands on his waist.

Pax crazily shook his head like a wet dog to get the sand out of his hair.

"I feel like I can't breathe," X said between labored breaths. "I need water."

"Maybe we should go look for the others," Vero said.

"How?" X asked. "I can barely stand up. I need water first, and then maybe my head will stop spinning, and I can help find them."

"Shh ... " Vero held his finger to his mouth. Something was making his skin tingle. Vero placed his hands on Pax's shoulders to stop him from moving.

The three listened intently. The sound was difficult to make out at first, but after a few moments, it became crystal clear. Water! Faint droplets echoed throughout the cavern. The boys' spirits immediately rose.

"Let's go!" X rasped. "I hear it coming from this tunnel!"

X followed the sound into one of the tunnels, but suddenly stopped short. Pax and Vero ran into him.

"What?" Vero asked.

"I don't hear it anymore," X said, and the excitement drained from his face.

"Let's try this one," Pax said as he walked to the entrance of another tunnel. But once again, the sound of water droplets disappeared.

Vero stuck his head into the remaining tunnel. "Guys, it's definitely this one!"

Pax and X raced over to Vero. But when they stepped into the tunnel, only the sound of their labored breathing could be heard.

"I know I heard it!" Vero yelled in frustration.

"Maybe we're hallucinating," Pax began. "That's what happens when you get dehydrated."

"We're going crazy," X panicked. "It's all in our heads!"

"How can that be if all three of us heard it?" Vero asked.

"Then we're all going nuts," Pax said.

"No, I can feel it. There's water here somewhere." And Vero knew it was true. "Raziel said this lesson will teach us to hear God's voice. It's our only way out."

Vero put his hand over his heart and spread his fingers apart like Raziel had shown them. He closed his eyes tight and concentrated as hard as he could. The next thing he knew, something inside of him was nudging him forward. Vero stepped into the tunnel directly in front of him. X and Pax followed.

The tunnel grew darker, so Pax grabbed Vero's shirt. X

also reached for Vero's shirt. Vero pushed on through the passageway.

Vero felt like a mole. Moles were completely blind, yet they could successfully claw their way through their burrows to find food. Despite all the rocks on the ground, Vero was amazed he never stumbled. Pax and X held firmly onto Vero as he snaked his way through the winding tunnel. Gradually, slivers of light began to break up the blackness. Vero looked around for its source, but there wasn't any. The light just … was. Then Vero heard a voice.

"What took you guys so long?"

It wasn't God, but Greer. She was perched on the edge of a heavily eroded rock wall above a small pool. Next to Greer was a small stream that flowed into the pool below, where Ada was madly scooping water into her hands and drinking her fill.

Vero, Pax, and X ran to the pool and began gulping up the water at a frenzied pace. It dripped down their chins and soaked their clothes. X dunked his entire head into the pool.

When he'd finished drinking, Pax asked Greer, "Is Kane with you?"

"No, I thought he was with you," she answered.

"Then he's probably still out there in the dust," Pax said.

Vero looked at Ada nervously. He couldn't imagine being trapped in that awful desert. "He could die out there," Vero said.

"Then I guess he's gonna be singing tenor for all eternity," Greer said.

"We have to go back for him," Vero said.

"Have fun," Greer said.

"I don't get you," Vero said. "One minute you're acting all

nice and being helpful, and the next minute you're all rough and tough. So which is it?"

"First of all, I'm never all that nice. And second, when I save you, it's only because I have zero tolerance for stupidity. Going after Kane fits into the stupidity category."

"It's the right thing to do," said Vero. "Even if it *is* stupid."

Greer hopped down off the wall and got up in Vero's face, glaring at him, daring him to go against her word. But Vero held her gaze and refused to back down. He sensed that X, Ada, and Pax were waiting nervously to see which one would cave first.

It was Greer. She ran a hand through her spiky hair and pulled at the strands until the blonde streaks stood on end. Then she nodded at Vero with a smug, sideways smile. "You're not as wimpy as I thought," she said.

Vero stood strong, making sure he didn't crack a smile or relax his body in any way that might give an indication of weakness.

"You guys better drink up if we're going back out there," Greer said to the others.

Vero breathed a little easier. He was glad he hadn't backed down. But then he thought of the horrid desert and wondered what he'd gotten himself into. Going back into that oppressive air would be agony.

"All right, tough guy, let's go," Greer said.

Vero took one last drink of water. Ada doused her head like X had done earlier, flattening her wild red hair into tight, dark ringlets. Pax took off his glasses and opened his mouth under the running spring.

The group turned to leave but then stopped short.

The landscape had completely changed.

Where moments before there had been a tunnel, now there was a solid rock wall.

"Okay, Genius," Greer said to Vero, "what's Plan B?"

Vero ran his fingers along the wall. But no matter how much he explored or felt for that internal nudge, Vero felt nothing. And the wall remained an impenetrable mass of stone.

Vero beat his fists against the rock repeatedly. After one particularly hard punch, Vero screamed as he smashed his knuckles against the stone.

Greer crossed her arms as she stood back, observing. As Vero tried to shake off the pain, he became aware of the others watching him. "You done?" Greer asked.

Vero nodded, feeling the weight of their stares upon him. A moment ago he'd felt proud of himself for standing up to Greer and setting a good example to the other fledglings. Now he just looked like a fool.

"So since you're done and all," Greer said, "could you please move? You're standing on the exit."

Vero looked down and realized he was standing on top of a wooden door that was carved into the ground. Vero stepped aside as Greer kneeled down and pulled on a clasp that had been indented into the wood.

"Wait!" Vero said, grabbing her arm.

Greer looked up at him.

"If we go through that door, we're only gonna be that much farther away from Kane."

"Well, that little voice inside of me is saying the only way out is through this door," Greer shot back. "And my intuition is a lot more developed than any of yours."

"Oh really? And why is that?" Vero asked.

"Because I wasn't raised with some perfect loving family like the rest of you. When I was sent to earth, I got one lousy foster family after the other. Each one was worse than the last. You wanna know how I got to the Ether my first time? Do you?"

Everyone looked at her, waiting. Vero let go of her arm.

"Foster mother number seven lost her temper when she saw that I'd forgotten to make my bed, so she picked up an aluminum baseball bat and mistook my head for the ball."

Vero fell silent, not sure how to respond. No one spoke. But Greer wasn't the type to want their pity anyway.

"So the bottom line is—I had to tap into that intuition sooner than the sorry lot of you, or else I wouldn't have made it this far. And besides, do any of you see another way out of here?"

Vero studied their surroundings. Greer was right. Solid stone walls enclosed them on every side. The pool of water was still there, but now it was as if they were trapped in a big rock box.

Greer pulled open the door. There was nothing to see, only darkness.

"Later," Greer said, and she jumped feet first into the complete unknown, disappearing without a sound.

Ada peered into the open hole. "I can't see her. She's really gone."

Vero looked into the uneasy faces of his fellow angels. *What to do?* X walked to the edge of the hole and stood tall. His hair was still wet from the spring, and his T-shirt was soaked. X saluted the others and took a step into the darkness.

Now it was down to three.

Ada turned to Vero, "I really don't want to go down there," she said, nervously twirling a finger through her curls.

Vero sighed heavily and said, "Greer's right. There's no other way out."

"How about we hold your hand, Ada," Pax said. "So whatever happens, we'll be together."

Vero nodded, though he couldn't help thinking Ada was going to have to toughen up if she was going to make it as a guardian. No one would be there to hold her hand if the maltures came for her. Still, he stepped to the edge of the hole and smiled at her.

"Come on," Vero said. "Let's get this over with."

Ada and Pax stood next to him with Ada in the middle, and the three joined hands. Vero didn't know what they would find in the unnatural darkness, but he had to admit that he felt a little better knowing he wouldn't be facing it alone.

"On the count of three … " Pax began, "One, two, three!"

Vero, Pax, and Ada jumped off the rim of the opening and blindly fell into the abyss.

Vero lost track of time as they plummeted through the darkness. It could have been two minutes or two hours. He was reminded of the time when he and Clover had made their way through a maze of mirrors at an amusement park. With strobe lights blasting and mirrors reflecting their distorted images, Vero had walked through it completely disoriented, as if in a dream.

This time, though, the feeling of Ada's fingernails digging into his palm kept him in reality.

Ha! Reality!

As they continued to fall, it suddenly occurred to Vero that if there would eventually be a bottom to this fall, then they could hit it at any moment.

"Open your wings!" he shouted. "Hurry!"

Vero willed his wings to open. But the space was tight, like they were falling down a narrow well. So his wings wouldn't fully extend. The others had trouble releasing their wings too. Flying was no longer an option.

"I can't fly!" Ada yelled.

"Just keep them open as far as you can! We have to slow our descent before we hit the bottom!"

As they continued to fall, Vero became aware of his outermost wing feathers as they scraped along the uneven crags of the rock walls. He shut his eyes, bracing for the inevitable impact. He hoped they wouldn't land on top of Greer and X.

Suddenly, his wings, even though they were still fairly close to his back, caught an updraft of wind. Finally his wings had some air to bite into, and he was no longer freefalling. The speed of his descent abruptly slowed to a leisurely glide, with his wings acting as a parachute. Vero had thought that his feathery appendages were only for flying distances, and he was never so glad to be wrong about something. Pax and Ada's wings had also caught the current.

As the three drifted down, a dull light began to illuminate their surroundings. It grew brighter and brighter until Vero had to blink repeatedly as his eyes adjusted to it. Suddenly, the stone walls disappeared, and their wings were able to fully extend. They all landed safely without so much as a sprained ankle.

But when Vero looked down, he understood why. They'd landed in mud up to their waists, and they were surrounded by tall, thick grass and reeds. Vero let Ada's hand drop.

"Thanks," Ada said to Vero.

"You're welcome," Vero said.

"Where are we?" Ada asked.

"Some kind of swamp," Pax answered.

"Gross!" Ada said. "The mud's on my wings, and it's so thick that I can't move them." She made a futile attempt to fly.

Vero parted the nearby reeds in the hopes of finding a way out. "Come on, let's get out of this muck," he said. But all he saw were more reeds and more marsh, no shore in sight, nothing to orient him. They couldn't just stand around in the waist-deep mud, so he began walking.

"Why that way?" Pax asked.

"We can't stay here," Vero answered. "We need to find the others."

"I feel like we should be going that way." Pax pointed behind them.

Vero wasn't going to fight Pax over the issue. The voice inside of him wasn't telling him anything except that he was thirsty again, so he turned and followed Pax, this time relying on Pax's intuition.

The mud was so dense that it felt like Vero had cinder blocks attached to his feet. *Please don't let this be quicksand.*

"I hope there aren't any leeches," Ada said. "I can't deal with leeches."

"It's the alligators that I'm worried about," Pax said.

"Now why'd you have to say that?" Vero asked.

"At least I didn't mention snakes," Pax said with a shrug.

This got to Vero. The thought of snakes swimming around made his chest tighten. "Let's just keep moving," Vero said.

"I'm glad we have daylight," Pax said, looking up at the bright sky above. "It's weird how the light in the Ether seems to appear out of nowhere."

"There's no sun in the Ether; only God's light. That's why the Ether doesn't follow the laws of day and night on earth," Ada said.

After a few minutes of trudging along, the group was exhausted. Pax stopped walking and tried to spread his wings to lift himself out of the muck, but the caked-on mud wouldn't allow it.

"My wings are pinned," Vero said.

"What if I climbed up on your shoulders? Then maybe I could see over the reeds," Ada said.

"It's worth a try," Vero said.

Ada faced Vero and placed her hands on his shoulders.

"Step on my knee and then try to climb up," Vero said.

Pax helped Ada balance as she attempted to hoist herself onto Vero's shoulders. She kneed Vero in the chest on the way up.

"Ouch!"

"Sorry ... " she said as Pax attempted to push her up from behind.

"Touch my butt again and you'll be missing some teeth," Ada snarled.

"I'm only trying to help!"

Pax moved behind Vero and tried to support him as Ada got situated. For just a moment, Vero imagined they looked like a really bad acrobatic act. And then Ada slipped. All her weight fell against Vero, and all three of them went down in the mud.

Great, Vero thought. *I've had sand in my eyeballs, and now I have mud everywhere!* He got to his feet first, grabbed Ada under her armpits, and pulled her up. Pax managed to stand on his own. They were completely covered in mud.

"Perfect!" Ada said with a look of disgust. "I think I'm gonna be picking mud out of places I never knew existed."

"Did you see anything before you fell?" Pax asked.

"There's land straight ahead of us," Ada said.

Vero spit sludge out of his mouth. He was beyond disgusted. "It's like we're swimming in a giant backed-up toilet!" Vero tried to wipe mud off his face.

Wait. What. Was. That? Vero frantically rubbed mud from his eyes so he could be sure of what he was seeing. It was a snake. But it was much bigger than any anaconda Vero had ever seen on the National Geographic channel. It made the snake that attacked Davina look like a night crawler! The enormous serpent was weaving through the reeds and gaining speed. It actually moved the mud with such force that it created a wake. The waves pushed Pax deeper into the reeds and out of sight.

"Pax!" Vero shouted.

With its head bobbing in and out of the sludge, the massive snake slithered over to Ada who was completely unaware of its presence.

"Ada!" Vero screamed. "Look out!"

Ada turned around, but it was too late. The snake was upon her. It began coiling.

"Vero!" Ada shouted just before the snake stole her breath. The snake violently tossed Ada. Vero broke off a piece of reed, intending to shove the end of it straight into the snake's eye. But as the horrific creature swam closer to Vero, he saw that it had no eyes!

The snake started to swim away with Ada firmly in its grasp. As its body swept past Vero, he grabbed Ada's legs. The snake shook both of them around as if they were rag dolls. It was like an amusement park ride neither one of them wanted to be on.

It took every ounce of Vero's strength to hang on while they were being viciously tossed from side to side. But Vero wouldn't let go of Ada's legs, hoping his weight alone would be enough to pull her free from the snake's grasp.

Suddenly, Vero and Ada were being lifted out of the swamp. They were still in the snake's embrace, but the height gave Vero a clearer view of their surroundings. And he realized the creature wasn't a snake at all, but some kind of dinosaur! They were in the clutches of its tail, and Vero wasn't sure if that was better or worse.

With one huge flick of its tail, the dinosaur uncurled its long extremity and flung Vero and Ada onto dry land. Ada heaved and coughed as the air came back into her lungs. Vero patted her on the back.

"What just happened?" Ada asked.

"I'm not sure, but I think that creature just helped us," Vero said. "But it swept Pax farther into the reeds."

"Maybe now we can clean off our wings and then fly out to find him," Ada said.

Vero didn't answer, but seconds later Ada tugged on his arm and pointed, speechless. Vero followed her gaze.

They were sitting on what seemed to be a bank along a mud river filled with patches of reeds and grasses. Farther inland Vero saw trees that looked like giant palms, and beyond the trees, a herd of sauropod dinosaurs peacefully grazed. Vero watched as their long necks stretched high into the air to eat leaves from the treetops. They moved gracefully, despite their massive bulk.

Months ago, Vero had gone on a field trip to a museum to see the dinosaur bones. He'd stood next to the display of reconstructed skeletons and reveled in their greatness. But that was nothing compared to seeing those bones with flesh over them . . . and they were moving! The scene before Vero and Ada was nothing less than extraordinary.

"Unbelievable . . . " Ada whispered.

"That must be what had us in its tail," Vero said.

Vero pointed to a dinosaur drinking from a pond. "That's a diplodocus. And over there is a brachiosaurus."

Ada stared at them and then quietly said, "Moves like a cedar . . . "

"What?" Vero asked.

"It has a tail that moves like a cedar!" Ada said. "From the book of Job!"

"A cedar tree?"

"Yes, they're behemoths," Ada said. "Creatures of immense proportions."

"They still look like dinosaurs to me," Vero said.

"Maybe that's all the behemoths ever were," Ada said. "Giant herbivores. And if they only eat grasses, I don't think we need to be afraid of them."

"Unless a T. rex shows up!"

"We just need to keep a safe distance," Ada said.

"How about 200 million years?" Vero studied the sauropods in the distance, and he noticed there were enormous mounds of dirt all around the behemoths. "Do you think those are anthills?" he asked.

"I hope not," Ada said. "I can't deal with giant ants right now."

Off in the distance, a sauropod lifted its tail, and they both made the connection at the same time.

"Oh lovely," Ada said.

"Hey, at least they aren't giant anthills."

A nearby rustling sound caused them to quickly duck behind a clump of reeds. Visions of *Jurassic Park* flashed through Vero's mind, and he expected a T. rex or a velociraptor to appear at any moment.

Instead, a miserable-looking, mud-covered creature slowly trudged out of the swamp.

"Pax!" Ada cried.

Vero couldn't help but laugh.

"Laugh all you want, but you guys don't look any better than I do," Pax said before he collapsed onto the ground, exhausted. "Why would anyone ever want to take a mud bath? I can't believe people pay money for this ... "

Suddenly, they heard a low rumbling, and the ground began to shake. Pax instantly bolted upright. "Earthquake!" he shouted.

"Worse!" Vero yelled. He grabbed Pax under his armpits and pulled him to his feet. "Behemoth stampede!"

Pax turned his head in the direction of the trembling ground. A herd of sauropods was charging straight at them. He did a double take.

"It's no dream!" Vero shouted.

The booming got louder.

"Run!" Ada screamed, but the heavy mud weighed them down.

"They're gaining on us!" Pax yelled. "An old person with a walker could move faster than us!"

Vero couldn't believe that something so big could move so fast! The herd of massive dinosaurs was nearly upon them. Vero tried moving his wings so he could fly to safety, but the hardened mud prevented them from flapping.

"Pax!" Ada yelled.

Vero turned and saw that Pax had fallen to the ground and was now struggling to get up under the weight of the mud. "Ada wait!" Vero cried, but she ran back to help Pax. They were sure to be crushed like little insects.

Then Vero recalled the day's lesson — allowing God's voice to guide him. So he did the only thing he could think of. He stood completely still and faced the charging creatures. Vero closed his eyes, placed his outstretched hand over his heart, and listened for the inner voice to lead him.

Once again, it was not easy to concentrate, but Vero focused and freed his mind of the impending danger. In seconds, Vero felt strength come over him and fill him with courage. He grabbed Pax by what little bit of his shirt collar he could find.

"Take his hand!" Vero shouted to Ada.

Ada grabbed Pax as the shadow cast from the charging dinosaurs overcame them, blocking out the daylight. The behemoths were massive at a distance, but up close ... images of giant redwood trees came to Vero's mind.

Following an inner pull, Vero dodged the gargantuan animals, guiding Pax and Ada between the legs of the beasts and through the stampede. They ducked, jumped, and skirted as the herd changed directions, and they were pelted by chunks of earth, rocks, and even dino muck kicked up by the herd.

Vero stumbled over a cluster of rocks. He was going down and he knew it. Pax and Ada fell with him onto the hard ground. An especially large behemoth charged. The beast's front leg lifted up and was poised to land on top of them! Vero refused to panic. He prayed hard and a way out presented itself to him—a ditch! Vero pulled Pax and Ada with him, and the three rolled into the safety of the trench. The beast's leg came down, narrowly missing them.

Finally, the last of the herd ran by. Safely hidden in the trench, the three angels eyed each other in a tense silence. Anger replaced the terror on Ada's face. And then she stood up and punched Vero squarely across his jaw.

17

THE BOOK OF RAZIEL

What was that for?" Vero asked, massaging his jaw.

"Because you made me jump into that hole!"

"I just saved your life!" Vero shot back.

"That's not the point!" yelled Ada.

Vero and Pax swapped looks, and then Pax shrugged his shoulders. Apparently Pax couldn't explain Ada's behavior either.

"Just *look* at us! Look what we're covered in!" Ada wailed.

A grin spread across Pax's face, and he began to laugh — shakily at first, but then his chuckles dissolved into all-out hysterical laughter until he was doubled over. Ada and Vero exchanged glances. Then Ada started laughing too. And finally Vero joined them.

"I don't know what's so funny," Greer said. "You guys stink! I can smell you all the way up here."

Vero looked up from the trench and saw Greer and X standing over them. They were perfectly clean—no mud or dino muck anywhere on them.

"If any of you swine would like our company," Greer said, holding her nose, "you'd better go wash yourselves in the river. Otherwise, it's been nice knowing you."

Vero, Pax, and Ada climbed out of the ditch and walked with X and Greer toward the river. The behemoths were no longer in sight.

"You guys didn't land in the swamp?" Vero asked.

"No, we glided to a smooth landing under a shade tree," X said.

"Maybe if you hadn't hesitated before jumping, you wouldn't have wound up in the swamp," Greer gloated.

Greer was right, and Vero knew it immediately. He hadn't listened to the inner voice when it told him to jump into the hole. As he washed himself off, Vero resolved to trust his instincts moving forward because he didn't want to pull dinosaur poop out of his ears ever again.

"Any sign of Kane?" Pax asked. They were now mud free, sitting by the river and eating wild berries with their wings retracted.

"He must be really lost," X said, shaking his head.

"That's *his* problem," Greer said.

"But aren't we all in this together?" Ada asked.

"No," Greer said. "Raziel made it very clear that this is a competition."

"No, he didn't. He said we were to push each other to our full potentials," Vero said.

"He also said we'd be judged based on our character and compassion," Pax added.

"Maybe, but you can't follow somebody down the wrong path," Greer explained. "I'm not gonna risk my chance to be a guardian for anyone."

"Did you ever think that maybe Kane's on the right path, and we're the lost ones?" Vero wondered aloud.

"I'm only doing what Raziel told us to do," Greer said. "And so far it's been working for me." She shot Vero a look, "And you're already on Raziel's bad side, so I'd recommend that you do what he says."

"Yeah, what's up with that?" Vero asked. "I just met him, and he hates me already."

"He doesn't hate you. Archangels do not hate," Ada said. "I think he's frustrated. He might feel like a failure. Did you ever learn about the Book of Raziel?"

Vero shook his head. He had no idea what she was talking about. The others were also listening closely.

"Raziel once stood close to God's throne. He was the Angel of Secrets. It was his job to write down everything he heard into a book made of blue sapphire. The book contained the entire history of mankind — past, present, and future. It included the secrets to the laws of the universe, the laws of creation, everything about the planets and stars, too. It named all of the angels and what they did, and it included information about how humans could summon angels and ward off demons."

Even Greer was giving Ada her undivided attention.

"After Adam was expelled from the garden, he was so

upset about what he'd done that God instructed Raziel to give
Adam the book. It was partly to comfort Adam, but mainly it
was to help him learn how to live outside the garden and show
Adam and Eve how to find their way back to God.

Raziel did as God asked. Through the book, Adam
gained great wisdom. He read about every single soul who
was yet to be born for all the generations to come. Adam
knew some things that many of the angels didn't know ...
things they'd never been privy to."

"That's amazing," Greer said. "When the serpent told
Eve that she and Adam would know all if they ate from
the tree of knowledge, in a way he was right. Yeah, they got
booted out of the garden, but the Book of Raziel really *did*
give them the knowledge and wisdom of God."

They all considered her idea for a moment.

"Anyway," Ada continued. "Some of the angels got jealous
that God had entrusted this book to man, his newest creation
who'd already let God down. So they stole the book from Adam
and threw it into the sea. But God ordered Rahab, the Angel
of the Seas, to retrieve the book and give it back to Adam, who
passed it down to his son Seth. It got passed on down through
the generations until it eventually reached Enoch, and then it
disappeared from man again. But Raziel gave the book to Noah
who used it to figure out how to build the ark."

"How do you know all this?" X asked.

"I've been studying this for my Bat Mitzvah," she replied.

Vero knew a little bit about Bat Mitzvahs. He understood
it was a ceremony that was done in the Jewish religion during which a kid becomes an adult. And then they have an
amazing party afterward.

"Noah placed the book in a golden box, and it was the

first thing he brought with him onto the ark. Later, Abraham was given the book, and then his son Jacob, and then *his* son Joseph who used it to learn the secrets of dreams. The book was buried with Joseph after he died. But years later, when Moses led the Israelites out of Egypt, he removed the bones of Joseph from the Nile and found the book with them. And it was Raziel who made sure the book always got into the proper hands. Eventually King Solomon used it to build a temple for God in Jerusalem."

"So where's the book now?" Vero asked.

"No one knows," Ada shrugged. "Some think it was destroyed when the temple was burned down."

"Does Raziel know where it is?" Pax asked.

"I don't think so. He used to be the archangel closest to God's throne. Now he teaches at C.A.N.D.L.E. My guess is that it disappeared on his watch. Even though its disappearance must be a part of God's bigger plan, Raziel probably took the blame for its loss."

"But Raziel knew what was in the book. Can't he just write everything down in a new book?" X wondered aloud.

"No, supposedly his memories regarding most of the information was taken from him."

"Well, God has to know where the book is," Pax said. "Why can't he just let the angels know?"

"Sure, and while God is at it, why can't he just stop wars? Or for that matter, every single bad thing that happens?" Ada asked.

Vero reflected for a moment. "Because he won't interfere with free will."

"Exactly," Ada replied. "Just like people, angels make decisions, and their actions have consequences. It's prophesied that the book will be found again, but nobody knows by whom. And I'm sure Raziel is worried about it because if that book lands in the wrong hands—as in, the hands of the Fallen—then Lucifer's power will increase tenfold."

Vero hoped the book had been destroyed in the fire. That was far better than the alternative.

The fledglings walked along the open plains. They had come a great distance from the swamp, but it felt as if they were walking to nowhere—almost like they were on a treadmill. The angels were searching for a way out, but to where?

"I think we passed that tree three times already," Pax informed the group.

"No, they're just all starting to look the same," X said.

"Does anyone know what we should be doing?" Ada asked. "Greer, what's your inner voice telling you?"

"Sorry, I got nothing," Greer answered.

"What about you, Vero?" Ada asked.

But Vero didn't answer her. While he was physically walking alongside the others, mentally he was somewhere else.

"I think Vero's got something," Greer said.

"Vero! Vero!" Greer smacked the back of his head to bring him out of his stupor.

Vero snapped out of it and turned to Greer. "Kane's in trouble."

18

❖

THE PIT
OF ACID

"I could see him." Vero said. "He's scared. Really scared."

"Where is he?" X asked.

"I'm not sure, but it's dark. It looked like he's underground."

"That narrows it down," Greer said.

"I'm sorry, did *you* take a class in interpreting visions?" Vero asked sarcastically.

Greer looked away.

"Didn't think so," Vero said.

"Look over here!" Pax yelled.

Vero, Greer, Ada, and X turned their heads toward Pax. He was on his knees looking at a sandy indentation within an otherwise grassy field.

As they approached, Pax extended his arm like a school crossing guard, stopping them from coming any closer.

"Watch this."

Pax picked up a stick and threw it into the hole. Instantly it disappeared into the sandy pit.

"It's a sinkhole," Pax told them. "They form when an underground cavern collapses. We have one near our house. People go there all the time to dump their old appliances and stuff, and the earth gulps 'em up. I've never heard of one forming in dry sand before."

"That's gotta be where Kane is!" Vero said.

"Great! Let's all jump right in!" Greer said.

Vero looked at Greer for a moment. In spite of her sarcasm, Vero knew Greer had taught them an important lesson with that last jump—don't hesitate. So almost together, the others all leapt into the sinkhole.

"Wait!" Greer shouted. "I didn't mean it!"

But it was too late.

This jump was completely different than the last one. Vero felt perfectly relaxed, and when he opened his eyes, he found himself inside an illuminated underground cavern with Ada, Pax, and X. A moment later, a hole appeared in the ceiling of the cavern, Greer fell through, and then the hole closed up again. Greer landed on her feet and stumbled to one knee, but she quickly stood up again and brushed the sand out of her hair. The rings on her ears caught the strange light and made sparkling reflections along the cavern walls.

"Okay, hotshot, now what?" she asked.

"We find Kane," Vero said. "Is anyone feeling anything?" he asked the group.

"Nope. This one is all you," Greer answered.

"Fine. Then we'll go this way," Vero said.

"You mean right through that giant spiderweb you just walked into?" Greer asked.

"Ahh!" Vero swatted the air wildly. "Where's the spider? Is it on me? Help!"

As he continued to jump around like a crazy man, he noticed a playful smile on Greer's face.

"What?"

"There's no spiderweb," X said, chuckling.

Vero stopped hopping around. At this moment he had two choices. He could either get mad at them, or he could laugh at himself. He chose the latter. A smile formed at the corners of his mouth.

"Now can we go find Kane?" X asked.

The group walked along an underground trail. The dull light that surrounded them seemed to emanate from the floor, casting odd, eerie shadows on the walls. Greer's hand shot up, indicating that everyone should stop walking. She'd heard something. It was a rustling sound like the flutter of wings. She turned to look behind the group and screamed, "BATS!"

Hundreds, maybe even thousands of bats swarmed overhead, and they were headed their way. Greer took off running. And X, Pax, and Ada followed on her heels. Only Vero continued walking at his leisurely pace.

"Nice try, guys. I'm not falling for that again," he said.

Suddenly, a cluster of the black-winged mammals swooped down onto Vero's head. Vero screamed and ran, but he lost his footing on the slippery ground and slid a few feet on his back. The bats descended upon him, and Vero curled into a ball, covered his head with his arms, and closed his eyes.

Vero braced for an attack, but several seconds passed and nothing happened. When Vero dared to open one eye, the cluster of bats were hovering a few feet above him, swarming like a hive of angry bees. Something was preventing them from flying any closer to him. Vero opened his other eye. A jagged object that looked like an upside down-icicle had grown up out of the ground next to his foot. Vero jerked his foot back. The giant icicle was red and shiny like a crystal with razor-sharp edges.

Without any warning, thousands of the daggerlike icicles sprouted from the ground. And when Vero turned his gaze upward, he saw more growing down from the cavern's ceiling, hanging like jewel-covered sword blades. They weren't just red, either, but a vivid array of colors, bursting with light like the wildflowers of the Ether.

"Stalactites," X said, coming up behind Vero. He stared open-mouthed at the cave's roof. "I studied them in my science class. They usually take thousands of years to form. Here . . . " X looked at his watch, "it took about ten seconds."

Greer, Pax, and Ada stood among the massive formations.

"It's too bright in here with all of these colors, so the bats won't come any closer," X said. "The ones jutting up from the ground are stalagmites. They're usually made up of mineral deposits, though I'm not sure what these are made of."

The stalactites hung so far down from the ceiling that they nearly touched the stalagmites that shot up from the cavern floor. So it appeared as if they were in the mouth of some hideous beast with really nasty teeth. A pathway through the formations looked nearly impossible to navigate.

The walls also glistened with countless formations. Helictites had grown horizontally from the walls at all different angles, though none vertical. The formations seemed to defy gravity. They shot out from the walls in strange configurations resembling curly fries or clumps of worms. Yet the ends of the helictites were pointed like sharp needles. Brushing up against them, Vero knew, would not be wise.

"It doesn't look like we can go that way," Ada announced.

"Yes, but the bats are saying that's the only way," X said, his eyes fixed on the horde of nocturnal creatures who were madly teeming on the other side of the stalactites.

Pax thought he heard something. He held his index finger to his mouth to shush the others.

"What is it?" Ada whispered.

"I think I hear Kane."

The others strained their ears to listen as well. After a few seconds, a boy's voice drifted through the cavern.

"It *is* Kane!" Pax shouted.

"Shhh … " Vero said. He craned his neck in the direction of the voice. He was able to make out the distant sound, and then the word *help* floated in the air. "He's in trouble!" Vero said.

Kane's pleas were coming from deeper inside the cavern.

"How can we get to him?" Ada asked.

"Fly," X said. "We can get airborne in here."

"But it's really narrow," Pax said. "Our wingspans are too wide."

"And besides, where are you gonna land? Right on some spiky stalagmite?" Greer asked.

"Maybe they're not as sharp as we think," X said. He tentatively ran his index finger over the tip of the nearest one, then quickly jerked it back. A bright red trickle of blood ran down his finger.

"Never mind."

"Somehow we have to navigate our way through this cave," Vero said.

No one looked too excited.

"You know what?" Vero said. "We slogged through the world's grossest swamp and outmaneuvered a herd of behemoths. So how much harder could this be?"

"I have a feeling those words are going to come back and bite you in the butt," Greer said.

"Keep your head down so you don't trip," Vero said. Slowly they weaved their way, single file, through the maze of razor-sharp stalactites and stalagmites, with Vero in the lead.

Each step needed to be deliberate and cautious. As they wove their way deeper into the cavern, Kane's cries for help became progressively clearer, guiding them like a compass.

"We're getting closer," Vero said. "Stay focused."

Pax had a definite advantage, being smaller than the others. But it was a much more difficult journey for X who was nearly six feet tall and had to manipulate the formations while hunching over awkwardly.

"I can't take this much longer," X said. "My back's killing me."

"And it's cold," Ada complained. By now they could all see their breath.

"We're getting closer," Vero said. "Just keep going."

"You don't get it! I'm in agony!" X snapped, and then he abruptly stopped walking.

Greer plowed into him, causing both of them to lose their balance and fall.

Vero whipped around and saw X's face land just millimeters away from a stalagmite.

"Watch out! I almost got shish kebabbed!" Greer protested. Then she got back on her feet while being careful to keep her head tucked low.

"Sorry," X said. "My back is killing me."

"When someone's on your tail, you can't stop like that. We're all tired and hurting. But we can't stop now. Kane needs our help." She offered a hand to help X up, and her gesture seemed to be just enough to keep X moving forward.

As they continued through the cavern, Vero noticed it was becoming more difficult to breathe. He felt his thighs burn with each step. *The ground must be sloping upward.*

Finally they reached a break in the rock formations, a small clearing where no more sharp formations pushed out from the cave's walls, ceiling, or floor. But best of all, the ceiling in this small chamber was tall enough for them all to stand fully upright.

"Oh man, I never thought standing up straight would feel so good!" X stretched as tall as he could.

Pax laid flat on his back on the cold ground, trying to catch his breath. Vero and Greer stood next to X and stretched.

"I can't hear Kane anymore," Vero said.

Pax rolled onto his stomach and looked toward the back of the chamber. "Uh, guys," he said. "Better take a look at this."

"What now?" Ada asked.

As they walked over, they all saw what Pax was pointing to. Right where the back wall of the cave hit the floor was a dark hole ... a hole just big enough for a fledgling to crawl through. It reminded Vero of a mousehole, only bigger.

Still lying on his stomach, Pax stuck his head through the opening and began crawling through it.

"Hold on!" Vero called, but Pax had already disappeared into the darkness.

Vero dropped to his hands and knees to follow him, but at that moment Pax called back, "It's Kane! I can see him!"

The others crowded around the hole as Vero disappeared into it, quick as a mouse.

Once through the hole, Vero noticed immediately that the floor and the walls of the narrow passage were very smooth and tilted downward at a steep slant. He felt like he was crawling down the tunnel in a waterslide, and he had to push his hands and feet against the walls to avoid sliding all the way. He carefully crawled forward and wedged himself tightly next to Pax who was looking over a ledge.

Swirling below them was a steaming pit of bubbling water. A number of rocks and eddies were peppered throughout the pit, and the churning liquid sloshed against them, making a gurgling sound. And there was Kane, sitting forlornly on the largest rock right in the middle of the pit. Vero yelled to him, and Kane looked up, his eyes squinting.

"I'm stuck! I can't get out! There's nowhere to fly!" Kane shouted over the loud bubbling noises of the water. "No way out!"

Vero could see a smooth, solid rock wall surrounding the pit. So there was no way for Kane to get out that way.

"What's beneath me? I can't tell! What kind of wall is it?" Vero called to Kane.

"You're on top of a sheer wall! There's no footing beneath you at all!"

"Can't you fly up here?" Vero asked.

"No. That hole is how I got into this stinkin' angel trap in the first place! I slid through it and now I can't get back to it. The entrance is too close to the ceiling! I've already tried a hundred times to fly back up there ... but I can't get close enough while my wings are out, and there's no foothold on the wall for me to land on."

"Too bad there aren't any stalactites around here," Vero told Pax. Vero felt something tug on his legs, and then Greer yanked him back from the edge. She was lying on her belly in the narrow tunnel.

"Move it, angel. I'll handle this," Greer said, and then she combat crawled right over Vero and landed on top of Pax who grimaced under her weight. She stuck her head out over the ledge and saw Kane sitting on the rock. "Kane, this is Greer! You need to just suck it up and swim over to us!"

"Can't!" Kane shouted.

"Don't tell me you can't swim!"

"No ... that's not it," Kane said.

"Look," Pax said, "the walls and rocks in here are limestone. That means that liquid in the pit is highly acidic. Watch ... " Pax reached around to his back and winced as he pulled out a small feather without extending his wings.

"Impressive trick," Greer said.

"Inch out a little more," Pax instructed.

Greer army crawled a little farther while bracing herself against the walls with both hands. She looked at the water below.

"Now watch." Pax held the feather over the slogging

liquid and let go. Greer watched as it floated gently downward. The lone feather hit the surface—and disintegrated into a puff of smoke upon impact.

"Okay, so swimming is out," Greer said. "I officially have no plan."

"Everyone, get out of the passage, now!" X boomed from behind them.

Vero, Greer, and then Pax all had to inch out of the tunnel backward and single file, using their hands to push them back up the narrow tunnel and into the chamber.

"We need a plan here!" X said, as he paced the small cavern. "What are we going to do?"

"The only way to get Kane out of there is to drag him back through that claustrophobic tunnel," Vero said.

"And he's going to have to fly up to the tunnel," Greer agreed. "Swimming is definitely out."

"But he can't get close enough to the entrance with his wings extended," Pax said.

"And if he tries to retract his wings, the pit of acid is right there, and he'll fall into it. He needs time to be able to pull in his wings," Ada said.

"I've got it!" shouted X. "We'll form a human chain through the tunnel. Whoever's at the front will have to dangle out over the edge and grab hold of him. That'll buy him the time he needs to withdraw his wings, and then we can all pull him back through the hole."

"That's a great plan," Ada said excitedly.

"Yeah, if you're looking for a one-way ticket to choir practice," Greer said. "We'll be burnt to a crisp in that drink!"

"X is right, though," Vero said. "It's the only way."

They looked at each other, silently weighing their options. Kane's faint cry for help drifted through the mouse hole.

X sighed heavily. "Okay, I have the best upper body strength from spending my life in a wheelchair, so I'll be the one to catch Kane."

"No," Vero said. "We need your strength to anchor the chain. I'll grab Kane."

"No arguments from me," Greer said.

The others solemnly nodded. Vero laid down on his belly and squirmed his way back down the steep tunnel. Pax went next and grabbed Vero's ankles. The others completed the remainder of the human chain with X holding Greer's feet as they stuck out through the mousehole.

When Vero's head reappeared over the edge, he shouted instructions to Kane. "You're going to have to fly over to me and grab my hands. Then—and do this as quick as you can—retract your wings, and we'll all pull you back through the tunnel!"

Kane looked uncertain. It was definitely a risky plan, but Kane stood on the tiny rock island and nodded.

"Wait 'til I give you the sign!" Vero shouted.

The others remained in position, with X serving as the anchor back in the chamber, then Greer, then Ada, and then Pax held Vero's ankles as Vero extended his entire body over the ledge. Using his left hand to brace himself against the ceiling, Vero extended his right hand as far as possible so he could grab and hold on to Kane. It would be close, but he knew they could do it.

"Ready?" Vero called down to Kane. When Kane nodded, Vero shouted, "Now!"

Kane opened his wings and lifted off the rock. He hovered in the air for a moment and then flew over to Vero.

As Kane approached, Vero held out both hands to grab Kane, but at the last moment, Kane hesitated.

He shook his head. "It won't work!" he said.

"Yes it will!" Vero yelled. "Come on, hurry! We're losing strength!"

Kane continued to waver. And every second of waiting depleted Vero's energy. He felt Pax's grip weakening too.

"Come on, Pax! I've seen you move SUVs with your bare hands!" Vero shouted. "Hold tight!"

"But I was answering a prayer at the time!" Pax yelled back.

"Yeah? Then hear MY prayer and ... DON'T LET GO!"

Pax tightened his grip on Vero.

"Kane, grab a hold of Vero's hands now or rot on that rock forever!" Greer shouted from the mouth of the tunnel.

A huge bubble burst in the acid below, and the spray reached Vero's face and singed off his right eyebrow. "NOW, Kane, or we're leaving you!" Vero shouted.

Kane flew up to Vero and clasped hands with him. His weight pulled Vero farther out over the ledge as he quickly retracted his wings.

"Got him!" Vero yelled to the others. "Now pull!"

The chain of angels tugged hard, but Kane was still suspended over the edge. And Vero's grip was loosening.

"Hurry!" Vero shouted.

X pulled Greer's ankles tight as she backed out of the tunnel and reentered the chamber. When she was clear of the mousehole, she told X to come grab Ada's other ankle. But as X let go of Greer, the whole line started sliding forward.

"Don't let go!" Pax shrieked. "Please!"

"I can't hold on any longer!" Ada yelled, feeling her fingers slipping away from Pax's ankles.

Suddenly, Ada felt a mighty force around her left ankle. The strength of the grip told her that X was now pulling her back toward the chamber. His power was incredible. Ada breathed a sigh of relief. But then X lost his footing. He pushed back on his heels, but he couldn't find any traction. They all started sliding back toward the acidic water.

"Your wings! Open your wings!" Ada shouted back to X. "They'll anchor you!"

X willed his wings to protrude, and they shot open with the force of an umbrella battling a windstorm. His wings wedged against the chamber walls, arresting his slide toward the hole. He was finally able to pull Ada safely inside the chamber, then Pax, Vero, and finally Kane.

As everyone caught their breath, Kane looked at his rescuers and muttered faintly, "Thanks, guys."

Thank you doesn't even begin to cover it, Vero thought, as he touched his missing eyebrow.

19

❖

THE NARROW
PATH

"How did you wind up on that rock?" Pax asked Kane.
"I'm not sure. I was standing out in that desert. It
was burning hot, and the sand was whipping against my face,
so I closed my eyes and tried to listen to the voice of truth like
Raziel said. Next thing I know, I'm in here—in this room."

"There were only two ways out ... through those stalagmite things or through that hole. I figured only an idiot
would try to go through those, I mean, did you see how
sharp they are? So, I decided to see what was on the other
side of that hole. I didn't realize it was a trap 'til I was sliding downhill into that cavern. I spread my wings and caught
my fall—thank you, God—and I managed to land on that
rock. But then I was stuck there."

Vero and the others stared at Kane as he finished his
story. Greer appeared as annoyed as Vero felt.

"What?" Kane asked.

"We were the big enough *idiots* to crawl through those stalagmites to rescue you," X said, still massaging his lower back.

"Oops. I'm sorry, guys," Kane said guiltily. "Here, let me just pull my foot out of my mouth."

"Good idea. That way, I can shove my fist in there instead," Greer said.

Vero thought for a moment. How was it that he and the others had wound up in the cool room with the pool of refreshing water, but not Kane? Why had the voice led Kane to a trap and not the stream? Why was Kane led to danger?

"Do you want to know why you ended up alone on that rock with no way out?" Greer asked Kane. "It's because you were being a total jerk. You were mad."

"Yeah, but if he was listening to his inner voice, and Raziel said that voice is God, then why was God punishing Kane?" Vero asked.

"No. It wasn't God's voice. It wasn't his *Vox Dei*. Didn't you hear what Raziel told us?" Greer asked.

Vero flashed her a puzzled look. He tried to recall Raziel's lesson, but he was on sensory overload.

"When you doubt or get angry with God, Lucifer seizes that opportunity. He sends his minions, and they slip in and cloud your thoughts, totally messing with you. That's what happened to Kane."

Vero silently pondered what Greer said. The thought of being under the devil's influence, especially here in the Ether, was terrifying. He was determined it wouldn't happen to him — no matter what.

Ada stood and looked up at the ceiling of the cave. "I'm

feeling really claustrophobic and kind of cold," she said. "I'd like to get out of here."

"Me too," Pax agreed.

Vero closed his eyes and focused his mind on doing the right thing. He tried to block out everything and concentrate. But thoughts raced in and out of his mind. Kane on the rock ... Ada in the tunnel ... Clover at dinner ... Danny and Davina at the movies. *No! I need to focus!*

He thought about the track meet and how good it felt to pass Danny. Then he recalled how he felt unexplainably guilty. He thought of Blake and Duff and how they seemed glad that Vero had won the race. He thought about the raven with the long tail, about the constant battle between good and evil—whether it was physical, like with the maltures, or mental, like how he constantly battled his innate nature.

No, he had to accept the goodness. God's goodness. He remembered the feeling of peace that overcame him on the night he made his snow angel, and he let that feeling fill him once again. *Please God, know my heart.*

Suddenly, Vero felt true goodness wash over him, and after a few moments, the path became clear to him. He opened his eyes.

"We need to keep moving forward through the stalactites," Vero said.

"I don't know how much more I can take in there," Ada said.

The angels surveyed the area that lay ahead of them, and then the area that lay behind them. Their options were limited. Either way looked pretty much the same—the roof, walls, and ground were decorated with stalactites, stalagmites, and helictites.

"I say we listen to Vero and move on," X said.

"You're only saying that because you don't want to walk hunched over," Pax said.

X nodded and said, "Maybe. But the truth is, it doesn't look much different either way."

X looked to Kane for his opinion.

"Don't look at me. You saw which way I picked," Kane said. "This time I'm keeping my mouth shut."

Pax turned to Greer, "I say we go back."

"I say we go ahead," Greer nodded to Vero. Then she turned to Pax and said, "But we could always split up if you feel strongly about it." She looked at each angel in turn. "If I had to go on my own, I would. I could do this alone."

Pax shook his head. "We stay together."

The angels snaked their way through a seemingly endless maze of stalactites and stalagmites. At times, the way was so narrow that Vero sucked in his breath and tried to make himself thinner. Vero sensed their reflexes dulling.

Suddenly Pax screamed out in pain. Vero carefully turned his head and saw the right side of Pax's face covered in what looked like dozens of cactus needles, from his forehead to his chin.

"He brushed up against some helictites!" Ada called to the others.

Pax cried out, "Get them out! Please! They burn!" Tears ran down his face.

Vero looked around. The space was way too tight for anyone to be able to stand next to Pax and pull them out.

"Pax, I'm sorry," Vero said. "But you're gonna have to keep walking until we find a place big enough where we can help you pull them out."

"Try not to think about them," Kane said, as they slowly made their way through the deadly obstacle course.

"I can't," Pax whimpered. "It hurts too much."

"We need to distract him," Ada told the others.

"Ninety-nine bottles of beer on the wall, ninety-nine bottles of beer ... " Greer began to sing. "Take one down, pass it around, ninety-eight bottles of beer ... "

"That'll really push him over the edge," X said to Greer, cutting her off.

"I'm only trying to help." Greer shrugged.

"Pax, what's your favorite color?" Vero asked, hoping to distract him from the pain.

"Blue."

"You like pizza?"

"Yeah."

"Good at sports?"

"No."

"Then I bet you get good grades?"

"I don't go to school."

"Really?" Vero said, surprised. "Why not?"

"I'm severely autistic on earth," Pax said. "I don't have any language. I wear a helmet all day to keep from hurting myself."

Vero stopped walking and carefully turned around to look at Pax. Vero's eyes were full of emotion as he said, "I'm sorry."

"Maybe that's why you're the only one of us who can hear thoughts," X said. "Maybe because you can't speak on earth, you've learned to communicate in other ways. My life on earth is tough too, but being in a wheelchair has made me stronger—and not just my arms, but mentally too. I think it's all part of our training."

Vero thought about that as the group walked on in silence. Compared to X, Pax, and Greer, Vero's life was pretty good. Was it sheer luck or was his family life preparing him for something? He didn't know.

Mercifully, the cavern's landscape began to change. Rocks and boulders gradually replaced the stalactites and stalagmites. Finally, the cavern widened, and the angels could stand and stretch.

"Hold still," X said to Pax. X gripped one of the needles and gently pulled it out.

"Thank you," Pax said softly. "It feels better already."

One by one, X pulled out the rest of them and let them drop to the ground.

"You okay?" Vero asked. Pax's face looked a bit swollen, but otherwise he seemed all right.

"Yeah," Pax replied. "But I have a headache."

"So do I," Kane said.

"Well suck it up, boys," Greer said. "We have a climb ahead of us."

The fledglings looked and saw their next adventure involved scaling a steep mountain of rocks and large stones.

X sighed heavily. "Well, at least we can stand up straight."

"I say we fly to the top," Pax suggested.

"Me too," Greer said. She began flapping her wings, but nothing happened. Then each of the other angels tried, but no one rose into the air.

"This makes no sense," Kane said.

"We must be at high altitude," Vero reasoned.

"How do you know?" Pax asked.

"My dad trained to be a pilot for the Navy. He used to explain to me that everything that uses air for flight propulsion—jets, helicopters, or even birds, has an altitude ceiling. Above that height, the air is just too thin for flight."

"Altitude sickness would explain the headaches," X said.

"And why I feel out of breath," Kane added.

"Okay, science class is now over," Greer said irritably. "Let's scale this baby."

As the angels climbed, X led the way, carefully placing each foot on the treacherous mountain of crumbled brown rock and shale. With each step, the unstable rubble would shift and sometimes roll downhill, causing other rocks and debris to slide.

Besides falling and cutting themselves on jagged rocks, Vero feared that upsetting the wrong rock could trigger an avalanche and bury them all.

"X, how much farther is it?" Pax asked, his face streaked with sweat.

"I can't tell," X answered. "I can't see the top."

As Ada grabbed onto a rock to pull herself up, the rock slipped out from under her and rolled straight toward Greer who was climbing behind her.

"Greer!" Ada yelled. "Look out!"

Greer looked up, saw the rock, and jerked her face out of its path just in time. The rock barely missed her head, but it smashed her left leg, shattering the bone.

Greer screamed in agony and grabbed her leg. Vero and the others watched helplessly as Greer lost her balance and plunged to the ground.

"Greer!" Ada shouted.

Greer didn't answer. X quickly maneuvered his way through a cluster of boulders and reached her side. Greer was sitting on the craggy ground, leaning against a smooth rock.

"Look," Greer said. She lifted her injured leg with her hands and let it drop back to the ground. It was completely useless.

"I guess walking is out," X thought aloud.

The others climbed back down to Greer.

Ada's normally olive skin was white as a sheet. "I'm so sorry . . . "

"Does it hurt?" Pax asked, bending down close to her.

"At first, but now it's just numb."

"I'm really sorry," Ada said again. "I didn't mean to . . . "

"Well you did," Greer said.

"It was an accident," Pax said. "It wouldn't have happened if we hadn't come this way."

Greer locked eyes with Vero, "Maybe it was the wrong way to come."

"I'm sorry you got hurt," Vero said. "But I really feel like we need to keep going."

"How?" Pax asked. "Do you think Greer's gonna be able to climb up there?"

"Yes," Vero said. "We'll help her."

"No. I'm taking her back the way we came, whether any of you come with us or not," Ada said.

"You think getting her through those stalactites will be any easier?" Vero asked.

"At least that way I know what we're dealing with."

Vero looked to the others for support, but he didn't find

any. Greer looked dazed and pale, Pax was shaking, Kane looked frustrated, and X ... "Where's X?"

"He was just here," Kane said.

Vero looked around and found X crouched behind several large boulders with a rock in his hand.

"What are you doing?" Vero asked.

"Watch," X said.

X chucked the rock as hard as he could, and it disappeared into the darkness.

Vero wasn't impressed. "Are you losing it?"

"You didn't hear it land, did you?"

X was right. Vero never heard the rock hit the ground. "I ... I don't know ... "

As X picked up another rock, Ada, Pax, and Kane helped a limping Greer hobble over to the boulder.

X gently threw the rock directly in front of them. It disappeared without a sound.

"It just vanished into thin air," Kane said.

"I say we do the same," X announced.

"Are you crazy?" Pax said.

"Are you willing to carry Greer back through the stalactite cave or up that hill of boulders?" X asked. Everyone was silent.

But something didn't feel right to Vero. "I don't know about this," he said.

"I say we take a chance," said X.

Vero once again looked to the others, and the fact that no one would look him in the eye gave Vero his answer. Kane stood and put one of Greer's arms around his neck, while X did the same with her other arm. They hoisted her to her feet.

"I'm sorry," Greer whispered.

Kane and X did a double take. "What?"

"As much as it kills me to say it," Greer said, "I really do need you guys."

Vero and Ada exchanged glances. Vero knew it was hard for Greer to admit that.

Pax smiled at Greer, and Ada gave her an awkward hug.

"Whatever," Greer said, feeling awkward with all of that positive attention.

Vero watched as Kane and X assisted Greer. Without looking back, the three of them walked toward the spot where the rock had vanished, and then they simply disappeared into thin air. Ada glanced at Vero and shrugged. Then she took Pax's hand in her own and followed the other three until they also vanished before Vero's eyes.

Everything inside of Vero was telling him not to move forward. He wanted to scream, *"Don't go!"* But then the fear of being left alone overshadowed his instincts, and so ignoring his own instincts, Vero ran after the others.

20

---✧---

GOLEMS

Vero found himself being pulled at an alarming rate, by an overpowering force, as if he were a tiny scrap of metal being yanked forward by a gigantic magnet. The rapid motion turned his stomach, and faster and faster he went until … *Bam!* He found himself flat on his back in the middle of another cavern. Only this one was fairly large and filled with light from the torches that lined the walls. Above him was a high domed ceiling carved out of stone.

As soon as he was able to sit up and take in his surroundings, Vero saw the other angels sprawled around the room. Greer was sitting against the cavern wall with her busted leg out straight in front of her, biting her fingernails. Vero thought she looked smaller and worn out due to the pain. She leaned her head back against the wall and closed her eyes. "I hate this. I hate not being able to walk on my own."

"Where are we?" Pax asked.

"Wherever we are, at least it's warmer in here," Ada said as she walked over to Vero.

"I'm starting to wonder if we'll ever see the green grass of the Ether again," said Kane.

"Don't blame me," Vero said, looking around nervously. "I didn't want to come this way. It doesn't feel right."

"When was the last time anyone heard their inner voice?" X asked.

"All I hear right now is a bunch of whining," Ada said.

"I have a good reason to whine," Greer moaned, massaging her leg.

"I'm starving and tired," X said, as he sat down on a large rock jutting out from the wall.

"Instead of worrying about how tired we are, I think we should be more worried about who lit these torches," Kane said.

The group fell silent.

Vero looked at X. Then he did a double take. "I think I'm seeing things. That rock you're sitting on looked like it just moved."

"I thought I felt something," X said. He looked down at the exposed rock between his legs.

They heard a muffled grunt. They all stood and looked around — all except Greer who could only scoot away from the wall — and everyone was on full alert.

Suddenly, the rock under X divided, and X fell between the moving ledges onto hard, stone ground! Massive chunks of stone began to break away from the cavern walls. The fledglings circled protectively around Greer, standing back-to-back, and they watched in horror as the gigantic rocks formed into the shape of an enormous creature. The rocks that X had been sitting on were actually monstrous feet!

Those feet were attached to legs, the legs were attached to a torso that had boulders for arms and fingers, and above them all—a massive head!

"Wh- ... wha- ... what ...?" X stammered.

The creature was made out of stone and hard clay, and it stood more than thirty feet tall.

The fledglings staggered backward and gathered even closer to Greer who grabbed ahold of Kane's shoulder and pulled herself to her feet. Her low groans revealed how much pain she was in with every move.

Her groans were echoed by the others—only ten times louder—when another hard-clay creature broke away from the opposite wall. Now two oversized, craggy ogres towered over the angels!

"Maybe they're friendly?" Greer said, though she sounded less than confident.

"Any ideas?" Pax asked, his face tense with fear.

No one had any.

The first creature blocked the way they'd come in. The other creature blocked what appeared to be a doorway carved in the stone. The fledglings were trapped.

"Fly!" X shouted.

"Where?" Vero yelled back.

"Up!"

Kane and X steadied Greer as she opened her wings and rose unsteadily into the air. Then they followed her, keeping close. Ada and Pax flew to the top of the domed ceiling. Vero now stood alone, trapped between the two creatures as they closed in on him. He looked for an escape route, but saw none.

"Vero! Up here!" Kane yelled. "What are you waiting for?"

"I can't just take off! I need a running start!"

"If I can do it with a broken leg, you definitely can!" Greer shouted.

The giant creature's hand swatted downward, and Vero jumped to the side, his hair ruffled by the giant's hand as it smashed into the ground where Vero had been standing just seconds before.

"Definitely not friendly!" Greer said.

Vero closed his eyes. *Fly ... fly ... fly!* he repeated in his head.

Nothing happened.

The creature's hand smashed down a second time with even greater force. Vero danced around it. Now the golem cupped its hands, intending to wrap them around Vero and crush him into dust.

He glimpsed Ada turning her head away, too afraid to see what would happen to him. Just as he felt the stiff clay brushing up against his body, a steely resolve came over Vero. In his mind he pictured himself as a strong, fierce angel with glorious wings. His eyes narrowed, and then he shot up into the air like a missile. He flew right past the creature's shoulder, and he didn't stop until he hit his head on the domed ceiling. Vero rubbed his head.

"Yeah, I guess there's no altitude problem in here!" X said to Vero.

The loud grunts coming from the stone creatures bounced off the chamber's walls. It was painful to their ears, and they had to shout to be heard.

"Now what do we do?" Ada asked as she dodged one of the creature's hands. They all hovered up by the ceiling, but they were still barely above the reach of the rock monsters.

"What are they?" Vero asked.

"I think they're golems," Ada said. "They're mentioned in the Talmud ... "

"The what?" Vero asked.

"The Talmud. It's one of the sacred Jewish books, a companion to the Torah," Ada said. "In it, golems are described as being crude and unthinking beings made of clay who could be brought to life by the high priests in times of great need. But I thought they were just Jewish folklore."

"Obviously they're not folklore," Kane said. He flew back against a wall to avoid a golem's fist that was coming straight toward him.

"Spit it out. What do you know about them?" Greer asked, her voice thick with pain.

"Golems were created by rabbis, or holy men, to be their servants or protectors. Only religious people who were close to God could create them, although they're inferior to any of God's creations. That's why they have no soul."

One of the golems jumped into the air and took a swipe at X, but it missed and landed heavily, causing the entire cavern to rumble and shake like an earthquake.

"Do they have any weaknesses?" X asked.

"They're not very smart," Ada shouted over the golems' bellows. "They don't have brains."

"I can tell," Pax said. "I'm trying to read their minds, and there's nothing there."

"Just tell us how to kill them!" Greer shouted.

"The only way is to destroy them," Ada answered. "But it's pretty dangerous."

"What? What is it?" Vero asked.

"In one version of the ancient texts, a golem comes to life when its maker inscribes a sacred word on its forehead, like the Jewish word for *life*. Another version claims the word is written on parchment and put into its mouth to bring it to life. A golem is brought to life by the power of that specific word."

"So if that's true, then it must be in their mouths," Vero reasoned, "because there's nothing written on their foreheads."

"I guess so," Ada said.

"So we need to get the parchment out of their mouths?" Kane asked.

"Yes, but in order to kill the creature, you have to read the word back to them."

"It sounds as simple as taking candy from a baby," Greer said matter-of-factly. "Except these big babies could bite your arm off."

"Maybe we use the Heimlich maneuver and make them spit it out," Pax suggested.

Greer flashed him an annoyed look, "I think I see a word written on your forehead ... it says *Idiot*."

Vero swallowed hard. This was not going to be an easy task. But why should he be the one to step forward? He'd volunteered when he grabbed Kane over the acidic pit. Why couldn't one of the other ones do it this time? But then he thought of his crown waiting for him in heaven—the crown Raziel spoke about. He wanted to fill it up with jewels. So he bravely faced the others.

"I'll give it a try," he said. "But I have no idea how to do it."

"We need to distract them," Greer said, "get them to open their mouths so somehow you can sneak attack and stick your hand in there."

"It's a well thought-out plan ... except for that *get them to open their mouths so somehow you can sneak attack* part," Vero said, rolling his eyes.

They hovered in the air, silently. Vero had no ideas, and he could see Greer was in a lot of pain, even though she was still acting all tough. If they didn't come up with something, and soon, they were going to start dropping.

Kane spoke up. "Ada, you and Pax fly around that one," he said, pointing to the smaller of the two golems, "and keep him busy. The rest of us can buzz around the other big guy so maybe he'll open his mouth and Vero can reach in. Everyone think like mosquitos!"

Ada and Pax flew circles around the smaller golem, while Kane and X glided around the other one. Greer started out with them, but then she pulled back, gasping. "I'm ... I'm sorry," she said. "It just hurts so bad."

"It's okay, Greer," Vero said. "Just stay as far back as possible."

The golems struck at them like King Kong swatting at fighter planes. The fledglings dodged the golems' wild grasps, but the creatures did not tire.

"Time for a little action!" Kane yelled. He swept down to the ground and picked up a large rock.

"Over here!" Kane shouted, as he hovered in the air once more.

When the ugly golem turned around, Kane threw the rock at its head. It was a perfect shot, hitting it right between the eyes. The golem opened its mouth and howled loudly. Vero flew to its mouth, but he was too late.

"Kane, throw another one!" Vero shouted.

Kane swooped to the ground, grabbed another rock, and dive-bombed the golem. He made another direct hit — this time hitting the back of the golem's head. The golem roared and focused his black, lifeless eyes on Kane, who flew within the golem's reach.

"Watch out!" Greer screamed.

But it was too late. The creature punched Kane with its full strength, slamming him against the rock wall. He fell to the ground, unconscious.

"Kane!" X yelled.

But Kane didn't move. Now the golem was moving toward Kane, ready to stomp the life from him, when Vero, looking for a distraction, shoved his arm deep inside the golem's nose.

Vero locked eyes with the creature but continued poking around, reaching through the nasal cavity.

"What are you doing?" Greer shouted.

"I'm going through its nose to get into its mouth!" Vero shouted back.

The creature tried to swipe at Vero but hit itself on the cheek. Then it roared in frustration, and Vero thought his eardrums would explode. But with its mouth open during that deafening roar, Vero got the chance he needed. He pulled his hand out of its nose and put it into the monster's ferocious mouth. He pulled out a piece of parchment and then flew out of reach again.

"Read it!" Greer shouted. She sounded desperate. "Quick!"

Vero's hands were shaking violently, so he couldn't open the parchment.

Vero could hear Pax and Ada trying to distract the other golem. But it must have realized that Vero's golem was in need because it started toward Vero with a thunderous roar.

Behind him, Ada screamed, "Hurry!"

Vero turned and saw that Ada and X had flown circles around the approaching golem's head and caused it to lose its balance. Vero saw the golem slowly tip sideways until it fell and bashed its head against the wall. The blow shook the entire chamber. Rocks broke free in an avalanche, and Vero watched in horror as the golem fell facedown and narrowly missed Kane who still lay unconscious on the ground.

The golem landed hard. It let out a tremendous *Oof!* as the wind was knocked out of it, and the parchment shot out of its mouth.

"Get it!" Ada shouted.

With lightning speed, X dove and grabbed the parchment while the golem struggled to regain its balance. A moment later, the golem was upright again, swatting furiously at Ada and Pax.

"Hurry up! Read it before one of 'em steps on Kane!" Ada yelled.

X and Vero feverishly opened the parchments while flying haphazardly through the air and trying to stay aloft. Vero got his open, only to be overcome with dread. "It's blank!"

"Mine too!" X said.

"It can't be!" Ada said, and she flew to Vero's side. Her curls flew wildly around her face as she attempted to see the piece of paper. "There has to be something on it ... "

Both golems lumbered over to Kane.

"Kane! Wake up!" Greer screamed.

The golems were now upon Kane. Ada turned the parchment over desperately hoping she could see some writing, but it was blank on both sides. Just as the golem raised its mammoth foot above Kane's body to crush him, Vero stared intently at the parchment in his hands.

Please, God, let me read it, Vero prayed. Then suddenly, symbols began to appear before his eyes. And they formed a word.

Behind him, Ada screamed, "Hurry!"

"Emeth!" Vero shouted as loud as he could.

The golem turned toward Vero. Greer and Pax seized the moment, and in a well-orchestrated move, they grabbed Kane. They lifted him into the safety of the air — and not a moment too soon because the golem began to crumble before their very eyes. Piece by piece, the hard clay that formed the largest golem broke off into rock chunks.

"Read this one!" X shouted as he handed his parchment to Vero.

Vero had an easier time reading the second parchment. The symbols quickly formed before his eyes. "Shamad!" he yelled.

The second golem also began to crumble, creating a massive rockslide in the chamber. The rumbling noise jostled Kane, who woke up just in time to see the last one collapse.

"Awesome," Kane muttered.

They swooped down and landed on the crumbled rocks, exhausted. Greer flew to the ground with a rough landing and sat down hard. Her leg was bent at an awkward angle in front of her.

Vero clutched the parchments tightly, but they began to

wither until all that remained was a tiny lump of dust in the palm of his hand.

As they caught their breath, Ada asked Vero, "Did you ever study Hebrew?"

"Me? No."

"You shouted the word *emeth* to the golem. It means 'truth.' And *shamad* means 'destroy.'"

Vero shrugged.

"When I looked at that parchment, there was nothing there," Ada said.

"I didn't see anything at first either," Vero said. "But then it was like lines appeared and then the symbols, and I could read them."

"But I didn't see it," Ada said.

Vero couldn't explain how the symbols hadn't been on the paper at first, and then suddenly they were. Looking around, he felt the intense scrutiny of the other angels. He couldn't read their thoughts, but he knew what they were thinking. *Freak.*

21

❖

THE BLACK
MIST

After the destruction of the golems, the young angels surveyed the damage. Unfortunately, the golems had collapsed right in front of one of the exits, so they had only one possible choice for making their escape—another small, dark, claustrophobic tunnel.

"It's not *too* small," Vero said, holding a torch near the opening. "And it seems like there's enough room that one person can help Greer. But there's definitely not enough room to fly."

"I'll help her," Kane said.

"Ha," Greer said.

"What?" Kane's perplexed look made Vero chuckle.

"I think what Greer is trying to say is that you're not in much better shape than she is," Vero said.

Kane's normally dark hair was plastered flat with red and

gray dust from the rocks. He had dried blood on his cheek from the cut on his nose, and his upper lip was split. All of their faces were covered with dust, and their lips were cracked and chapped.

"Let's see where this tunnel leads us," X said, pulling another torch off the wall. "Hopefully to a hot shower."

Vero and X took the lead, holding their torches out in front of them. The others followed close behind, and Greer leaned on Kane for support. Worn out, they all walked in silence. Vero glanced over his shoulder. Greer was grimacing with every step.

"Everything we've gone through so far was supposed to be one huge training exercise," Ada said, breaking the silence. "What lesson do you think we're supposed to learn from the golems?"

"That we're resourceful," X said.

"And pretty smart," Pax added.

"We outsmarted two brainless creatures," Greer pointed out. "Think about it: How smart does that really make us?"

Kane chuckled, "Good point."

Vero noticed they were now walking through a low-lying mist, about shin deep. "Hold up," he said, raising his arm to signal that the others should stop. He shuffled forward while fully expecting to hit something. But after taking a dozen steps without bumping into anything, Vero relaxed. "I guess it's okay," he said. The group continued on ahead.

Soon, the fog grew denser, and it was now up to their waists. Within two more steps, it swirled all around them, thickening and getting darker. They breathed it in, but it had no scent. It filled their ears, but it was silent. It filled their mouths when they spoke, but it had no taste.

"You know what? Maybe we weren't supposed to learn anything from the golems except that we shouldn't have been in that cavern in the first place," Vero said. "It never felt right going that way. I went against my inner voice. And now that I think about it, I feel like ever since we rescued Kane, we've been getting farther and farther away from God."

"What?" Kane asked sharply. "So this is all *my* fault?"

"Yeah," Vero answered. "Pretty much."

"Why don't you do me a favor and not talk to me anymore!" Kane yelled.

"With pleasure!" Vero yelled back.

"Shut up, Vero. I think we've all heard enough out of you and your *special* voice and your *special* ideas!" X's raised voice echoed through the tunnel.

Pax tripped and bumped into Ada.

"You're such a stupid klutz," Ada said.

"Why don't you whine about it a little more!" Pax shot back. "That's all you do!"

How could Vero have been so thankful for these other *fledglings* just a short time ago? X said it himself: Vero *was* special! He didn't need them. He didn't care about them. Why should he?

From behind, Vero heard Kane sigh in frustration. "I'm tired of you leaning against me. You're nothing but dead weight! We should have left you behind!"

"Go ahead and leave me!" Greer shouted. "It sure beats hanging out with you losers. I don't need you guys to help me!"

"Cool," Kane replied.

With that, he let go of Greer, and she collapsed to the ground. Luckily, her hands helped break her fall.

"You heartless jerk!" she shouted up at Kane.

"How do *you* like it?" X yelled, as he marched over and shoved Kane to the ground.

Furious, Kane sprung to his feet and pulled his arm back in one smooth motion. Then he swung his fist hard across X's mouth.

"Get him good!" Now seemingly oblivious to her injured leg, Greer sat up and cheered, though Vero didn't know which one she was cheering for. And he didn't care either.

Ada grabbed Vero's arm. "Stop them!"

But Vero just smirked and yelled, "Deck him!"

"We have to get out of here!" Ada cried. "This isn't right!"

Suddenly, the fog grew thicker. It was so heavy that it extinguished the torches, plunging the fledglings into darkness. A wet clamminess wrapped around Vero. He called to the other angels, but they were no longer there. Silhouettes began to emerge out of the heavy mist. Vero tried to make sense of them, but they were only shapes without any tangible form. The hairs on his neck bristled.

Suddenly he heard a strange noise, like the clanging of chains. It was still totally black in the tunnel no matter which direction he looked. Without warning, ear-piercing shrieks emanated from the shadows, like the war cries of men charging into battle. The dark shadows began to swarm, and then the horrifying wails changed to creepy clicking sounds, causing Vero to envision first a locust and then a swarm of locusts devouring a farmer's field full of crops. A chill rose from the depths of his soul, and he knew he'd stumbled into the presence of pure evil.

"Ada! Kane!" he yelled, as panic seized him.

Nothing. The other angels were all gone. No one would

be coming to his rescue. And how could he blame them after the things he'd said? Why did he say those awful things after everything they'd been through together? Shame enveloped Vero followed by a feeling of being utterly alone.

And then, a horrific creature broke through the black void. It had the head of a man with long black hair and a hideous mouth filled with sharp teeth that looked like they belonged to a lion.

The man's body resembled that of a locust, but with scales like iron breastplates and a scorpion's tail full of venom. His fluttering wings sounded like chariots and hundreds of thundering horses running into battle.

An immense fear gripped Vero—a fear so deep it took his breath away. He gasped for air.

The creature glared at him with a ravenous look as it came closer, closer. Its mouth full of lion teeth opened, clicked, and then hissed, "Vero ... "

Vero's legs buckled, and he collapsed under the weight of his own terror. He registered a sudden flash of white—and then nothing.

22

THE KING OF THE BOTTOMLESS PIT

Ve-ro! Ve-ro!" Chanting voices.

Vero opened his eyes. He was back on earth! In fact, he was in the middle of jumping a track hurdle, leaping in midair as the crowd cheered him on.

Tack's shot put throw was still on target for his head. But with lightning-fast reflexes, Vero jerked his head back just in time. The maneuver ultimately saved his life but cost him his balance. He crashed down hard onto the hurdle, which knocked the wind out of him. He was still lying on the ground and holding his side when Coach Randy raced over to him.

"Vero, are you okay?"

Vero attempted to sit up.

"Take it easy," Coach Randy said.

Then Tack appeared. "Dude, I'm so sorry!"

"I'm okay," Vero managed to say.

"Thank God," Coach Randy said.

"It was so weird. That shot put just slipped out of my hands," Tack said.

"Do you think you can run the next race?" Coach Randy asked with a hopeful look.

"No," Vero shook his head. "I think my days on the track team are over."

Tack extended his hand, and Vero grabbed hold of it. Coach Randy pulled Vero's opposite hand, and the two of them helped Vero to his feet.

Coach sighed heavily. "I'm glad you're okay, Vero, really. It's just, I had such hopes … such high hopes … "

With his free hand, Coach pulled a sweat rag from his belt and let loose with a loud bellow as he blew his nose into it. "Yes, well … let's get you checked out."

"Hey, don't cry, Coach! You've still got me on the team," Tack said.

"Uh, yeah," Coach said. Then he blew his nose into the rag again.

Nervously watching from the stands, Nora breathed a huge sigh of relief when Tack lifted Vero to his feet. Vero was all right.

Nora saw Dennis drop his big foam hand as a runner

from Lexington Junior High crossed the finish line first, and Danny took second. Seeing her husband's disappointment, Nora linked arms with Dennis, and together they made their way through the crowd to Vero's side.

Clover watched as Blake and Duff stomped their feet, pointed at Vero, and laughed obnoxiously.

"What a loser!" Blake yelled as Vero limped off the track. "Hey, Danny! You whipped him good!"

But Danny didn't acknowledge Blake. He was bent over at the waist with his hands on his hips, still trying to catch his breath.

"And there goes mommy to kiss his boo-boos!" Duff mocked, as Nora felt Vero's ribs for any injury.

What is up *with those guys?* Clover thought. She had a mind to go over there and let them have it. But they seriously creeped her out. Still, she didn't take well to people giving her brother a hard time—even though she'd been doing that a lot herself lately.

Clover thought that if she distanced herself from Vero, then maybe her problems would go away—the problems with Vero and her "overactive imagination," as her parents liked to call it whenever they dismissed her concerns.

For her whole life, Clover had had a special awareness, an ability to look at Vero and know what he was thinking. And she could always tell when something was bothering him. For instance, that when he was in third grade and he fell off the stage during a musical number in the school's production of *Beauty and the Beast*. He'd laughed along with the audience, but Clover knew her brother was totally embarrassed.

But she could also see things that she knew couldn't

really be there, like a man in a tree on a wintery afternoon eight years ago, or a raven with red eyes and a rat tail.

So over the years, Clover had tried to ignore her feelings and these visions. She'd watched endless reruns and reality shows on television. She'd played online games with anonymous gaming partners for hours, or wasted time texting her friends. Anything to distract herself.

And she'd been downright nasty to Vero just to try and get him to stay away from her, since most of her imaginings revolved around him. But it only made her miss her brother more. And lately, she'd been finding it harder and harder to ignore her visions or feelings. Whatever you wanted to call it, Clover was seeing things.

And seeing Vero lying hurt on the track made her think about what could have happened if the shot put had actually hit him in the head. What if Vero had died and she'd never gotten a chance to make things right with him?

Clover stood up and flashed her nastiest look at Blake and Duff. Blake glanced in her direction with eyes that were so icy blue, she was convinced they had to be contact lenses. A strand of dark, oily hair flopped down and covered half his face as he opened his mouth in a nasty, crooked grin. Clover turned and walked away, feeling a chill along her neck despite the heat.

Uriel bent down and picked up a handful of tiny stones, then let them sift through his fingers. He turned his gaze to Raziel, who solemnly looked back at him.

It's been centuries since anyone's gotten past the golems, Uriel directed his thoughts to Raziel.

The two archangels were now standing in the very spot where Vero and the other fledglings had beaten the golems. Raziel looked around the chamber, which resembled the aftermath of an earthquake.

It's the sign we've been waiting for. This confirms he's the one, Uriel wordlessly conveyed to Raziel.

Raziel nodded in agreement and turned his gaze upward. *It has begun.*

As Vero lay on his bed, he kept replaying the events leading up to his departure from the Ether, hoping to reach some kind of understanding about what exactly had happened. What was that scorpion creature whose image now haunted his memories? And what happened to the other angels? Had they made it back to safety, or was he the only one who'd escaped to earth? Would Greer's leg still be broken when she returned home? What happened between all of them at the end? Why had Vero been so *hateful* toward everyone? But most importantly, Vero wanted to know why he no longer felt safe in his own home.

In that dark tunnel, Vero had felt such evil, he wasn't sure he'd ever be able to shake it.

An abrupt knock on the door startled him, and Clover walked in without waiting for his response.

"Mom said dinner's in five minutes."

"Okay," he said softly, as his blood pressure slowly returned to normal.

Clover turned to leave, but she paused at the last moment, looking at Vero with a strange expression on her face. Vero tried to sit up but then grabbed his ribs in pain.

"Sorry about the meet," Clover said. "You should have won that last race."

"I'm done with track. The doctor said I have to let my ribs heal for a few weeks."

"I'm glad they're only bruised. But it's probably smart that you quit. It's become too much of a high-risk sport with Tack out there." She smiled at him.

And there it was. Clover had finally cracked open the door, inviting Vero back into her life. Vero knew this was an apology of sorts. He'd waited such a long time for his sister to come back, he'd wanted it so badly. But now as he looked at her sloppy, sideways smile and those green, green eyes, Vero knew he couldn't tell her the truth. She was better off not knowing all the things he'd seen and learned in the Ether.

"Tell Mom I'm not hungry," he said, rolling over to face the wall. "And please close the door on your way out."

Creatures formed a circle around Vero. There were three of them, and Vero saw they all looked the same. Each had hollow, black eyes that were sunk deep into their skulls. Their partially decomposed faces were streaked with dried blood, and a few pale hairs sprouted from the tops of their heads. Vero's white outfit was a stark contrast to their dark figures.

The creatures threw something black and furry to one another as Vero tried to snatch it away from them. He wasn't sure what the object was, but he knew he desperately wanted it. They hurled insults at him, but Vero didn't care because behind them, Vero glimpsed Davina. She looked beautiful in a simple white dress that clasped over her left shoulder like a Roman toga. She was also visibly upset. Her eyes darted around, searching—searching for what? Vero didn't know. But her worry became his worry. He desperately wanted to help her, but he had to get past these creatures first ...

Vero woke up drenched in sweat. It had all been a dream.

But he knew this dream had meaning. The Ether, or someone from the Ether, was trying to reveal something to him.

The dream played over and over in Vero's mind as he made his way through the school parking lot after school. He needed answers. What had the dream meant? Did it have to do with the evil presence he'd stumbled upon back in the dark tunnel?

The unmistakable sound of brakes skidding against the pavement made Vero's heart skip a beat. His whipped around and found himself staring down the grill of a yellow school bus.

"Watch where you're going!" the bus driver yelled out the window.

It was Mr. Harmon.

"Do you want me to file another report on you?" he asked.

Vero ignored him.

Tack, having seen the encounter, briskly walked over to Vero.

"Hey, Wayne!" Tack shouted. "Chill!"

"That's 'Mr. Harmon' to you."

"Well, I'm not on the bus right now, *Wayne*," Tack said.

Mr. Harmon laid on the horn, which startled Vero and Tack, and then they rapidly stepped out of the bus's way as it drove past them.

Tack turned to Vero and said, "There goes our ride home."

"I was planning to go to the library to study anyway," Vero said.

"Oh, c'mon! You're already the smartest kid in class! You don't need to study any more. Take your mom's advice and dumb yourself down a little."

Vero walked away without replying.

Tack chased after him, grabbed him by the arm and spun him around. "What's your problem? Are you mad at me about the shot put?"

"No!" Vero said. "I know that was an accident."

"Then why don't you want to hang out with me?" Tack asked. He looked hurt.

Vero's face softened. "I'm not mad at you."

Vero *was* feeling angry, but not at Tack. He was mad at Uriel and the other archangels. How could they expect him to keep his two worlds separate? It's impossible! Oh, how he wished he could tell Tack the truth.

"You act like you don't even want to be friends anymore," Tack said. "Are you hanging out with new people?"

Vero put both hands on Tack's shoulders and flashed him a heartfelt smile, "You're always gonna be my best friend." Then Vero dropped his hands and walked away. He hoped his words would be enough to reassure Tack, because they'd have to be. Right now he needed to get to the library and try to figure out what he'd encountered in the Ether.

But as he raced up the library steps two at a time, Vero got the feeling that someone was following him. He glanced over his shoulder and saw Tack quickly duck behind a maple tree. Somehow he had the sneaking suspicion that Tack would have to see for himself whether or not Vero was hanging with a new crowd.

Vero knew Tack had never felt comfortable inside a library. It was too quiet for him. So as Vero entered through the main doors, he hoped Tack wouldn't follow him inside but just go on home.

The library was two stories tall with stairs that led to the second floor. Upstairs, row upon row of dark wooden bookshelves formed a circle overlooking the main floor. Vero walked to the second story and immediately pulled several books from the shelves.

"Can I *help* you?" a woman's voice asked rather loudly on the main floor.

Vero leaned over the balcony and saw Tack spin around to face a thin older woman with her hair pulled back in a tight bun. She was one of the librarians, and she looked just like what Vero would expect a librarian to look like. The woman had a very serious demeanor. She probably hadn't cracked a smile in decades.

"You must be looking for the comic book section," she said.

Offended, Tack's eyes narrowed. "Actually, I was looking for something——"

"Shhhhh!!" the librarian cut him off and whispered, "We whisper in here."

Tack rolled his eyes.

"I'm not looking for comics. I'm looking for something in today's news, for a report," he whispered loudly.

"That's called a *periodical*," the librarian whispered back. "The newspaper and magazine section is upstairs."

"Thanks," he said in a normal voice, forgetting all about the whisper rule.

The librarian shot him a nasty look before she turned around to restack some books.

Vero watched as Tack made his way up the stairs and over to the periodicals, passing men and women sitting at worktables engrossed in their books, papers, and laptops, while little kids sat quietly on tiny chairs, flipping through picture books.

Vero sat at a table with a stack of books scattered in front of him. He carefully combed through each one, intently studying them. He no longer cared that Tack was spying on him from just a few feet away, hiding his face behind a copy of *The Wall Street Journal*.

Vero had already looked through copies of *Connect with Your Angel*, *Angels and the Bible*, and *Celestial Beings*. But when he turned a page in a book titled *Heavenly Warriors*, Vero felt the blood drain from his face. He sat back in his chair and looked across the room, feeling dazed. His eyes met Tack's. Tack immediately put down the newspaper and walked over to Vero.

"Dude, what's wrong?" Tack asked.

Vero didn't answer.

Tack's eyes dropped down to the open book. He saw a hand-drawn illustration of a frightening creature. It had a face like a man but with fangs. His body resembled a cricket with arms wearing armor, and it had claws for hands. His tail had spikes on the end of it.

Tack read the caption beneath the sketch. "Abaddon, the Angel of the Bottomless Pit."

Vero felt his face flush as a shiver traveled up his spine.

"What are you so upset about?" Tack asked. "It's not like he's real."

Vero's face bunched up. "Is that what you think? Do you think angels and demons and everything are just made-up stuff? That the Bible is nothing but a bunch of fairy tales?" Vero asked angrily.

With a guilty expression on his face, Tack said, "I don't really think about it much." He shrugged.

"Well, you'd better!" Vero shouted, then he slammed the chair back under the table and stormed out of the library.

Vero now knew he'd encountered Abaddon in that black tunnel. According to Revelation 9:11, Abaddon was the king of the locust-like creatures who guarded the bottomless pit—or the lake of fire. Abaddon was given the task of the Destroyer. He'd set the Great Flood upon the earth, sparing only Noah and his ark. He'd demolished the cities of Sodom and Gomorrah.

God created Abaddon to be different from the other angels. Their nature was goodness and kindness, while Abaddon's nature was destruction. And because of that nature, Abaddon does God's will but doesn't live in the presence of God.

He's a very complicated guy, Vero thought.

It was written that Abaddon would open the bottomless pit and release the locust creatures upon the earth when God said it was time. And he was also the one who would seize Satan and throw him into the pit.

So basically, Vero figured, Abaddon wasn't really on anyone's side—he just wanted souls for his pit. He didn't care if they were good or bad, human or angel. Body count was what mattered to him.

Vero couldn't understand how he'd come face-to-face with this creature and yet managed to escape. An angel in training was no match for Abaddon. What had happened down there? Vero was desperate to find out.

Then a new thought occurred to him—Ada. The other fledglings lived all over the world, but Ada said she lived in a large city on the East Coast. That's all he knew. She'd never told him which city, and he'd never asked. If Vero could reach her, maybe Ada could shed some light on all of this. That is, if she wasn't already singing with the choir of angels.

As soon as he got home, Vero used his family's computer to search the Internet and try to locate Ada. He knew her last name was Brickner, so he searched through online phone books starting with Boston and working his way down to New York City. He called every Brickner he could find, but there were no matches to Ada.

"I need to use the computer," Clover said as she walked into the office. "You've been hogging it ever since you got home. And no one can get on the phone because you're using that too."

"You have a cell phone," Vero said, not taking his eyes off the computer screen.

"I don't want to use up my minutes."

"Vero, I need you to take out the garbage!" Nora called from the kitchen.

Vero finally looked up at Clover. "Five minutes."

Clover gave him a look as he clicked the mouse and then left the room. Once he was gone, she sat at the computer and watched as the screen saver flashed photos of the Leland family. A wistful look came over Clover's face. There was a photo of a young Vero and Clover body surfing in the ocean, another one of little Vero and Clover wearing matching cowboy hats and riding a pony, and one of Vero flashing the victory sign after winning his first track race.

Feeling curious, she clicked on the "History" icon to see what Vero had been researching. Her brow furrowed when the name "Ada Brickner" came up on the screen multiple times. She wondered who that could be.

Vero came back into the office. "Time's up," he said.

"Who's Ada Brickner?" Clover asked in a half-teasing voice.

"None of your business."

"I think it's a girl you like."

"Fine," Vero sighed. "I do like her."

"Where'd you meet her?"

Vero hesitated. "Um … well … uh … " he stammered.

Clover scrutinized him.

"At the last track meet!" he quickly covered. "But she doesn't go to our school, and I didn't get her address."

Clover eyeballed Vero. She knew he wasn't telling her the whole truth; he was hiding something.

"Clover, come set the table for dinner!" Nora called.

Clover gave Vero one last suspicious look and then walked out of the office.

Over the next two days, Vero spent every spare moment making phone calls. He was driving his family crazy because no one else could use the phone. Clover squealed to her parents that he was trying to find his "crush." Nora thought it was cute. Dennis was just grateful their long distance plan had unlimited minutes.

By the time Vero got to the Philadelphia phone book, he was becoming discouraged. At least there were only seven Brickners listed in Philly—wait a minute! One listing was actually for an Ada Brickner! Vero couldn't believe it! His fingers trembled as he dialed the number. He waited for the phone to connect, and as soon as someone answered, Vero said excitedly, "Ada, it's me! Vero!"

"Speak up!" an old woman's voice came through the receiver. "My hearing aid ran out of batteries!"

"Oh, I'm sorry. I was looking for a younger Ada," Vero said.

"Well, I look a lot better than I sound," the old lady replied. "But maybe you're looking for my granddaughter, Ada."

"Yes, I am!"

"Get a pen, and I'll give you her number," the lady instructed. "And hurry before I forget what it is."

Ada was alive! Vero hoped that meant the others were all right as well. He dialed her number and felt his heart pounding. Were the guardian angels allowed to have contact with one another outside of the Ether? He reasoned they must be, or else Uriel would have intervened by now.

The phone rang a few times, and then a voice picked up on the other end.

"Hello?"

It was a voice Vero recognized.

"Ada, it's Vero!" he said.

There was a moment of silence. Not the response he was hoping for.

"Excuse me while I go to my room where it's a bit more quiet. My brothers have the TV on too loud."

Vero heard a door shut and then Ada came back on the line. "Thank God, you're alive!"

It was definitely Ada. Vero was thrilled.

"How did you find me?" Ada asked.

"The Internet. I really need to talk to you."

"We thought they got you," Ada said in a rush.

"No, I'm alive. But what happened to you and the others?"

Vero could hear Ada's brother banging on her bedroom door and yelling, "I need the phone!" Then another brother picked up the kitchen phone and sang, "Ada's got a boyfriend! Ada's got a boyfriend!"

"Get off the phone!" Ada yelled.

He made kissing sounds into the phone before he hung up.

"Could you come to my bat mitzvah this weekend? It's here in Philly. We can talk there. I'll just say you're a friend from summer camp."

Ada gave Vero all of the necessary information just before a third brother picked the lock and opened her bedroom door. She quickly hung up the phone.

And Vero realized he was going to his first-ever bat mitzvah.

"No way!" Tack shouted as they shot hoops in Tack's

backyard. "You expect me to cover for you, and you're not even gonna tell me why?"

"It's important," Vero said. "I told my parents I'm spending the weekend at your house."

"Well I might just have to call and tell them otherwise. And here I thought you actually came over to hang out," Tack caught the ball and headed inside the house with Pork Chop at his heels.

Vero needed to come up with something quick.

"Okay! The truth is . . . I met this girl. She invited me to her bat mitzvah this weekend. She's really cute, so I want to go. I've got enough allowance money for the train ticket, and I can go up for the day and come back without anyone knowing about it. They're gonna have a live band and everything."

Tack spun around and a smile erupted across his face.

"A bat mitzvah?" Tack pulled off his Attleboro Middle baseball cap and ran his fingers through his sweaty hair so it stuck straight up. "That means there will be lots of thirteen-year-old girls there. Older women. I'm coming with you."

Vero shook his head and chuckled. "Fine," he said. "But you definitely need to get a haircut first."

Then a thought occurred to Vero. "Since you're coming along, can you get Martha to go too?"

"My sister? What? Why? She's no fun."

"Um, she's seventeen and she drives . . . " Vero explained. "It would solve how we're going to get to and from the train station. And no one will question us if she's with us."

"It's risky, but I know something that could help," Tack said, as he held the back door open for Vero and Pork Chop.

"What do you two want?" Martha asked suspiciously, as Vero and Tack walked into her bedroom. Vero was holding a tray full of food, and Tack was holding Pork Chop.

"Nothing more than your happiness," Tack smiled. "Right, Vero?"

Vero nodded eagerly.

Tack put Pork Chop in bed with Martha. "Here's your favorite puppy."

Hugging the dog, Martha sat up on her bed and stared the boys down. She was waiting for one of them to crack. Vero noted her eyes were the same deep blue as Tack's. And with her messy strawberry-blonde hair, there was no denying the two were brother and sister.

"We made your favorite: a potato chip omelet," Vero said, placing the tray on her bed.

Martha's eyes narrowed.

"How would you like an all-expense-paid day trip to The City of Brotherly Love in exchange for giving us a ride ... this Saturday?" Tack asked.

Martha bolted out of bed. Vero took a step back, suddenly feeling a bit afraid for his life. Pork Chop scooted under the bed with a whimper.

But then Martha did something completely unexpected. She ran over and gave Tack a big bear hug. He was totally caught off guard by her display of affection.

"I've always wanted to see the Liberty Bell!" Martha exclaimed. "Mom and Dad never took us there!"

Over Martha's shoulder, Tack winked at Vero. "Who knew?" he asked.

23

❖

PHILLY

The train ride from DC to Philadelphia took less than two hours, and Tack ate the entire time—mostly mini microwave pizzas that were being served in the café car. As the three of them sat at a table, Vero watched the landscape go by, feeling very much as though his life was moving as fast as the trees, houses, and cars that whipped past the train window.

"Ouch!" Tack said.

Vero turned and saw that Tack was holding his hand across his mouth. "I burned my tongue," he explained.

As Vero watched Tack pant to get some cool air on his tongue, a wave of sadness hit him. Vero knew that eventually these ordinary moments would be a thing of the past. In just a few years, he'd be gone from the earth for good.

Tack took a huge bite of pizza that left a string of melted cheese dangling from his chin. Tack pulled the cheese off and shoved it into his mouth.

Vero would miss Tack.

In a stroke of good luck, Tack's parents were out of town that weekend, and they'd put Martha in charge of her little brother. Their father had a dowsing job down in Texas, and their mother had tagged along so she could visit her sister who lived outside of Dallas.

"I'm so glad I didn't go to Texas with Mom and Dad," Tack said with his mouth full. "I would have missed out on these pizzas."

Martha looked up from her tourism book on Philadelphia.

"You didn't go because they didn't invite you," she said. "Dad knows you're totally worthless on dowsing jobs."

Vero saw Tack's face drop. He knew this was a sore subject for Tack.

"Don't worry, Tack," Vero said, trying to encourage him. "Didn't you tell me that your mom is always saying she knows the dowsing gene is in you because no matter where she hides the Ding Dongs, you always find them?"

Rolling her eyes, Martha stood and walked down the aisle. "I need to use the ladies' room."

Tack had apparently lost his appetite. He dropped his slice of pizza on the plate.

Vero looked at him, not sure if he should say anything more.

But then Tack said, "You remember the other day, when you asked me about God? The reason I don't think much about him is because I know he doesn't listen to me."

Vero gave him a curious look.

"Every night I prayed that he would let me be a dowser, but it's never happened."

"Not yet," Vero said.

"But what if it *never* happens?" Tack asked miserably.

"Then it means he wants you to do something else with your life."

As Tack contemplated Vero's words, an announcement came over the PA system: "Next stop. Thirtieth Street Station, Philadelphia."

"Tack, you have your cell phone, right?"

The boys looked up to see Martha standing over them. Tack nodded.

"We'll meet back here at the train station at four o'clock sharp. We're on the four-thirty train to DC. Don't make me sorry I trusted you, or you'll regret the day you were born!"

"Are you sure you don't want to come with us?" Vero asked. Tack kicked him under the table.

"No, thanks. I'm spending the day sightseeing — the Liberty Bell, Ben Franklin's printing press, the Schuylkill boathouses, the Philadelphia Museum of Art ... "

Tack rolled his eyes. "Boring."

"And then I'll top it off with my very first authentic Philly cheesesteak sandwich."

Tack did a double take, "Hey! Bring me one, too!"

"Shalom," said a middle-aged man, as he held out his hand to the boys.

Vero shook the man's hand, "Um ... shalom."

"Yeah, shalom right back at ya," Tack said.

Vero and Tack had just arrived at the synagogue. As soon as they'd stepped outside the train station, Martha put them in a cab while she went in search of the Liberty Bell.

"I'm Ada's father," the man said. "But I'm sorry, I don't believe I know either of you."

"Oh, we're friends of Ada's. We met her at summer camp," Vero told him. "I'm Vero, and this is Tac—um, this is Thaddeus."

"Yeah, we went to camp together. I remember when I first met Ada. The counselors were teaching us how to surf," Tack said.

"In upstate New York?" Ada's father asked.

Tack froze. Luckily, Vero was quick on his feet.

"Um . . . he means surf the Internet."

"Ah, yes, of course." Ada's father handed both of them a small cap and said, "Please go in and find a seat. We're about to begin."

Vero and Tack placed the caps on their heads.

"What is this?" Tack whispered. "A beret?"

"It's a yarmulke," Vero whispered back. "It's worn in the synagogue as a sign of respect to God."

Tack raised his eyebrows as Vero. "How do you know that?"

Vero felt his face flush. "Uh, I learned it in school."

"They don't reach religion in school."

"I meant Sunday school," Vero said quickly.

"Oh," Tack said.

How could Vero explain that Old Testament and Jewish traditions are things he's learned about at C.A.N.D.L.E.? Once again, Vero felt shame in having to lie to his best friend.

The synagogue didn't seem all that different from his church at home. Light streamed in through stained-glass windows. The rows of pews faced a large, raised platform

with an altar like the one at Vero's church. And behind
the altar, beautiful embroidered curtains in shades of deep
purple and royal blue were pulled back to reveal the ark,
the cabinet where the Torah scrolls are kept. But today, the
scrolls were laid out on a table.

Ada stood in front of them, looking nervous. Her olive
skin looked flushed, as though she'd just run a mile. But she
looked really pretty in her simple white dress.

A woman primped Ada's hair, kissed her, and then sat
down in the front row. Vero thought she had to be Ada's
mother. Sitting on her mother's right were two older boys —
probably high school age, or maybe even college — and next
to them were two younger boys, maybe six and seven years
old. Vero knew these younger two were probably the ones
who'd tormented Ada when he'd called her.

An elderly woman slowly walked down the aisle on the
arm of Ada's father and then sat with the family. Vero heard
one of the brothers call her *Bubbe*, which somehow he knew
meant "Grandma." And he noticed that she *did* look as old
as her voice had sounded on the phone.

The ceremony began. Everyone grew quiet.

As Ada read in Hebrew from the Torah, the congregation
replied with the appropriate prayers. Without realizing it,
Vero answered in perfect Hebrew right along with the rest
of the congregation.

Tack looked at Vero with a strange, almost scared expression on his face. "When did you learn Hebrew?" Tack
whispered.

"What do you mean?" Vero asked.

"You're speaking perfect Hebrew."

This came as a surprise to Vero. He'd never spoken a

single word of Hebrew in his life, save for that incident back in the Ether with the golems. He was as confused as Tack was, but he couldn't show it.

"Um, I've been studying it," he said matter-of-factly.

"Wow, you must have it *bad* for this girl," Tack said.

Loud music filled the hotel ballroom as two DJs whipped up the bat mitzvah crowd. Guests of all ages showed off their best moves on the multicolored dance floor. Bussing dirty dessert plates and silverware, the serving staff skirted around the dancers as they headed back to the kitchen with their arms full. Vero killed time by dipping strawberries on long toothpicks into the chocolate fountain.

He was growing worried. He still hadn't had a moment alone with Ada because it seemed like every single one of her friends and relatives had come up to congratulate her. And now Vero was running out of time. He and Tack needed to catch the train back to DC; and from the look of things, it was going to be hard to drag Tack off the dance floor.

Ada glanced across the room at Vero. He locked eyes with her and then motioned with his head for her to follow him. Ada finally excused herself and walked over. She led him down a hallway away from the noise of the party, and they sat beside each other on a bench.

"Mazel tov," Vero said.

"Thanks. I'm guessing you didn't know you speak perfect Hebrew?"

"Yeah ... "

"It happens when you enter the synagogue. "It's one of those hidden guardian angel talents."

Vero glanced at his watch. "Ada, I need some information, and I'm almost out of time. What happened down in that tunnel?"

"Well, as you'll recall, after we got past the golems, everyone was fighting with each other. It was really bad—and really strange. Then all of a sudden, you just disappeared. And a moment later, Uriel and Raziel appeared and took us back to the Ether—the nice part of the Ether."

"Did Uriel or Raziel say anything?"

Ada shook her head. "They wouldn't tell us anything. But Pax picked up some of their thoughts. They were really worried about you, and they couldn't go after you."

"So how did I get back to earth?"

Ada shrugged, "I don't know. But here's another thing Pax heard: No one has been able to read those parchments for centuries."

Vero tried to make sense of it all, but it was hard to put the pieces together when he didn't even know what the pieces were.

Ada locked eyes with him. "Vero, where did you go?"

Vero looked away, not wanting to answer.

"What did you see down there?" she persisted.

Finally, Vero looked into her eyes. He wanted so badly to tell her. He needed someone else to know the truth about what had happened to him. "Abaddon," he said.

Ada gasped and started nervously twirling a finger in her hair. "How do you know?"

"Because I researched it," Vero told her. "Pure evil, face-to-face."

Ada leaned back with a troubled expression on her face. "That explains why we were at each other's throats. The presence of Abaddon was seeping into us."

She flicked at a spot on her white dress, lost in thought. Vero wished he knew what she was thinking. Once he learned how to silently communicate in the Ether, would he be able to communicate with angels while here on earth?

"How did you get away from him?" she asked.

Vero shook his head and stood. "I don't know. I was so scared that I couldn't breathe. He literally stole my breath from me. It actually hurt. I remember falling to the ground, a flash of white light, and then I was back on earth."

Ada looked intense as she sat there thinking. Her eyes held a ferocity Vero hadn't seen in her before.

Suddenly the music from the party got louder, and then a conga line burst through the doors and down the hallway— with Tack right in the mix.

Vero knew time was short, so he grabbed Tack out of the conga line.

"Hey!" Tack protested.

"We have to go," Vero said. "Or else we're going to miss the train." Vero turned back to Ada. "Thanks for inviting us. I'll call you."

Ada flashed Vero a smile, "Too bad you can't just fly back to DC."

"No way!" Tack said. "Then we'd miss out on the awesome microwave pizza."

24

❖

THE RED
MARBLE

O kay, everyone open your yoga mats," Coach Randy told the class.

Vero sat on the gym floor next to Davina. "Since when do we do yoga in gym class?" Vero asked.

"Since Tack joined the track team," she chucked. "I think Coach Randy is looking for ways to lower his stress level."

"Come on, now get on your mats ... " Coach said.

"Hey, thanks for saving me a spot," Danny said to Davina. He squeezed in between Vero and Davina and "accidentally" pushed Vero over as he unrolled his mat. Danny snickered as Vero righted himself. Vero knew Danny wasn't about to let him have any alone time with Davina.

"Now, close your eyes and slowly inhale ... "

The gym full of students had become silent. Vero snuck a peek at Davina with her eyes closed. She looked so beautiful.

Vero especially loved the little smile that formed at the corner of her lips as she began to relax. Clearly, the Ether wasn't the only place where beauty existed.

"When you exhale, push all of your negative emotions out of your body . . . "

Vero closed his eyes and tried to meditate. It took a few moments for him to be able to let his mind go, what with Davina being so close. But finally, he was totally relaxed—and then someone let one rip.

"Oh, gross, Tack!" Missy Baker yelled.

"What? Why do you think it was me?" Tack asked, laughing.

"It smells like a stinking Ding Dong!"

"I was just doing what Coach said—pushing all of the bad stuff out of my body."

"Shhh! Let's try again," Coach Randy said. "And Tack, this time please don't push so hard."

The class was silent once again. Vero stole another glance at Davina and then closed his eyes. This wasn't too unlike the exercise that Raziel had been trying to teach the fledglings when he'd urged them to clear their minds and listen for God's voice. Angels weren't the only ones who needed to master it; humans did too.

Vero relaxed and as he retreated into his mind, his surroundings gradually began to disappear. He became completely unaware of the gym and the other kids around him. It was as if he were seeing a movie playing right before his eyes.

Vero saw himself running through thick woods. It was dark outside, but the moon was bright. He was scared. His face stung where tree branches had scratched him while he ran. Vero could feel burrs from the underbrush clinging to his clothes and piercing his skin. When he finally came to a clearing, he saw a new house under construction sitting on a patch of earth where no grass grew. An ominous feeling of dread plagued him. Hesitantly he approached the house. As Vero got closer, his eyes could just make out a form lying on the front porch.

Vero knew that whatever he found lying there would bring him great pain, but something urged him on. He reached the top stair of the porch and realized it was a person, lying lifeless on the cold floor. Agony filled his heart when Vero recognized the person's outfit. It was a toga. He bent down on one knee, placed his hand beneath the person's shoulder, and rolled the body over. It was an exercise in futility because Vero already knew who was lying there. Even so, he was struck with a feeling of horror when Davina's face came into focus. She lay there motionless with blood trickling from her left temple. And he noticed a single red marble lying next to her.

Grief paralyzed him, but it wasn't just his grief alone. Someone else was there. He could feel it. Vero looked up and saw Danny's tear-streaked face looking down at him. Vero knew Danny was the one who had done this to Davina.

Danny dropped his slingshot onto the porch and began weeping. "I'm sorry! I didn't know she was there!" he confessed between sobs. "It was an accident ... "

"Yoga is not supposed to move you to violence!" Coach Randy yelled, snapping Vero out of his daydream.

Vero's eyes quickly scanned his surroundings. He was back in the school gym. But now his hands were clenching the front of Danny's shirt, and Vero was violently shaking him. When Vero realized what he was doing, he let go of Danny and stood up. Everyone was looking at him, and no one dared move. Even Davina inched away from him.

Danny glared at Vero. "You're dead meat," he growled.

Vero faked a migraine so Nurse Kunkel would send him home early. This way he figured he'd avoid getting another after-school beating from Danny and his thugs. As Vero walked down the hallway to meet his mother, he saw a boy stealing a kiss from a girl as they pretended to look inside his locker. Two jocks high-fived each other and reminisced about winning some basketball game. Three girls were sitting beneath a huge banner and selling tickets for the upcoming dance. A display case showed off various trophies and ribbons won by the school's students. Everything Vero saw defined an ordinary day in the life of a middle school— a life that Vero no longer felt connected to. Sadly, he walked through the front doors and got into his mother's car.

"How's your head?" Nora asked.

Vero didn't answer. Instead, he reached over and pulled the key out of the ignition so she couldn't drive away. Vero locked eyes with his mother. "Tell me about the night you found me."

"What?"

"I need to know every detail."

Nora had known this day would eventually come. She'd had twelve years to come up with a story, to carefully prepare her answers. But when Nora saw the conviction in her son's eyes, she decided to tell him the truth. A tear ran down her cheek, and she quickly brushed it away.

"There had been a terrible storm that night," she began. "I was working the night shift in the ER. An elderly man came in. His head was bleeding pretty bad. There was something about him, some connection. I don't know what it was, but I felt really upset when he died. As I went to close his eyes to give him some peace, he grabbed my arm and said, "Name the baby Vero. Raise him as your own."

Vero gave her a look of complete surprise.

"I guess the doctors had called his death too early. He died moments later. I went out to the nurses' station and there you were. Just lying on a chair. I've replayed that night over and over in my mind, and the best I can come up with is that the old man either brought you in to the ER or somehow knew you. Or … Vero, I've watched a lot of people die in the ER. And sometimes they see or know things that go beyond our normal perceptions. I think it's because they have one foot in this world and one in the next. I truly believe God sent that elderly man to me. Or maybe he was an angel."

"They're real, Mom," Vero said as his eyes drifted up to the patch of sky gleaming through the sunroof.

"Who?"

"Angels. They love us and they want to help us," Vero said with conviction.

Nora looked at her son, not sure where this was coming from. "I believe that's true," Nora said.

"So was that it?" Vero asked. "Was that all that happened that night?"

Nora hesitated. She knew she could bail out at this point,

and Vero would accept what she'd told him as being the whole truth. She could get away with it. Since the day she'd brought Vero home, Nora had tried to keep his world as normal as possible. She'd never wanted to scare him. She'd even tried to convince herself that Vero was just a typical little boy.

However, deep in her heart she'd known differently. Sheltering him from the truth had done no good. Strange things still occurred. In that moment, Nora realized that if she really loved Vero, she owed him the truth.

"On the way home after my shift ended, I took you into the grocery store so I could buy some diapers and formula. A man wearing a long black coat began to follow me. I was terrified of him. He was wearing a hood, so I never did see his face. But something told me he was pure evil."

"What did he want?" Vero asked.

Nora looked at him with the utmost seriousness, "You."

Vero dropped his head. It was overwhelming to hear.

Nora held his face between her hands and locked eyes with him. "I'm sorry, Vero, but you needed to know the truth."

Vero nodded. He understood. Just then Uriel's words came to mind, "everything in its own time."

Nora put her hands back on the steering wheel and continued, "The man chased me into the storeroom and we were trapped. I thought it was the end for both of us. But then that huge steel gate—you know, the one that lifts up by the loading docks so the truck drivers can deliver their goods? Well, that gate flew up and this light—"

"What kind of light?" Vero was giving Nora his undivided attention by this point.

"It was brighter than any light I'd ever seen before — or since. I couldn't even look at it for fear of being blinded. Yet at the same time, the light was comforting and I no longer felt afraid. When the light faded, the man in black had vanished. Run off, I guess. I never saw him again. Thank God that produce deliveryman showed up right then."

Nora began to sob. She unlatched her seatbelt, reached over, and hugged her son tight. She never wanted to let him go. But by telling Vero his story, she'd unknowingly taken the first step toward doing so.

A few days passed and Vero somehow managed to avoid Danny and Blake and Duff. He'd stayed close to Tack at all times and made sure he was always the first one on the bus. He knew that if he were to miss it, he'd be easy pickings if he walked home alone. It really ticked Vero off that while he could defeat golems and dodge behemoths, he still ran scared of a thirteen-year-old bully and his pals. He felt helpless on earth — especially when it came to Davina.

His vision of Davina lying lifeless on that porch continued to plague him. He feared for her, but he didn't know how to help her. Sometimes when he was home alone, he'd call on Uriel and Raphael for guidance — screaming their names at the top of his lungs. But he never received a response. It was as if everyone from the Ether had forgotten him.

Whenever he felt utterly abandoned, he'd pick up the phone and call Ada. Just hearing her voice confirmed that his life in the Ether was real, that he hadn't imagined it after all.

Neither Ada nor Vero had returned to the Ether since their last training exercise.

"They'll call us back when we're needed," she reassured him.

But Vero wasn't so sure. He sensed that Davina's life was in trouble, and he couldn't just sit around twiddling his thumbs. So Vero kept a close eye on her both during school and after. Davina's house was near enough to Vero's that he could ride his bike to it. So he pedaled past it as often as he could. He'd ditch his bike in a nearby field and climb a tree across the street to keep watch. Sometimes he'd keep watch for hours until he had to go home for dinner.

One late afternoon as Vero kept watch in the tree, Danny and Davina walked out of her house together. They were laughing and obviously enjoying one another's company. Surprised to see Danny there, Vero lost his footing and had to grab onto a lower branch to keep himself from falling to the pavement below. He held his breath as Danny and Davina crossed the street and sat on the curb directly beneath the tree's wide branches. He prayed they wouldn't notice him up there. He'd never be able to live it down if they did. He could hear the gossip now: "I heard Vero Leland was spying on Davina Acker from up in a *tree*. Can you believe it? What'll he do next?" Even Tack wouldn't understand it.

"I think my mom really liked you," Davina said to Danny.

"Where's your dad?" Danny asked.

"He's on a business trip until next week. Maybe when he gets back, your parents could go out with mine?"

Danny's face flushed. He looked down at the street and kicked some pebbles with his foot.

"What? What's wrong?" Davina asked.

"My mom left us a few months ago. She moved to Arizona with her boyfriend."

"I'm so sorry, Danny. I didn't know. Do you visit her?"

Vero hadn't known either. He felt bad for Danny.

Danny shook his head. "Every time I ask if I can, she always says she's too busy or it's not a good time. Me and my older brother live with my dad. But Dad drives a tractor trailer and has to haul loads to Colorado three times a month. So I don't see much of him either. It's so quiet in my house that sometimes I turn on the TV just to hear people's voices."

Davina held Danny's hand, "I'm sorry."

Danny looked over at her. "Why do you hang out with me?"

"'Cause you're nice."

Danny hung his head, "I don't always do nice things."

"Well, that's true about everybody."

"No, I ... I ... " Danny stuttered.

"Is it true what the kids are saying at school?" Davina asked. "Did you shatter the windows on that new house?"

Davina looked straight into his eyes, and Danny didn't look away. He nodded.

"Why?"

"I don't know. I just get so mad at my parents ... I know I shouldn't do it, but it makes me feel better."

"Promise me you won't do it anymore," Davina said. "The next time you feel mad at your parents, call me instead of going out to that house. Okay?"

Danny's lips formed a tight smile. He nodded.

Davina stood and turned to head home. Danny quickly got to his feet.

"Do you want to go to the dance with me?" Danny asked shyly, with his eyes cast down, and his hands shoved deep in his pockets.

"Sure," Davina said with a smile. Then she turned and crossed the street.

For the first time ever, Vero saw a genuine look of happiness on Danny's face.

"Elvis, baby!" Tack yelled, waving a white sequined jumpsuit in Vero's face.

"What?" Vero asked, truly confused.

"It's for the dance. We're gonna be the Elvis brothers!"

Oh, that. Vero had let Tack talk him into going to the school dance — their very first one. The thought of dancing with girls was more frightening to Vero than facing craggy golems. He had no idea how to dance, but Tack had convinced him it wouldn't be a huge deal because everybody had to wear a costume. If they made complete fools of themselves, no one would ever know who they were.

"Here's an Elvis wig and a pair of sunglasses," Tack said, shoving them into Vero's hands. "Try 'em on."

Vero put on the oversized rhinestone sunglasses, which covered most of his face. The wig made his head itch, but he could deal with that.

"Are you going to ask someone to go with you? Maybe that girl from the bat mitzvah?" Tack asked.

"No," Vero said.

"Good answer. You're smart to keep your options open," Tack said. "I don't want to be tied down to just one girl either."

Vero laughed. He knew they'd be lucky if Nurse Kunkel agreed to dance with them.

The real reason Vero was going to the dance was to keep an eye on Davina. And it wasn't just because she was going with Danny. Sure, he was jealous. Sure, it hurt. Why did she like Danny more than him? But regardless of his personal feelings, Vero's dream still haunted him. He was determined to be near Davina any chance he could.

On the night of the dance, Vero and Tack walked into the Lelands' living room wearing their Elvis outfits. Nora snapped a photo.

"My baby's first dance," she said, pretending to be misty-eyed.

Next, Clover walked in wearing a hippie outfit from the sixties. After Nora snapped photos of the three of them together, Clover laughed and pointed at Vero. "You look like the young Elvis," she said, "and Tack looks like the old fat Elvis."

"Oh yeah, cupcake? That kind of talk won't get you a slow dance with me," Tack warned her.

"Be nice, Clover," Dennis said as he walked into the room. "Besides, nasty comments like that really clash with your outfit. You dig?"

Clover instantly began to rethink her costume choice. Maybe a peace-loving flower child from the sixties wasn't a good fit for her personality. But she sure loved the white go-go boots.

As Dennis drove them to the dance, Vero peered out the car window when they passed Davina's house. Vero couldn't see her, but all appeared calm.

"There's Danny!" Tack said.

Sure enough, Danny was walking in the opposite direction and headed toward Davina's house. He was dressed in an old-fashioned convict's uniform—a pair of baggy black-and-white striped pants and a matching shirt. Vero couldn't help but feel a pang of jealousy when he noticed Danny was carrying a corsage in a clear plastic box.

Tack rolled down the car window and yelled, "Hey, Konrad! Didn't you hear? It's supposed to be a *costume* party!"

"Shut up!" Vero hissed and elbowed Tack in the ribs—hard.

Clover rolled her eyes. "Tack, you seriously need to get a life," she said.

"No, don't you get it? He's headed for prison one day," Tack explained matter-of-factly.

"Get down! He's gonna see us!" Vero hissed again.

"Relax. We're in disguise, buddy," Tack reassured him.

With that, Dennis steered the car closer to the curb and pulled up alongside Danny.

Danny stopped walking and stared at Tack and Vero sitting in the backseat.

"Tack, you should apologize," Dennis said.

Tack's eyes went wide and he turned beet red. "Um, sorry, Danny," Tack stammered through the open car window.

Danny didn't say a word. He just kept staring at Tack.

"Okay, well ... enjoy the dance!" Dennis said, giving Danny a little wave before he drove off.

Vero shot daggers at Tack while Tack rolled up the window.

"Don't worry about Konrad," Tack said under his breath. "There's only one of him and two of us."

"Don't forget his goon friends. That makes *three* of them and only *two* of us," Vero whispered.

"What friends? The guy's got no friends," Tack said.

"What do you mean? What about Blake and Duff?"

"You're dreaming, dude," Tack said. "No one would be friends with that guy."

Using the mirror on the passenger side sun visor, Clover looked at her brother in the backseat. From the expression on his face, she could tell he was totally confused by what Tack had just said. She opened her mouth to argue with Tack but thought better of it.

25

THE DANCE

A disco ball hung from the center of the gym ceiling. Multicolored twisted streamers stretched from the ball to each corner of the gym. Strobe lights flashed, and a professional disc jockey played dance music through an elaborate sound system.

Cupcakes, cookies, potato chips, pretzels, and all kinds of other snacks filled a huge table, and there were two punch bowls—one at each end. Nurse Kunkel was watching over the food, and Vero had seen her sneak at least two cupcakes so far.

Parent chaperones and teachers circled the gym, and they had the focus of a hawk. Albert Atwood walked around with a field hockey stick in his hands, poking kids who were dancing too closely.

"There will be no dirty dancing on my watch!" he said, poking Missy Baker and her date as they slow danced to a rap song.

Vero stood off to the side, watching Tack dance. He was out there in the middle of the floor, not dancing with anyone in particular, and he displayed no grace whatsoever. He just jerked his body around as if someone had poured a jar of spiders down his shirt. And he was having a total blast.

Clover walked up behind Vero. "Is Tack okay? I mean, is that voluntary, or should we call 9 – 1 – 1?"

"And those are his best moves," Vero said. He continued scanning the room, looking everywhere for Danny and Davina. *They should have been here by now,* he thought.

Vero was so preoccupied by his search that he barely appreciated the fact that Clover was talking to him … in public … at a school function.

Clover followed Vero's gaze to the gym doors. She knew something was going on. "Are you worried that Danny and his buddies are coming to get you? Because Tack was pretty stupid to egg him on like that."

Danny was exactly who Vero wanted to see right now, because if Danny walked through those doors, then Davina would be with him, and that would mean she's safe. Before he could answer his sister, a guy dressed in a Batman costume grabbed Clover.

"Let's dance," Batman said.

Clover went along with Batman but gave Vero a little wave and a shrug as she was being pulled onto the dance floor. Something was going on, and she had a bad feeling about it.

"Hey, it's Elvis," someone said.

Vero turned around. Three big kids wearing identical masks circled Vero. The rubber masks were made to look as if the facial features had been partially decomposed. They were streaked with blood. Vero had a hard time seeing their eyes as the mask made the sockets appear hollow. They looked like zombies. One of them grabbed Vero's black wig off his head and threw it to one of the other guys.

"Monkey in the middle!"

Vero lunged for his wig, but they quickly chucked it from one to another before Vero could snatch it back.

"Seriously?" Vero asked. "Are we in first grade again?"

I don't have time for this, Vero thought, and he was just about to walk away and forget the wig when he noticed some stray hairs sprouting from the tops of their masks. Those hairs triggered a memory. He'd seen these masks before in his daydream during gym class. But in his daydream, he'd assumed he was surrounded by demons. Now he realized they were only middle school boys wearing masks.

Whatever the Ether had been trying to show him that night was happening now! Vero looked over the guys' shoulders and knew exactly who he'd see — Davina, wearing a toga and scanning the room with panic in her eyes. And there she was!

Vero's heart leapt into his throat, and he pushed his way past the trio of tormentors. In his race to reach Davina, he bumped into some kids on the dance floor.

Clover watched her brother hurry past and saw Vero tap Davina's shoulder. When Davina spun around, Clover saw the worried expression on her face.

"Have you seen Danny?" Davina asked Vero. "Did he come in here?"

"He's not here," Vero said.

"I have to find him!" Davina shouted over the music.

"I saw him walking to your house earlier," Vero said.

"He came to my house, but then he got really upset and

stormed off," Davina said. She was visibly upset. "I really need to find him!"

She turned to leave, but Vero stepped in front of Davina and blocked her exit.

From Clover's vantage point, it looked like Davina was trying to get around him. *Something is seriously up*, she thought.

"Please, Davina, don't go out there!" Vero pleaded. He grabbed her hand and tried to hold her back.

"I have to go, Vero," Davina said, trying to pull free.

The next thing Vero knew, Mr. Atwood's field hockey stick jabbed him hard in the back.

"Let's keep our hands to ourselves, eh, Vero?" Mr. Atwood said.

Seizing the moment, Davina escaped and scurried across the crowded dance floor.

Vero chased after her. "Davina, wait!"

Clover watched as Mr. Atwood dropped his field hockey stick and grabbed Vero from behind, locking his arm across Vero's chest. Vero struggled to get free as a group of onlookers formed.

Angus walked over to help his dad restrain Vero, but Mr. Atwood waved him off. Vero heard Angus say to one of the onlookers, "We live next door to him. He pulls this kind of stuff all the time."

"Let go of me, Mr. Atwood!" Vero yelled.

"You're going home! Now!"

"Davina!" Vero fought to free himself, but he gave up as soon as Davina had disappeared from view.

As soon as Vero stopped fighting him, Mr. Atwood let him go. "We're calling your parents, Vero," he said. "This party is over for you."

Vero's mind raced frantically. *He had to stop Davina!* He'd seen what would happen if he didn't.

Clover sensed her brother's panic. She had no idea why he was so desperate to stop Davina from leaving the dance, but she instinctively knew he would never hurt the girl. He must have a good reason. The next thing Clover knew, she was pulling the fire alarm. With the same conditioning as Pavlov's dogs, kids ran to the exits in droves. And in all of the chaos, Vero disappeared into the crowd and escaped through a side door.

Vero searched the school grounds for Davina, but she was long gone. He closed his eyes and calmed his mind. Then he recalled the events in his daydream: the shattered window, the house under construction, Danny with his slingshot, and Davina dead on the porch.

Vero's eyes shot open. He knew where to go! And he had to get there before Davina did. Vero looked around for some sort of transportation and saw the bike rack by the school's front doors. He ran over and frantically started checking the bikes. Luckily, he found a red mountain bike that had been left unlocked. Vero pulled the bike out of the rack.

"Taking that bike would be *stealing*," Blake hissed.

The sound of his voice sent a wave of chills down Vero's spine. Vero whipped his head around and saw Blake and Duff perched on the bench near the front door. "Mind your own business!" Vero said sharply. His strong voice disguised the fear he felt rising in his gut.

"But this *is* our business," Duff replied. He stood and walked toward Vero with a maniacal smirk.

Vero froze, mesmerized by Duff's unnaturally blue eyes. Duff peered down at him before grabbing Vero's wrist and squeezing it. Vero screamed as an excruciating pain shot through his body.

Behind Duff, Blake pulled a black iron chain from under the bench.

"You're going to leave Danny alone, once and for all," Blake sneered. "He's ours."

"You're coming with us," said Duff.

Duff held Vero's wrist in an agonizing grip, while Blake bent down and tried to wrap the chains around Vero's feet.

Vero had his hands on the bike's handlebars, but he remained frozen, hypnotized by Duff's eyes. He felt helpless as Blake approached him with the chain.

"Soon, you'll be ours as well," Duff said, and his eyes flashed from brilliant blue to red.

Vero blinked. Duff's hold on him was momentarily broken, and as he looked straight into the depths of Duff's eyes, Vero understood that Blake and Duff were maltures! They'd been plaguing Danny this whole time. No wonder Tack couldn't see them!

Duff leaped on top of Vero and attempted to pin him down, but Vero thrashed wildly. Then seemingly out of nowhere, Blake pulled out a metal wrist cuff to use with the chains and attempted to fasten it around Vero's arm.

Vero fought with all his might, but the maltures were stronger than Vero.

"Uriel! Help!" he screamed.

But Uriel did not come.

Vero then realized that as long as he was on earth, he would remain a powerless guardian angel. Somehow he had to get to the Ether and fight them there—that was the only way to defeat the maltures and make them release their hold on Danny.

Suddenly, a girl's voice cut through the darkness. "Get off my brother!"

Vero turned his head and saw Clover charging toward them, swinging Mr. Atwood's field hockey stick like a sword. Her outfit might have said peace and love, but her face said warrior.

Wait. Clover could see them? Surprised, Blake and Duff hesitated, and that was all Vero needed. He rolled out from under Duff's grasp and scrambled to his feet.

Clover continued to charge, more fearsome than Vero had ever seen her.

"You're dead meat!" she shouted.

Suddenly, sirens wailed, and the flashing lights of a fire truck appeared from around the corner of the building. Vero paused for a moment and looked at Clover. He wanted to explain, but there was no time. Grabbing Duff and Blake by the backs of their shirts, he stepped right into the path of the speeding fire truck.

Clover's screams penetrated the night air.

Completely hysterical, Clover searched under the fire truck for her brother as a fireman shined a flashlight underneath.

"He's under there!" she cried.

The fireman turned off the flashlight and stood up, pulling Clover up with him.

"There's no one under the truck," he said.

"No ... my brother," Clover insisted.

Spotting another fireman talking to the crowd that had gathered, Clover ran over to him. "Fireman Bob! You remember Vero. Please, did you see him step in front of the fire truck?"

"No, I didn't see him," he said. "And I know Vero well. Why don't I call your parents and ask them to come take you home?"

Something shiny on the ground near the fire truck's wheels caught her attention. Clover bent and picked up the sunglasses from Vero's Elvis costume.

"Are those yours?" Fireman Bob asked.

Clover didn't answer. As she held the glasses in her hand, Clover could no longer brush off all of the instances she knew to be true. Yes, she'd seen the man who twisted Vero's ankle when they were little. Yes, she'd seen Vero grow a pair of massive wings when he was making a snow angel. Yes, she'd been having vivid dreams about angels and demons that seemed completely real. She knew Vero was different, and she could no longer deny the fact that she saw things beyond her earthly eyes.

Since Blake and Duff had disappeared into thin air with her brother, Clover now understood that they were more than just a couple of school bullies. And she knew Vero was in grave danger. Wherever the three of them had gone to, Clover wouldn't be able to help her brother. She knelt on the ground and closed her eyes. "Please God. Please help my brother."

Unbeknownst to Clover, five young hands shot up and caught streaking bursts of light in their palms. She had been heard.

26

❖

FIVE ANSWERS TO A PRAYER

Vero landed in what appeared to be the Arctic. Everywhere he looked, he saw snow and ice. And mammoth glaciers surrounded him. He was standing on a frozen ocean. Blake and Duff were gone. Vero was alone and shivering violently. His sequined Elvis jumpsuit was definitely not the proper attire for Arctic conditions. Vero needed to get out of there, or he'd surely freeze to death.

As the winds whipped across the tundra and pelted him with icy snow, Vero regretted falling into the fire truck's path — but especially now that Blake and Duff were nowhere to be seen. Tiny icicles formed on his eyelashes. He tried to walk, but there was nowhere to go — the floating icebergs seemed infinite against the horizon. He was a mere blemish in the white vastness. Even if Vero had tried to cry, he couldn't — his tear ducts were frozen.

To think that he'd come this far and then failed completely! He'd allowed himself to die in front of Clover; he'd allowed Blake and Duff to get away. And after all that, Davina was still about to die.

Vero lifted his head and screamed at the frozen sky. He felt so angry that he needed the release. But then, in the midst of his rage, Vero remembered Uriel's promise to him — that he would never be alone. Even in this barren, icy wasteland, someone was keeping watch over him. Vero forced himself to practice what he'd learned during his training in the Ether. He calmed his mind, closed his eyes, and placed his hand over his heart. Then he listened for God's voice, his *Vox Dei*. Gradually, Vero became impervious to the harsh elements around him.

The voice directed him to dig away at the snow beneath his feet. Vero dropped to his knees and, despite his numb fingers, furiously swept the snow out from under him. Within moments, he reached a sheet of clear ice. And through that thick ice, he clearly saw X, Kane, Pax, Ada, and Greer about fifteen feet below him. It felt like he was peering down at them through a glass-bottom boat. Vero saw his fellow fledglings standing in a passageway, looking up at him in astonishment.

Suddenly, the ice began to crack. The cracks quickly grew, and then the ice shattered like a mirror. Vero fell through and landed on top of the other angels.

"Ouch! Get off!" Greer yelled.

It took Vero a few moments to realize that he was no longer *on* the iceberg, but *underneath* it — sprawled on the floor of an icy hallway, a channel that ran through the glacier. The first thing that registered was that it was surprisingly warm and bright in there. And then he became aware of Greer's elbow poking him in the chest.

"There's nothing like dropping in on your friends," Ada said, smiling warmly.

Suddenly, they heard thunder overhead, and the hole in the ice began shaking violently. They looked up to see the hole shrinking until it had completely closed over. The fledglings were now trapped under sheets of ice.

"I guess flying out of that hole is no longer an option," X said. His brown skin glowed golden in the strange light of the tunnel.

"Trust me, you wouldn't want to," Vero said. "Boy, am I glad to see you guys!"

"Likewise," Kane said. "We thought we'd lost you."

For the first time in a long time, Vero got a good look at his new friends. Ada slipped on the icy floor and grabbed onto X to steady herself. Pax adjusted his glasses. Kane stood with his arms crossed, smiling at Vero. And Greer gave him her customary smirk. Vero noticed that her leg was better. He pointed at it, and she said, "Uriel took care of it."

Only a short time ago, Vero had felt like an outsider with this group, and yet now they all stood here, a true team. A fierce loyalty and love for these friends filled Vero's chest.

"Ada filled us in on the whole Abaddon thing," Pax said.

"It's amazing that any of us survived after being so close to him like that," Kane said.

Vero swallowed hard. "Yeah, well, I need to go back there."

The group fell silent as the seriousness of his words sank in.

"Are you insane?" Greer asked.

"Some maltures have a hold over a kid at my school," Vero said. "And if we don't break it ... Davina will die tonight."

"Davina?" Kane asked.

"She's a friend of mine," Vero said, but the emotion in his voice betrayed him.

"Sounds like she's more than just a friend," Kane said.

Vero looked down, embarrassed.

"I get it," Kane said sadly. "I've been in love with a girl since kindergarten. She's even come up with names for our kids. There's a part of me that doesn't want to complete my training so I won't have to leave her."

Vero looked at him. It was nice to know someone understood how he felt.

"But we don't have our swords yet," Ada said. "We have nothing to fight with."

"You're wrong," Vero said. "We have something stronger than swords."

"Me," Greer said, stepping forward.

"I was thinking more along the lines of faith," Vero said. But he couldn't help smiling.

"Well, yeah, that too." Greer flashed him a big smile.

"But you guys need to understand what you're getting yourselves into," Vero said. "To find the maltures, we need to go to the entrance of the bottomless pit ... "

"Where Abaddon reigns," Ada said somberly.

The fledglings exchanged glances, and Vero felt their concern. "That's right," Vero said.

"That was bad down there," Kane said, running his fingers nervously through his dark hair.

"It's where we need to go," Vero said.

Vero saw the fear in their eyes.

"I know all of you vowed to help me; but I can't lie to you, it's a dangerous mission. If any of you want to bail, I'll understand. No hard feelings."

The angels considered for a few moments.

"Forget you," Greer said. "You just want to hog all the glory." She sounded different, and Vero realized she didn't have that subtle sneer in her voice anymore. Vero studied her and finally figured out that her I-got-someplace-better-to-be stance and her this-had-better-be-good look were both gone. Yet she was still every bit the fierce warrior who'd bumped into him on his first day at C.A.N.D.L.E. She looked ready for battle. "I say bring it."

Ada had a determined look on her face, but she began twirling her curls. She nodded at Vero.

"I'm also with you," X said. He looked like he was already formulating tactics and evasive maneuvers in his mind. "After all, we are answering a prayer, so we should get extra strength to carry it out."

Kane walked up to Vero. "Aren't you wondering how we found you here in the middle of nowhere?"

"Well, yeah, now that you mention it ... "

"We all got a hit from the prayer grid," Kane said. "All of us got the exact same prayer. We were told to help you, so here we are. If you need to battle a couple of maltures, then I won't let you down." Kane stood up straight and strong.

Vero looked over at Pax with his oversized glasses; the familiar worry shone in his eyes.

"Do you believe you're better than us?" Pax asked Vero.

"No, I don't."

"Sometimes I can hear angels' thoughts, and I've heard

some things I wasn't supposed to hear. For instance, Uriel said you're special."

Vero collected his thoughts for a moment.

"I'm Vero Leland. I get beat up by bullies on earth. I have trouble flying in the Ether. I can't even carry out a simple little prayer like flagging down a cab on my own. I *know* I'm not better than anyone else."

Pax mulled Vero's response. "That's too bad. If we're going over to malture territory, then I was really hoping you had something good up your sleeve."

"Sorry, I don't."

"Are you in or not?" Greer asked impatiently.

"A prayer is a prayer," Pax said, "and I'm an angel of God. I'm in." Pax knuckle-bumped Vero.

Greer turned to Vero, "When you were giving your little speech about not being better than anyone else, you forgot to add that you have the worst taste in clothes. What the heck are you wearing?"

Vero looked down at his outfit. He'd forgotten about the Elvis jumpsuit.

"Yeah, the maltures might not take you very seriously in that getup," X added.

"Long story," Vero said.

He took off the jumpsuit, revealing a red T-shirt and jeans underneath. Vero dropped the jumpsuit to the icy floor. The temperature was comfortable inside the ice tunnel, so he was relieved he wouldn't need it for extra warmth.

"So where to now?" Kane asked, looking to Vero.

Vero's eyes took in their surroundings. There were two options—travel ahead in the tunnel or turn around and go in the opposite direction. Vero placed his hand over his heart, took a deep breath, and closed his eyes. After a moment, his eyes opened.

"My *Vox Dei* is telling me we should go straight ahead. Trust me. I know I can find it."

Moving unsteadily on the slippery ground, Ada tugged at X until they both fell flat on the ice.

"I hope we're gonna fly there," Ada said as Vero helped her and then X stand up. "I was never great at ice skating."

The angels flew at breakneck speed underneath the ice as Vero guided them. They followed his *Vox Dei* like it was an internal radar system. When he was a little kid, Vero had watched a news story about a dog that got separated from his family while they were on vacation. The family searched for the dog for days until they'd finally had to go back home without him, heartbroken. Miraculously, three months later the dog showed up at their doorstep. He'd traveled over three hundred miles to find his way home. Vero had been amazed by the story, but now he understood.

Vero led the others in a V shape. Just like geese, their bodies naturally formed the pattern. By having each fledgling fly slightly higher than the one in front, the formation caused a decrease in the wind resistance, which helped them conserve energy and keep track of one another.

The snowy white ice above their heads began to grow darker. The bright light, which had shone through it, now dimmed while the temperature warmed even more. Vero noticed the walls and floors of ice were progressively transforming into walls and floors of stone.

They flew faster, and gradually the tunnel walls widened. And as the walls grew farther apart, the tunnel's height also grew taller and taller. Eventually, Vero saw twilight above them, and he knew they were no longer inside the tunnel. The sky was dark and filled with black clouds that obscured the tops of the stone walls.

The next thing Vero became aware of was a strong smell of salt. Then humidity. Droplets of water hit his face. And there before them, the angels saw a vast ocean framed by massive rock cliffs.

This ocean wasn't the beautiful crystal blue of the Caribbean Sea. Rather, it was dark, completely black, and it matched the clouds overhead. The water appeared to be thick and move slowly, like bubbly mud. *Was it an illusion?* Vero wasn't sure, but he wasn't going to let this unsightly body of water slow their progress as the angels continued to fly well over the sea.

"Don't think I'll be swimming down there," Ada said.

"It looks like sewage plant runoff gone way wrong," Kane said.

The black clouds cast shadows on the angels' lily-white wings, making them appear gray and gloomy. Their V formation broke as each flew in closer to one another, afraid of the sinister water below.

From behind them they heard an ear-splitting scream, which stopped them mid-flight. Vero saw Greer and Pax fall into the water. And his eye glimpsed something long and scaly disappearing quickly into the water.

"What was that?" X shouted.

Whatever it was, it rose up out of the murky water again and slashed at them, throwing them into the sea along with

Pax and Greer. Vero tried opening his eyes under the water to see what they were up against, but it was too dark to make out anything. He accidentally swallowed some water, noting that this was probably what motor oil tasted like. When he resurfaced, Vero saw the others bobbing up and down as they treaded water to stay afloat.

A gurgled "Help!" caught Vero's attention. He swam in the direction of the plea and saw Pax's arms thrashing about as he desperately tried to keep his head above water. Dense waves of water rushed into Pax's mouth, and then he went under.

"Pax!" Vero shouted.

Vero swam to Pax, grabbed him around the chest, and pulled his head up out of the water. Pax wasn't responsive. Vero looked in all directions until he spotted a small cluster of rocks. He tried swimming toward the rocks while dragging Pax behind him. Pax sputtered and coughed, but at least he was alive!

Pax began to slip out of Vero's grip. Vero struggled to hold on to him, but Pax was like dead weight. He pulled Vero under.

"Hold on!" Kane shouted, and he swam over and pulled Pax away from Vero.

"Over there!" Vero told Kane.

Kane hooked his arm over Pax's chest and swam with him to the rocks while Vero followed. Kane pushed Pax up to safety. Greer, Ada, and X were already there. Pax was unconscious.

"I don't know how long that thing had Pax under the water," Vero said, panting, "but I saw him take a mouthful of that noxious water."

"Let me try," Greer said. She turned Pax onto his stomach

and pushed on his back as hard as she could. Pax's wings were gone. Everyone's wings had disappeared when they hit the water.

"Come on, Pax!" Greer cried, and she gave another mighty heave.

"Please, Pax," Ada said. Her long auburn curls appeared black from the seawater. She struggled to regain her breath as she watched Greer work on Pax.

Finally, Pax coughed out great bursts of dark, slushy water. Greer helped him turn onto his side, away from the waves that crashed along their tiny outcrop of rocks. Vero sent up a silent prayer of thanks.

"What *was* that thing?" X asked, wiping the water from his eyes.

"Is it gone?" Pax whispered hoarsely.

"I don't know," Vero said. "But we need to keep going. Can everyone fly?"

"I don't think my lungs can take it," Pax said between coughs.

"That thing might have gotten us just by pure luck," Vero said.

"Twice?" Kane asked.

"I'll try flying past, and then you can follow."

Vero concentrated and his wings appeared. He rose into the air and flew straight over the water. Five yards, twenty, fifty—the farther he went, the more sure he was of his escape.

Vero looked back and flashed the others the thumbs-up sign. "Come on, we're clear!" he called to them.

"Vero!" X shouted.

Vero turned in time to see an enormous sheet of scales rising from the sea—right before he was smacked back down into the water like a fly getting hit by a fly swatter. Momentarily stunned, he swam back to the rocks.

"Got any other brilliant ideas?" Greer asked.

"As a matter of fact, I do. I'll just have to fly higher."

Vero stood on the rocks, opened his wings and shot high into the air. Vero was rising faster than he'd ever flown and gaining altitude quickly—until he was slapped back down into the water again.

The others winced. Whatever they were dealing with, it was apparently massive. It smacked Vero like a volleyball getting stuffed at the net.

"It won't let him go higher," X said.

"Very observant," Greer said.

But Vero would not be deterred. He swam back to the rocks, got himself airborne for a third time, only to be smacked back into the water.

Finally, Greer had enough. "Hey, moron! Do you know what Albert Einstein said the definition of *insanity* is?"

Vero didn't answer her.

"It's doing the same thing over and over again and expecting different results. That thing will *not* let us pass!"

Greer was right. Vero needed to come up with a new tactic. He swam back to the rock cluster and Kane pulled him up. He sat down and gazed out over the black ocean. "If we only knew what that thing was, we could figure out how to get around it," Vero said.

Without warning, the water all around them began to bubble like a tarpit. As a few specks landed on his arm, Vero yelled, "It's boiling!"

"Oh, no … " X stuttered.

"What?"

"Now I know what we're up against."

Before X could say more, a gigantic creature resembling a dragon lifted its ugly head out of the water. Its eyes shone like a lighthouse beacon. The beast was covered in scales that were as thick as iron. Its mouth was lined with rows of sharp teeth. The teeth alone were easily two stories tall. Smoke billowed from its nostrils. As the rest of its body rose, the angels could see sharp fins running the length of its back. Now they knew what had been knocking them into the water—it was the creature's tail.

"And I thought the behemoth was big," Pax said. "This thing is the size of a roller coaster!"

"X, what is it?" Vero asked.

"It's the Leviathan from Job 41!" X said. "An invincible, fire-breathing sea monster. Nothing on earth is its equal."

Vero's heart sank. He looked at X for anything more that might help them. Some glimmer of hope.

"Job was pretty specific in his description. I won't go into all of it; but basically, we have no chance here."

"Then what do we do?" Ada asked.

"Turn back," Kane answered.

That was the last thing Vero wanted to do because the voice inside of him had only grown stronger. And it was urging him to continue in the direction they'd been headed.

"We're already in the middle of his ocean," Vero said. "I don't think he'd let us go back even if we wanted to."

Everyone was at a loss. The sky turned darker as a storm began to brew. Then Vero noticed that Greer had her eyes closed in concentration, praying for direction. Her fingers were stretched over her heart.

"Wait . . . Greer might have something," Vero said.

Her eyes fluttered open as she came back to them. "Seriously? For real?" Greer said, questioning whatever directions she'd received.

"What is it?" X asked. "What did you hear?"

"Well, it's not for the faint of heart," she began. "But I know how to get around this overgrown crocodile."

27

❖

CATCHING
A WAVE

Fly *into* its mouth?" Pax exclaimed. "Are you crazy?"

"It's like Jonah and the big fish. He was able to live in the fish's belly for three days and three nights until the whale finally spit Jonah onto dry land," Greer said.

"But a whale doesn't have fangs that are two stories tall!" Ada said.

"We'll have to get the Leviathan to swallow us whole in one gulp," Greer said.

"Do you know what the *real* definition of *insanity* is?" Pax asked. "Your plan!"

"Greer, we don't have three days and three nights to spare," Vero said.

"We won't need that long. Once we get in there, we'll wait until its head is pointed beyond here, you know, to the land on the other side. And then we'll use our wings to tickle its throat until it spits us out. We just need to hit his gag reflex."

There was a moment of silence as everyone considered Greer's plan. It was far-fetched, but what other ideas did they have?

Vero stretched out his arm, palm down, toward the others. "It's so crazy, it just might work."

Greer placed her hand on top of his. "I'm in."

X and Kane put their hands on top of the others. "Us too."

Pax reluctantly nodded his approval and placed his hand on the pile.

Only Ada was left. She shrugged and said, "Okay, fine. But I just want to state for the record that I'm totally against this whole thing."

"Noted." Vero smiled.

"Okay, so we'll need to hold on to each other. When a huge wave comes along, we'll all jump on top of it and ride the wave straight into its mouth," Greer said.

"That's a fine idea, except the water is boiling," Pax said.

Kane stuck his finger in the water to test it.

"It's not boiling anymore. I think the water must only heat up when the thing breathes fire."

"Oh, yes. Now it's perfectly safe," Pax said, pushing his glasses higher up on his nose with his index finger.

The storm was now beginning to churn the water. The winds whipped the waves higher and higher, smashing them against the rocks. Vero knew the angels' strength was waning.

"I can't hold on much longer!" X yelled, as if he'd read Vero's mind.

"Wait for it … wait," Greer said. "Just a few seconds more until it opens its mouth … "

As the waves tormented the Leviathan, the creature grew angry. It raised its head. And when it opened its mouth to howl, Greer saw their opportunity.

"Now!" she cried.

Clinging to each other, the angels jumped off the rocks into the water below. Then a huge wave came up from behind them.

"Hold tight!" Vero shouted.

When the sea monster wailed at an ear-splitting level, the angels all body-surfed straight into the Leviathan's mouth and landed safely on the other side of those two-story fangs. Its mouth closed, and the creature began to gag when it felt the intruders inside.

"Oh no, it's going to spit us out! But it's too soon!" Greer yelled. "We're in too deep! We're too close to its throat! Quick, run back toward the front of its mouth!"

The angels quickly ran forward, and the gagging motions stopped.

"I thought the idea was for it to barf us out?" Pax said.

"Only after it turns around so it shoots us in the other direction," Greer explained.

Ada looked around. Being in the Leviathan's mouth was like being inside a cavern—a cavern with a squishy, fleshy ceiling and floor.

"It reeks like rotten fish in here," Ada said pinching her nose.

No one contradicted her.

X cupped his mouth and said, "I might puke before the Leviathan does."

"So now what do we do?" Kane asked.

"We wait," Greer said. "We wait until we feel it turn around."

So they waited and waited, but the Leviathan never turned its body around. Vero grew impatient with each passing moment. Plus, it was no thrill sitting in the dark inside a creature's disgusting mouth. The only relief came when the Leviathan opened its mouth and a wave of fresh air and light came through.

"I can't wait any longer. I've already wasted too much time," Vero told the others. "I have to get out of here."

"It'll just spit us back onto the rocks, and then we're back to square one," Greer said.

Everyone took a moment to consider their predicament. Pax then broke the silence. "I'm gonna hate myself for saying this, but there is another way out to the other side."

"How?" Vero asked.

"We could follow his stomach down through his digestive system and then … "

A look of horror crossed Ada's face. "And then it passes us out … you mean, *that* end?" she demanded.

Pax nodded.

"No way!" Ada yelled. "I've done enough for you guys, but I have to draw the line somewhere! Some prayers go too far!"

Greer winced. X and Kane had similar looks on their faces.

"We're already inside its mouth, so how much worse could it be?" Vero offered.

"You know, I should be home right now relaxing on the sofa and watching TV. Instead, I'm here trying to help you! And now I'm about to be pooped out into a black ocean by some sea monster?" Ada punched Vero hard in his gut. He fell backward. The release made Ada feel better.

"Thanks, I needed that," Ada said. "Okay, let's go."

Vero and the others flew past the Leviathan's throat and into its massive stomach. They landed in the knee-deep, rancid, disgustingness. What little light they'd had within the Leviathan's open mouth was extinguished once they entered its gut.

"I hate you!" Ada yelled to Vero as the darkness set in.

"Angels aren't allowed to hate, Ada," Vero shot back.

"It's creepy in here," Ada said. "I can't see."

"I don't like this," Pax said, echoing her sentiment.

Vero could hear the panic in their voices. "It's okay," he said. "Let's move together." But then a huge rush of gastric juices knocked him down and completely submerged him. He came up sputtering and gagging.

"Oh this is just perfect," Vero said. "I can feel fish guts in my wings."

"And I can smell 'em," X said.

"Wait!" Kane shouted. "I just remembered something." Kane clicked on a small LED flashlight attached to a keychain, and the beast's belly lit up.

"That's so much better!" Ada said.

"Yeah, now we can actually see the chewed fish guts and bloody fish carcasses," Greer said.

"That's pretty powerful for such a small flashlight," Vero remarked.

"My mom worries about me coming home in the dark," Kane admitted a bit sheepishly.

Occasionally, a huge rush of water would knock them all down. The water carried them farther along as if they were on a slide at a water park. They could make more ground riding the waves than by flying.

"Does this thing ever end?!" Kane yelled.

"Do you think we're getting any closer?" X asked.

"Who knows?" Pax said.

Something brushed against X's leg. He looked down and his eyes went wide. X tried to scream, but no words came out. All he could do was point. Kane shined his light in X's direction. A crocodile's headless body floated past them.

"A crocodile?" Kane yelled. "Man, that is just wrong."

"Do you know why Leviathan lives alone?" Pax asked, as they waded through the massive beast. "Because he ate his chum."

"Real funny, Pax. Remind me to throw up on you," Ada said.

"C'mon, Ada, sometimes being an angel is more than just a job, it's a doody," Greer smirked. "Get it? Doody?"

"Not funny," Ada said.

"I agree. We really need to get to the bottom of this," X chimed in.

"Not you too, X!" Ada groaned.

"Yeah, well, I can't wait to finish this program so we can *log out*," Kane added.

Ada looked like she was going to be sick.

Greer laughed, "C'mon, Ada. Would it hurt you to tell a joke just once?"

"Get me out of this beast, and I'll be the first one to tell a joke," Ada retorted.

Just then, an enormous wave rushed toward them. It was so high that it reached the top of the stomach roof. It was like a tsunami, taking everything in its path.

"Hold your breath!" Vero yelled.

The wave swept them farther down the stomach before it finally dropped them over a waterfall into a pool below. One by one, the angels poked their heads up through all the liquid muck. The water slowly receded and they were finally able to stand. Kane shined the flashlight at them while Vero took a head count.

"We're all here," Vero announced.

"Talk about catching a wave," X said.

"The good thing is, it pushed us a lot farther," Pax noted, looking around.

"The bad news is ... " Ada said as she pulled something blue and squishy out of her hair, "now I have whale blubber in my hair."

"You mean the Leviathan just snacked on a whale?" X asked.

"That explains the huge wave," Pax said.

The angels continued on. The more they walked, the more the walls began to narrow.

"Hopefully, we'll be out soon," Vero said as he sniffed the air with a wrinkled nose. "You guys smell that?"

Ada looked at Vero, disgusted. "Eww, Vero!"

"It's not me! It's the Leviathan. We're in its bowels now!"

The foul stench wafted through the whole place.

"I need to get out of here!" Ada yelled. "I can't take it any longer!" Ada grabbed the flashlight from Kane and plowed ahead.

"Ada, come back!" Greer yelled.

She wasn't stopping, so the others ran after her. The odor grew more and more putrid the farther they went. As Vero covered his mouth and nose, he kept telling himself that the offending odor was a good thing. It meant that soon they would be out. Vero slipped in something, which he quickly tried to convince himself was only mud.

Before he could get back up, some unseen force shot him out into the sea. He swam to the surface and saw land just a few feet away. Pax, Greer, Ada, Kane, and X popped up like fishing bobbers next to him.

"Land ho!" Greer shouted.

The angels swam to shore and plopped down on the beach, exhausted. They were covered with sea sludge, but at least the seawater had washed off the monster's waste.

True to her word, Ada raised her head and looked at the other angels. "Thank God that's over," she said. "I'm just happy everything came out okay in the end."

"I guess the girl has a sense of humor after all," Greer smiled.

28

CHASING MALTURES

Vero was the first to stand up on the rocky shore. A feeling of dread formed in the pit of his stomach as his eyes took in the sight before him.

A forest — trees everywhere he looked. But they weren't green, leafy trees ... these trees were grotesque, gnarled. They were naked with no leaves to cover their branches. Twisted trunks. Branches contorted like distorted limbs. And thick sheets of moss hung off the sickly trees like decayed flesh.

"Out of the belly of the Leviathan and straight into hell," Greer said, as she took in the landscape.

"Stay together," Vero said.

Silvery moonlight provided enough light for the fledglings to navigate their way through the dead forest. Vero noticed it was eerily silent. There were only the sounds of their feet crashing through the underbrush. Vero's eyes darted between the nearest diseased trees. He had the feeling they were being watched.

Kane's foot caught on a fallen branch. "Aahh!" he cried out as he face-planted. "This whole thing is a bad idea!" Kane sat up and tugged on his foot, wrenching it free from the branch.

"Yeah, Vero, why do we have to do everything *your* way? You think you're so much better than us!" Ada snarled.

"We're starting to fight. That means we're close to the maltures' territory," Pax said. "Resist their influence! We need to be strong. We need to do this together."

"If we turn on one another," Vero said, "we're all doomed."

"It's not easy," Ada said. "I feel angry and scared. Everything is hopeless and so dark."

"No, it's not. It just feels that way here. We're approaching their side of the Ether, and it's a world filled with hatred, deceit, and hopelessness. For demons and maltures, these feelings are the air they breathe. It's their essence. But it's not ours," Vero said.

Vero stood in front of Ada and grabbed her shoulders. He locked eyes with her and said, "Ada Brickner, you are an angel of light, full of love and goodness. That is your essence. Remember that, and nothing can harm you."

Vero looked over at the others. "That goes for all of us."

"Send forth your light and truth, let them guide me," X recited.

"Psalm 43," said Ada.

X nodded.

The verse helped fortify them. Vero removed his hands from Ada's shoulders and walked ahead of the others. As they journeyed deeper into the putrid forest, it became darker as the trees grew thicker. The wind howled as if it were the cries of a horrible beast.

All kinds of crazy thoughts swirled around in Vero's mind. He, too, felt the harmful influences surrounding them. Confusion and feelings of despair tormented him. Vero pressed his temples and repeated over and over, "Your Light. Your Truth, let them guide me."

Suddenly, Vero was attacked from behind. Someone—or something—jumped on his back and pounded his face into the ground over and over again. His nose smashed against a rock, and blood flowed down his face. Vero heard Ada shrieking. *A malture!*

Vero craned his head and saw not a malture, but Kane! His eyes were wild with fury.

"You think you're so special! Well, you're not!" Kane shouted.

"Kane! Get off of him!" X yelled.

But Kane couldn't hear him. When Vero looked into his eyes, he knew Kane had checked out. Greer and X pulled Kane off of Vero, only to have Kane turn around and punch Greer in the mouth. He was like a caged animal who'd finally been set free. He shoved Greer up against a thick tree trunk and pinned her.

"Do you think I've forgotten how you rubbed my face in that dirt? Do you think it's over?"

Greer looked terrified.

"Well, now it's payback time!" Kane shouted.

Kane slammed Greer against a tree trunk. Vero, Pax, and X pulled him off of her.

"Kane! Remember, his Light. His Truth. Let them guide you!" Vero shouted in his face.

As X and Vero restrained him, Vero's words seemed to have some positive effect. Kane calmed slightly as he noticed Vero's bleeding nose. It looked as if he was coming back. Then, from out of the dark shadows, a thick black chain sailed through the air and lassoed Kane around his torso. The chain coiled itself the same way a snake snares its prey. Then it squeezed Kane until he could no longer move. The chain didn't stop coiling until it had bound Kane up to and around his mouth. Kane lost the ability to speak. But what his mouth couldn't say, his eyes conveyed clearly.

His previous rage was replaced with raw fear. Vero and X were trying to free him from the shackle when Vero heard a stirring in the trees overhead. His heart thundering, Vero lifted his head toward the treetops. The blackened clawlike branches swayed ominously as the wind picked up. Goose bumps spread across his body. He could feel the hair on his arms stand on end. Yet no one was there.

Greer screamed.

Vero whirled around to see two sets of red eyes glowing through the thick moss that drooped from a knotty branch toward the ground. He stretched out his arms and pushed the others behind him as Blake and Duff walked through the moss. They looked exactly as they had appeared on earth — two teenage thugs with pimply faces and greasy hair.

"We'll be taking this guy as a souvenir," Blake said, picking up the end of the chain and holding it like a leash. "He was such an easy target."

"No!" Vero shouted.

With lecherous grins, Blake and Duff looked at the other angels and eagerly sized them up.

"The rest of them should be easy to take down, too," Duff said with a cruel laugh.

"Don't give in to them!" Vero cried.

X cried out, "We are light!"

Duff walked over to X.

"Oh, we've got a tough guy here. Let me ask you something, X," Duff said in a mocking tone. "The Light, the Light, where is your precious Light when you're sitting in that wheelchair? Huh? When you can't even raise your arms to give mommy a hug?"

X's face lost all color.

"Why would you feel any loyalty toward someone who did that to you?" Duff asked as he bent down and picked up a rock. "Perhaps it's because you have rocks in your head?" Duff slammed the rock against X's skull, and X went down. He was out cold.

"Leave him alone!" Greer shouted. She raced over to help X.

In the blink of an eye, Duff rushed her and caught her in his grip. She winced and couldn't escape his hold. He began stroking her face.

"Oh, you may talk tough, sister. But how about you … how was that tenth birthday, Greer? If memory serves me correctly, you spent it locked in the closet of what? Foster family number five?"

Greer began shaking.

"Two whole days in a closet without any light. You thought darkness was your only companion. But we were there with you. We kept you company in that closet while your precious Light turned his back on you—just like he's doing again today."

Duff punched Greer in the stomach. With the wind knocked out of her, she doubled over and sank to her knees.

"Greer!" Vero yelled as he ran to her and put his hand on her back. She slumped the rest of the way to the ground, fighting for a breath.

Ada began crying. Pax gripped her hand.

"Oh, look how touching," Blake said to Duff. Then he turned to Pax and said, "Is that bogus little gesture of support supposed to comfort your crybaby girlfriend?"

"It's not bogus. There is only Truth and Light here," Pax said calmly.

"It *is* bogus," Blake said. "Because when I wrap you up in my chains — trust me, you're gonna let go of her hand real fast."

Blake snapped off a twig and threw it at Ada and Pax. In midair the twig spun several times end over end, and then it transformed into a heavy, black chain.

"Run!" Vero shouted.

But the chain was too fast. With lightning speed, it coiled itself around Ada and Pax, tightly tying them together.

Blake laughed as he looked at their hands, still clasped. "Guess I was wrong."

Vero had seen enough. He left Greer and charged at Blake. But when Vero angrily shoved him, Blake barely flinched.

"You have unfinished business with me, *not* them!" Vero shouted.

Blake got right up in Vero's face and snarled, "And what unfinished business are you talking about?"

"Release your hold on Danny," Vero said, wiping a trickle of blood from his nose.

"Danny Konrad? A kid nobody cares about? His own mother and father don't even care," Blake smirked. "Isn't he the same kid who loves beating the crap out of you? Who stole pretty little Davina away from you?"

Vero grew enraged. The blood pumped to his face.

"And how are you going to make us do that anyway?" Blake asked. "Are your friends really here to help you?" He laughed.

Blake motioned to X who was still out cold on the ground. Blood trickled down his forehead from where the rock smashed his head. Greer was lying in the fetal position clutching her stomach. Kane, Ada, and Pax all struggled to break free of their chains.

"Pathetic," Duff scoffed.

"If I were you, I'd get revenge on a guy like Danny," Blake said. "It's so much more satisfying."

Vero grabbed Blake by the shoulders and shook him. Blake laughed maniacally, unfazed and unthreatened. Next, Duff jumped in Vero's face.

"Your angelic efforts have all been in vain anyway, Vero," Duff said. "You're too late!"

"That's a lie!"

"Think so? Then why don't we all take a look, shall we?"

In a dramatic gesture, Duff swept his hands apart, revealing a festering black light. The blackness grew wider the farther apart he spread his hands. Eventually, the dark mist clouded all of their vision. Then, in the cloudy darkness, Vero heard someone walking. Slowly, the darkness cleared. Although they were all standing in the same positions, their surroundings had changed. They were now on earth, standing in front of the abandoned house from Vero's daydream.

Only this wasn't a dream. Danny was now walking toward them headed up the driveway. His face was consumed with anger, and he had a slingshot firmly in hand. He gave no indication that he could see any of them.

Vero lunged toward Danny, but Blake and Duff grabbed Vero and held him down.

"Easy there, hotshot. This is for viewing pleasure only," Blake snarled. "We thought it would be fun for everyone to watch your little girlfriend die."

Vero tried to escape, but their hold on him was too strong.

"It's a trick, Vero!" Pax shouted, while still trying to free himself and Ada from the black chain. "Remember, this hasn't happened yet! Time on earth stops when we're called to the Ether!"

"Is that what you learned in class? Well, what if Vero wasn't exactly called back to the Ether?" Duff said with an evil smile. "There wasn't any class scheduled for today, was there, Fledgling? If I recall, you jumped in front of that fire truck and took us with you. And that was what? A good hour ago?"

Vero's heart sank. It was true. He'd returned to the Ether of his own accord.

"Because of that, what you're seeing is happening right now — live," Blake told Vero.

"Or didn't they teach you that in angel school?" Duff snickered.

Vero looked toward the woods behind the house. If what Blake said was true and if Vero was now watching his daydream happening in real life, then Davina should come running through those woods any minute now, and Danny's red marble should strike her in the temple, killing her instantly.

Vero knew he had to stop it from happening. But how? Vero closed his eyes and tried listening for his *Vox Dei*. But he heard nothing. A look of disappointment crossed his face when he opened his eyes again.

"I guess just like your teachers at C.A.N.D.L.E., that voice in your heart deceived you again," Duff taunted him.

X began stirring. "X, wake up," Ada whispered.

Pax shushed her, and then Vero sent this thought to Pax: *Try to get into X's mind! Try to reach his consciousness.* Vero prayed that Pax could read his thoughts. *Please, God . . .*

Pax's head whipped around. He'd heard Vero!

"Poor Danny finally thought someone cared about him. He even bought Davina a corsage," Duff said.

Danny stopped walking and was sizing up the windows on the house.

"What a loser," Duff scoffed.

Duff and Blake laughed, and Vero experienced an overwhelming feeling of compassion for Danny.

"Davina never cared about you," Blake said.

"Davina's not like that!" Vero yelled.

"Nobody on earth cares about anyone but himself," Blake said. "Do they?"

"Danny, please!" Vero shouted.

Vero's desire to save both Danny and Davina became overpowering, and suddenly he was just as consumed as he'd been on the day when that corn snake had attacked Davina during science class. With a deafening roar, he threw off

Blake and Duff with newfound strength. His wings shot out, and he flew to Danny's side.

"Davina cares about you!" Vero yelled in Danny's ear. "She's on her way! Don't do this!"

Stunned by Vero's sudden surge of power, Blake and Duff appeared even more shocked when Danny hesitated. So with renewed force, they sprang into action.

"You're gonna pay dearly for that," Duff hissed, and he tackled Vero to the ground.

"Hold on, Vero!" Greer shouted as her breathing finally returned to normal. She got to her feet and began unraveling the chains that were constricting Kane.

Blake ran at Danny and began whispering in his ear again. "No one cares about you, Danny. Davina was just toying with you. She sure made a big fool out of you tonight."

Danny furrowed his brow and started walking toward the house again, completely unaware that the hateful thoughts in his mind were being planted there.

As Vero saw Blake yelling in Danny's ear, he had an epiphany. He remembered how Blake had yelled in Danny's ear in that exact same way on that day when Danny had beat up Vero. Danny had apparently never even been aware of Blake and Duff's presence. Even though they'd always been with him, they'd been invisible to him!

Duff smashed Vero hard into the ground, and then he quickly rejoined Blake, whispering negative encouragement in Danny's other ear. As he did this, Vero noticed something different about Blake and Duff ... *was it panic?*

"You have every right to be angry, Danny. You're not loved," Duff whispered. "You never have been."

Blake whispered in the other ear, and their words dripped like poison.

Vero flew at Duff and tried to pull him away from Danny, but Duff was too strong.

Vero shouted to his fellow angels, "Guys, I need your help *now*!"

X sat up quickly, feeling confused and rubbing his head. As he took in the scene, he didn't recognize the environment, but he saw that Vero needed help.

"I'll be back," Greer said to Kane, and she sprang to her feet, leaving him still partially chained.

Greer and X released their wings. Then they swooped down on top of Duff and attacked. They pulled him away from Danny, giving Vero a clear shot at Danny's ear instead.

Vero desperately yelled into it, "Don't listen to their hateful thoughts, Danny!" Vero shouted. "It's all lies!"

Danny looked down at the driveway for a moment, his concentration on the house now clearly interrupted. Vero's words were getting through!

Blake and Duff grew enraged. With astonishing strength, Duff grabbed Greer and X simultaneously and threw them onto Pax and Ada who were still bound together by the black chains. They landed in a bone-bruising heap.

Blake tackled Vero, pinned him down by his arms, and sat on him. "That's enough out of you, angel boy!"

"Your own mother doesn't care about you, so why would Davina?" Duff shouted in Danny's ear.

Danny's momentary hesitation quickly passed as Duff's words sank in. The anger returned to Danny's face, and he stormed over to the house.

"No!" Vero cried.

Blake gritted his teeth as he screamed angrily in Vero's face. "He's *ours*! We'll never let him go!"

A feeling of dire urgency came over Vero as he saw Duff whispering in Danny's ear, "Smash some more of those windows. It'll feel good . . . "

Danny reached into his pocket and pulled out a red marble. He loaded it into the elastic band of the slingshot. Vero watched in horror as he saw Davina running through the woods. She was about to burst through those trees and run straight for the house, right on time.

"No! Danny! No!" Vero yelled.

Suddenly, a black chain struck Blake hard across the face, knocking him backward and off of Vero. He was momentarily stunned. Surprised, Duff looked up to see Kane holding the chain. He'd freed himself!

"The next one's for you!" Kane growled in fury.

Kane swung the chain around his head lasso-style, readying to strike Duff.

"You guys aren't so scary after all," Kane taunted as he swung the chain at Duff. But in a peevish rage, Duff grabbed the chain with his hand and jerked hard, flinging Kane high into the air.

Kane managed to grab a tree branch as he sailed through the air. And then right before the fledglings' eyes, Duff began to morph. His boyish appearance turned monstrous, with burn marks stretching from ear to ear. His flesh boiled into a slimy hide. His hands became claws, and his feet were now talons. And that single eye that had haunted Vero ever since his first run-in with maltures went all the way through his head and burned with pure hatred. "Am I scary now?" Duff grinned, showing rotted, sharp fangs.

Blake also mutated into his hideous self. Turns out they were the same maltures that had attacked him in the bathroom at Dr. Weiss's office! It was clear they intended to finish the job this time.

"Oh man ... " X said with his mouth hanging open. He freed Pax and Ada, letting the chain drop to the ground.

The angels watched in total fear as Blake lifted his arm toward the sky. His claw grew into a scythe, and the long curved blade became an extension of his arm.

"It's perfect for a beheading," Greer said, mesmerized by the terrifying blade.

Vero heard a swish of air as Blake swung the scythe at Vero's head. He quickly ducked and narrowly missed the lethal blow.

Roaring in frustration, Blake turned to Pax and Ada who recoiled. "How about if I behead one of your friends instead? Who will you save?"

"No!" Vero cried racing over to them.

As Blake swiped at them, Greer and X flew full speed onto Blake's back, knocking him to the ground for a moment.

"Vero, look!" Kane shouted, as he flew down from the tree.

Vero whipped around and saw Duff whispering into Danny's ear. Vero's heart nearly stopped as he watched Danny pull the red marble back in the elastic part of the slingshot. At that same moment, Davina burst through the thicket of trees. But Danny didn't see her, just like in Vero's daydream.

"Danny, no!" Vero shouted.

Blake jumped to his feet and swung his scythe at Vero who retreated from the blade. Just as Danny was about to release the marble into the air, Vero screamed with every ounce of his being, "Danny, we are here! You are not alone!"

Danny hesitated for a moment. He didn't release the marble.

"God loves you!" Vero shouted.

The maltures grew more enraged at the mention of God. They hissed and charged at Vero with scythes raised. Vero braced himself for the worst; but in that split second, Vero read Danny's mind. And he saw that Danny was having his own epiphany. Danny remembered how when he was a little kid, his mother would tuck him into bed and shower him with kisses. He remembered how his father spent hours with him carving a car out of wood that they hoped would win the Cub Scouts' Pinewood Derby. Danny remembered carefree days spent riding bikes with his older brother. But most of all, he remembered that he was loved.

Danny slowly lowered the slingshot. He felt ashamed of what he'd become. Out of a pure and simple desperation, he uttered the words, "Please, God, help me."

In that moment Vero learned just how powerful simple prayers can be. For in that precise moment, gold streaks appeared on Vero's forearm and shot up to his fingers. A magnificent sword blade sprang forth from Vero's right hand. From the inside of his palm, the sword continued to grow until a handle appeared, and Vero clutched it in his grasp. The sleek, solid-gold blade with its handle covered in vibrant gems fit Vero's hand so perfectly that it seemed as if his hand and the sword were one. The other angels looked on with their mouths hanging wide open in astonishment.

"Get them!" Greer shouted to Vero. "You are a warrior!"

Blake and Duff charged at Vero in a blind fury, and in

one clean swipe, Vero blocked both of their thrusts with the scythes. The maltures exchanged confused looks, obviously surprised by Vero's prowess. They charged Vero again, slicing at him. Vero fended off their blows with an agility he didn't know he possessed. Then he swung his sword and met their every thrust. The sound of clanking metal reverberated throughout the air. It was a sound Vero had heard while Uriel was sparring with the maltures on the rooftop while Vero hung from the ledge.

Pax and Ada flew over to Danny and stood on either side of him, creating a buffer between Danny and the maltures. Greer and X flew to Davina's side as Kane stood and watched Vero in stunned awe.

"Awesome ... " Kane muttered, his mouth agape.

Vero deflected their every stab. And as his confidence grew, Vero was no longer dodging jabs, but thrusting forward, slashing at the maltures, and forcing them to back away from Danny and head toward the house.

"Release Danny!" Vero demanded as he continued to advance.

After he'd backed them all the way to the house, he kept them both at bay, parrying blow for blow.

"Release him!" Vero shouted.

"If we release him, what will you do to us, Vero?" Blake asked. "Kill us?"

Blake's question threw Vero. A flicker of uncertainty came to his mind. Did he really have it in him to finish them off?

"Vero Leland ... track star, loyal friend, dutiful son, guardian angel ... *killer!*" Blake snarled.

The word *killer* resonated through Vero's head. He could never imagine himself killing anyone. But these were maltures. As his confidence wavered, his concentration broke.

In that moment of confusion, Duff spun away from the house and his blade sliced Vero's shoulder with great precision as Duff tried to jump clear of the fray. Vero was overcome with excruciating pain, and he slumped to the ground.

"Vero!" Kane yelled. He ran over to help Vero, but the hissing creatures swung violently at him, stopping him in his tracks. Vero clutched his shoulder, his energy was starting to drain right along with the blood that was now seeping from his gash.

"Vero! Behind you!" Greer screamed.

Vero turned and saw Duff charging at him with a raised scythe. The curved blade swung at Vero with deadly force. But with incredible swiftness, Vero rolled out of its path. The maltures shrieked.

Vero had allowed those fiends to distract him! *You fool!* he thought, and his anger brought him strength. Vero rose from the ground and held his sword out in front of him.

"Release Danny!" he said, unflinching.

His voice echoed voluminously, deep and commanding. He no longer feared. He no longer felt pain. His only thought was of Danny. If Vero died, so be it. He would fight for Danny and Davina to the death.

Blake and Duff went back on the offensive and charged Vero, but Vero was ready for them. He effortlessly somersaulted over their heads and landed squarely on his feet behind them.

The maltures turned around and engaged Vero, scythes against sword. Vero was equal to their challenge, thwarting each and every slice of their blades.

Then Blake's blade cut close to Vero's chest, but Vero pulled back quickly so the blade only caught his shirt, ripping the red material. Vero recoiled, and that little step back helped him avoid an erratic swipe from Duff. The swing went wide missing Vero completely, and instead it found Blake and cut off his arm at the elbow.

Blake shrieked in pain and fury. His scythe clanged to the ground where it instantly withered. Blake hissed at Duff who showed no concern for his fellow malture.

Defeated and with his scythe gone, Blake turned to run. But Kane flew right at him and knocked him to the driveway. "Not so fast!" Kane put his foot on Blake's chest as the beaten malture whimpered.

"One down!" Greer shouted.

Vero and Duff circled each other—waiting for someone to make a move.

"Yes, Vero, you are a real prize, and you know it, don't you?" Duff said.

Vero was curious, but he didn't let down his guard. Vero continued circling, never taking his eyes off of Duff.

"They're setting you up, Vero. Do your friends know about you?" Duff continued. "They'll tell you that it's all for the greater good, that it's *his* will. But you'll be the one to pay the price, not him."

"Light, Vero. You are light!" Ada called.

"Don't let him get up in your head, Vero. You've got this!" Pax shouted.

Yet, Duff's words bothered Vero.

"If you're not just a pawn, why haven't they told you everything? What are their plans for you, Vero . . ., hmmm?"

Duff's malicious words found their mark. Vero wondered

why he was special and what the plan for him was. Why did the maltures seem to know more about him than Vero did? Vero was wrestling with his doubt. His hands began trembling. Duff smiled.

Vero caught his own reflection in his blade, and in his eyes he no longer saw a timid young angel. Uriel's words came rushing back to him: *"The opposite of faith is not doubt. The opposite of faith is fear."* Vero would not give in to his fear. He wielded his sword at the demonic creature with such conviction that Duff fell backward to the ground.

"Release Danny!" Vero said, his blade pointed at Duff's chest.

"You understand nothing. We can't release Danny. We have no authority."

Duff rolled out from underneath Vero's sword and jumped to his feet. As he swiped at Vero's head with his scythe, Vero ducked, spun around, and sliced his sword blade clear through Duff's wrist.

Duff looked down, and as he watched his scythe wither, he let out a screeching howl.

And then the earth around them began to rumble. Between the two miserable maltures, a mound of earth rose up.

"No!" Duff screamed. "It's not our fault!"

As the mound continued to grow, Vero and Kane backed away. Vero held his sword in front of him, shielding the other angels. A resounding clicking sound began to emanate from the mound until it finally burst open, and millions of insect-like creatures emerged.

They had the heads of men, the bodies and wings of locusts, and the tails of scorpions. They grabbed the flailing maltures and dragged them, kicking and screaming, down into the hole.

Their shrieks made Vero think of the cries of wild beasts' prey, as they're being dismembered by their predators.

Once the maltures disappeared into the ground, a few remaining locust-men buzzed around the entrance to the hole. The wind from their wings picked up a huge cloud of dirt all around them, and a face flashed through the haze — a face Vero recognized. Abaddon. Then the buzzing stopped.

A moment later, the dirt settled. The hole had sealed itself shut, and Abaddon and his locust creatures were gone.

Then everything flashed white.

29

✦

THE WHITE
LIGHT

Vero was sitting under a shade tree on the banks of a sparkling river in the Ether. He blinked his eyes and massaged his temples, trying to focus on something, anything. After a few moments, he could make out a figure. A powerfully built angel with handsome, rugged features and penetrating violet eyes came into view. He was enormous! At least ten feet tall. His stature was completely intimidating, but there was a kindness to his face that put Vero at ease.

"Hello, Vero. I'm Michael."

The mightiest of all of God's warriors walked over and placed his massive hand on Vero's shoulder. Vero didn't feel worthy of the gesture.

"The others?" Vero asked.

"They're fine."

Vero sighed with relief.

"You were very brave. Look at what your actions have done."

Michael waved his hand, and an image appeared in mid-air of Davina running up the porch steps of that new home being built on Fairburn.

"Danny! Danny!" she shouted.

Danny turned and saw her. He dropped the slingshot to the ground, and the red marble rolled away. Davina was safe. She sat on the top step with Danny.

"I want to explain … " she began.

Danny looked at her.

"I really wanted to go to the dance with you. But my dad came back from his trip this afternoon, and when he found out about the dance, he wouldn't let me go. It's not that he doesn't like you; he just thinks I'm too young to go to a dance with a boy."

Danny looked relieved. "Really?" he whispered.

"Yes, Danny," Davina said. "I really do like you. And I'll save a dance for you someday."

A smile broke over Danny's face. He had a nice smile. It was the second time Vero had seen it.

"It's like a miracle that you found me here," Danny said, as he took Davina's hand in his own.

She nodded and laid her head on his shoulder.

"All of your efforts paid off," Michael told Vero.

"I guess," Vero said, feeling a strange mix of emotions.

He was happy for Danny, but a piece of his own heart was breaking. Vero thought of his journey through the belly of the Leviathan, his battle with the maltures—he did all of that to get Danny to lower his hand … a tiny gesture that had saved Davina's life.

Michael read his mind. "You were able to fight through it all to reach the goodness in Danny's heart. Tonight you helped turn the direction of that boy's life. You brought him a step closer to God." Michael paused thoughtfully. "And he was able to help you."

"What do you mean? How did Danny help me?" Vero asked.

"A guardian angel's purpose is to protect humans. But we can only do so much on our own. God gives humans free will, and we can never dictate to them what they should or must do. However, when a person asks God for help, they are inviting us into their lives. And in return, we become empowered by their hope, their belief. As our power strengthens, we will stop at nothing to help them."

"That's where the extra strength comes from when we're answering prayers?"

"Yes. You grew your sword at the exact same moment that Danny asked God for help. All of you young angels received more strength today."

Vero tried to make sense of it all, but he was still confused.

"If God hears everyone's prayers, then why didn't Danny's guardian angel show up to help him?" Vero asked.

Michael smiled. "He did. And he fought magnificently."

And suddenly, Vero understood.

"I'm Danny's guardian angel."

Michael nodded.

Vero watched as Davina held Danny's hand and the two of them walked away from the house. Michael swept his hands, and Danny and Davina disappeared. Michael understood what Vero was feeling.

"Jealousy is never a good thing, Vero," Michael said

gently. "We have such great love for humans; but Vero, we are not to fall in love with them."

"I can't just turn off my feelings."

"That's because you still live in the earthly world. But I promise you, it will get easier the more time you spend in the Ether. It has to, because, Vero, we have high hopes for you."

Vero looked at Michael.

"Only a handful of beings since the beginning of time have ever been able to get past the golems and the Leviathan and the behemoths. They are there to stop beings from reaching the lake of fire. They may seem like horrible creatures, but God placed them there to prevent fledglings like yourself from reaching Abaddon and his pit."

"But I *did* reach the pit. I saw Abaddon. What happened when I got there? Was I in real danger?"

"Abaddon guards the pit and the lake of fire within. That is his domain. You were standing at the entrance. Not even *I* can enter that pit—not even to rescue someone because once a being is thrown in, there is no return from that pit of despair. The entrance is as far as I'm allowed to go."

Vero became frightened as Michael's words sunk in. "So it was you? You rescued me that day?"

Michael nodded, his face serious.

"Raziel didn't tell us the whole truth," Vero realized. "He said that if we fail in our training, we'll wind up in the choir of angels. He neglected to tell us that we could also wind up in the lake of fire for all eternity."

Michael sighed. "No one likes to think about that. It's too painful. You were never supposed to get that far."

"But then why would God let me get past the Leviathan and the golems and put the other angels in danger?"

"Because apparently God gave you the skills to handle them." Michael sat down next to Vero under the tree, and together they gazed at the fields and flowers before them. "In time you will discover, Vero, that you have been given much more than most angels ... so much more is expected of you."

The gravity of Michael's words hit Vero hard.

"And because you have been entrusted with much," Michael continued, "Lucifer and his maltures will come after you relentlessly."

"Is Lucifer the one who chased me in the grocery store when I was a baby?"

"Yes. He suspects that you are special. And those first few hours when an infant guardian is placed upon the earth are when he or she is the most vulnerable. But we had you covered. The produce deliveryman showing up when he did was no coincidence."

"And the old man who died in the ER?"

"Not an angel. That was Mr. Jenkins. He'd recently passed away, and we asked him if he'd go back to earth for a few moments and deliver a message to your mother."

Vero smiled at the explanation, but then another thought worried him. "Michael, why do they think I'm special?"

"You know of Raziel's book?"

Vero nodded.

"In the book there is a mention of an angel who will tip the scales for good in the final war between good and evil. The identity of the angel was hidden even from the archangels, but the date in which he or she would come down to earth is ... the same night that you were delivered to the ER."

Vero's head sunk to his chest. It was all too much.

"But you were not the only angel delivered that night. A few others came down to earth on that same day. So that is why we were not sure of your identity at first. But now we are."

"But how does Lucifer know?"

"Raziel's book did not always fall into the right hands. Lucifer still doesn't know for certain that it is you. But he suspects and that is enough. He will stop at nothing to thwart God's plan for you. He'll attack you any way he can. And as you saw with Davina, the ones you love the most are now the most vulnerable."

Vero was scared. Michael placed his hand under Vero's chin, making sure Vero didn't miss out on what he was about to say.

"But just like humans, Vero, we angels are never alone."

The blinding white light flashed, and Michael was gone. Vero now realized that he'd seen that white flash before — many times before. When he saw the face of Abaddon, the white light was Michael rescuing him. When he was on the school bus, he thought heavy snow had covered the windshield, but it was Michael protecting him from the malture in that oncoming car. When he was a baby and his mother ran through the grocery store with him, it was Michael who'd saved them. And Vero realized it was true. He would never be alone.

After the light vanished completely, Vero saw something glistening before his eyes. It was a single jewel — a simple yet exquisite gemstone that sparkled radiantly. Vero looked closer and saw it was inlaid on a golden crown, his crown. The crown that Raziel said they all had waiting for them in heaven. He reached out to touch it, and it disappeared.

The water crashed over the three waterfalls and into the serene pool below. As Vero stood off in the distance, he listened to the thunderous, yet calming roar of the cascading water. He turned his face up to the sky, soaking in its warmth as he silently prayed, thanking God for safely delivering him from the maltures.

"Hey, Vero!" Greer yelled.

Greer, Pax, X, and Ada ran toward Vero, and Vero smiled at the sight of them. They were cleaned up, no ripped clothes, no cuts or bruises. No one would have ever guessed that only a short time ago, they'd trekked through the gut of a sea monster and battled maltures. Vero looked down at his own clothes. His jeans and red T-shirt also looked freshly washed.

"And you said you had nothing up your sleeve," Pax chuckled.

Vero shrugged and smiled. "And hey, I was able to communicate with you mind to mind."

"Pretty cool," Pax answered. "It only gets easier."

"How's your shoulder?" X asked Vero.

Vero had forgotten all about his injury. He put his hand on his shoulder and examined it. He rotated his arm, and to his surprise, there was no pain.

"All healed."

"Where did you learn to sword fight like that?" X asked.

"I don't know," Vero said. "Probably the same place I learned to speak Hebrew. But when I get back to earth, I think I may take up fencing. Seems like I might have a knack for it."

"Did you get a vision of your crown? Was there a jewel in it?" Pax asked.

"Yeah," Vero said.

"Pretty cool," Pax said.

Vero noticed Kane was standing away from them, looking nervous. They briefly locked eyes, and then Kane looked away. Vero understood. He walked over to him as the others watched.

"Are you okay?" Vero asked.

Kane nodded.

"Are you sure?"

Kane shook his head.

"I'm the weak link. Everyone got a vision of their crown but me. I guess it's because I've messed up twice now." Kane looked at his feet. "I'm not as strong as the rest of you."

Vero knew how that felt. He'd had plenty of his own failures during training. He couldn't fly at first. He'd humiliated Danny. In the caverns, Vero had refused to listen to his inner voice and wound up in the golems' cavern. "All I can say is that you saved me from the maltures. If you hadn't been there, I doubt it would have turned out so well."

"Thanks," Kane said. "And I'm sorry I attacked you."

Vero knew there would be many more tests to come. Their faith would be challenged at every turn. No one wanted to fail.

"My grandmother says faith takes practice. So maybe the more we do this, the easier it'll get," Pax offered.

Uriel walked up to the fledglings. "I'm very proud of all of you," he said, making sure to extend his gaze to Kane and intentionally include him. "Few fledglings have ever come up against what you five have encountered. And despite a few setbacks, you learned well to rely on your *Vox Dei*. It is the greatest gift you possess. As you progress with your training, listening to the voice should eventually become as natural as breathing ... because dark times are coming."

The group flashed anxious looks at Uriel.

"But for now, you will go back and enjoy your time on earth," Uriel said.

"Usually I hate leaving the Ether, but this time I'm okay with it," Ada said. "I want to go home and do nothing for a few days."

"Agreed," X said.

"In a big way," said Greer. "After seeing a malture, my latest foster mom doesn't seem so bad."

One by one, they closed their eyes and disappeared. As Vero closed his eyes, he felt a hand on his shoulder.

"Hold up a minute," Uriel said. He removed his hand and looked at Vero with those intense violet eyes. "Take a walk with me. I want to show you something."

Uriel and Vero walked over the rolling hills toward the waterfalls.

"I'm extremely proud of you, Vero, " Uriel said. "You don't realize it yet, but every action in the world, no matter how small or seemingly trivial, produces a ripple effect. Even when one person smiles at another, that tiny gesture isn't wasted. It gets passed along. Saving Davina's life has far-reaching implications that you cannot even begin to fathom, and the heavens are grateful to you."

"I'm sorry, Uriel," Vero said, and then paused to choose his words. "I'm sorry for blaming you for that whole garden of Eden thing. It's not so easy, is it?"

"No, it's not."

As they got closer to the waterfalls' shore, Uriel held out his arm and stopped Vero.

"You won't be able to go any farther. I wouldn't want you to bang your head."

"Thanks for the heads-up."

Uriel took a few steps closer to the pool. He bent down and stuck his hand into the still water of the lake. And then he walked back to Vero.

"Close your eyes."

Vero did as he was told. Just as Raphael had done to him in New York City, Uriel placed his thumbs — now wet with the waterfalls' water — on Vero's eyelids. After a moment, Uriel removed his thumbs, and Vero opened his eyes.

The sight before him caused Vero to take a step back. There in the lake, scores of humans were frolicking in the water. They splashed one another, some cupped the water into their hands and let it drip over their heads, others laid on their backs and just floated in it. The humans were of all nationalities and all ages, from little children to the elderly. They were laughing, smiling, and radiating pure joy. Their bodies were shimmering, glowing even. Scores of angels lined the shore and watched their humans proudly, the joy evident on their faces as well.

"Who are those people?" Vero asked.

"The recently deceased. They're being bathed. All souls must be purified before they meet God."

"They're going to heaven?"

Uriel nodded. Vero watched as one by one, the humans walked out of the water and clasped hands with a waiting angel.

"Those are their guardian angels?" Vero asked.

"Yes. This is the greatest moment of a guardian angel's life, when we take our humans to be with God."

Vero, his eyes misty, was overcome with emotion. He knew why Uriel had shown this to him. It was to remind him of what he must do—to one day be standing on that shore with Danny.

With hands still clasped, the angels and humans walked through the waterfall; and one by one, they vanished from sight.

Uriel closed Vero's eyelids with his thumbs, and when Vero opened his eyes again, the humans and angels had disappeared.

"It's time for you to return to earth," Uriel said.

Vero nodded.

"Oh, and when you get back, Vero, I think your sister will finally be ready to talk to you. You're not the only one with secrets in the Leland household. And you can talk openly with her. I won't send any ambulances racing past this time."

Uriel disappeared in a blur. Vero took in one last view of the Ether. He wasn't sure when he would return, but he never doubted that he would be back someday. Something flew past him and landed on a tree branch. It was a dove. The dove stared at him for a moment, and Vero could have sworn that it smiled at him.

30

A SISTER'S CONFESSION

Vero found himself wearing an Elvis jumpsuit and standing on the curb where the fire truck had hit him. For a moment, he thought time had stood still while he'd been in the Ether, but then he noticed he was the only person outside the gym, and there was no fire truck anywhere. Music blasted through the gym windows, and Vero looked at his watch. Time had not stood still. He'd traveled through the Leviathan and had battled the maltures all in the course of an evening. The fire drill was over, and the dance was back in full swing.

Vero peered through a gym window. Kids were dancing up a storm and having a blast. He spotted Davina dancing with Danny. It was bittersweet for him. Danny looked up and caught Vero staring at them. He flashed Vero a haughty smile. Vero sighed. Being Danny's guardian angel was really going to be a challenge.

"Vero!"

Vero whipped around to see Clover running full force at him. She grabbed him and hugged him tight. In fact, she squeezed Vero so tightly that he thought his head would pop off.

"Are you all right?" she asked.

"Yeah, I'm fine."

"But what happened? I mean, where were you?"

Vero wanted so badly to tell her the truth. And Uriel had given him permission to do so. And yet, he was afraid. How could he expect her to accept who he really was? What if she freaked? Or worse, what if it pushed her even farther away?

"I just went for a walk."

"No, you fell in front of the fire truck. I saw it!"

Vero looked down, not wanting to answer. Clover realized that if she was going to earn her brother's trust, she could no longer lie to him. She'd been just as deceitful as him. So she mustered up her courage and faced him.

"I remember the man who twisted your ankle. I remember everything about him. And I saw you sprout wings that day when you were making a snow angel. And even though Tack couldn't see them, I saw Blake and Duff. I know they're real. And my dreams, they seem like they're really happening. I can't shake them the next morning. Vero, I see things that normal people can't. For years, I thought if I denied seeing all that stuff, then it would just go away, but it hasn't. And I actually think it's getting stronger."

Vero looked at her, completely surprised. He hadn't been expecting to hear this.

"They're true, aren't they? All the things I see?"

Vero nodded, hoping his limited response would suffice.

"You're an angel, aren't you?"

Vero's first reaction was to lie and call her crazy, but then he remembered Uriel's words to him. "Yes," he said.

Clover's eyes filled with tears—not sad ones, but joyous tears. "Well that explains a lot," she said.

"But not enough," Vero replied. He hesitated for a moment. "Clover, in your dream journal there is a drawing..." Vero began.

"You looked in my diary?"

"It was by accident! But there is a drawing of a man, and he has three other faces: a lion, an ox and an eagle—"

"That's the Cherubim," Clover said. "The angels who guard God's throne."

Vero gave her a curious look.

"You really should pay closer attention during Sunday school," Clover grinned.

"I saw him in my dream too," Vero said.

"Why do you think we got to see him?" Clover asked.

"I don't know. But something tells me we'll know why someday."

"Are you sure? Because even though I see all these things... sometimes it just doesn't make any sense," Clover said. "Sometimes I'm not sure of anything."

"Can you see the wind?" Vero asked.

"What?"

"Can you see the wind?" Vero asked again.

"No."

"But it topples trees, moves oceans, shapes mountains, and even holds birds up in flight. You can feel it, and you can hear it. And even though you can't see it, Clover, you know it's there."

Clover understood that he was talking about God. She nodded and then looked up at the night sky—a sky full of endless wonder.

"Is it as wonderful as they taught us in Sunday school?"

"I haven't been to heaven yet," Vero smiled. "But from what I've seen so far, wonderful doesn't even begin to cover it."

Tack came barreling through the gym doors.

"Hey, you two! There's a dance going on in there!"

"We know," Clover said, rolling her eyes.

"And I promised to save a slow dance for you," Tack said with a wink.

"In your dreams, Tack!" she said.

Vero pulled Clover aside and whispered, "Don't forget ... around us, dreams have a way of coming true."

Clover's eyes went wide. Then a car horn blared next to them as Nora and Dennis pulled into the school parking lot.

"Sorry, Tack. Ten o'clock curfew. No dance tonight," Clover said with definite glee.

"Ah, man! Why do your parents always have to be on time?"

As they walked over to the car, Nora rolled down her window. "If you hurry, we might be able to get in a game of pajama Twister before bed," she said.

"Yes!" Tack shouted, punching his fist in the air, and he broke into a sprint for the car.

"They are so embarrassing," Clover said to Vero.

Vero smiled. He was determined to savor every single embarrassing moment.

"Race you!" Vero said.

ACKNOWLEDGMENTS

I wish to personally thank the following people for their contributions that were so helpful in creating this book:

For my husband, Chris, who majorly helped me to define the angelic realm of *The Ether* ... he was my story consultant, sounding board, and enthusiastic supporter from day one.

For my daughter, Grace, the best little reader in the City of Angels, who devoured each chapter as I wrote it. And for my son, Luke, from whom I gleaned many of Vero's and Tack's youthful characteristics.

For my mother, Joan Elehwany, who encouraged me as a child to tell stories, especially during long road trips. And for my brothers, David and Michael, who had no choice but to listen to them.

For my Hollywood screenplay manager and friend, David Greenblatt, whose years of support and sage advice have greatly inspired my writings.

For my brother-in-law and attorney, Guy N. Molinari, who gave generously of his time and considerable talents.

For Larry A. Thompson, book packager and producer extraordinaire, who originally read the manuscript and shepherded *The Ether* to market.

For my wonderful agents at DMA, Jan Miller and Nena Madonia, whose enthusiasm and constant encouragement was a true blessing for this neophyte novelist.

And for the wonderful folks at Zondervan, especially my editor, Kim Childress, whose continual guidance, advice, and support helped transform *The Ether* from manuscript to novel.

Thank you, one and all. Your help and assistance has been a true Godsend.

Check out this exclusive bonus chapter from the next Ether novel, *Pillars of Fire*, available January 2015!

CHAPTER ONE

The moon hid itself in the night sky, providing no light to the forest below. The woods were dark and deadly still—not even the music of the evening crickets could be heard. The air was thick and heavy as black smoke wafted through the trees. The silence was broken by the sounds of screeching birds and wooded animals as they desperately fled and crashed through the underbrush. Something was not right.

Deep within the heart of the forest, a fire burned, creating the smothering air. A shadowy figure sought the warmth of that unnatural fire, slowly approaching the burning embers, maneuvering around trees and rocks with the agility of a serpent.

The figure was a woman, and behind her trailed a carpet

of black, coarse hair that was revealed by the dancing flames as it weaved its way over the craggy ground, longer than a hundred wedding trains sewn together.

When the woman reached the fire, she dropped to her knees in reverence. As she leaned toward the flames, her face became illuminated, and the wrinkles running from her chin to her forehead and ear to ear appeared like deep crevices in earth's surface. She looked to be thousands of years old.

"I am listening, my prince," the grotesque hag spoke to the sharp, reddish-orange blaze before her. Her voice sounded like the screech of a hundred owls shrieking at once.

"Our time runs short." The fire gave voice, the flames rising and falling with the intensity of its sound. "The others have disappointed me. But you shall not."

A white-tailed buck unknowingly sniffed at fallen leaves that lay beneath a portion of the long hair.

"Is the young angel the one?" the hag asked.

"His identity will be become obvious during the trials. Then we will know with certainty," the inferno answered, its tone equally matched with menace and coldness. "He cannot live."

Without warning, the end of the hair chain rose up. The buck's eyes went wide with alarm when the hair coiled itself around its body. The deer lost the ability to breathe as the hair strangled it. Within seconds, the buck was completely encased by the hair, swallowed whole, then disappeared.

"I see you are hungry for fresh souls," the fire said. "And this one will be the prize of all prizes. You will no longer have to feed off the creatures of the forest."

"I will do as my prince commands," the hag said. The fire cast shadows against the thick clusters of trees, creating the illusion that the tangled branches were moving of their own volition. And perhaps they were. "He will not live."

She stood up and turned to leave, the hair moving with her. The blaze called out to her, "Do you loathe me?"

The ancient woman stopped and spun back around to face the fire—her eyes, hollow.

"I despise everything He has created. So you are no different."

Pleased with her answer, the fire let out a haughty laugh as the ugly hag disappeared into the darkness of the forest.

Vero Leland stood with his back up against the stark wall. His ever-changing grey eyes nervously scanned the room looking for things that could hurt him. There were long needles and razor-sharp scissors and something that looked like a scalpel on the counter. Vero was scared. Yet he was more frightened that the paper gown he was wearing would open and expose his backside. He tightly clutched the opening shut.

"Sit down. You're going to rip the gown," his mother, Nora, told him. "Really, Vero, you're too old to be so afraid of the doctor."

"Easy for you to say. You're not the one who's getting a shot. Look at those needles on the counter!" Vero shouted.

"I'm sure they're not all for you."

Tenderness came into Nora's eyes as she gazed upon her son.

"I remember your very first set of shots like it was yesterday. You were so tiny. When the doctor pricked you, you cried and cried. Then I joined in," Nora said, tearing up. "It broke my heart. The doctor thought I took it harder than you."

"Knock it off, Mom." Vero rolled his eyes. "You're gonna embarrass me."

"No more embarrassing than a knobby knee thirteen-year-old boy in a paper dress," Nora replied with a hurt look.

"Well, it's just that I'm old enough to get my physical by myself. You don't need to be in here with me."

"But I've always taken you to your physical."

"You say you want me to take on more responsibility," Vero stated in his defense.

"What if the doctor has questions and you can't answer them?"

"Then I'll come find you in the waiting room. I'm not a baby."

Nora looked at Vero. She knew he was right, but it was so hard to let go. Nora had always struggled to give Vero more independence. She feared for him more than for her daughter. Thirteen years later, she would still wake up in a cold sweat after nightmares in which she relived the night of Vero's arrival. The night she found Vero abandoned in the hospital. The night a figure in a dark robe chased her through a grocery store while she clutched Vero to her chest. The night she so desperately wanted to shake from her memory, but knew she never would.

"Hello, Vero," the doctor said as he walked into the room, snapping Nora out of her thoughts. "How's my medical wonder doing?"

Dr. Walker had known Vero all his life, but he really only saw Vero once a year for his physical because Vero rarely got sick. Nora had brought Vero to see him a few times to discuss how to put more weight on him, but other than that, Vero never saw the doctor.

Nora stood up and headed for the door.

"I'll be out in the waiting room if you need me," she said.

"You're not staying?" the doctor asked.

"No, he can handle himself."

Vero smiled gratefully. Taking one last look at her son, Nora slipped out, leaving him alone with the white-haired doctor.

"So, Vero, how is everything?"

"Pretty good."

"You feeling okay? Any complaints?" Dr. Walker asked as he listened to Vero's heart with his stethoscope.

"No."

"Breathe."

The doctor checked Vero's lungs as Vero sucked in deep breaths. Dr. Walker smiled to him.

"Very nice. So how's your back?

His question threw Vero.

"Oh, um … my back?"

"Your mother called a while ago, said you were complaining it hurt?"

"Oh, that. Yeah, they bought me a new mattress, and then it cleared up."

Vero felt bad about the lie, but there was no way he could tell him the truth. That all his back pain had completely disappeared the first time he had sprouted his wings. That it had been nothing more than guardian angel growing pains.

"Let's check your vision. Put your hand over your left eye and read the chart."

Vero covered his eye and read the chart hanging on the other side of the room.

"E, F, P, T, O, Z ..." he shouted out.

"Just read the lowest line you can see clearly," Dr. Walker interrupted.

Vero squinted as his eye scanned down the chart. When he reached the last line, the letters came into focus.

"I can make out the last line. F, E, A ..." he read aloud. "R, M, E."

"Nope, you got every letter wrong," Dr. Walker told him. "Try the line above it."

"But I see 'em clearly."

"Remove your hand and read it with both eyes."

Vero dropped his hand. His eyes stared intently at the last line.

"F, E ... A, R, M, E," Vero confidently blurted out.

Dr. Walker quickly scribbled something on his prescription pad and tore it off.

"Here's a prescription to see an eye doctor," he said as he handed it to Vero.

"But I'm sure I'm reading them right!"

Vero walked over to the eye chart and stuck his face right up to it.

"See? I'm right. Look. F, E, A, R, M, E."

"Not are you only nearsighted, you're also farsighted."

Then it hit Vero. The letters, F, E, A, R, M, E—they spelled out Fear me! He was getting a message that the doctor could not see—a message from the Ether. Fear me? Who was threatening him? It had been several months since he had heard anything from the Ether. And he missed it. Vero longed for the vast fields full of wildflowers, with colors so bright he had to shield his eyes. He longed for the warmth of the Ether's eternal light. And he so badly wanted to sprout his wings and soar into the Ether's brilliant blue sky.

Fear me. A chill ran through Vero, because he knew that not everything in the Ether was good.

"Any questions, Vero?" Dr. Walker asked.

"No," Vero answered, relieved that there was no mention of any shots.

"Then I'll see you next year," the doctor said on his way out. "You can get dressed."

After the door shut, Vero reached down to grab his clothes off the chair. As he untied the thin plastic belt from around his waist, a nurse knocked then entered without waiting for a response. Vero quickly spun around. His hand instinctively pulled the back of the gown shut, hiding his backside.

"Time for your shot," the nurse announced.

"But Dr. Walker didn't say I needed one!" Vero panicked.

"They never like to deliver bad news," the nurse answered. "They make us nurses be the bad guys. Sorry, sweetie."

Vero looked at the woman. Even though she gave him a smile, Vero saw it was forced. That she wasn't really all that sorry for what she was about to do to him. That perhaps after years of dealing with screaming scared kids, her sympathy turned to indifference or worse—annoyance. He got up on the examination table. As the nurse rubbed down his arm with an alcohol swab, Vero swallowed hard. Now that he was a teenager, he would put on a brave face and take his shot without incident. But secretly he regretted sending his mom out to the waiting room. He wished she were there to hold his hand.

"It'll be over before you know it," the nurse said in a flat voice. "Hold still."

Vero looked into her eyes for reassurance, but found none. Instead, he saw red. Glowing little flecks of red. He knew what those flecks meant. He'd seen them many times before. He became alarmed.

The nurse gripped his arm, ready to shove the needle into it, when Vero jumped up from the examination table. He grabbed whatever he could find on the counter to defend himself. Vero looked down into his hand—a stethoscope! It would be about as much help as the Q-Tips that had been lying next to it.

"Tell us who it is!" the nurse yelled as she backed him into a corner.

"Who are you?" Vero screamed.

She growled, exposing crooked, rotted teeth, then lunged at Vero. He rolled underneath her legs, getting away. But there was no time to catch his breath. The nurse spun and wildly jabbed the syringe at Vero, trying to stab him with it. He fell back onto the examination table. As the needle came straight between his eyes, he picked up a pillow and blocked it.

"Tell us which one of you it is!" she commanded.

Vero bolted to the door when she flew onto his back. He felt the tip of the needle press against his neck. He grabbed her wrist and twisted it, thrusting the needle deep into her shoulder. He compressed the plunger, releasing whatever poisons lay inside. The nurse snarled her teeth while letting out a dying shriek. Vero turned his head and watched as she tumbled off his back onto the hard floor. He was breathing so heavily, Vero thought he'd pass out. But more importantly how was he going to explain the dead nurse, or whatever creature it was, lying in the middle of the room?

As Vero stared at her, he noticed the stethoscope had fallen to the floor. He bent down and picked it up. He wanted to make sure she was totally dead, so he kneeled, put the earpieces into his ears, and held the other end to her heart. There was no heartbeat. Relief swept over him. But then he heard something … a faint sound came through the stethoscope. It was the distant sound of eerie laughter. It grew louder and louder. He yanked out the earpieces and chucked the instrument to the ground. He looked at the nurse. A smile was plastered on her face that hadn't been there previously. Puffs of black smoke began to waft from her mouth.

Vero backed away as the nurse's body blackened, until she became a shadowy layer of black dust. Vero had seen enough. He ran out the door and raced down the hallway into the waiting room.

He wanted to hug his mother so badly, to know that everything would be all right. So he could feel safe again. When he saw his mother casually leafing through a magazine, sitting in the crowded waiting room, Vero ran into her arms. Nora was caught off guard by his embrace. Parents and kids looked upon Vero with interest.

"Vero, what's wrong?"

"The shot … they're going to give me a shot," he blurted out.

Dr. Walker stood behind the appointment desk reading a patient's file. He overheard.

"No shot today, Vero. Your vaccines are all up to date."

Nora stared at Vero intently, then she said, "Come on, you need to get to school."

Vero let go of his mother, his fear dissipating.

A five-year-old boy walked over to him, laughing and pointing. "You're wearing a paper dress," he said.

Vero turned beet red.

"And I can see your underwear."

Vero hid behind his mom.

LOOKING FOR MORE FROM THIS AUTHOR?

Be sure to connect with her
at www.LauriceMolinari.com

Share Your Thoughts

With the Author: Your comments will be forwarded to the author when you send them to *zauthor@zondervan.com*.

With Zondervan: Submit your review of this book by writing to *zreview@zondervan.com*.

Free Online Resources at
www.zondervan.com

Daily Bible Verses and Devotions: Enrich your life with daily Bible verses or devotions that help you start every morning focused on God. Visit www.zondervan.com/newsletters.

Free Email Publications: Sign up for newsletters on Christian living, academic resources, church ministry, fiction, children's resources, and more. Visit www.zondervan.com/newsletters.

Zondervan Bible Search: Find and compare Bible passages in a variety of translations at www.zondervanbiblesearch.com.

Other Benefits: Register to receive online benefits like coupons and special offers, or to participate in research.

Wild at
Heart

This Large Print Book carries the
Seal of Approval of N.A.V.H.

Wild at

Heart

Discovering the Secret of a Man's Soul

JOHN ELDREDGE

Thorndike Press • **Waterville, Maine**

Published in 2003 by arrangement with Thomas Nelson, Inc.

Thorndike Press® Large Print Christian Living Series.

The tree indicium is a trademark of Thorndike Press.

The text of this Large Print edition is unabridged.
Other aspects of the book may vary from the original edition.

Set in 16 pt. Plantin by Al Chase.

Printed in the United States on permanent paper.

Library of Congress Cataloging-in-Publication Data

Eldredge, John.
    Wild at heart : discovering the secret of a man's soul /
John Eldredge.
        p. cm.
    ISBN 0-7862-5642-7 (lg. print : hc : alk. paper)
    1. Christian men — Religious life.   2. Masculinity —
Religious aspects — Christianity.   I. Title.
BV4528.2.E4519 2003
    248.8′42—dc21   2003052687

For Samuel, Blaine, and Luke.

I love your warrior hearts. You definitely have what it takes.

As the Founder/CEO of NAVH, the only national health agency solely devoted to those who, although not totally blind, have an eye disease which could lead to serious visual impairment, I am pleased to recognize Thorndike Press★ as one of the leading publishers in the large print field.

Founded in 1954 in San Francisco to prepare large print textbooks for partially seeing children, NAVH became the pioneer and standard setting agency in the preparation of large type.

Today, those publishers who meet our standards carry the prestigious "Seal of Approval" indicating high quality large print. We are delighted that Thorndike Press is one of the publishers whose titles meet these standards. We are also pleased to recognize the significant contribution Thorndike Press is making in this important and growing field.

Lorraine H. Marchi, L.H.D.
Founder/CEO
NAVH

★ Thorndike Press encompasses the following imprints: Thorndike, Wheeler, Walker and Large Print Press.

I have just finished reading John Eldredge's new work, *Wild at Heart*. I was deeply moved by this excellent book. I believe it is the best, most insightful book I have read in at least the last five years. I plan to read it again through the summer, only this next time, much more slowly. Eldredge shares splendid ideas that he has stated so creatively and, thankfully, free of cliché. New vistas will appear in the readers' minds as they take the wonderful journey of reading this book. His insights on identifying the wound, facing it head-on, then staying with it until the healing transpires will be immensely helpful to many folks. Every man and his wife and every mother of a boy really should read this book.

CHARLES R. SWINDOLL
June 28, 2001

Acknowledgments

My deep thanks to those who have helped me climb this mountain:

Sam, Blaine, Jenny, Aaron, Morgan, Cherie, Julie, Gary, Leigh, Travis, Sealy, and Stasi. Brian and Kyle at Thomas Nelson. The Thursday night poker group. And all those who have been praying for me, near and far.

Brent, for teaching me more about what it means to be a man than anyone else ever has, and Craig, for taking up the sword.

Contents

Introduction

I know. I almost want to apologize. *Dear Lord — do we really need another book for men?*

Nope. We need something else. We need *permission.*

Permission to be what we are — men made in God's image. Permission to live from the heart and not from the list of "should" and "ought to" that has left so many of us tired and bored.

Most messages for men ultimately fail. The reason is simple: They ignore what is deep and true to a man's *heart,* his real passions, and simply try to shape him up through various forms of pressure. "This is the man you *ought* to be. This is what a good husband/father/Christian/churchgoer *ought* to do." Fill in the blanks from there. He is responsible, sensitive, disciplined, faithful, diligent, dutiful, etc. Many of these are good qualities. That these messengers are well-intentioned I have no doubt. But the road to hell, as we remember, is paved with good intentions. That they are a near total failure should seem obvious by now.

No, men need something else. They need a deeper understanding of why they long for adventures and battles and a Beauty — and why God made them *just like that.* And they need a deeper understanding of why women long to be fought for, to be swept up into adventure, and to *be* the Beauty. For that is how God made them as well.

So I offer this book, not as the seven steps to being a better Christian, but as a safari of the heart to recover a life of freedom, passion, and adventure. I believe it will help men get their heart back — and women as well. Moreover, it will help women to understand their men and help them live the life they both want. That is my prayer for you.

It is not the critic who counts, not the man who points out how the strong man stumbles, or where the doer of deeds could have done them better. The credit belongs to the man in the arena, whose face is marred by dust and sweat and blood, who strives valiantly . . . who knows the great enthusiasms, the great devotions, who spends himself in a worthy cause, who at the best knows in the end the triumph of high achievement, and who at the worst, if he fails, at least fails while daring greatly, so that his place shall never be with those cold and timid souls who have never known neither victory nor defeat.
— TEDDY ROOSEVELT

The kingdom of heaven suffers violence, and violent men take it by force.
— MATTHEW 11:12 NASB

Chapter One

WILD AT HEART

The heart of a man is like deep water . . .
— PROVERBS 20:5 NKJV

The spiritual life cannot be made suburban. It is always frontier, and we who live in it must accept and even rejoice that it remains untamed.
— HOWARD MACEY

I want to ride to the ridge where the west
   commences
I can't look at hobbles and I can't stand fences
Don't fence me in.
— COLE PORTER
"Don't Fence Me In"

At last, I am surrounded by wilderness. The wind in the top of the pines behind me sounds like the ocean. Waves are rushing in from the great blue above, cresting upon the ridge of the mountain I have climbed, somewhere in the Sawatch Range of central Colorado. Spreading out below me the landscape is a sea of sagebrush for mile after lonesome mile. Zane Grey immortalized it as the purple sage, but most of the year it's more of a silver gray. This is the kind of country you could ride across for days on horseback without seeing another living soul. Today, I am on foot. Though the sun is shining this afternoon, it will not warm above thirty here near the Continental Divide, and the sweat I worked up scaling this face is now making me shiver. It is late October and winter is coming on. In the distance, nearly a hundred miles south by southwest, the San Juan Mountains are already covered in snow.

The aroma of the pungent sage still clings to my jeans, and it clears my head as I gasp for air — in notably short supply at 10,000 feet. I am forced to rest again, even though I know that each pause broadens the distance between me and my quarry. Still, the advantage has always been his. Though the tracks I found this morning were fresh — only a few hours old — that holds little promise. A bull elk can easily cover miles of rugged country in that amount of time, especially if he is wounded or on the run.

The wapiti, as the Indians called him, is one of the most elusive creatures we have left in the lower forty-eight. They are the ghost kings of the high country, more cautious and wary than deer, and more difficult to track. They live at higher elevations, and travel farther in a day, than nearly any other game. The bulls especially seem to carry a sixth sense to human presence. A few times I've gotten close; the next moment they are gone, vanishing silently into aspen groves so thick you wouldn't have believed a rabbit could get through.

It wasn't always this way. For centuries elk lived out on the prairies, grazing together on the rich grasses in vast numbers. In the spring of 1805 Meriwether Lewis described passing herds lolling about in the thousands as he made his way in search of a Northwest Passage. At times the curious wandered so close he could throw sticks at them, like bucolic dairy cows blocking the road. But by the end of the century westward expansion had pushed the elk high up into the Rocky Mountains. Now they are elusive, hiding out at timberline like outlaws until heavy snows force them down for the winter. If you would seek them now, it is on their terms, in forbidding haunts well beyond the reach of civilization.

And that is why I come.

And why I linger here still, letting the old bull get away. My hunt, you see, actually has little to do with elk. I knew that before I came. There is something else I am after, out here in the wild. I am searching for an even more elusive prey . . . something that can only be found through the help of wilderness.

I am looking for my heart.

WILD AT HEART

Eve was created within the lush beauty of Eden's garden. But Adam, if you'll remember, was created *outside* the Garden, in the wilderness. In the record of our beginnings, the second chapter of Genesis makes it clear: Man was born in the outback, from the untamed part of creation. Only afterward is he brought to Eden. And ever since then boys have never been at home indoors, and men have had an insatiable longing to explore. We long to return; it's when most men come alive. As John Muir said, when a man comes to the mountains, he comes home. The core of a man's heart is undomesticated *and that is good.* "I am not alive in an office," as one Northface ad has it. "I am not alive in a taxi cab. I am not alive on a sidewalk." Amen to that. Their conclusion? "Never stop exploring."

My gender seems to need little encouragement. It comes naturally, like our innate love of maps. In 1260 Marco Polo headed off to find China, and in 1967, when I was seven, I tried to dig a hole straight through from our backyard with my friend Danny Wilson. We gave up at about eight feet, but it made a great fort. Hannibal crosses his famous Alps, and there comes a day in a boy's life when he first crosses the street and enters the company of the great explorers. Scott and Amundsen race for the South Pole, Peary and Cook vie for the North, and when last summer I gave my boys some loose change and permission to ride their bikes down to the store to buy a soda, you'd have thought I'd given them a charter to go find the equator. Magellan sails due west, around the tip of South America — despite warnings that he and his crew will drop off the end of the earth — and Huck Finn heads off down the Mississippi ignoring similar threats. Powell follows the Colorado into the Grand Canyon, even though — no, *because* — no one has done it before and everyone is saying it can't be done.

And so my boys and I stood on the bank of the Snake River in the spring of '98, feeling that ancient urge to shove off. Snow melt was high that year, unusually high, and the river had overflowed its banks and was surging through the trees on both sides. Out in the middle of the river, which is crystal clear in late summer but that day looked like chocolate milk, logs were floating down, large tangles of branches bigger than a car, and who knows what else. High and muddy and fast, the Snake was forbidding. No other rafters could be seen. Did I mention it was raining? But we had a brand-new canoe and the paddles were in hand and, sure, I have never floated the Snake in a canoe, nor any other river for that matter, but what the heck. We jumped in and headed off into the unknown, like Livingstone plunging into the interior of dark Africa.

Adventure, with all its requisite danger and wildness, is a deeply spiritual longing written into the soul of man. The masculine heart needs a place where nothing is prefabricated, modular, nonfat, zip lock, franchised, on-line, microwavable. Where there are no deadlines, cell phones, or committee meetings. Where there is room for the soul. Where, finally, the geography around us corresponds to the geography of our heart. Look at the heroes of the biblical text: Moses does not encounter the living God at the mall. He finds him (or is found by him) somewhere out in the deserts of Sinai, a long way from the comforts of Egypt. The same is true of Jacob, who has his wrestling match with God not on the living room sofa but in a wadi somewhere east of the Jabbok, in Mesopotamia. Where did the great prophet Elijah go to recover his strength? To the wild. As did John the Baptist, and his cousin, Jesus, who is *led by the Spirit* into the wilderness.

Whatever else those explorers were after, they were also searching for themselves. Deep in a man's heart are some fundamental questions that simply cannot be answered at the kitchen table. Who am I? What am I made of? What am I destined for? It is fear that keeps a man at home where things are neat and orderly *and under his control*. But the answers to his deepest questions are not to be found on television or in the refrigerator. Out there on the burning desert sands, lost in a trackless waste, Moses received his life's mission and purpose. He is called out, called up into something much bigger than he ever imagined, much more serious than CEO or "prince of Egypt." Under foreign stars, in the dead of night, Jacob received a new name, his real name. No longer is he a shrewd business negotiator, but now he is one who wrestles with God. The wilderness trial of Christ is, at its core, a test of his *identity*. "If you are who you think you are . . ." If a man is ever to find out who he is and what he's here for, he has got to take that journey for himself.

He has got to get his heart back.

WESTWARD EXPANSION AGAINST THE SOUL

The way a man's life unfolds nowadays tends to drive his heart into remote regions of the soul. Endless hours at a computer screen; selling shoes at the mall; meetings, memos, phone calls. The business world — where the majority of American men live and die — requires a man to be efficient and punctual. Corporate policies and procedures are designed with one aim: to harness a man to the plow and make him produce. But the soul refuses to be harnessed; it knows nothing of Day Timers and deadlines and P&L statements. The soul longs for passion, for freedom, for *life*. As D. H. Lawrence said, "I am not a mechanism." A man needs to feel the rhythms of the earth; he needs to have in hand something real — the tiller of a boat, a set of reins, the roughness of rope, or simply a shovel. Can a man live all his days to keep his fingernails clean and trim? Is that what a boy dreams of?

Society at large can't make up its mind about men. Having spent the last thirty years redefining masculinity into something more sensitive, safe, manageable and, well, feminine, it now berates men for not being men. Boys will be boys, they sigh. As though if a man were to truly grow up he would forsake wilderness and wanderlust and settle down, be at home forever in Aunt Polly's parlor. "Where are all the *real* men?" is regular fare for talk shows and new books. *You asked them to be women,* I want to say. The result is a gender confusion never experienced at such a wide level in the history of the world. How can a man know he is one when his highest aim is minding his manners?

And then, alas, there is the church. Christianity, as it currently exists, has done some terrible things to men. When all is said and done, I think most men in the church believe that God put them on the earth to be a good boy. The problem with men, we are told, is that they don't know how to keep their promises, be spiritual leaders, talk to their wives, or raise their children. But, if they will try real hard they can reach the lofty summit of becoming . . . a nice guy. That's what we hold up as models of Christian maturity: Really Nice Guys. We don't smoke, drink, or swear; that's what makes us *men*. Now let me ask my male readers: In all your boyhood dreams growing up, did you ever dream of becoming a Nice Guy? (Ladies, was the Prince of your dreams dashing . . . or merely nice?)

Really now — do I overstate my case? Walk into most churches in America, have a look around, and ask yourself this question: What is a Christian man? Don't listen to what is said, look at what you find there. There is no doubt about it. You'd have to admit a Christian man is . . . bored. At a recent church retreat I was talking with a guy in his fifties, listening really, about his own journey as a man. "I've pretty much tried for the last twenty years to be a good man as the church defines it." Intrigued, I asked him to say what he thought that was. He paused for a long moment. "Dutiful," he said. "And separated from his heart." *A perfect description*, I thought. *Sadly right on the mark.*

As Robert Bly laments in *Iron John*,

"Some women want a passive man if they want a man at all, the church wants a tamed man — they are called priests, the university wants a domesticated man — they are called tenure-track people, the corporation wants a . . . sanitized, hairless, shallow man." It all comes together as a sort of westward expansion against the masculine soul. And thus the *heart* of a man is driven into the high country, into remote places, like a wounded animal looking for cover. Women know this, and lament that they have no access to their man's heart. Men know it, too, but are often unable to explain why their heart is missing. They know their heart is on the run, but they often do not know where to pick up the trail. The church wags its head and wonders why it can't get more men to sign up for its programs. The answer is simply this: We have not invited a man to know and live from his deep heart.

AN INVITATION

But God made the masculine heart, set it within every man, and thereby offers him an *invitation:* Come, and live out what I meant you to be. Permit me to bypass the entire nature vs. nurture "is gender really built-in?" debate with one simple observation: Men and women are made in the image of God *as men* or *as women.* "So God created man in his own image, in the image of God he created him, male and female he created them" (Gen. 1:27). Now, we know God doesn't have a body, so the uniqueness can't be physical. Gender simply must be at the level of the soul, in the deep and everlasting places within us. God doesn't make generic people; he makes something very distinct — a man or a woman. In other words, there is a masculine heart and a feminine heart, which in their own ways reflect or portray to the world God's heart.

God *meant* something when he meant man, and if we are to ever find ourselves we must find that. What has he set in the masculine heart? Instead of asking what you think you ought to do to become a better man (or woman, for my female readers), I want to ask, *What makes you come alive?* What stirs your heart? The journey we face now is into a land foreign to most of us. We must head into country that has no clear trail. This charter for exploration takes us into our own hearts, into our deepest desires. As the playwright Christopher Fry says,

> Life is a hypocrite if I can't live
> The way it moves me!

There are three desires I find written so deeply into my heart I know now I can no longer disregard them without losing my soul. They are core to who and what I am and yearn to be. I gaze into boyhood, I search the pages of literature, I listen carefully to many, many men, and I am convinced these desires are universal, a clue into masculinity itself. They may be misplaced, forgotten, or misdirected, but in the heart of every man is a desperate desire for a battle to fight, an adventure to live, and a beauty to rescue. I want you to think of the films men love, the things they do with their free time, and especially the aspirations of little boys and see if I am not right on this.

A BATTLE TO FIGHT

There's a photo on my wall of a little boy about five years old, with a crew cut, big cheeks, and an impish grin. It's an old photograph, and the color is fading, but the image is timeless. It's Christmas morning, 1964, and I've just opened what may have been the best present any boy received on any Christmas ever — a set of two pearl-handled six-shooters, complete with black leather holsters, a red cowboy shirt with two wild mustangs embroidered on either breast, shiny black boots, red bandanna, and straw hat. I've donned the outfit and won't take it off for weeks because, you see, this is not a "costume" at all, it's an *identity*. Sure, one pant leg is tucked into my boot and the other is hanging out, but that only adds to my "fresh off the trail" persona. My thumbs are tucked inside my gun belt and my chest is out because I am armed and dangerous. Bad guys beware: This town's not big enough for the both of us.

Capes and swords, camouflage, bandannas and six-shooters — these are the *uniforms* of boyhood. Little boys yearn to know they are powerful, they are dangerous, they are someone to be reckoned with. How many parents have tried in vain to prevent little Timmy from playing with guns? Give it up. If you do not supply a boy with weapons, he will make them from whatever materials are at hand. My boys chew their graham crackers into the shape of hand guns at the breakfast table. Every stick or fallen branch is a spear, or better, a bazooka. Despite what many modern educators would say, this is not a psychological disturbance brought on by violent television or chemical imbalance. Aggression is part of the masculine *design;* we are hardwired for it. If we believe that man is made in the image of God, then we would do well to remember that "the LORD is a warrior, the LORD is his name" (Ex. 15:3).

Little girls do not invent games where large numbers of people die, where bloodshed is a prerequisite for having fun. Hockey, for example, was not a feminine creation. Nor was boxing. A boy wants to attack something — and so does a man, even if it's only a little white ball on a tee. He wants to whack it into kingdom come. On the other hand, my boys do not sit down to tea parties. They do not call their friends on the phone to talk about relationships. They grow bored of games that have no element of danger or competition or bloodshed. Cooperative games based on "relational interdependence" are complete nonsense. "No one is killed?" they ask, incredulous. "No one wins? What's the point?" The universal nature of this ought to have convinced us by now: The boy is a warrior, the boy is his name. And those are not boyish antics he is doing. When boys play at war they are rehearsing their part in a much bigger drama. One day, you just might need that boy to defend you.

Those Union soldiers who charged the stone walls at Bloody Angle; the Allied troops that hit the beaches at Normandy or the sands of Iwo Jima — what would they have done without this deep part of their heart? Life *needs* a man to be fierce — and fiercely devoted. The wounds he will take throughout his life will cause him to lose heart if all he has been trained to be is soft. This is especially true in the murky waters of relationships, where a man feels least prepared to advance. As Bly says, "In every relationship something *fierce* is needed once in a while."

Now, this longing may have submerged from years of neglect, and a man may not feel that he is up to the battles he knows await him. Or it may have taken a very dark turn, as it has with inner-city gangs. But the desire is there. Every man wants to play the hero. Every man *needs* to know that he is powerful. Women didn't make *Braveheart* one of the best-selling films of the decade. *Flying Tigers*, *The Bridge on the River Kwai*, *The Magnificent Seven*, *Shane*, *High Noon*, *Saving Private Ryan*, *Top Gun*, the *Die Hard* films, *Gladiator* — the movies a man loves reveal what his heart longs for, what is set inside him from the day of his birth.

Like it or not, there is something fierce in the heart of every man.

"My mother loves to go to Europe on her vacations." We were talking about our love of the West, a friend and I, and why he moved out here from the East Coast. "And that's okay for her, I guess. There's a lot of culture there. But I need wildness." Our conversation was stirred by the film *Legends of the Fall*, the story of three young men coming of age in the early 1900s on their father's ranch in Montana. Alfred, the eldest, is practical, pragmatic, cautious. He heads off to the Big City to become a businessman and eventually, a politician. Yet something inside him dies. He becomes a hollow man. Samuel, the youngest, is still a boy in many ways, a tender child — literate, sensitive, timid. He is killed early in the film and we know he was not ready for battle.

Then there is Tristan, the middle son. He is wild at heart. It is Tristan who embodies the West — he catches and breaks the wild stallion, fights the grizzly with a knife, and wins the beautiful woman. I have yet to meet a man who wants to be Alfred or Samuel. I've yet to meet a woman who wants to marry one. There's a reason the American cowboy has taken on mythic proportions. He embodies a yearning every man knows from very young — to "go West," to find a place where he can be all he knows he was meant to be. To borrow Walter Brueggeman's description of God: "wild, dangerous, unfettered and free."

Now, let me stop for a moment and make something clear. I am no great white hunter. I have no dead animals adorning the walls of my house. I didn't play college football. In fact, in college I weighed 135 pounds and wasn't much of an athlete. Despite my childhood dreams, I have never been a race car driver or a fighter pilot. I have no interest in televised sports, I don't like cheap beer, and though I do drive an old jeep its tires are not ridiculously large. I say this because I anticipate that many readers — good men and women — will be tempted to dismiss this as some sort of macho-man pep rally. Not at all. I am simply searching, as many men (and hopeful women) are, for an authentic masculinity.

When winter fails to provide an adequate snow base, my boys bring their sleds in the house and ride them down the stairs. Just the other day, my wife found them with a rope out their second-story bedroom window, preparing to rappel down the side of the house. The recipe for fun is pretty simple raising boys: Add to any activity an element of danger, stir in a little exploration, add a dash of destruction, and you've got yourself a winner. The way they ski is a perfect example. Get to the top of the highest run, point your skis straight downhill and go, the faster the better. And this doesn't end with age, the stakes simply get higher.

A judge in his sixties, a real southern gentleman with a pinstriped suit and an elegant manner of speech, pulled me aside during a conference. Quietly, almost apologetically, he spoke of his love for sailing, for the open sea, and how he and a buddy eventually built their own boat. Then came a twinkle in his eye. "We were sailing off the coast of Bermuda a few years ago, when we were hit by a northeaster (a raging storm). Really, it came up out of nowhere. Twenty-foot swells in a thirty-foot homemade boat. I thought we were all going to die." A pause for dramatic effect, and then he confessed, "It was the best time of my life."

Compare your experience watching the latest James Bond or Indiana Jones thriller with, say, going to Bible study. The guaranteed success of each new release makes it clear — adventure is written into the heart of a man. And it's not just about having "fun." Adventure *requires* something of us, puts us to the test. Though we may fear the test, at the same time we yearn to be tested, to discover that we have what it takes. That's why we set off down the Snake River against all sound judgment, why a buddy and I pressed on through grizzly country to find good fishing, why I went off to Washington, D.C., as a young man to see if I could make it in those shark-infested waters. If a man has lost this desire, says he doesn't want it, that's only because he doesn't know he has what it takes, believes that he will fail the test. And so he decides it's better not to try. For reasons I hope to make clear later, most men hate the unknown and, like Cain, want to settle down and build their own city, get on top of their life.

But you can't escape it — there is something wild in the heart of every man.

A BEAUTY TO RESCUE

Romeo has his Juliet, King Arthur fights for Guinevere, Robin rescues Maid Marian, and I will never forget the first time I kissed my grade school sweetheart. It was in the fall of my seventh-grade year. I met Debbie in drama class, and fell absolutely head over heels. It was classic puppy love: I'd wait for her after rehearsals were over, carry her books back to her locker. We passed notes in class, talked on the phone at night. I had never paid girls much attention, really, until now. This desire awakens a bit later in a boy's journey to manhood, but when it does his universe turns on its head. Anyway, I longed to kiss her but just couldn't work up the courage — until the last night of the school play. The next day was summer vacation, she was going away, and I knew it was now or never. Backstage, in the dark, I slipped her a quick kiss and she returned a longer one. Do you remember the scene from the movie *E.T.*, where the boy flies across the moon on his bike? Though I rode my little Schwinn home that night, I'm certain I never touched the ground.

There is nothing so inspiring to a man as a beautiful woman. She'll make you want to charge the castle, slay the giant, leap across the parapets. Or maybe, hit a home run. One day during a Little League game, my son Samuel was so inspired. He likes baseball, but most boys starting out aren't sure they really have it in them to be a great player. Sam's our firstborn, and like so many firstborns he is cautious. He always lets a few pitches go by before he takes a swing, and when he does, it's never a full swing; every one of his hits up till this point were in the infield. Anyway, just as Sam steps up to bat this one afternoon, his friend from down the street, a cute little blonde girl, shows up along the first-base line. Standing up on tiptoe she yells out his name and waves to Sam. Pretending he doesn't notice her, he broadens his stance, grips the bat a little tighter, looks at the pitcher with something fierce in his eye. First one over the plate he knocks into center field.

A man wants to be the hero to the beauty. Young men going off to war carry a photo of their sweetheart in their wallet. Men who fly combat missions will paint a beauty on the side of their aircraft; the crews of the WWII B-17 bomber gave those flying fortresses names like *Me and My Gal* or the *Memphis Belle*. What would Robin Hood or King Arthur be without the woman they love? Lonely men fighting lonely battles. Indiana Jones and James Bond just wouldn't be the same without a beauty at their side, and inevitably they must fight for her. You see, it's not just that a man needs a battle to fight; he needs someone to fight *for*. Remember Nehemiah's words to the few brave souls defending a wall-less Jerusalem? "Don't be afraid . . . fight for your brothers, your sons and your daughters, your wives and your homes." The battle itself is never enough; a man yearns for romance. It's not enough to be a hero; it's that he is a hero *to someone* in particular, to the woman he loves. Adam was given the wind and the sea, the horse and the hawk, but as God himself said, things were just not right until there was Eve.

Yes, there is something passionate in the heart of every man.

THE FEMININE HEART

There are also three desires that I have found essential to a woman's heart, which are not entirely different from a man's and yet they remain distinctly feminine. Not every woman wants a battle to fight, but every woman yearns to be fought *for*. Listen to the longing of a woman's heart: She wants to be more than noticed — she wants to be *wanted*. She wants to be pursued. "I just want to be a priority to someone," a friend in her thirties told me. And her childhood dreams of a knight in shining armor coming to rescue her are not girlish fantasies; they are the core of the feminine heart and the life she knows she was made for. So Zach comes back for Paula in *An Officer and a Gentleman*, Frederick comes back for Jo in *Little Women*, and Edward returns to pledge his undying love for Eleanor in *Sense and Sensibility*.

Every woman also wants an adventure *to share*. One of my wife's favorite films is *The Man from Snowy River*. She loves the scene where Jessica, the beautiful young heroine, is rescued by Jim, her hero, and together they ride on horseback through the wilds of the Australian wilderness. "I want to be Isabo in *Ladyhawk*," confessed another female friend. "To be cherished, pursued, fought for — yes. But also, I want to be strong and a *part* of the adventure." So many men make the mistake of thinking that the woman *is* the adventure. But that is where the relationship immediately goes downhill. A woman doesn't want to be the adventure; she wants to be caught up into something greater than herself. Our friend went on to say, "I know myself and I know I'm not the adventure. So when a man makes me the point, I grow bored immediately. I know that story. Take me into one I don't know."

And finally, every woman wants to have a beauty to unveil. Not to conjure, but to unveil. Most women feel the pressure to be beautiful from very young, but that is not what I speak of. There is also a deep desire to simply and truly *be* the beauty, and be delighted in. Most little girls will remember playing dress up, or wedding day, or "twirling skirts," those flowing dresses that were perfect for spinning around in. She'll put her pretty dress on, come into the living room and twirl. What she longs for is to capture her daddy's delight. My wife remembers standing on top of the coffee table as a girl of five or six, and singing her heart out. *Do you see me?* asks the heart of every girl. *And are you captivated by what you see?*

The world kills a woman's heart when it tells her to be tough, efficient, and independent. Sadly, Christianity has missed her heart as well. Walk into most churches in America, have a look around, and ask yourself this question: What is a Christian woman? Again, don't listen to what is said, look at what you find there. There is no doubt about it. You'd have to admit a Christian woman is . . . tired. All we've offered the feminine soul is pressure to "be a good servant." No one is fighting for her heart, there is no grand adventure to be swept up in, and every woman doubts very much that she has any beauty to unveil.

BY WAY OF THE HEART

Which would you rather be said of you: "Harry? Sure I know him. He's a real sweet guy." Or, "Yes, I know about Harry. He's a dangerous man . . . in a really good way." Ladies, how about you? Which man would you rather have as your mate? (Some women, hurt by masculinity gone bad, might argue for the "safe" man . . . and then wonder why, years later, there is no passion in their marriage, why he is distant and cold.) And as for your own femininity, which would you rather have said of you — that you are a "tireless worker," or that you are a "captivating woman"? I rest my case.

What if? What if those deep desires in our hearts are telling us the truth, revealing to us the life we were *meant* to live? God gave us eyes so that we might see; he gave us ears that we might hear; he gave us wills that we might choose, and he gave us hearts that we might *live*. The way we handle the heart is everything. A man must *know* he is powerful; he must *know* he has what it takes. A woman must *know* she is beautiful; she must *know* she is worth fighting for. "But you don't understand," said one woman to me. "I'm living with a hollow man." No, it's in there. His heart is there. It may have evaded you, like a wounded animal, always out of reach, one step beyond your catching. But it's there. "I don't know when I died," said another man. "But I feel like I'm just using up oxygen." I understand. Your heart may feel dead and gone, but it's there. Something wild and strong and valiant, just waiting to be released.

And so this is not a book about the seven things a man ought to do to be a nicer guy. It is a book about the recovery and release of a man's heart, his passions, his true nature, which he has been given by God. It's an invitation to rush the fields at Bannockburn, to go West, to leap from the falls and save the beauty. For if you are going to know who you truly are *as a man,* if you are going to find a life worth living, if you are going to love a woman deeply and not pass on your confusion to your children, you simply must get your heart back. You must head up into the high country of the soul, into wild and uncharted regions and track down that elusive prey.

Chapter Two

THE WILD ONE WHOSE IMAGE WE BEAR

*How would telling people to be nice to one an-
other get a man crucified? What government
would execute Mister Rogers or Captain Kan-
garoo?*

— Philip Yancey

*Safe? Who said anything about safe? 'Course he
isn't safe. But he's good.*

— C. S. Lewis

*This is a stem
Of that victorious stock, and let us fear
The native mightiness and fate of him.*

— Henry V

Remember that little guy I told you about, with the shiny boots and a pair of six-shooters? The best part of the story is that it wasn't all pretend. I had a place to live out those dreams. My grandfather, my father's father, was a cowboy. He worked his own cattle ranch in eastern Oregon, between the desert sage and the Snake River. And though I was raised in the suburbs, the redemption of my life and the real training grounds for my own masculine journey took place on that ranch, where I spent my boyhood summers. Oh, that every boy should be so lucky. To have your days filled with tractors and pickup trucks, horses and roping steers, running through the fields, fishing in the ponds. I was Huck Finn for three wonderful months every year. How I loved it when my grandfather — "Pop" is what I called him — would look at me, his thumbs tucked in his belt, smile, and say, "Saddle up."

One afternoon Pop took me into town, to my favorite store. It was a combination feed and tack/hardware/ranch supply shop. The classic dry goods store of the Old West, a wonderland of tools and equipment, saddles, bridles and blankets, fishing gear, pocketknives, rifles. It smelled of hay and linseed oil, of leather and gunpowder and kerosene — all the things that thrill a boy's heart. That summer Pop was having a problem with an overrun pigeon population on the ranch. He hated the dirty birds, feared they were carrying diseases to the cattle. "Flying rats," is what he called them. Pop walked straight over to the firearms counter, picked out a BB rifle and a quart-sized milk carton with about a million BBs in it, and handed them to me. The old shop-keeper looked a bit surprised as he stared down at me, squinting over his glasses. "Isn't he a bit young for that?" Pop put his hand on my shoulder and smiled. "This is my grandson, Hal. He's riding shotgun for me."

WHERE DO WE COME FROM?

I may have walked into that feed store a squirrelly little kid, but I walked out as Sheriff Wyatt Earp, the Lone Ranger, Kit Carson. I had an identity and a place in the story. I was invited to be dangerous. If a boy is to become a man, if a man is to know he is one, this is not an option. A man *has* to know where he comes from, and what he's made of. One of the turning points in my good friend Craig's life — maybe *the* turning point — was the day he took back his father's name. Craig's father, Al McConnell, was killed in the Korean War when Craig was only four months old. His mother remarried and Craig was adopted by his stepdad, a sour old navy captain who would call Craig a "seagull" whenever he was angry with him. Talk about an identity, a place in the story. He'd say, "Craig, you're nothing but a seagull — all you're good for is sitting, squawking, and . . ." (you get the idea).

When Craig was a man he learned the truth of his heritage — how his dad was a warrior who had been cut down in battle. How if he had lived, he was planning on going to the mission field, to take the gospel to a place no one else had ever gone before. Craig discovered that his real great-grandfather was William McConnell, the first missionary to Central America, a man who risked his life many times to bring Christ to a lost people. Craig changed his name to McConnell and with it took back a much more noble identity, a much more dangerous place in the story. Would that we were all so fortunate. Many men are ashamed of their fathers. "You're just like your father," is an arrow many a bitter mother fires at her son. Most of the men I know are trying hard *not* to become like their fathers. But who does that leave them to follow after? From whom will they derive their sense of strength?

Maybe it would be better to turn our search to the headwaters, to that mighty root from which these branches grow. Who is this One we allegedly come from, whose image every man bears? What is he like? In a man's search for his strength, telling him that he's made in the image of God may not sound like a whole lot of encouragement at first. To most men, God is either distant or he is weak — the very thing they'd report of their earthly fathers. Be honest now — what is your image of Jesus *as a man?* "Isn't he sort of meek and mild?" a friend remarked. "I mean, the pictures I have of him show a gentle guy with children all around. Kind of like Mother Teresa." Yes, those are the pictures I've seen myself in many churches. In fact, those are the *only* pictures I've seen of Jesus. As I've said before, they leave me with the impression that he was the world's nicest guy. Mister Rogers with a beard. Telling me to be like him feels like telling me to go limp and passive. Be nice. Be swell. Be like Mother Teresa.

I'd much rather be told to be like William Wallace.

Wallace, if you'll recall, is the hero of the film *Braveheart*. He is the warrior poet who came as the liberator of Scotland in the early 1300s. When Wallace arrives on the scene, Scotland has been under the iron fist of English monarchs for centuries. The latest king is the worst of them all — Edward the Longshanks. A ruthless oppressor, Longshanks has devastated Scotland, killing her sons and raping her daughters. The Scottish nobles, supposed protectors of their flock, have instead piled heavy burdens on the backs of the people while they line their own purses by cutting deals with Longshanks. Wallace is the first to defy the English oppressors. Outraged, Longshanks sends his armies to the field of Sterling to crush the rebellion. The highlanders come down, in groups of hundreds and thousands. It's time for a showdown. But the nobles, cowards all, don't want a fight. They want a treaty with England that will buy them more lands and power. They are typical Pharisees, bureaucrats . . . religious administrators.

Without a leader to follow, the Scots begin to lose heart. One by one, then in larger numbers, they start to flee. At that moment Wallace rides in with his band of warriors, blue warpaint on their faces, ready for battle. Ignoring the nobles — who have gone to parley with the English captains to get another deal — Wallace goes straight for the hearts of the fearful Scots. "Sons of Scotland . . . you have come to fight as free men, and free men you are." He gives them an identity and a reason to fight. He reminds them that a life lived in fear is no life at all, that every last one of them will die some day. "And dying in your beds, many years from now, would you be willing to trade all the days from this day to that to come back here and tell our enemies that they may take our lives, but they'll never take our freedom!" He tells them they have what it takes. At the end of his stirring speech, the men are cheering. They are ready. Then Wallace's friend asks,

> "Fine speech. Now what do we do?"
> "Just be yourselves."
> "Where are you going?"
> "I'm going to pick a fight."

Finally, someone is going to stand up to the English tyrants. While the nobles jockey for position, Wallace rides out and interrupts the parley. He picks a fight with the English overlords and the Battle of Sterling ensues — a battle that begins the liberation of Scotland.

Now — is Jesus more like Mother Teresa or William Wallace? The answer is . . . it depends. If you're a leper, an outcast, a pariah of society whom no one has *ever* touched because you are "unclean," if all you have ever longed for is just one kind word, then Christ is the incarnation of tender mercy. He reaches out and touches you. On the other hand, if you're a Pharisee, one of those self-appointed doctrine police . . . watch out. On more than one occasion Jesus "picks a fight" with those notorious hypocrites. Take the story of the crippled woman in Luke 13. Here's the background: The Pharisees are like the Scottish nobles — they, too, load heavy burdens on the backs of God's people but do not lift a finger to help them. What is more, they are so bound to the Law that they insist it is a sin to heal someone on the Sabbath, for that would be doing "work." They have twisted God's intentions so badly they think that man was made for the Sabbath, rather than the Sabbath for man (Mark 2:27). Christ has already had a number of skirmishes with them, some over this very issue, leaving those quislings "wild with rage" (Luke 6:11 NLT).

Does Jesus tiptoe around the issue next time, so as not to "rock the boat" (the preference of so many of our leaders today)? Does he drop the subject in order to "preserve church unity"? Nope. He walks right into it, he baits them, he picks a fight. Let's pick up the story there:

> One Sabbath day as Jesus was teaching in a synagogue, he saw a woman who had been crippled by an evil spirit. She had been bent double for eighteen years and was unable to stand up straight. When Jesus saw her, he called her over and said, "Woman, you are healed of your sickness!" Then he touched her, and instantly she could stand straight. How she praised and thanked God! But the leader in charge of the synagogue was indignant that Jesus had healed her on the Sabbath day. "There are six days of the week for working," he said to the crowd. "Come on those days to be healed, not on the Sabbath." (Luke 13:10–14 NLT)

Can you believe this guy? What a weasel. Talk about completely missing the point. Christ is furious:

> But the Lord replied, "You hypocrite!

You work on the Sabbath day! Don't you untie your ox or your donkey from their stalls on the Sabbath and lead them out for water? Wasn't it necessary for me, even on the Sabbath day, to free this dear woman from the bondage in which Satan has held her for eighteen years?" This shamed his enemies. And all the people rejoiced at the wonderful things he did. (Luke 13:15–17 NLT)

A BATTLE TO FIGHT

Christ draws the enemy out, exposes him for what he is, and shames him in front of everyone. The Lord is a *gentleman???* Not if you're in the service of his enemy. God has a battle to fight, and the battle is for our freedom. As Tremper Longman says, "Virtually every book of the Bible — Old and New Testaments — and almost every page tells us about God's warring activity." I wonder if the Egyptians who kept Israel under the whip would describe Yahweh as a Really Nice Guy? Plagues, pestilence, the death of every firstborn — that doesn't seem very gentlemanly now, does it? What would Miss Manners have to say about taking the promised land? Does wholesale slaughter fit under "Calling on Your New Neighbors"?

You remember that wild man, Samson? He's got a pretty impressive masculine résumé: killed a lion with his bare hands, pummeled and stripped thirty Philistines when they used his wife against him, and finally, after they burned her to death, he killed a thousand men with the jawbone of a donkey. Not a guy to mess with. But did you notice? All those events happened when *"the Spirit of the LORD* came upon him" (Judges 15:14, emphasis added). Now, let me make one thing clear: I am not advocating a sort of "macho man" image. I'm not suggesting we all head off to the gym and then to the beach to kick sand in the faces of wimpy Pharisees. I am attempting to rescue us from a very, very mistaken image we have of God — especially of Jesus — and therefore of men as his image-bearers. Dorothy Sayers wrote that the church has "very efficiently pared the claws of the Lion of Judah," making him "a fitting household pet for pale curates and pious old ladies." Is that the God you find in the Bible? To Job — who has questioned God's strength, he replies:

> Do you give the horse his strength
> or clothe his neck with a flowing
> mane?

Do you make him leap like a locust,
striking terror with his proud
snorting?
He paws fiercely, rejoicing in his
strength,
and charges into the fray.
He laughs at fear, afraid of nothing;
he does not shy away from the
sword.
The quiver rattles against his side,
along with the flashing spear and
lance.
In frenzied excitement he eats up the
ground,
he cannot stand still when the
trumpet sounds.
At the blast of the trumpet he snorts,
"Aha!"
He catches the scent of battle from
afar,
the shout of commanders and the
battle cry. (Job 39:19–25)

The war horse, the stallion, embodies the
fierce heart of his Maker. And so do we;
every man is "a stem of that victorious
stock." Or at least, he was originally. You
can tell what kind of man you've got simply
by noting the impact he has on you. Does he
make you bored? Does he scare you with his

doctrinal nazism? Does he make you want to scream because he's just so very nice? In the Garden of Gesthemane, in the dead of night, a mob of thugs "carrying torches, lanterns and weapons" comes to take Christ away. Note the cowardice of it — why didn't they take him during the light of day, down in the town? Does Jesus shrink back in fear? No, he goes to face them head-on.

Jesus, knowing all that was going to happen to him, went out and asked them, "Who is it you want?"

"Jesus of Nazareth," they replied.

"I am he," Jesus said. (And Judas the traitor was standing there with them.) When Jesus said, "I am he," *they drew back and fell to the ground.*

Again he asked them, "Who is it you want?"

And they said, "Jesus of Nazareth."

"I told you that I am he," Jesus answered. "If you are looking for me, then let these men go." (John 18:4–8, emphasis added)

Talk about strength. The sheer force of Jesus' bold presence knocks the whole posse over. A few years ago a good man gave me a copy of a poem Ezra Pound wrote about

Christ, called "Ballad of the Goodly Fere." It's become my favorite. Written from the perspective of one of the men who followed Christ, perhaps Simon Zelotes, it'll make a lot more sense if you know that *fere* is an Old English word that means *mate,* or *companion:*

Ha' we lost the goodliest fere o' all
For the priests and the gallows tree?
Aye lover he was of brawny men,
O' ships and the open sea.

When they came wi' a host to take Our
    Man
His smile was good to see,
"First let these go!" quo' our Goodly
    Fere,
"Or I'll see ye damned," says he.

Aye he sent us out through the crossed
    high spears
And the scorn of his laugh rang free,
"Why took ye not me when I walked
    about
Alone in the town?" says he.

Oh we drunk his "Hale" in the good
    red wine
When we last made company,

No capon priest was the Goodly Fere
But a man o' men was he.

I ha' seen him drive a hundred men
Wi' a bundle o' cords swung free,
That they took the high and holy house
For their pawn and treasury . . .

I ha' seen him cow a thousand men
On the hills o' Galilee.
They whined as he walked out calm
   between,
Wi' his eyes like the grey o' the sea,

Like the sea that brooks no voyaging
With the winds unleashed and free,
Like the sea that he cowed at Genseret
Wi' twey words spoke' suddenly.

A master of men was the Goodly Fere,
A mate of the wind and sea,
If they think they ha' slain our Goodly Fere
They are fools eternally.

Jesus is no "capon priest," no pale-faced
altar boy with his hair parted in the middle,
speaking softly, avoiding confrontation,
who at last gets himself killed because he
has no way out. He works with wood, commands the loyalty of dockworkers. He is the

Lord of hosts, the captain of angel armies. And when Christ returns, he is at the head of a dreadful company, mounted on a white horse, with a double-edged sword, his robe dipped in blood (Rev. 19). Now that sounds a lot more like William Wallace than it does Mother Teresa.

No question about it — there is something fierce in the heart of God.

WHAT ABOUT ADVENTURE?

If you have any doubts as to whether or not God loves wildness, spend a night in the woods . . . alone. Take a walk out in a thunderstorm. Go for a swim with a pod of killer whales. Get a bull moose mad at you. Whose idea was this, anyway? The Great Barrier Reef with its great white sharks, the jungles of India with their tigers, the deserts of the Southwest with all those rattlesnakes — would you describe them as "nice" places? Most of the earth is not safe, but it's good. That struck me a little too late when hiking in to find the upper Kenai River in Alaska. My buddy Craig and I were after the salmon and giant rainbow trout that live in those icy waters. We were warned about bears, but didn't really take it seriously until we were deep into the woods. Grizzly sign was everywhere — salmon strewn about the trail, their heads bitten off. Piles of droppings the size of small dogs. Huge claw marks on the trees, about head-level. *We're dead*, I thought. *What are we doing out here?*

It then occurred to me that after God made all this, he pronounced it *good*, for heaven's sake. It's his way of letting us know he rather prefers adventure, danger, risk, the element of surprise. This whole creation is unapologetically *wild*. God loves it that way. But what about his own life? We know he has a battle to fight — but does God have an *adventure* to live? I mean, he already knows everything that's going to happen, right? How could there be any risk to his life; hasn't he got everything under absolute control?

In an attempt to secure the sovereignty of God, theologians have overstated their case and left us with a chess-player God playing both sides of the board, making all his moves and all ours too. But clearly, this is not so. God is a person who takes immense risks. No doubt the biggest risk of all was when he gave angels and men free will, including the freedom to reject him — not just once, but every single day. Does God cause a person to sin? "Absolutely not!" says Paul (Gal. 2:17). Then he can't be moving all the pieces on the board, because people sin all the time. Fallen angels and men use their powers to commit horrendous daily evil. Does God stop every bullet fired at an innocent victim? Does he prevent teenage liaisons from producing teenage pregnancies? There is something much more risky going on here than we're often willing to admit.

Most of us do everything we can to *reduce* the element of risk in our lives. We wear our seat belts, watch our cholesterol, and practice birth control. I know some couples who have decided against having children altogether; they simply aren't willing to chance the heartache children often bring. What if they are born with a crippling disease? What if they turn their backs on us, and God? What if . . . ? God seems to fly in the face of all caution. Even though he *knew* what would happen, what heartbreak and suffering and devastation would follow upon our disobedience, God chose to have children. And unlike some hyper-controlling parents, who take away every element of choice they can from their children, God gave us a remarkable choice. He did not *make* Adam and Eve obey him. He took a risk. A staggering risk, with staggering consequences. He let others into his story, and he lets their choices shape it profoundly.

This is the world he has made. This is the world that is still going on. And he doesn't walk away from the mess we've made of it. Now he lives, almost cheerfully, certainly heroically, in a dynamic relationship with us and with our world. "Then the Lord intervened" is perhaps the single most common phrase about him in Scripture, in one form or another. Look at the stories he writes. There's the one where the children of Israel are pinned against the Red Sea, no way out, with Pharaoh and his army barreling down on them in murderous fury. Then God shows up. There's Shadrach, Meshach, and Abednego, who get rescued only *after* they're thrown into the fiery furnace. Then God shows up. He lets the mob kill Jesus, bury him . . . then he shows up. Do you know why God loves writing such incredible stories? Because *he loves to come through.* He loves to show us that he has what it takes.

It's not the nature of God to limit his risks and cover his bases. Far from it. Most of the time, he actually lets the odds stack up against him. Against Goliath, a seasoned soldier and a trained killer, he sends . . . a freckle-faced little shepherd kid with a slingshot. Most commanders going into battle want as many infantry as they can get. God cuts Gideon's army from thirty-two thousand to three-hundred. Then he equips the ragtag little band that's left with torches and watering pots. It's not just a battle or two that God takes his chances with, either. Have you thought about his handling of the gospel? God needs to get a message out to the human race, without which they will perish . . . forever. What's the plan? First, he starts with the most unlikely group ever: a couple of prostitutes, a few fishermen with no better than a second-grade education, a tax collector. Then, he passes the ball to us. Unbelievable.

God's relationship with us and with our world is just that: a *relationship*. As with every relationship, there's a certain amount of unpredictability, and the ever-present likelihood that you'll get hurt. The ultimate risk anyone ever takes is to love, for as C. S. Lewis says, "Love anything and your heart will be wrung and possibly broken. If you want to make sure of keeping it intact you must give it to no one, not even an animal." But God does give it, again and again and again, until he is literally bleeding from it all. God's willingness to risk is just astounding — far beyond what any of us would do were we in his position.

Trying to reconcile God's sovereignty and man's free will has stumped the church for ages. We must humbly acknowledge that there's a great deal of mystery involved, but for those aware of the discussion, I am not advocating open theism. Nevertheless, there is definitely something wild in the heart of God.

A BEAUTY TO FIGHT FOR

And all his wildness and all his fierceness are inseparable from his romantic heart. That theologians have missed this says more about theologians than it does about God. Music, wine, poetry, sunsets . . . those were *his* inventions, not ours. We simply discovered what he had already thought of. Lovers and honeymooners choose places like Hawaii, the Bahamas, or Tuscany as a backdrop for their love. But whose idea was Hawaii, the Bahamas, and Tuscany? Let's bring this a little closer to home. Whose idea was it to create the human form in such a way that a kiss could be so delicious? And he didn't stop there, as only lovers know. Starting with her eyes, King Solomon is feasting on his beloved through the course of their wedding night. He loves her hair, her smile, her lips "drop sweetness as the honeycomb" and "milk and honey are under her tongue." You'll notice he's working his way *down:*

Your neck is like the tower of David,
    built with elegance . . .
Your two breasts are like two fawns . . .

Until the day breaks
    and the shadows flee
I will go to the mountain of myrrh
    and to the hill of incense. (Song 4:4–6)

And his wife responds by saying, "Let my lover come into his garden and taste its choice fruits" (Song 4:16). What kind of God would put the Song of Songs in the canon of Holy Scripture? Really, now, is it conceivable that such an erotic and scandalous book would have been placed in the Bible by the Christians *you* know? And what a delicate, poetic touch, "two fawns." This is no pornography, but there is no way to try to explain it all as "theological metaphor." That's just nonsense. In fact, God himself actually speaks in person in the Songs, once in the entire book. Solomon has taken his beloved to his bedchamber and the two are doing everything that lovers do there. God blesses it all, whispering, "Eat, O friends, and drink; drink your fill, O lovers" (Song 5:1), offering, as if needed, his own encouragement. And then he pulls the shades.

God is a romantic at heart, and he has his

own bride to fight for. He is a jealous lover, and his jealousy is for the hearts of his people and for their freedom. As Francis Frangipane so truly states, "Rescue is the constant pattern of God's activity."

For Zion's sake I will not keep silent,
    for Jerusalem's sake I will not remain quiet,
till her righteousness shines out like the
        dawn,
    her salvation like a blazing torch . . .

As a bridegroom rejoices over his bride,
    so will your God rejoice over you.
        (Isa. 62:1, 5)

And though she has committed adultery against him, though she has fallen captive to his enemy, God is willing to move heaven and earth to win her back. He will stop at nothing to set her free:

Who is this coming from Edom,
    from Bozrah, with his garments stained
        crimson?
Who is this, robed in splendor,
    striding forward in the greatness of his
        strength?
"It is I, speaking in righteousness,
    mighty to save."

64

Why are your garments red,
  like those of one treading the
    winepress?
"I have trodden the winepress alone;
  from the nations no one was with me.
I trampled them in my anger
  and trod them down in my wrath;
their blood spattered my garments,
  and I stained all my clothing.
For the day of vengeance was in my heart,
  and the year of my redemption has
    come. (Isa. 63:1–4)

Whoa. Talk about a Braveheart. This is one fierce, wild, and passionate guy. I have never heard Mister Rogers talk like that. Come to think of it, I have never heard anyone in church talk like that, either. But this is the God of heaven and earth. The Lion of Judah.

LITTLE BOYS AND LITTLE GIRLS

And this is our true Father, the stock from which the heart of man is drawn. Strong, courageous love. As George MacDonald wrote,

Thou art my life — I the brook, thou the
  spring.

Because thine eyes are open, I can see;
Because thou art thyself, 'tis therefore I
am me. (*Diary of an Old Soul*)

I've noticed that so often our word to boys is *don't*. Don't climb on that, don't break anything, don't be so aggressive, don't be so noisy, don't be so messy, don't take such crazy risks. But God's design — which he placed in boys as the picture of himself — is a resounding *yes*. Be fierce, be wild, be passionate. Now, none of this is to diminish the fact that a woman bears God's image as well. The masculine and feminine run throughout all creation. As Lewis says, "Gender is a reality and a more fundamental reality than sex . . . a fundamental polarity which divides all created beings." There is the sun and then there are the moon and stars; there is the rugged mountain and there is the field of wildflowers that grows upon it. A male lion is awesome to behold, but have you ever seen a lioness? There is also something wild in the heart of a woman, but it is feminine to the core, more *seductive* than fierce.

Eve and all her daughters are also "a stem of that victorious stock," but in a wonderfully different way. As a counselor and a friend, and especially as a husband, I've been honored to be welcomed into the deep heart of Eve. Often when I am with a woman, I find myself quietly wondering, *What is she telling me about God? I know he wants to say something to the world through Eve — what is it?* And after years of hearing the heart-cry of women, I am convinced beyond a doubt of this: God wants to be loved. He wants to be a priority to someone. How could we have missed this? From cover to cover, from beginning to end, the cry of God's heart is, "Why won't you choose Me?" It is amazing to me how humble, how *vulnerable* God is on this point. "You will . . . find me," says the Lord, "when you seek me with all your heart" (Jer. 29:13). In other words, "Look for me, pursue me — I want you to pursue me." Amazing. As Tozer says, "God waits to be wanted."

And certainly we see that God wants not merely an adventure, but an adventure to *share*. He didn't have to make us, but he *wanted* to. Though he knows the name of every star and his kingdom spans galaxies, God delights in being a part of our lives. Do you know why he often doesn't answer prayer right away? Because he wants to talk to us, and sometimes that's the only way to get us to stay and *talk* to him. His heart is for relationship, for shared adventure to the core.

And yes, God has a beauty to unveil. There's a reason that a man is captivated by a woman. Eve is the crown of creation. If you follow the Genesis narrative carefully, you'll see that each new stage of creation is better than the one before. First, all is formless, empty and dark. God begins to fashion the raw materials, like an artist working with a rough sketch or a lump of clay. Light and dark, land and sea, earth and sky — it's beginning to take shape. With a word, the whole floral kingdom adorns the earth. Sun, moon, and stars fill the sky. Surely and certainly, his work expresses greater detail and definition. Next come fish and fowl, porpoises and red-tailed hawks. The wild animals are next, all those amazing creatures. A trout is a wonderful creature, but a horse is truly magnificent. Can you hear the crescendo starting to swell, like a great symphony building and surging higher and higher?

Then comes Adam, the triumph of God's handiwork. It is not to any member of the animal kingdom that God says, "You are my very image, the icon of my likeness." Adam bears the likeness of God in his fierce, wild, and passionate heart. And yet, there is one more finishing touch. There is Eve. Creation comes to its high point, its climax with her. She is God's finishing touch. And all Adam can say is, "Wow." Eve embodies the beauty and the mystery and the tender vulnerability of God. As the poet William Blake said, "The naked woman's body is a portion of eternity too great for the eye of man."

The reason a woman wants a beauty to unveil, the reason she asks, *Do you delight in me?* is simply that God does as well. God is captivating beauty. As David prays, "One thing I ask of the LORD, this is what I seek: that I may . . . gaze upon the beauty of the LORD" (Ps. 27:4). Can there be any doubt that God wants to be *worshiped?* That he wants to be seen, and for us to be captivated by what we see? As C. S. Lewis wrote, "The beauty of the female is the root of joy to the female as well as to the male . . . to desire the enjoying of her own beauty is the obedience of Eve, and to both it is in the lover that the beloved tastes of her own delightfulness."

This is far too simple an outline, I admit. There is so much more to say, and these are not hard and rigid categories. A man needs to be tender at times, and a woman will sometimes need to be fierce. But if a man is only tender, we know something is deeply wrong, and if a woman is only fierce, we sense she is not what she was meant to be. If you'll look at the essence of little boys and little girls, I think you'll find I am not far from my mark. Strength and beauty. As the psalmist says,

> One thing God has spoken,
> two things have I heard:
> that you, O God, are strong,
> and that you, O Lord, are loving.
>   (Ps. 62:11–12)

Chapter Three

THE QUESTION THAT HAUNTS EVERY MAN

The tragedy of life is what dies inside a man while he lives.

— ALBERT SCHWEITZER

He begins to die, that quits his desires.

— GEORGE HERBERT

Are you there?
Say a prayer for the Pretender
Who started out so young and strong
Only to surrender.

— JACKSON BROWNE
"The Pretender"
(© 1976 by Swallow Turn Music)

Our local zoo had for years one of the biggest African lions I've ever seen. A huge male, nearly five hundred pounds, with a wonderful mane and absolutely enormous paws. *Panthera leo.* The King of the Beasts. Sure, he was caged, but I'm telling you the bars offered small comfort when you stood within six feet of something that in any other situation saw you as an easy lunch. Honestly, I felt I ought to shepherd my boys past him at a safe distance, as if he could pounce on us if he really wanted to. Yet he was my favorite, and whenever the others would wander on to the monkey house or the tigers, I'd double back just for a few more minutes in the presence of someone so powerful and noble and deadly. Perhaps it was fear mingled with admiration, perhaps it was simply that my heart broke for the big old cat.

This wonderful, terrible creature should have been out roaming the savanna, ruling his pride, striking fear into the heart of every wildebeest, bringing down zebras and gazelles whenever the urge seized him. Instead, he spent every hour of every day and every night of every year alone, in a cage smaller than your bedroom, his food served to him through a little metal door. Sometimes late at night, after the city had gone to sleep, I would hear his roar come down from the hills. It sounded not so much fierce, but rather mournful. During all of my visits, he never looked me in the eye. I desperately wanted him to, wanted for his sake the chance to stare me down, would have loved it if he took a swipe at me. But he just lay there, weary with that deep weariness that comes from boredom, taking shallow breaths, rolling now and then from side to side.

For after years of living in a cage, a lion no longer even believes it is a lion . . . and a man no longer believes he is a man.

THE LION OF JUDAH??

A man is fierce . . . passionate . . . wild at heart? You wouldn't know it from what normally walks around in a pair of trousers. If a man is the image of the Lion of Judah, how come there are so many lonely women, so many fatherless children, so few *men* around? Why is it that the world seems filled with "caricatures" of masculinity? There's the guy who lives behind us. He spends his entire weekend in front of the tube watching sports while his sons play outside — without him. We've lived here nine years and I think I've seen him play with his boys maybe twice. What's with that? Why won't he *engage?* And the guy the next street over, who races motorcycles and drives a huge truck and wears a leather jacket and sort of swaggers when he walks. I thought James Dean died years ago. What's with him? It looks manly, but it seems cartoonish, overdone.

How come when men look in their hearts they don't discover something valiant and dangerous, but instead find anger, lust, and fear? Most of the time, I feel more fearful than I do fierce. Why is that? It was one hundred and fifty years ago that Thoreau wrote, "The mass of men lead lives of quiet desperation," and it seems nothing has changed. As the line from *Braveheart* has it, "All men die; few men ever really live." And so most women lead lives of quiet resignation, having given up on their hope for a true man.

The real life of the average man seems a universe away from the desires of his heart. There is no battle to fight, unless it's traffic and meetings and hassles and bills. The guys who meet for coffee every Thursday morning down at the local coffee shop and share a few Bible verses with each other — where is their great battle? And the guys who hang out down at the bowling alley, smoking and having a few too many — they're in the exact same place. The swords and castles of their boyhood have long been replaced with pencils and cubicles; the six-shooters and cowboy hats laid aside for minivans and mortgages. The poet Edwin Robinson captured the quiet desperation this way:

> Miniver Cheevy, child of scorn,
> Grew lean while he assailed the
>   seasons;
> He wept that he was ever born
> And he had reasons.
>
> Miniver loved the days of old
> When swords were bright and steeds
>   were prancing;
> The vision of a warrior bold
> Would set him dancing.
>
> Miniver Cheevy, born too late,
> Scratched his head and kept on
>   thinking;
> Miniver coughed, and called it fate,
> And kept on drinking. ("Miniver
>   Cheevy")

Without a great battle in which a man can live and die, the fierce part of his nature goes underground and sort of simmers there in a sullen anger that seems to have no reason. A few weeks ago I was on a flight to the West Coast. It was dinnertime, and right in the middle of the meal the guy in front of me drops his seat back as far as it can go, with a couple of hard shoves back at me to make sure. I wanted to knock him into First Class. A friend of mine is having trouble with his toy shop, because the kids who come in "tick him off" and he's snapping at them. Not exactly good for business. So many men, good men, confess to losing it at their own children regularly. Then there's the guy in front of me at a stoplight yesterday. It turned green, but he didn't move; I guess he wasn't paying attention. I gave a little toot on my horn to draw his attention to the fact that now there were twenty-plus cars piling up behind us. The guy was out of his car in a flash, yelling threats, ready for a fight. Truth be told, I wanted desperately to meet him there. Men are angry, and we really don't know why.

And how come there are so many "sports widows," losing their husbands each weekend to the golf course or the TV? Why are so many men addicted to sports? It's the biggest adventure many of them ever taste. Why do so many others lose themselves in their careers? Same reason. I noticed the other day that the *Wall Street Journal* advertises itself to men as "adventures in capitalism." I know guys who spend hours on-line, e-trading stocks. There's a taste of excitement and risk to it, no question. And who's to blame them? The rest of their life is chores and tedious routine. It's no coincidence that many men fall into an affair not for love, not even for sex, but, by their own admission, for adventure. So many guys have been told to put that adventurous spirit behind them and "be responsible," meaning, live only for duty. All that's left are pictures on the wall of days gone by, and maybe some gear piled in the garage. Ed Sissman writes,

> Men past forty
> Get up nights, Look out at city lights
> And wonder
> Where they made the wrong turn
> And why life is so long.

I hope you're getting the picture by now. If a man does not find those things for which his heart is made, if he is never even invited to live for them from his deep heart, he will look for them in some other way. Why is pornography the number one snare for men? He longs for the beauty, but without his fierce and passionate heart he cannot find her or win her or keep her. Though he is powerfully drawn to the woman, he does not know how to fight for her or even that he *is* to fight for her. Rather, he finds her mostly a mystery that he knows he cannot solve and so at a soul level he keeps his distance. And privately, secretly, he turns to the imitation. What makes pornography so addictive is that more than anything else in a lost man's life, it makes him *feel* like a man without ever requiring a thing of him. The less a guy feels like a real man in the presence of a real woman, the more vulnerable he is to porn.

And so a man's heart, driven into the darker regions of the soul, denied the very things he most deeply desires, comes out in darker places. Now, a man's struggles, his wounds and addictions, are a bit more involved than that, but those are the core reasons. As the poet George Herbert warned, "he begins to die, that quits his desires." And you know what? We all know it. Every man knows that something's happened, something's gone wrong . . . we just don't know what it is.

OUR FEAR

I spent ten years of my life in the theater, as an actor and director. They were, for the most part, joyful years. I was young and energetic and pretty good at what I did. My wife was part of the theater company I managed, and we had many close friends there. I tell you this so that you will understand what I am about to reveal. In spite of the fact that my memories of theater are nearly all happy ones, I keep having this recurring nightmare. This is how it goes: I suddenly find myself in a theater — a large, Broadway-style playhouse, the kind every actor aspires to play. The house lights are low and the stage lights full, so from my position onstage I can barely make out the audience, but I sense it is a full house. Standing room only. So far, so good. Actors love playing to a full house. But I am not loving the moment at all. I am paralyzed with fear. A play is under way and I've got a crucial part. But I have no idea what play it is. I don't know what part I'm supposed to be playing; I don't know my lines; I don't even know my cues.

This is every man's deepest fear: to be exposed, to be found out, to be discovered as an impostor, and not really a man. The dream has nothing to do with acting; that's just the context for my fear. You have yours. A man bears the image of God in his strength, not so much physically but soulfully. Regardless of whether or not he knows the biblical account, if there's one thing a man does know he knows he is made to *come through*. Yet he wonders . . . *Can I? Will I?* When the going gets rough, when it really matters, will he pull it off? For years my soul lived in this turmoil. I'd often wake in the morning with an anxiousness that had no immediate source. My stomach was frequently tied in knots. One day my dear friend Brent asked, "What do you do now that you don't act anymore?" I realized at that moment that my whole life felt like a performance, like I am always "on." I felt in every situation that I must prove myself again. After I spoke or taught a class, I'd hang on what others would say, hoping they would say it went well. Each counseling session felt like a new test: *Can I come through, again? Was my last success all that I had?*

One of my clients got a great promotion and a raise. He came in depressed. *Good grief*, I thought. *Why?* Every man longs to be praised, and paid well on top of it. He confessed that although the applause felt great, he knew it only set him up for a bigger fall. Tomorrow, he'd have to do it all over, hit the ball out of the park again. Every man feels that the world is asking him to be something he doubts very much he has it in him to be. This is universal; I have yet to meet an honest man who won't admit it. Yes, there are many dense men who are wondering what I'm talking about; for them, life is fine and they are doing great. Just wait. Unless it's really and truly a reflection of genuine strength, it's a house of cards, and it'll come down sooner or later. Anger will surface, or an addiction. Headaches, an ulcer, or maybe an affair.

Honestly — how do you see yourself as a man? Are words like *strong, passionate,* and *dangerous* words you would choose? Do you have the courage to ask those in your life what *they* think of you as a man? What words do you fear they would choose? I mentioned the film *Legends of the Fall*, how every man who's seen it wants to be Tristan. But most see themselves as Alfred or Samuel. I've talked to many men about the film *Braveheart* and though every single one of them would love to be William Wallace, the dangerous warrior-hero, most see themselves as Robert the Bruce, the weak, intimidated guy who keeps folding under pressure. I'd love to think of myself as Indiana Jones; I'm afraid I'm more like Woody Allen.

The comedian Garrison Keillor wrote a very funny essay on this in his *The Book of Guys*. Realizing one day that he was not being honest about himself as a man, he sat down to make a list of his strengths and weaknesses:

USEFUL THINGS I CAN DO:

Be nice.

Make a bed.

Dig a hole.

Write books.

Sing alto or bass.

Read a map.

Drive a car.

USEFUL THINGS I CAN'T DO:

Chop down big trees and cut them into lumber or firewood.

Handle a horse, train a dog, or tend a herd of animals.

Handle a boat without panicking the
others.

Throw a fastball, curve, or slider.

Load, shoot, and clean a gun. Or bow
and arrow. Or use either of them,
or a spear, net, snare, boomerang,
or blowgun, to obtain meat.

Defend myself with my bare hands.

Keillor confesses: "Maybe it's an okay
report card for a *person* but I don't know any
persons . . . For a guy, it's not good. A
woman would go down the list and say,
'What does it matter if a guy can handle a
boat? Throw a curveball? Bag a deer?
Throw a left hook? This is 1993.' But that's
a womanly view of manhood." Craig and I
were joking about this as we hacked our way
through grizzly-infested woods in Alaska.
The only other guys we met all day were a
group of locals on their way out. They
looked like something out of *Soldier of Fortune* magazine — sawed-off shotguns, pistols, bandoleers of ammo slung across their
chests, huge knives. They were ready. They
had what it takes. And we? We had a
whistle. I'm serious. That's what we

brought for our dangerous trek through the wild: a whistle. Talk about a couple of pansies. Craig confessed, "Me — what can I really do? I mean really? I know how to operate a fax machine."

That's how most men feel about their readiness to fight, to live with risk, to capture the beauty. We have a whistle. You see, even though the *desires* are there for a battle to fight, an adventure to live, and a beauty to rescue, even though our boyhood dreams once were filled with those things, we don't think we're up to it. Why don't men play the man? Why don't they offer their strength to a world desperately in need of it? For two simple reasons: We doubt very much that we have any real strength to offer, and we're pretty certain that if we did offer what we have it wouldn't be enough. Something has gone wrong and we know it.

What's happened to us? The answer is partly back in the story of mankind, and partly in the details of each man's story.

WHAT IS A MAN FOR?

Why does God create Adam? What is a man for? If you know what something is designed to do, then you know its purpose in life. A retriever loves the water; a lion loves the hunt; a hawk loves to soar. It's what they're made for. Desire reveals design, and design reveals destiny. In the case of human beings, our design is also revealed by our desires. Let's take adventure. Adam and all his sons after him are given an incredible mission: rule and subdue, be fruitful and multiply. "Here is the entire earth, Adam. Explore it, cultivate it, care for it — it is your kingdom." Whoa . . . talk about an invitation. This is permission to do a heck of a lot more than cross the street. It's a charter to find the equator; it's a commission to build Camelot. Only Eden is a garden at that point; everything else is wild, so far as we know. No river has been charted, no ocean crossed, no mountain climbed. No one's discovered the molecule, or fuel injection, or Beethoven's Fifth. It's a blank page, waiting to be written. A clean canvas, waiting to be painted.

Most men think they are simply here on earth to kill time — and it's killing them. But the truth is precisely the opposite. The secret longing of your heart, whether it's to build a boat and sail it, to write a symphony and play it, to plant a field and care for it — those are the things you were made to do. That's what you're here for. Explore, build, conquer — you don't have to tell a boy to do those things for the simple reason that it *is his purpose.* But it's going to take risk, and danger, and there's the catch. Are we willing to live with the level of risk God invites us to? Something inside us hesitates.

Let's take another desire — why does a man long for a battle to fight? Because when we enter the story in Genesis, we step into a world at war. The lines have already been drawn. Evil is waiting to make its next move. Somewhere back before Eden, in the mystery of eternity past, there was a coup, a rebellion, an assassination attempt. Lucifer, the prince of angels, the captain of the guard, rebelled against the Trinity. He tried to take the throne of heaven by force, assisted by a third of the angelic army, in whom he instilled his own malice. They failed, and were hurled from the presence of the Trinity. But they were not destroyed, and the battle is not over. God now has an enemy . . . and so do we. Man is not born into a sitcom or a soap opera; he is born into a world at war. This is not *Home Improvement*; it's *Saving Private Ryan*. There will be many, many battles to fight on many different battlefields.

And finally, why does Adam long for a beauty to rescue? Because there is Eve. He is going to need her, and she is going to need him. In fact, Adam's first and greatest battle is just about to break out, as a battle for Eve. But let me set the stage a bit more. Before Eve is drawn from Adam's side and leaves that ache that never goes away until he is with her, God gives Adam some instructions on the care of creation, and his role in the unfolding story. It's pretty basic, and very generous. "You may freely eat any fruit in the garden except fruit from the tree of the knowledge of good and evil" (Gen. 2:16–17 NLT). Okay, most of us have heard about that. But notice what God *doesn't* tell Adam.

There is no warning or instruction over what is about to occur: the Temptation of Eve. This is just staggering. Notably missing from the dialogue between Adam and God is something like this: "Adam, one more thing. A week from Tuesday, about four in the afternoon, you and Eve are going to be down in the orchard and something dangerous is going to happen. Adam, are you listening? The eternal destiny of the human race hangs on this moment. Now, here's what I want you to do . . ." he doesn't tell him. He doesn't even mention it, so far as we know. Good grief — *why not?!* Because God *believes* in Adam. This is what he's designed to do — to come through in a pinch. Adam doesn't need play-by-play instructions because this is what Adam is *for*. It's already there, everything he needs, in his design, in his heart.

Needless to say, the story doesn't go well. Adam fails; he fails Eve, and the rest of humanity. Let me ask you a question: Where is Adam, while the serpent is tempting Eve? He's standing right there: "She also gave some to her husband, who was with her. Then he ate it, too" (Gen. 3:6 NLT). The Hebrew for "with her" means right there, elbow to elbow. Adam isn't away in another part of the forest; he has no alibi. He is standing right there, watching the whole thing unravel. What does he do? Nothing. Absolutely nothing. He says not a word, doesn't lift a finger.* He won't risk, he won't fight, and he won't rescue Eve. Our first father — the first real man — gave in to paralysis. He denied his very nature and went passive. And every man after him, every son of Adam, carries in his heart now the same failure. Every man repeats the sin of Adam, every day. We won't risk, we won't fight, and we won't rescue Eve. We truly are a chip off the old block.

Lest we neglect Eve, I must point out that

*I'm indebted to Crabb, Hudson, and Andrews for pointing this out in *The Silence of Adam*.

she fails her design as well. Eve is given to Adam as his *ezer kenegdo* — or as many translations have it, his "help meet" or "helper." Doesn't sound like much, does it? It makes me think of Hamburger Helper. But Robert Alter says this is "a notoriously difficult word to translate." It means something far more powerful than just "helper"; it means *"lifesaver."* The phrase is only used elsewhere of God, when you need him to come through for you desperately. "There is no one like the God of Jeshurun, who rides on the heavens to help you" (Deut. 33:26). Eve is a life giver, she is Adam's ally. It is to *both* of them that the charter for adventure is given. It will take both of them to sustain life. And they will both need to fight together.

Eve is deceived . . . and rather easily, as my friend Jan Meyers points out. In *The Allure of Hope*, Jan says, "Eve was convinced that God was withholding something from her." Not even the extravagance of Eden could convince her that God's heart is good. "When Eve was [deceived], the artistry of being a woman took a fateful dive into the barren places of control and loneliness." Now every daughter of Eve wants to "control her surrounding, her relationships, her God." No longer is she vulnerable, now she will be grasping. No longer does she want simply to share in the adventure; now, she wants to control it. And as for her beauty, she either hides it in fear and anger, or she uses it to secure her place in the world. "In our fear that no one will speak on our behalf or protect us or fight for us, we start to re-create both ourselves and our role in the story. We manipulate our surroundings so we don't feel so defenseless." Fallen Eve either becomes rigid or clingy. Put simply, Eve is no longer simply *inviting*. She is either hiding in busyness or demanding that Adam come through for her; usually, an odd combination of both.

POSERS

Adam knows now that he has blown it, that something has gone wrong within him, that he is no longer what he was meant to be. Adam doesn't just make a bad decision; he *gives away* something essential to his nature. He is marred now, his strength is fallen, and he knows it. Then what happens? Adam hides. "I was afraid because I was naked; so I hid" (Gen. 3:10). You don't need a course in psychology to understand men. Understand that verse, let its implications sink in, and the men around you will suddenly come into focus. We are hiding, every last one of us. Well aware that we, too, are not what we were meant to be, desperately afraid of exposure, terrified of being seen for what we are and *are not,* we have run off into the bushes. We hide in our office, at the gym, behind the newspaper and mostly *behind our personality.* Most of what you encounter when you meet a man is a facade, an elaborate fig leaf, a brilliant disguise.

Driving back from dinner one night, a friend and I were just sort of shooting the breeze about life and marriage and work. As the conversation deepened, he began to admit some of the struggles he was having. Then he came out with this confession: "The truth is, John, I feel like I'm just [bluffing] my way through life . . . and that someday soon I'll be exposed as an impostor." I was so surprised. This is a popular, successful guy who most people like the moment they meet him. He's bright, articulate, handsome, and athletic. He's married to a beautiful woman, has a great job, drives a new truck, and lives in a big house. There is nothing on the outside that says, "not really a man." But inside, it's another story. It always is.

Before I ever mentioned my nightmare about being onstage with nothing to say, another friend shared with me that he, too, is having a recurring nightmare. It involves a murder, and the FBI. Apparently, in his dream, he has killed someone and buried the body out back of his house. But the authorities are closing in, and he knows that any moment they'll discover the crime scene and he'll be caught. The dream always ends just before he is found out. He wakes in a cold sweat. "Any day now, I'll be found out" is a pretty common theme among us guys. Truth be told, most of us are faking our way through life. We pick only those battles we are sure to win, only those adventures we are sure to handle, only those beauties we are sure to rescue.

Let me ask the guys who don't know much about cars: How do you talk to your mechanic? I know a bit about fixing cars, but not much, and when I'm around my mechanic I feel like a weenie. So what do I do? I fake it; I pose. I assume a sort of casual, laid-back manner I imagine "the guys" use when hanging around the lunch truck, and I wait for him to speak. "Looks like it might be your fuel mixture," he says. "Yeah, I thought it might be that." "When was the last time you had your carb rebuilt?" "Oh I dunno . . . it's probably been years." (I'm guessing he's talking about my carburetor, and I have no idea if it's ever been re-built.) "Well, we'd better do it now or you're going to end up on some country road miles from nowhere and then you'll have to do it yourself." "Yeah," I say casually, as if I don't want to be bothered having to rebuild that thing even though I know I wouldn't have the slightest idea where to begin. All I have is a whistle, remember? I tell him to go ahead, and he sticks out his hand, a big, greasy hand that says *I know tools real well* and what am I supposed to do? I'm dressed in a coat and tie because I'm supposed to give a talk at some women's luncheon, but I can't say, "Gee, I'd rather not get my hands dirty," so I take his hand and pump it extra hard.

Or how about you fellas who work in the corporate world: How do you act in the boardroom, when the heat is on? What do you say when the Big Boss is riding you hard? "Jones, what the devil is going on down there in your division? You guys are three weeks late on that project!!" Do you try to pass the buck? "Actually, sir, we got the plans over to McCormick's department to bid the job weeks ago." Do you feign ignorance? "Really? I had no idea. I'll get right on it." Maybe you just weasel your way out of it: "That job's a slam dunk, sir . . .

we'll have it done this week." Years ago I did a tour of duty in the corporate world; the head man was a pretty intimidating guy. Many heads rolled in his office. My plan was basically to try to avoid him at all costs; when I did run into him in the hallway, even in "friendly" conversation, I always felt about ten years old.

How about sports? A few years ago I volunteered to coach for my son's baseball team. There was a mandatory meeting that all coaches needed to attend before the season, to pick up equipment and listen to a "briefing." Our recreation department brought in a retired professional pitcher, a local boy, to give us all a pep talk. The posing that went on was incredible. Here's a bunch of balding dads with beer bellies sort of swaggering around, talking about their own baseball days, throwing out comments about pro players like they knew them personally, and spitting (I kid you not). Their "attitude" (that's a tame word) was so thick I needed waders. It was the biggest bunch of posers I've ever met . . . outside of church.

That same sort of thing goes on Sunday mornings, it's just a different set of rules. Dave runs into Bob in the church lobby. Both are wearing their happy faces, though neither is happy at all. "Hey, Bob, how are ya?" Bob is actually furious at his wife and ready to leave her, but he says, "Great, just great, Dave. The Lord is good!" Dave, on the other hand, hasn't believed in the goodness of God for years, ever since his daughter was killed. "Yep — God is good, all the time. I'm just so glad to be here, praising the Lord." "Me too. Well, I'll be praying for you!" I would love to see a tally of the number of prayers actually *prayed* against the number of prayers promised. I bet it's about one in a thousand. "And I'll be praying for you too. Well, gotta go! You take care." "Take care" is our way of saying, "I'm done with this conversation and I want to get out of here but I don't want to appear rude so I'll say something that sounds meaningful and caring," but in truth, Dave doesn't give a rip about Bob.

STRENGTH GONE BAD

Adam falls, and all his sons with him. After that, what do you see as the story unfolds? Violent men, or passive men. Strength gone bad. Cain kills Abel; Lamech threatens to kill everybody else. God finally floods the earth because of the violence of men, but it's still going on. Sometimes it gets physical; most of the time, it's verbal. I know Christian men who say the most awful things to their wives. Or they kill them with their silence; a cold, deadly silence. I know pastors, warm and friendly guys in the pulpit, who from the safety of their office send out blistering E-mails to their staff. It's cowardice, all of it. I was intrigued to read in the journals of civil war commanders how the men you thought would be real heroes end up just the opposite. "Roughs that are always ready for street fighting are cowards on the open battlefield," declared one corporal. A sergeant from the same division agreed: "I don't know of a single fist-fighting bully but what he makes a cowardly soldier." The violence, no matter what form, is a cover-up for *fear*.

What about the achievers, the men running hard at life, pressing their way ahead? Most of it is fear-based as well. Not all of it, but most of it. For years, I was a driven, type A, hard-charging perfectionist. I demanded a lot of myself and of those who worked for me. My wife didn't like to call me at work, for as she said, "You have your work voice on." In other words, your fig leaf is showing. All that swaggering and supposed confidence and hard charging came out of fear — the fear that if I did not, I would be revealed to be less than a man. Never let down, never drop your guard, give 150 percent.

Achievers are a socially acceptable form of violent men, overdoing it in one way or another. Their casualties tend to be their marriages, their families, and their health. Until a man faces this honestly, and what's really behind it, he'll do great damage.

Then there's the passive men. Abraham is a good example. He's always hiding behind his wife's skirt when the going gets rough. When he and his household are forced by a famine down to Egypt, he tells Pharaoh that Sarah is his sister so that he won't be killed; he jeopardizes her in order to save his own skin. Pharaoh takes Sarah into his harem, but the whole ruse is exposed when God strikes the Egyptians with diseases. You'd think Abraham would have learned his lesson, but no — he does it again years later when he moves to the Negev. In fact, his son Isaac carries on the tradition, jeopardizing Rebekah in the same way. The sins of the father passed along. Abraham is a good man, a friend of God. But he's also a coward. I know many like him. Men who can't commit to the women they've been dragging along for years. Men who won't stand up to the pastor and tell him what they really think. Pastors and Christian leaders who hide behind the fig leaf of niceness and "spirituality" and never, ever confront a difficult situation. Guys who organize their paper clips. Men who hide behind the newspaper or the television and won't really talk to their wives or children.

I'm like him too — a true son of Abraham. I mentioned that the early years of our life in the theater were good ones — but that's not the full story. I also had an affair . . . with my work. I married my wife without ever resolving or even knowing the deeper questions of my own soul. Suddenly, the day after our wedding, I am faced with the reality that I now have this woman as my constant companion and I have no idea what it really means to love her, nor if I have whatever it is she needs from me. *What if I offer her all I have as a man and it's not enough?* That's a risk I was not willing to take. But I knew I had what it took at the theater, and so slowly I began to spend more and more time there. Late nights, weekends, eventually every waking moment. I was hiding, like Adam, running from the fact that my strength was being called for and I really doubted I had any.

The evidence is clear: Adam and Eve's fall sent a tremor through the human race. A fatal flaw entered the original, and it's been passed on to every son and daughter. Thus every little boy and every little girl comes into the world set up for a loss of heart. Even if he can't quite put it into words, every man is haunted by the question, "Am I really a man? Have I got what it takes . . . when it counts?" What follows is the story we are personally much, much more familiar with.

Chapter Four

THE WOUND

Little Billy's mother was always telling him exactly what he was allowed to do and what he was not allowed to do. All the things he was allowed to do were boring. All the things he was not allowed to do were exciting. One of the things he was NEVER NEVER allowed to do, the most exciting of them all, was to go out through the garden gate all by himself and explore the world beyond.

— ROALD DAHL,
THE MINPINS

*In the clearing stands a boxer
And a fighter by his trade
And he carries the reminders
Of every glove that laid him down
and cut him till he cried out
in his anger and his shame
"I am leaving, I am leaving"*

But the fighter still remains.

— PAUL SIMON
"The Boxer"
(© 1968 by Paul Simon)

I believe I was the only one in the entire company to come all the way through Normandy without getting wounded.

— PVT. WILLIAM CRAFT,
314TH INFANTRY REGIMENT

The story of Adam's fall is every man's story. It is simple and straightforward, almost mythic in its brevity and depth. And so every man comes into the world set up for a loss of heart. Then comes the story we are much more aware of — our own story. Where Adam's story seems simple and straightforward, our own seems complex and detailed; many more characters are involved, and the plot is sometimes hard to follow. But the outcome is always the same: a wound in the soul. Every boy, in his journey to become a man, takes an arrow in the center of his heart, in the place of his strength. Because the wound is rarely discussed and even more rarely healed, every man carries a wound. And the wound is nearly always given by his father.

A MAN'S DEEPEST QUESTION

On a warm August afternoon several years ago my boys and I were rock climbing in a place called Garden of the Gods, near our home. The red sandstone spires there look like the dorsal fins of some great beast that has just surfaced from the basement of time. We all love to climb, and our love for it goes beyond the adventure. There's something about facing a wall of rock, accepting its challenge and mastering it that calls you out, tests and affirms what you are made of. Besides, the boys are going to climb everything anyway — the refrigerator, the banister, the neighbor's grape arbor — so we might as well take it outside. And it's an excuse to buy some really cool gear. Anyway, when I climb with the boys we always top-rope, meaning that before the ascent I'll rig protection from the top of the rock down, enabling me to belay from the bottom. That way I can coach them as they go, see their every move, help them through the tough spots. Sam was the first to climb that afternoon, and after he clipped the rope into his harness, he began his attempt.

Things were going well until he hit a bit of an overhang, which even though you're roped in makes you feel exposed and more than a little vulnerable. Sam was unable to get over it and he began to get more and more scared the longer he hung there; tears were soon to follow. So with gentle reassurance I told him to head back down, that we didn't need to climb this rock today, that I knew of another one that might be more fun. "No," he said, "I want to do this." I understood. There comes a time when we simply have to face the challenges in our lives and stop backing down. So I helped him up the overhang with a bit of a boost, and on he went with greater speed and confidence. "Way to go, Sam! You're looking good. That's it . . . now reach up to your right . . . yep, now push off that foothold . . . nice move."

Notice what a crucial part of any male sport this sort of "shop talk" is. It's our way of affirming each other without looking like we're affirming. Men rarely praise each other directly, as women do: "Ted, I absolutely love your shorts. You look terrific today." We praise indirectly, by way of our accomplishments: "Whoa, nice shot, Ted. You've got a wicked swing today." As Sam ascended, I was offering words of advice and exhortation. He came to another challenging spot, but this time sailed right over it. A few more moves and he would be at the top. "Way to go, Sam. You're a *wild man*." He finished the climb, and as he walked down from the back side I began to get Blaine clipped in. Ten or fifteen minutes passed, and the story was forgotten to me. But not Sam. While I was coaching his brother up the rock, Sam sort of sidled up to me and in a quiet voice asked, "Dad . . . did you really think I was a wild man up there?"

Miss that moment and you'll miss a boy's heart forever. It's not a question — it's *the* question, the one every boy and man is longing to ask. Do I have what it takes? Am I powerful? Until a man *knows* he's a man he will forever be trying to prove he is one, while at the same time shrink from anything that might reveal he is not. Most men live their lives haunted by the question, or crippled by the answer they've been given.

WHERE DOES MASCULINITY COME FROM?

In order to understand how a man receives a wound, you must understand the central truth of a boy's journey to manhood: Masculinity is *bestowed.* A boy learns who is he and what he's got from a man, or the company of men. He cannot learn it any other place. He cannot learn it from other boys, and he cannot learn it from the world of women. The plan from the beginning of time was that his father would lay the foundation for a young boy's heart, and pass on to him that essential knowledge and confidence in his strength. Dad would be the first man in his life, and forever the most important man. Above all, he would answer *the question* for his son and give him his name. Throughout the history of man given to us in Scripture, it is the father who gives the blessing and thereby "names" the son.

Adam receives his name from God, and also the power of naming. He names Eve, and I believe it is therefore safe to say he also names their sons. We know Abraham names Isaac, and though Isaac's sons Jacob and Esau are apparently named by their mother, they desperately crave the *blessing* that can only come from their father's hand. Jacob gets the blessing, and nearly a century later, leaning on his staff, he passes it on to his sons — he gives them a name and an identity. "You are a lion's cub, O Judah . . . Issachar is a rawboned donkey . . . Dan will be a serpent . . . Gad will be attacked by a band of raiders, but he will attack them at their heels . . . Joseph is a fruitful vine . . . his bow remained steady" (Gen. 49:9, 14, 17, 19, 22, 24). The Baptist's father names him John, even though the rest of the family was going to name him after his father, Zechariah. Even Jesus needed to hear those words of affirmation from his Father. After he is baptized in the Jordan, before the brutal attack on his identity in the wilderness, his Father speaks: "You are my Son, whom I love; with you I am well pleased" (Luke 3:22). In other words, "Jesus, I am deeply proud of you; you have what it takes."

One father-naming story in particular intrigues me. It centers around Benjamin, the last son born to Jacob. Rachel gives birth to the boy, but she will die as a result. With her last breath she names him Ben-Oni, which means "son of my sorrow." But Jacob intervenes and names him Benjamin — "son of my right hand" (Gen. 35:18). This is the critical move, when a boy draws his identity no longer from the mother, but from the father. Notice that it took an active *intervention* by the man; it always does.

MOTHERS AND SONS

A boy is brought into the world by his mother, and she is the center of his universe in those first tender months and years. She suckles him, nurtures him, protects him; she sings to him, reads to him, watches over him, as the old saying goes, "like a mother hen." She often names him as well, tender names like "my little lamb," or "Mama's little sweetheart," or even "my little boyfriend." But a boy cannot grow to manhood with a name like that, let alone a name like "son of my sorrow," and there comes a time for the shift when he begins to seek out his father's affection and attention. He wants to play catch with Dad, and wrestle with him, spend time outside together, or in his workshop. If

Dad works outside the home, as most do, then his return in the evening becomes the biggest event of the boy's day. Stasi can tell you when it happened for each of our boys. This is a very hard time in a mother's life, when the father replaces her as the sun of the boy's universe. It is part of Eve's sorrow, this letting go, this being replaced.

Few mothers do it willingly; very few do it well. Many women ask their sons to fill a void in their soul that their husband has left. But the boy has a question that needs an answer, and he cannot get the answer from his mother. Femininity can never bestow masculinity. My mother would often call me "sweetheart," but my father called me "tiger." Which direction do you think a boy would want to head? He will still turn to his mother for comfort (who does he run to when he skins his knee?), but he turns to Dad for adventure, for the chance to test his strength, and most of all, to get the answer to his question. A classic example of these dueling roles took place the other night. We were driving down the road and the boys were talking about the kind of car they want to get when it comes time for their first set of wheels. "I was thinking about a Humvee, or a motorcycle, maybe even a tank. What do you think, Dad?" "I'd go with the Humvee.

We could mount a machine gun on top." "What about you, Mom — what kind of car do you want me to have?" You know what she said . . . "A safe one."

Stasi is a wonderful mother; she has bitten her tongue so many times I wonder that she still has one, as she holds her peace while the boys and I rush off to some adventure begging destruction or bloodshed. Her first reaction — "a safe one" — is so natural, so understandable. After all, she is the incarnation of God's tenderness. But if a mother will not allow her son to become dangerous, if she does not let the father take him away, she will emasculate him. I just read a story of a mother, divorced from her husband, who was furious that he wanted to take the boy hunting. She tried to get a restraining order to prevent him from teaching the boy about guns. That is emasculation. "My mom wouldn't let me play with GI Joe," a young man told me. Another said, "We lived back east, near an amusement park. It had a roller coaster — the old wooden kind. But my mom would never let me go." That is emasculation, and the boy needs to be rescued from it by the active intervention of the father, or another man.

This kind of intervention is powerfully

portrayed in the movie *A Perfect World*. Kevin Costner plays an escaped convict who takes a young boy hostage and heads for the state line. But as the story unfolds, we see that what looks like the boy's ruin is actually his *redemption*. The boy is in his underpants when Costner abducts him. That is where many mothers want to keep their sons, albeit unconsciously. She wants her little lamb close by. Over the days that follow, days "together on the road" I might add, Costner and the boy — who has no father — grow close. When he learns that the boy's mother has never allowed him to ride a roller coaster, Costner is outraged. The next scene is the boy, arms high in the air, rolling up and down country roads on the roof of the station wagon. That's the invitation into a man's world, a world involving danger. Implicit in the invitation is the *affirmation*, "You can handle it; you belong here."

There comes a moment when Costner buys the boy a pair of pants (the symbolism in the film is amazing), but the boy won't change in front of him. He is a shy, timid boy who has yet to even smile in the story. Costner senses something is up.

"What's the matter — you don't want

me to see your pecker?"
"It's . . . puny."
"What?"
"It's puny."
"Who told you that?"

The boy, Phillip, is silent. It is the silence of emasculation and shame. The absence of the father's voice is loud and clear. So Costner intervenes, and speaks. "Lemme see . . . go on, I'll shoot you straight." The boy reluctantly bares himself. "No, Phillip. That's a good size for a boy your age." A smile breaks out on his face, like the sun coming up, and you know a major threshold has been crossed for him.

FROM STRENGTH TO STRENGTH

Masculinity is an *essence* that is hard to articulate but that a boy naturally craves as he craves food and water. It is something passed between men. "The traditional way of raising sons," notes Robert Bly, "which lasted for thousands and thousands of years, amounted to fathers and sons living in close — murderously close — proximity, while the father taught the son a trade: perhaps farming or carpentry or blacksmithing or tailoring." My father taught me to fish. We would spend long days together, out in a boat on a lake, trying to catch fish. I will never, ever forget his delight in me when I'd hook one. But the fish were never really the important thing. It was the delight, the contact, the masculine presence gladly bestowing itself on me. "Atta boy, Tiger! Bring him in! That's it . . . well done!" Listen to men when they talk warmly of their fathers and you'll hear the same. "My father taught me to fix tractors . . . to throw a curveball . . . to hunt quail." And despite the details, what is mostly passed along is the masculine blessing.

"Fathers and sons in most tribal cultures live in an amused tolerance of each other," says Bly. "The son has a lot to learn, and so the father and son spend hours trying and failing together to make arrowheads or to repair a spear or track a clever animal. When a father and son spend long hours together, which some fathers and sons still do, we could say that a substance almost like food passes from the older body to the younger." This is why my boys love to wrestle with me — why any healthy boy wants the same with his father. They love the physical contact, to brush against my cheek, feel the sandpaper of my whiskers, my strength all around them, and to test theirs on me.

And it's that *testing* that is so essential. As they've gotten older, they love to start punching matches with me. Luke just did it this morning. I'm downstairs fixing breakfast; Luke senses the opportunity, and he sneaks downstairs and silently stalks me; when he's in range, he lets loose a wallop. It hurts, and *they need to see* that it hurts. Do they have a strength like Dad's? Is it growing, real, substantive? I'll never forget the day when Sam gave me a bloody lip, quite by accident, when we were wrestling. At first he drew back in fear, waiting, I'm sorry to admit, for my anger. Thankfully, on this occasion I just wiped the blood away, smiled, and said, "Whoa . . . nice shot." He beamed; no, he *strutted.* Shook his antlers at me. Word quickly spread through the house and his younger brothers were on the scene, eyes wide at the fact that one of them had drawn blood. New possibilities opened up. Maybe young bucks can take on the old bull.

"The ancient societies believed that a boy becomes a man only through ritual and effort — only through the 'active intervention of the older men,'" Bly reminds us. The father or another man must actively intervene, and the mother must let go. Bly tells the story of one tribal ritual, which involves as they all do the men taking the boy away for initiation. But in this case, when he returns, the boy's mother pretends not to know him. She asks to be introduced to "the young man." That is a beautiful picture of how a mother can cooperate in her son's passage to the father's world. If she does not, things get very messy later — especially in marriage. The boy develops a bond with his mother that is like emotional incest. His loyalties are divided. That is why Scripture says, "For this reason *a man will leave* his father and mother and be united to his wife" (Gen. 2:24, emphasis added).

Sometimes, when the mother clings, the boy will try to tear himself away, violently. This typically comes in the teenage years and often involves some ugly behavior, maybe some foul words on the part of the young man. She feels rejected, and he feels guilty, but he knows he *must* get away. This was my story, and my relationship with my mother has never been good since. I've found that many, many adult men resent their mothers but cannot say why. They simply know they do not want to be close to them; they rarely call. As my friend Dave confessed, "I hate calling my mom. She always says something like, 'It's so good to hear your little voice.' I'm twenty-five and she still wants to call me her little lamb." Somehow, he senses that proximity to his mother endangers his masculine journey, as though he might be sucked back in. It is an irrational fear, but it reveals that both essential ingredients in his passage were missing: Mom did not let go, and Dad did not take him away.

Whatever the mother's failure, it can be overcome by the father's engagement. Let's come back to the rock climbing story with Sam. "Did you really think I was a wild man up there?" He did not ask, "Do you think I am a nice boy?" He asked about his strength, his dangerous capacity to really come through. A boy's passage into manhood involves many of those moments. The father's role is to arrange for them, invite his boy into them, keep his eye out for the moment the question arises and then speak into his son's heart *yes, you are.* You have what it takes. And that is why the deepest wound is always given by the father. As Buechner says, "If strangers and strange sights can shake the world of children, it takes the people they know and love best to pull it out from under them like a chair."

THE FATHER-WOUND

Dave remembers the day the wound came. His parents were having an argument in the kitchen, and his father was verbally abusing his mother. Dave took his mom's side, and his father exploded. "I don't remember all that was said, but I do remember his last words: 'You are such a mama's boy,' he yelled at me. Then he walked out." Perhaps if Dave had a strong relationship with his dad most of the time, a wound like this might be lessened, healed later by words of love. But the blow came after years of distance between them. Dave's father was often gone from morning till night with his own business, and so they rarely spent time together. What is more, Dave felt a lingering disappointment from his dad. He wasn't a star athlete, which he knew his dad highly valued. He had a spiritual hunger and often attended church, which his dad did not value. And so those words fell like a final blow, a death sentence.

Leanne Payne says that when the father-son relationship is right, "the quiet tree of masculine strength within the father protects and nurtures the fragile stripling of masculinity within his son." Dave's father took an ax and gave his hardest blow to his young tree. How I wish it were a rare case, but I am deeply sorry to say I've heard countless stories like it. There's a young boy named Charles who loved to play the piano, but his father and brothers were jocks. One day they came back from the gym to find him at the keyboard, and who knows what else had built up years of scorn and contempt in his father's soul, but his son received both barrels: "You are such a faggot." A man my father's age told me of growing up during the depression; times were hard for his family, and his father, an alcoholic rarely employed, hired him out to a nearby farmer. One day while he was in the field he saw his father's car pull up; he hadn't seen him for weeks, and he raced to meet his dad. Before he could get there his father had grabbed the check for his son's wages, and, spying the boy running toward him, he jumped in the car and sped away. The boy was five years old.

In the case of violent fathers, the boy's question is answered in a devastating way. "Do I have what it takes? Am I a man, Papa?" No, you are a mama's boy, an idiot, a faggot, a seagull. Those are defining sentences that shape a man's life. The assault wounds are like a shotgun blast to the chest. This can get unspeakably evil when it involves physical, sexual, or verbal abuse carried on for years. Without some kind of help, many men never recover. One thing about the assault wounds — they are obvious. The passive wounds are not; they are pernicious, like a cancer. Because they are subtle, they often go unrecognized as wounds and therefore are actually more difficult to heal.

My father was in many ways a good man. He introduced me to the West, and taught me to fish and to camp. I still remember the fried egg sandwiches he would make us for dinner. It was his father's ranch that I worked on each summer, and my dad and I saw a lot of the West together as we'd make the long drive from southern California to Oregon, often with fishing detours through Idaho and Montana. But like so many men of his era, my father had never faced the issues of his own wounds, and he fell to drinking when his life began to take a downhill turn. I was about eleven or twelve at the time — a very critical age in the masculine journey, the age when the question really begins to surface. At the very moment when I am desperately wondering what it means to be a man, and do I have what it takes, my father checked out, went silent. He had a workshop out back, attached to the garage, and he would spend his hours out there alone, reading, doing crossword puzzles, and drinking. That is a major wound.

As Bly says, "Not receiving any blessing from your father is an injury . . . Not seeing your father when you are small, never being with him, having a remote father, an absent father, a workaholic father, is an injury." My friend Alex's father died when he was four years old. The sun in his universe set, never to rise again. How is a little boy to understand that? Every afternoon Alex would stand by the front window, waiting for his father to come home. This went on for almost a year. I've had many clients whose fathers simply left and never came back. Stuart's dad did that, just up and left, and his mother, a troubled woman, was unable to raise him. So he was sent to his aunt and uncle. Divorce or abandonment is a wound that lingers because the boy (or girl) believes if they had done things better, Daddy would have stayed.

Some fathers give a wound merely by their silence; they are present, yet absent to their sons. The silence is deafening. I remember as a boy wanting my father to die, and feeling immense guilt for having such a desire. I understand now that I wanted someone to validate the wound. My father was gone, but because he was physically still around, he was not gone. So I lived with a wound no one could see or understand. In the case of silent, passive, or absent fathers, the question goes unanswered. "Do I have what it takes? Am I a man, Daddy?" Their silence is the answer: "I don't know . . . I doubt it . . . you'll have to find out for yourself . . . probably not."

THE WOUND'S EFFECT

Every man carries a wound. I have never met a man without one. No matter how good your life may have seemed to you, you live in a broken world full of broken people. Your mother and father, no matter how wonderful, couldn't have been perfect. She is a daughter of Eve, and he a son of Adam. So there is no crossing through this country without taking a wound. And every wound, whether it's assaultive or passive, delivers with it a *message*. The message feels final and true, absolutely true, because it is delivered with such force. Our reaction to it shapes our personality in very significant ways. From that flows the false self. Most of the men you meet are living out a false self, a pose, which is directly related to his wound. Let me try to make this clear.

The message delivered with my wound (my father disappearing into his own battles) was simply this: *You are on your own, John. There is no one in your corner, no one to show you the way and above all, no one to tell you if you are or are not a man. The core question of your soul has no answer, and can never get one.* What does a boy do with that? First, I became an unruly teen. I got kicked out of school, had a police record. We often misunderstand that behavior as "adolescent rebellion," but those are cries for involvement, for *engagement.* Even after God's dramatic rescue of me at the age of nineteen, when I became a Christian, the wound remained. As my dear friend Brent said, "Becoming a Christian doesn't necessarily fix things. My arrows were still lodged deep and refused to allow some angry wounds inside to heal."

I mentioned earlier that for years I was a very driven man, a perfectionist, a hard-charger, and a fiercely independent man. The world rewards that kind of drivenness; most of the successful men reading this book are driven. But behind me was a string of casualties — people I had hurt, or dismissed — including my own father. There was the near casualty of my marriage and there was certainly the casualty of my own heart. For to live a driven life you have to literally shove your heart down, or drive it with whips. You can never admit need, never admit brokenness. This is the story of the creation of that false self. And if you had asked my wife during the first ten years of our marriage if we had a good relationship, she probably would have said yes. But if you had asked her if something was missing, if she sensed a fatal flaw, she would have immediately been able to tell you: he doesn't need me. That was my vow, you see. *I won't need anyone.* After all, the wound was deep and unhealed, and the message it brought seemed so final: I am on my own.

Another friend, Stan, is a successful attorney and a genuinely good guy. When he was about fifteen, his father committed suicide — stuck a gun in his mouth and pulled the trigger. His family tried to put it all behind them, sweep it under the rug. They never spoke of it again. The message delivered by that gruesome blow was something like this: *Your background is very dark, the masculine in your family cannot even be spoken of, anything wild is violent and evil.* The effect was another sort of vow: "I will never do anything even remotely dangerous, or risky, or wild. I will never be like my dad (how many men live with that vow?). I won't take one step in that direction. I will be the nicest guy you ever met." You know what? He is. Stan's the nicest guy you could meet — gentle, creative, caring, soft-spoken. And now he hates that about himself; he hates the thought that he's a pushover, that he won't take you on, can't say no, can't stand up for himself.

Those are the two basic options. Men either overcompensate for their wound and become driven (violent men), or they shrink back and go passive (retreating men). Often it's an odd mixture of both. Witness the twin messages sported by young college-age men especially: a goatee, which says, "I'm kind of dangerous," and a baseball hat turned backward, which says, "But really I'm a little boy; don't require anything of me." Which is it? Are you strong, or are you weak? Remember Alex, who stood at the door waiting for a daddy who would never return? You wouldn't in a million years have guessed that was his story if you'd known him in college. He was a man's man, an incredible football player. A hard-drinking, hard-living man every guy looked up to. He drove a truck, chewed tobacco, loved the outdoors. He used to eat glass. I'm serious. It was a sort of frat party trick he took on, the ultimate display of dangerous strength.

He'd literally take a bite out of a glass, chew it slowly and swallow it. When he worked as a bouncer for a tough bar, it made a pretty impressive show to get the roughnecks in line. But it was a show — the whole macho-man persona.

Charles, the artistic boy, the piano player whose father called him a "faggot" — what do you think happened there? He never played the piano again after that day. Years later, as a man in his late twenties, he does not know what to do with his life. He has no passion, cannot find a career to love. And so he cannot commit to the woman he loves, cannot marry her because he is so uncertain of himself. But of course — his heart was taken out, way back there in his story. Dave is also in his twenties now, drifting, deeply insecure, and loaded with a great deal of self-hatred. He does not feel like a man and he believes he never will. Like so many, he struggles with confidence around women and around men he sees as real men. Stuart, whose father abandoned him, became a man without emotion. His favorite character as a boy was Spock, the alien in *Star Trek* who lives solely from his mind. Stuart is now a scientist and his wife is immensely lonely.

On and on it goes. The wound comes,

and with it a message. From that place the boy makes a vow, chooses a way of life that gives rise to the false self. At the core of it all is a deep uncertainty. The man doesn't live from a center. So many men feel stuck — either paralyzed and unable to move, or unable to stop moving. Of course, every little girl has her own story too. But I want to save that for a later chapter, and bring it together with how a man fights for a woman's heart. Let me say a few more words about what happens to a man after the wound is given.

Chapter Five

THE BATTLE FOR A MAN'S HEART

Now you're out there God knows where
You're one of the walking wounded.

> — JAN KRIST
> "Walking Wounded"
> by Ian Krist
> and Paul Murphy

To give a man back his heart is the hardest mis-
sion on earth.

> — FROM THE MOVIE *MICHAEL*

Nothing worth having comes without some kind
of fight.

> — BRUCE COCKBURN
> "Lovers in a Dangerous Time"
> (written in 1982 for *Stealing Fire*)

A few years ago now my middle son, Blaine, made the big transition to first grade. That's a huge step for any child — leaving the comfort and safety of Mom's side, spending all day at school, being among the "big kids." But Blaine's a very outgoing and winsome boy, a born leader, and we knew he'd handle it swimmingly. Every night at the dinner table he regaled us with tales of the day's adventures. It was fun to recall with him the joys of those early school days — a shiny new lunchbox, brand-new yellow No. 2 pencils, a box of Crayolas with a *built-in sharpener,* a new desk, and new friends. We heard all about his new teacher, gym class, what they played at recess, how he was emerging as a leader in all the games. But then one night he was silent. "What's wrong, Tiger?" I asked. He wouldn't say, wouldn't even look up. "What happened?" He didn't want to talk about it. Finally, the story came out — a bully. Some first-grade poser had pushed him down on the playground in front of all his friends. Tears were streaming down his cheeks as he told us the story.

"Blaine, look at me." He raised his tearful eyes slowly, reluctantly. There was shame written all over his face. "I want you to listen very closely to what I am about to say. The next time that bully pushes you down, here is what I want you to do — are you listening, Blaine?" He nodded, his big wet eyes fixed on mine. "I want you to get up . . . and I want you to hit him . . . as hard as you possibly can." A look of embarrassed delight came over Blaine's face. Then he smiled.

THE BATTLE FOR A MAN'S HEART

Good Lord — why did I give him such advice? And why was he delighted with it? Why are some of *you* delighted with it, while others are appalled?

Yes, I know that Jesus told us to turn the other cheek. But we have really misused that verse. You cannot teach a boy to use his strength *by stripping him of it*. Jesus was able to retaliate, believe me. But he chose not to. And yet we suggest that a boy who is mocked, shamed before his fellows, stripped of all power and dignity should stay in that beaten place because Jesus wants him there? You will emasculate him for life. From that point on all will be passive and fearful. He will grow up never knowing how to stand his ground, never knowing if he is a man indeed. Oh yes, he will be courteous, sweet even, deferential, minding all his manners. It may look moral, it may look like turning the other cheek, but it is merely *weakness*. You cannot turn a cheek you do not have. Our churches are full of such men.

At that moment, Blaine's soul was hanging in the balance. Then the fire came back into his eyes and the shame disappeared. But for many, many men their souls still hang in the balance because no one, *no one* has ever invited them to be dangerous, to know their own strength, to discover that they have what it takes. "I feel there is this stormy ocean within me, and I keep trying to make those waters calm and placid," confessed a young friend in his early twenties. "I would love to be dangerous," he said, sighing. "You mean . . . it's possible? I feel like I have to ask permission." Why on earth would a young man have to ask permission to be a man? Because the assault continues long after the wound has been given. I don't mean to create a wrong impression — a man is not wounded once, but many, many times in the course of his life. Nearly every blow ends up falling in the same place: against his strength. Life takes it away, one vertebra at a time, until in the end he has no spine at all.

FINISHING HIM OFF

I read a case a few years ago about a baby boy who suffered a terrible blow during surgery: his penis was "accidentally removed." The event took place back in the '70s, and a decision was made that reflected the widely held belief that "sex roles" are not truly part of our design, but merely shaped by culture and therefore interchangeable. His genitalia were reconstructed in female form, and he was raised as a girl. That story is a parable of our times. It is exactly what we've tried to do to boys, starting from when they are very young. As Christina Hoff Sommers says in her book *The War Against Boys*, "It's a bad time to be a boy in America." Our culture has turned against the masculine essence, aiming to cut it off early. As one example she points to the way in which the shootings at Columbine High School in Littleton, Colorado, are being used against boys in general.

Most of you will remember the tragic story from April 1999. Two boys walked into the school library and began shooting; when it was all over, thirteen victims and their two assailants were dead. Sommers is alarmed about the remarks of William Pollack, director of the Center for Men at McLean Hospital, and so am I. Here is what he said: "The boys in Littleton are the tip of the iceberg. And the iceberg is *all* boys." The idea, widely held in our culture, is that the aggressive nature of boys is inherently bad, and we have to make them into something more like girls. The primary tool for that operation is our public school system. The average schoolteacher faces an incredible challenge: to bring order to a room of boys and girls, and promote learning. The main obstacle to that noble goal is getting the boys to sit still, keep quiet, and pay attention . . . for an entire day. You might as well hold back the tide. That's not the way a boy is wired, and it's not the way a boy learns. Rather than changing the way we do male education, we try to change males.

As Lionel Tiger reports in his book *The Decline of Males*, boys are three to four times more likely than girls to be diagnosed as suffering from attention deficit disorder (ADD). But maybe they're not sick, maybe, as Tiger says, "This may simply mean they enjoy large-muscle movements and assertive actions . . . Boys as a group appear to prefer relatively boisterous and mobile activities to the sedate and physically restricted behavior that school systems reward and to which girls seem to be more inclined."

Tell me about it. This guy ought to come over to our house for dinner. With three boys at the table (and one man, but with a boyish heart), things get pretty wild at times. Chairs, for the most part, are an option. The boys use them more like gymnastic equipment than restraints. Just the other night, I look over to see Blaine balancing across his chair on his stomach, like an acrobat. At the same moment Luke, our youngest, is nowhere to be seen. Or rather, in the place at the table where his head should be, we can only see a pair of socks, pointing straight up. My wife rolls her eyes. But not our school systems. As Tiger says,

> At least three to four times as many boys than girls are essentially defined as ill because their preferred patterns of play don't fit easily into the structure of the school. Well-meaning psycho-managers then prescribe tranquilizing drugs for ADD, such as Ritalin . . . The situation is scandalous. The use of drugs so disproportionately among boys betrays the failure of school authorities to understand sex differences . . . The only disease these boys may have is being male.

But it's not just the schools. (Many of

them, by the way, are doing a heroic job.) How about our churches? A young man recently came to me very angry and distraught. He was frustrated at the way his father, a church leader, was coaching him in sports. He's a basketball player and his team had made the city finals. The night of the big game, as he was heading out the door, his father literally stopped him and said, "Now don't go out there and 'kick butt' — that's just not a nice thing to do." I am not making this up. What a ridiculous thing to say to a seventeen-year-old athlete. Go out there and give 'em . . . well, don't give 'em anything. Just be nice. Be the nicest guy the opposing team has ever met. In other words, be *soft*. That is a perfect example of what the church tells men. Someone I read said the church may have a masculine exterior, but its soul has turned feminine.

Emasculation happens in marriage as well. Women are often attracted to the wilder side of a man, but once having caught him they settle down to the task of domesticating him. Ironically, if he gives in he'll resent her for it, and she in turn will wonder where the passion has gone. Most marriages wind up there. A weary and lonely woman asked me the other day, "How do I get my husband to come alive?"

"Invite him to be dangerous," I said. "You mean, I should let him get the motorcycle, right?" "Yep." She shrank back, disappointment on her face. "I know you're right, but I hate the idea. I've made him tame for years."

Think back to that great big lion in that tiny cage. Why would we put a man in a cage? For the same reason we put a lion there. For the same reason we put God there: he's dangerous. To paraphrase Sayers, we've also pared the claws of the Lion *Cub* of Judah. A man is a dangerous thing. Women don't start wars. Violent crimes aren't for the most part committed by women. Our prisons aren't filled with women. Columbine wasn't the work of two young girls. Obviously, something has gone wrong in the masculine soul, and the way we've decided to handle it is to take that dangerous nature away . . . entirely.

"We know that our society produces a plentiful supply of boys," says Robert Bly, "but seems to produce fewer and fewer men." There are two simple reasons: We don't know how to initiate boys into men; and second, *we're not sure we really want to.* We want to socialize them, to be sure, but *away from* all that is fierce, and wild, and passionate. In other words, away from masculinity and toward something more feminine. But as Sommers says, we have forgotten a simple truth: "The energy, competitiveness, and corporal daring of normal, decent males is responsible for much of what is right in the world." Sommers reminds us that during the Columbine massacre, "Seth Houy threw his body over a terrified girl to shield her from the bullets; fifteen-year-old Daniel Rohrbough paid with his life when, at mortal risk to himself, he held a door open so others could escape."

That strength so essential to men is also what makes them *heroes*. If a neighborhood is safe, it's because of the strength of men. Slavery was stopped by the strength of men, at a terrible price to them and their families. The Nazis were stopped by men. Apartheid wasn't defeated by women. Who gave their seats up on the lifeboats leaving the *Titanic*, so that women and children would be saved? And have we forgotten — it was a Man who let himself be nailed to Calvary's cross. This isn't to say women can't be heroic. I know many heroic women. It's simply to remind us that God made men the way they are because we desperately *need* them to be the way they are. Yes, a man is a dangerous thing. So is a scalpel. It can wound or it can save your life. You don't make it safe by making it dull; you put it in the hands of someone who knows what he's doing.

If you've spent any time around horses, you know a stallion can be a major problem. They're strong, very strong, and they've got a mind of their own. Stallions typically don't like to be bridled, and they can get downright aggressive — especially if there are mares around. A stallion is hard to tame. If you want a safer, quieter animal, there's an easy solution: castrate him. A gelding is much more compliant. You can lead him around by the nose; he'll do what he's told without putting up a fuss. There's only one problem: Geldings don't give life. They can't come through for you the way a stallion can. A stallion is dangerous all right, but if you want the life he offers, you have to have the danger too. They go together.

WHAT'S REALLY GOING ON HERE, ANYWAY?

Let's say it's June 6, 1944, about 0710. You are a soldier in the third wave onto Omaha Beach. Thousands of men have gone before you and now it is your turn. As you jump out of the Higgins boat and wade to the beach, you see the bodies of fallen soldiers everywhere — floating in the water, tossing in the surf, lying on the beach. Moving up the sand you encounter hundreds of wounded men. Some are limping toward the bluffs with you, looking for shelter. Others are barely crawling. Snipers on the cliffs above continue to take them out. Everywhere you look, there are pain and brokenness. The damage is almost overwhelming. When you reach the cliffs, the only point of safety, you find squads of men with no leader. They are shell-shocked, stunned and frightened. Many have lost their weapons; most of them refuse to move. They are paralyzed with fear. Taking all this in, what would you conclude? What would be your assessment of the situation? Whatever else went through your mind, you'd have to admit, *This is one brutal war*, and no one would have disagreed or thought you odd for having said so.

But we do not think so clearly about life and I'm not sure why. Have a look around you — what do you observe? What do you see in the lives of the men that you work with, live by, go to church alongside? Are they full of passionate freedom? Do they fight well? Are their women deeply grateful for how well their men have loved them? Are their children radiant with affirmation? The idea is almost laughable, if it weren't so tragic. Men have been taken out right and left. Scattered across the neighborhood lie the shattered lives of men (and women) who have died at a soul-level from the wounds they've taken. You've heard the expression, "he's a shell of a man?" They have lost heart. Many more are alive, but badly wounded. They are trying to crawl forward, but are having an awful time getting their lives together; they seem to keep taking hits. You know others who are already captives, languishing in prisons of despair, addiction, idleness, or boredom. The place looks like a battlefield, the Omaha Beach of the soul.

And that is precisely what it is. We are now in the late stages of the long and vicious war against the human heart. I know — it sounds overly dramatic. I almost didn't use the term "war" at all, for fear of being dismissed at this point as one more in the group of "Chicken Littles," Christians who run around trying to get everybody worked up over some imaginary fear in order to advance their political or economic or theological cause. But I am not hawking fear at all; I am speaking honestly about the nature of what is unfolding around us . . . *against us.* And until we call the situation what it is, we will not know what to do about it. In fact, this is where many people feel abandoned or betrayed by God. They thought that becoming a Christian would somehow end their troubles, or at least reduce them considerably. No one ever told them they were being moved to the front lines, and they seem genuinely shocked at the fact that they've been shot at.

After the Allies took the beachhead at Normandy, the war wasn't over. In some ways, it had just begun. Stephen Ambrose has given us many unforgettable stories of what followed that famous landing in *Citizen Soldiers*, his record of how the Allies won the war. Many of those stories are almost parables in their meaning. Here is one that followed on the heels of D-Day. It is June 7, 1944:

Brig. Gen. Norman "Dutch" Cota, assistant division commander of the 29th, came on a group of infantry pinned down by some Germans in a farmhouse. He asked the captain in command why his men were making no effort to take the building. "Sir, the Germans are in there, shooting at us," the captain replied. "Well, I'll tell you what, captain," said Cota, unbuckling two grenades from his jacket. "You and your men start shooting at them. I'll take a squad of men and you and your men watch carefully. I'll show you how to take a house with Germans in it." Cota led his squad around a hedge to get as close as possible to the house. Suddenly, he gave a whoop and raced forward, the squad following, yelling like wild men. As they tossed grenades into the windows, Cota and another man kicked in the front door, tossed a couple of grenades inside, waited for the explosions, then dashed into the house. The surviving Germans inside were streaming out the back door, running for their lives. Cota returned to the captain. "You've seen how to take a house," said the general, still out of breath. "Do you understand? Do you know how to do it now?" "Yes, sir."

What can we learn from the parable? Why were those guys pinned down? First, they seemed almost surprised that they were being shot at. "They're shooting at us, sir." Hello? That's what happens in war — you get shot at. Have you forgotten? We were born into a world at war. This scene we're living in is no sitcom; it's bloody battle. Haven't you noticed with what deadly accuracy the wound was given? Those blows you've taken — they were not random accidents at all. They hit dead center. Charles was meant to be a pianist, but he never touched the piano again. I have a gift and calling to speak into the hearts of men and women. But my wound tempted me to be a loner, live far from my heart and from others. Craig's calling is to preach the gospel, like his father and great-grandfather. His wound was an attempt to take that out. He's a seagull, remember? All he can do is "squawk." I failed to mention Reggie earlier. His dad wounded him when he tried to excel in school. "You are so stupid; you'll never make it through college." He wanted to be a doctor, but he never followed his dream.

On and on it goes. The wound is too well aimed and far too consistent to be accidental. It was an attempt to take you out; to cripple or destroy your strength and get you out of the action. The wounds we've taken were leveled against us with stunning accuracy. Hopefully, you're getting the picture. Do you know why there's been such an assault? The Enemy fears you. You are dangerous big-time. If you ever really got your heart back, lived from it with courage, you would be a huge problem to him. You would do a lot of damage . . . on the side of good. Remember how valiant and effective

God has been in the history of the world? You are a stem of that victorious stalk.

Let me come back to the second lesson of the parable from D-Day plus one. The other reason those men were lying there, pinned down, unable to move is because no one had ever shown them how to take a house before. They had been trained, but not for that. Most men have never been initiated into manhood. They have never had anyone show them how to do it, and especially, how to fight for their heart. The failure of so many fathers, the emasculating culture, and the passive church have left men without direction.

That is why I have written this book. I am here to tell you that you *can* get your heart back. But I need to warn you — if you want your heart back, if you want the wound healed and your strength restored and to find your true name, you're going to have to fight for it. Notice your reaction to my words. Does not something in you stir a little, a yearning to live? And doesn't another voice rush in, urging caution, maybe wanting to dismiss me altogether? *He's being melodramatic. What arrogance.* Or, *maybe some guys could, but not me.* Or, *I don't know . . . is this really worth it?* That's part of the battle, right there. See? I'm not making this up.

OUR SEARCH FOR AN ANSWER

First and foremost, we still need to know what we never heard, or heard so badly, from our fathers. We *need to know* who we are and if we have what it takes. What do we do now with that ultimate question? Where do we go to find an answer? In order to help you find the answer to The Question, let me ask you another: What *have* you done with your question? Where have you taken it? You see, a man's core question does not go away. He may try for years to shove it out of his awareness, and just "get on with life." But it does not go away. It is a hunger so essential to our souls that it will compel us to find a resolution. In truth, it drives everything we do.

I spent a few days this fall with a very successful man I'll call Peter. He was hosting me for a conference on the East Coast, and when Peter picked me up at the airport he was driving a new Land Rover with all the bells and whistles. *Nice car,* I thought. *This guy is doing well.* The next day we drove around in his BMW 850CSi. Peter lived in the largest house in town, and had a vacation home in Portugal. None of this wealth was inherited; he worked for every dime. He loved Formula One racing, and fly-fishing for salmon in Nova Scotia. I genuinely liked him. *Now here's a man,* I said to myself. And yet, there was something missing. You'd think a guy like this would be confident, self-assured, centered. And of course, he seemed like that at first. But as we spent time together I found him to be . . . hesitant. He had all the appearances of masculinity, but none of it felt like it was coming from a true center.

After several hours of conversation, he admitted he was coming to a revelation. "I lost my father earlier this year to cancer. But I did not cry when he died. You see, we were never really close." Ah yes, I knew what was coming next. "All these years, knocking myself out to get ahead . . . I wasn't even enjoying myself. What was it for? I see now . . . I was trying to win my father's approval." A long, sad silence. Then Peter said quietly, through tears, "It never worked." Of course not; it never does. No matter how much you make, no matter how far you go in life, that will never heal your wound or tell you who you are. But, oh how many men buy into this one.

After years of trying to succeed in the world's eyes, a friend still clings stubbornly to that idea. Sitting in my office, bleeding from all his wounds, he says to me, "Who's the real stud? The guy making money." You understand that he's not making much, so he can still chase the illusion.

Men take their souls' search for validation in all sorts of directions. Brad is a good man who for so many years now has been searching for a sense of significance through belonging. As he said, "Out of my wounds I figured out how to get life: I'll find a group to belong to, do something incredible that others will want, and I'll be somebody." First it was the right gang of kids in school; then it was the wrestling team; years later, it was the right ministry team. It has been a desperate search, by his own admission. And it hasn't gone well. When things didn't work out earlier this year at the ministry he was serving, he knew he had to leave. "My heart has burst and all the wounds and arrows have come pouring out. I have never felt such pain. The sentences scream at me, 'I do not belong. I am wanted by no one. I am alone.' "

Where does a man go for a sense of validation? To what he owns? To who pays attention to him? How attractive his wife is? Where he gets to eat out? How well he plays sports? The world cheers the vain search on: Make a million, run for office, get a promotion, hit a home run . . . *be* somebody. Can you feel the mockery of it all? The wounded crawl up the beach while the snipers fire away. But the deadliest place a man ever takes his search, the place every man seems to wind up no matter what trail he's followed, is the woman.

TAKING IT TO EVE

Remember the story of my first kiss, that little darling I fell in love with in the seventh grade and how she made my bicycle fly? I fell in love with Debbie the very same year my father checked out of my story, the year I took my deepest wound. The timing was no coincidence. In a young boy's development, there comes a crucial time when the father must intervene. It arrives early in adolescence, somewhere between the ages of eleven and fifteen, depending on the boy. If that intervention does not happen, the boy is set up for disaster; the next window that opens in his soul is sexuality. Debbie made me feel like a million bucks. I couldn't have put words to it at the time; I had no idea what was really going on. But in my heart I felt I had found the answer to my question. A pretty girl thinks I'm the greatest. What more can a guy ask for? If I've found Juliet, then I must be Romeo.

When she broke up with me, it began

what has been a long and sad story of searching for "the woman that will make me feel like a man." I went from girlfriend to girlfriend trying to get an answer. To be the hero to the beauty — that has been my longing, my image of what it means to really, finally be a man. Bly calls it the search for the Golden-haired Woman.

> He sees a woman across the room, knows immediately that it is "She." He drops the relationship he has, pursues her, feels wild excitement, passion, beating heart, obsession. After a few months, everything collapses; she becomes an ordinary woman. He is confused and puzzled. Then he sees once more a radiant face across the room, and the old certainty comes again. (*Iron John*)

Why is pornography the most addictive thing in the universe for men? Certainly there's the fact that a man is visually wired, that pictures and images arouse men much more than they do women. But the deeper reason is because that seductive beauty reaches down inside and touches your desperate hunger for validation as a man you didn't even know you had, touches it like nothing else most men have ever experienced. You must understand — this is deeper than legs and breasts and good sex. It is mythological. Look at the lengths men will go to find the golden-haired woman. They have fought duels over her beauty; they have fought wars. You see, every man remembers Eve. We are haunted by her. And somehow we believe that if we could find her, get her back, then we'd also recover with her our own lost masculinity.

You'll recall the little boy Philip, from the movie *A Perfect World*? Remember what his fear was? That his penis was puny. That's how many men articulate a sense of emasculation. Later in life a man's worst fear is often impotence. If he can't get an erection, then he hasn't got what it takes. But the opposite is also at work. If a man can feel an erection, well then, he feels powerful. He feels strong. I'm telling you, for many men The Question feels hardwired to his penis. If he can feel like the hero sexually, well, then mister, he's the hero. Pornography is so seductive because what is a wounded, famished man to think when there are literally hundreds of beauties willing to give themselves to him? (Of course, it's not just to him, but when he's alone with the photos, it feels like it's just for him.)

It's unbelievable — how many movies center around this lie? Get the beauty, win her, bed her, and you are the man. You're James Bond. You're a stud. Look carefully at the lyrics to Bruce Springsteen's song, *Secret Garden* (from his *Greatest Hits* recording, 1995):

> She'll let you in her house
> If you come knockin' late at night
> She'll let you in her mouth
> If the words you say are right
> If you pay the price
> She'll let you deep inside
> But there's a secret garden she hides.
> She'll lead you down a path
> There'll be tenderness in the air
> She'll let you come just far enough
> So you know she's really there
> She'll look at you and smile
> And her eyes will say
> She's got a secret garden
> Where everything you want
> Where everything you need
> Will always stay
> A million miles away.

It's a deep lie wedded to a deep truth. Eve *is* a garden of delight (Song 4:16). But she's not everything you want, everything you need — not even close. Of course it will stay a million miles away. You can't get there from here because it's not there. *It's not there.* The answer to your question can never, ever be found there. Don't get me wrong. A woman is a captivating thing. More captivating than anything else in all creation. "The naked woman's body is a portion of eternity too great for the eye of man." Femininity can *arouse* masculinity. Boy oh boy can it. My wife flashes me a little breast, a little thigh, and I'm ready for action. All systems alert. She tells me in a soft voice that I'm a man and I'll leap tall buildings for her. But femininity can never *bestow* masculinity. It's like asking a pearl to give you a buffalo. It's like asking a field of wildflowers to give you a '57 Chevy. They are different substances entirely.

When a man takes his question to the woman what happens is either addiction or emasculation. Usually both.

Dave, whose father blew a hole in his chest when he called him "mama's boy," took his question to the woman. Recently he confessed to me that younger women are his obsession. You can see why — they're less of a threat. A younger woman isn't half the challenge. He can feel more like a man there. Dave's embarrassed by his obsession, but it doesn't stop him. A younger woman feels like the answer to his question *and he's got to get an answer.* But he knows his search is impossible. He admitted to me just the other day, "Even if I marry a beautiful woman, I will always know there is an even more beautiful woman out there somewhere. So I'll wonder — could I have won her?"

It's a lie. As Bly says, it's a search without an end. "We are looking at the source of a lot of desperation in certain men here, and a lot of suffering in certain women." How often I have seen this. A friend's brother hit rock bottom a few years back when his girlfriend broke up with him. He was a really successful guy, a high school star athlete who became a promising young attorney. But he was carrying a wound from an alcoholic, workaholic father who never gave him what every boy craves. Like so many of us, he took his heart with its question to the woman. When she dumped him, my friend said, "it blew him out of the water. He went into a major nosedive, started drinking heavily, smoking. He even left the country. His life was shattered."

This is why so many men secretly fear their wives. She sees him as no one else does, sleeps with him, knows what he's made of. If he has given her the power to validate him as a man, then he has also given her the power to *invalidate* him too. That's the deadly catch. A pastor told me that for years he's been trying to please his wife and she keeps giving him an "F" "What if she is not the report card on you?" I suggested. "She sure feels like it . . . and I'm failing." Another man, Richard, became verbally abusive toward his wife in the early years of their marriage. His vision for his life was that he was meant to be Romeo and therefore, she must be Juliet. When she turned out not to be the Golden-haired Woman, he was furious. Because that meant, you see, that he was not the heroic man. I remember seeing a picture of Julia Roberts without costume and makeup; *Oh,* I realized, *she's just an ordinary woman.*

"He was coming to me for his validation," a young woman told me about the man she was dating. Or, had been dating. She was drawn to him at first, and certainly drawn to the way he was taken with her. "That's why I broke up with him." I was amazed at her perceptiveness and her courage. It's very rare to find, especially in younger women. How wonderful it feels at first to be his obsession. To be thought of as a goddess is pretty heady stuff. But eventually, it all turns from romance to immense pressure on her part. "He kept saying, 'I don't know if I have what it takes and you're telling me I don't.' He'll thank me for it some day."

What's fascinating to note is that homosexuals are actually more clear on this point. They know that what is missing in their hearts is *masculine* love. The problem is that they've sexualized it. Joseph Nicolosi says that homosexuality is an attempt to repair the wound by filling it with masculinity, either the masculine love that was missing or the masculine strength many men feel they do not possess. It, too, is a vain search and that is why the overwhelming number of homosexual relationships do not last, why so many gay men move from one man to another and why so many of them suffer from depression and a host of other addictions. What they need can't be found there.

Why have I said all this about our search for validation and the answer to our question? Because we cannot hear the real answer until we see we've got a false one. So long as we chase the illusion, how can we face reality? The hunger is there; it lives in our souls like a famished craving, no matter what we've tried to fill it with. If you take your question to Eve, it will break your heart. I know this now, after many, many hard years. You can't get your answer there. In fact, you can't get your answer from any of the things men chase after to find their sense of self. There is only one source for the answer to your question. And so no matter where you've taken your question, you've got to take it back. You have to walk away. That is the beginning of your journey.

Chapter Six

THE FATHER'S VOICE

No man, for any considerable period of time, can wear one face to himself and another to the multitude without finally getting bewildered as to which may be the truth.
— NATHANIEL HAWTHORNE

Esse quam videri
To be, rather than to appear

Who can give a man this, his own name?
— GEORGE MACDONALD

Summers in the eastern Oregon sagebrush are hot, dry, and dusty. When the sun was high the temperature could soar into the 90s, so whenever possible we saved most of the hard labor on the ranch for the early morning or late afternoon and evening, when the cool air drifted up from the river valley below. Sometimes we'd fix irrigation ditches during the heat of the day, which for me was a great excuse to get really wet. I'd tromp along in the ditch, letting the warm muddy water soak my jeans. But most of the time we'd head back to the ranch house for a glass of iced tea. Pop loved his tea sweetened with a healthy dose of sugar, the way they drink it in the South. We'd sit at the kitchen table and have a glass or two and talk about the events of the morning, or a plan he had to sell some cattle at the auction, or how he thought we'd spend the afternoon.

One day late in the summer of my thirteenth year, Pop and I had just come in for our ritual when he stood up and walked over to the window. The kitchen faced south and from there gave a view over a large alfalfa field and then on toward the pastureland. Like most ranchers Pop grew his own hay, to provide feed for cattle and horses he kept over the winter. I joined him at the window and saw that a steer had gotten out of the range and into the alfalfa. I remembered my grandfather telling me that it's dangerous for a cow to stuff itself on fresh alfalfa; it expands in their stomach like rising bread and could rupture one of their four chambers. Pop was clearly irritated, as only a cowboy can be irritated at cattle. I, on the other hand, was excited. This meant adventure.

"Go saddle up Tony and get that steer," he said, sitting back in his chair and kicking his boots up on the one in front of him. His demeanor made it clear that he was not going with me; he was, in fact, not going anywhere. As he poured himself another glass of tea my mind raced through the implications of what he'd said. It meant I first had to go catch Tony, the biggest horse on the ranch. I was scared of Tony, but we both knew he was the best cattle horse. I had to saddle him up by myself and ride out to get that steer. Alone. Having processed this information I realized I had been standing there for who knows how long and it was time I got going. As I walked out the back porch toward the corral I felt two things and felt them strongly: fear . . . and honor.

Most of our life-changing moments are realized as such later. I couldn't have told you why, but I knew I'd crossed a threshold in my life as a young man. Pop believed in me, and whatever he saw that I did not, the fact that he believed made me believe it too. I got the steer that day . . . and a whole lot more.

DESPERATE FOR INITIATION

A man needs to know his name. He needs to know he's got what it takes. And I don't mean "know" in the modernistic, rationalistic sense. I don't mean that the thought has passed through your cerebral cortex and you've given it intellectual assent, the way you know about the Battle of Waterloo or the ozone layer — the way most men "know" God or the truths of Christianity. I mean a deep knowing, the kind of knowing that comes when you have been there, entered in, experienced firsthand in an unforgettable way. The way "Adam knew his wife" and she gave birth to a child. Adam didn't know *about* Eve; he knew her intimately, through flesh-and-blood experience at a very deep level. There's knowledge *about* and knowledge *of.* When it comes to our question, we need the latter.

In the movie *Gladiator*, set in the second century A.D., the hero is a warrior from Spain called Maximus. He is the commander of the Roman armies, a general loved by his men and by the aging emperor

Marcus Aurelius. The emperor's foul son Commodus learns of his father's plan to make Maximus emperor in his place, but before Marcus can pronounce his successor, Commodus strangles his father. He sentences Maximus to immediate execution and his wife and son to crucifixion and burning. Maximus escapes, but too late to save his family. Captured by slave traders, he is sold as a gladiator. That fate is normally a death sentence, but this is Maximus, a valiant fighter. He more than survives; he becomes a champion. Ultimately he is taken to Rome to perform in the Coliseum before the emperor Commodus (who of course believes that Maximus is long dead). After a remarkable display of courage and a stunning upset, the emperor comes down into the arena to meet the valiant gladiator, whose identity remains hidden behind his helmet.

MAXIMUS:	My name is Gladiator. (He turns and walks away.)
COMMODUS:	How dare you show your back to me?! Slave! You will remove your helmet and tell me your name.
MAXIMUS:	(Slowly, very slowly

lifts his helmet and
turns to face his
enemy)
My name is Maximus
Decimus Meridius;
Commander of the
Armies of the North;
General of the Felix
Legions;
loyal servant to the
true emperor, Marcus
Aurelius;
father to a murdered
son;
husband to a mur-
dered wife;
and I will have my
vengeance, in this life
or in the next.

His answer builds like a mighty wave,
swelling in size and strength before it
crashes on the shore. Where does a man go
to learn an answer like that — to learn his
true name, a name that can never be taken
from him? That deep heart knowledge
comes only through a process of *initiation*.
You have to know where you've come from;
you have to have faced a series of trials that
test you; you have to have taken a journey;

and you have to have faced your enemy. But as a young man recently lamented to me, "I've been a Christian since I was five — no one ever showed me what it means to really be a man." He's lost now. He moved across the country to be with his girlfriend, but she's dumped him because he doesn't know who he is and what he's here for. There are countless others like him, a world of such men — a world of uninitiated men.

The church would like to think it is initiating men, but it's not. What does the church bring a man into? What does it call him out to be? Moral. That is pitifully insufficient. Morality is a good thing, but morality is never the point. Paul says the Law is given as a tutor to the child, but not to the son. The son is invited up into something much more. He gets the keys to the car; he gets to go away with the father on some dangerous mission. I'm struck by the poignancy of the scene at the end of the Civil War, just after Appomattox, where General Robert E. Lee has surrendered to General Ulysses S. Grant. For five years Lee has led the Army of Northern Virginia through some of the most terrible trials men have ever known. You would think they'd be glad to have it over. But Lee's men hang upon the reins of his horse and beg him not to go, plead for one more chance to "whip those Yankees." Lee had become their father, had given those men what most of them had never had before — an identity and a place in a larger story.

Every man needs someone like Robert E. Lee, or that brigadier general from the 29th: "You've seen how to take a house. Do you understand? Do you know how to do it now?" "Yes, sir." We need someone like my grandfather, who can teach us how to "saddle up." But Lee is long gone, brigadier generals are rare, and my grandfather has been dead for many years. Where do we go? To whom can we turn? To a most surprising source.

HOW GOD INITIATES A MAN

A number of years ago, at a point in my own journey when I felt more lost than ever, I heard a talk given by Gordon Dalby, who had just written *The Healing of the Masculine Soul.* He raised the idea that despite a man's past and the failures of his own father to initiate him, God could take him on that journey, provide what was missing. A hope rose within me, but I dismissed it with the cynicism I'd learned to use to keep down most things in my soul. Several weeks, perhaps months later, I was downstairs in the early morning to read and pray. As with so many of my "quiet times," I ended up looking out the window toward the east to watch the sun rise. I heard Jesus whisper a question to me: "Will you let me initiate you?" Before my mind ever had a chance to process, dissect, and doubt the whole exchange, my heart leaped up and said *yes*.

"Who can give a man this, his own name?" George MacDonald asks. "God alone. For no one but God sees what the man is." He reflects upon the white stone that Revelation includes among the rewards God will give to those who "overcome." On that white stone there is a new name. It is "new" only in the sense that it is not the name the world gave to us, certainly not the one delivered with the wound. No man will find on that stone "mama's boy" or "fatty" or "seagull." But the new name is really not new at all when you understand that it is your *true* name, the one that belongs to you, "that being whom he had in his thought when he began to make the child, and whom he kept in his thought throughout the long process of creation" and redemption. Psalm 139 makes it clear that we were personally, uniquely planned and created, knit together in our mother's womb by God himself. He had someone in mind and that someone has a name.

That someone has also undergone a terrible assault, and yet God remains committed to the realization of that same someone. The giving of the white stone makes it clear — that is what he is up to. The history of a man's relationship with God is the story of how God calls him out, takes him on a journey and gives him his true name. Most of us have thought it was the story of how God sits on his throne waiting to whack a man broadside when he steps out of line. Not so. He created Adam for adventure, battle and beauty; he created us for a unique place in his story and he is committed to bringing us back to the original design. So God calls Abram out from Ur of the Chaldeas to a land he has never seen, to the frontier, and along the way Abram gets a new name. He becomes Abraham. God takes Jacob off into Mesopotamia somewhere, to learn things he has to learn and cannot learn at his mother's side. When he rides back into town, he has a limp and a new name as well.

Even if your father did his job, he can only take you partway. There comes a time when you have to leave all that is familiar, and go on into the unknown with God. Saul was a guy who really thought he understood the story and very much liked the part he had written for himself. He was the hero of his own little miniseries, "Saul the Avenger." After that little matter on the Damascus road he becomes *Paul,* and rather than heading back into all of the old and familiar ways he is led out into Arabia for three years to learn directly from God. Jesus shows us that initiation can happen even when we've lost our father or grandfather. He's the carpenter's son, which means Joseph was able to help him in the early days of his journey. But when we meet the young man Jesus, Joseph is out of the picture. Jesus has a new teacher — his true Father — and it is from him he must learn who he really is and what he's really made of.

Initiation involves a journey and a series of tests, through which we discover our real name and our true place in the story. Robert Ruark's book *The Old Man and the Boy* is a classic example of this kind of relationship. There's a boy who needs a lot of teaching, and there's an old man who's got a lot of wisdom. But the initiation doesn't take place at a school desk; it takes place *in the field,* where simple lessons about the land and animals and seasons turn into larger lessons about life and self and God. Through each test comes a *revelation*. The boy must keep his eyes open and ask the right questions. Learning to hunt quail helps you learn about yourself: "He's smart as a whip, and every time you go up against him you're proving something about yourself."

Most of us have been misinterpreting life and what God is doing for a long time. "I think I'm just trying to get God to make my life work easier," a client of mine confessed, but he could have been speaking for most of us. We're asking the wrong questions. Most of us are asking, "God, why did you let this happen to me?" Or, "God, why won't you just . . ." (fill in the blank — help me succeed, get my kids to straighten out, fix my marriage — you know what you've been whining about). But to enter into a journey of initiation with God requires a new set of questions: What are you trying to teach me here? What issues in my heart are you trying to raise through this? What is it you want me to see? What are you asking me to let go of? In truth, God has been trying to initiate you for a long time. What is in the way is how you've mishandled your wound and the life you've constructed as a result.

CONTEMPT FOR THE WOUND

"Men are taught over and over when they are boys that a wound that hurts is shameful," notes Bly. "A wound that stops you from continuing to play is a girlish wound. He who is truly a man keeps walking, dragging his guts behind." Like a man who's broken his leg in a marathon, he finishes the race even if he has to crawl and he doesn't say a word about it. That sort of misunderstanding is why for most of us, our wound is an immense source of shame. A man's not supposed to get hurt; he's certainly not supposed to let it really matter. We've seen too many movies where the good guy takes an arrow, just breaks it off, and keeps on fighting; or maybe he gets shot but is still able to leap across a canyon and get the bad guys. And so most men minimize their wound. "It's not a big deal. Lots of people get hurt when they're young. I'm okay." King David (a guy who's hardly a pushover) doesn't act like that at all. "I am poor and needy," he confesses openly, "and my heart is wounded within me" (Ps. 109:22).

Or perhaps they'll admit it happened, but deny it was a wound because they deserved it. After many months of counseling together about his wound, his vow, and how it was impossible to get The Answer from women, I asked Dave a simple question: "What would it take to convince you that you are a man?" "Nothing," he said. "Nothing can convince me." We sat in silence as tears ran down my cheeks. "You've embraced the wound, haven't you, Dave? You've owned its message as final. You think your father was right about you." "Yes," he said, without any sign of emotion at all. I went home and wept — for Dave, and for so many other men I know and for myself because I realized that I, too, had embraced my wound and ever since just tried to get on with life. Suck it up, as the saying goes. The only thing more tragic than the tragedy that happens to us is the way we handle it.

God is fiercely committed to you, to the restoration and release of your masculine heart. But a wound that goes unacknowledged and unwept is a wound that cannot heal. A wound you've embraced is a wound that cannot heal. A wound you think you deserved is a wound that cannot heal. That is why Brennan Manning says, "The spiritual life begins with the acceptance of our wounded self." Really? How can that be? The reason is simple: "Whatever is denied cannot be healed." But that's the problem, you see. Most men deny their wound — deny that it happened, deny that it hurt, certainly deny that it's shaping the way they live today. And so God's initiation of a man must take a very cunning course; a course that feels very odd, even cruel.

He will wound us in the very place where we have been wounded.

THWARTING THE FALSE SELF

From the place of our woundedness we construct a false self. We find a few gifts that work for us, and we try to live off them. Stuart found he was good at math and science. He shut down his heart and spent all his energies perfecting his "Spock" persona. There, in the academy, he was safe; he was also recognized and rewarded. Alex was good at sports and the whole macho image; he became a glass-eating animal. Stan became the nicest guy you could ever meet. "In the story of my life," he admitted, "I want to be seen as the Nice Guy." I became a hard-charging perfectionist; there, in my perfection, I found safety and recognition. "When I was eight," confesses Brennan Manning, "the impostor, or false self, was born as a defense against pain. The impostor within whispered, 'Brennan, don't ever be your real self anymore because nobody likes you as you are. Invent a new self that everybody will admire and nobody will know.' " Notice the key phrase: "as a defense against pain," as a way of saving himself. The impostor is our plan for salvation.

So God must take it all away. This often happens at the start of our initiation journey. He thwarts our plan for salvation; he shatters the false self. In the last chapter I told you of Brad's plan for self-redemption: he would belong to the "inside group." Even after it failed him time and again, breaking his heart over and over, he wouldn't give it up. He simply thought his aim was off; if he found the *right* group, then his plan would work. Our plan for redemption is hard to let go of; it clings to our hearts like an octopus. So what did God do for Brad? He took it all away. God brought Brad to the point where he thought he had found *the* group, and then God prevented him from maneuvering his way in. Brad wrote me a letter to describe what he was going through:

God has taken all that away, stripped me of all the things I used to earn people's admiration. I knew what he was up to. He put me in a place where my heart's deepest wounds and arrows — and sin

170

— came out. As I was weeping all these pictures of what I want to belong to came up — speaker, counselor, in a group — and it was as if Jesus asked me to give them up. What came from my heart was surprising — incredible *fear*. And then the image of never getting them. A sentence arose in my heart: "You want me to die! If I give those up then I'll never belong and be somebody. You are asking me to die." It has been my hope of salvation.

Why would God do something so cruel? Why would he do something so terrible as to wound us in the place of our deepest wound? Jesus warned us that "whoever wants to save his life will lose it" (Luke 9:24). Christ is not using the word *bios* here; he's not talking about our physical life. The passage is not about trying to save your skin by ducking martyrdom or something like that. The word Christ uses for "life" is the word *psyche* — the word for our soul, our inner self, our heart. He says that the things we do to save our psyche, our self, those plans to save and protect our inner life — those are the things that will actually destroy us. "There is a way that seems right to a man but in the end it leads to death" says

Proverbs 16:25. The false self, our plan for redemption, seems so right to us. It shields us from pain and secures us a little love and admiration. But the false self is a lie; the whole plan is built on pretense. It's a deadly trap. God loves us too much to leave us there. So he thwarts us, in many, many different ways.

In order to take a man into his wound, so that he can heal it and begin the release of the true self, God will thwart the false self. He will take away all that you've leaned upon to bring you life. In the movie *The Natural*, Robert Redford is a baseball player named Roy Hobbs, perhaps the most gifted baseball player ever. He's a high school wonder boy, a natural who gets a shot at the big leagues. But his dreams of a professional career are cut short when Hobbs is wrongly sentenced to prison for murder. Years later, an aging Hobbs gets a second chance. He's signed by the New York Knights — the worst team in the league. But through his incredible gift, untarnished by the years, Hobbs leads the Knights from ignominy to the play-off game for the National League pennant. He rallies the team, becomes the center of their hopes and dreams.

The climax of the film is the game for the championship. It's the bottom of the ninth;

the score is Pittsburgh 2, Knights 0. The Knights have 2 outs; there's a man on first and third when Hobbs steps up to the plate. He's their only chance; this is his moment. Now, there's something you must know, something absolutely crucial to the story. Ever since his high school days, Hobbs has played with a bat he made himself from the heart of a tree felled by lightning in his front yard. Burned into the bat is a lightning bolt and the words "wonder boy." That bat is the symbol of his greatness, his giftedness. He has never, ever played with another. Clutching "wonder boy," Hobbs steps to the plate. His first swing is a miss; his second is a foul ball high and behind. His third is a solid hit along the first-base line; it looks like it's a home run, but it also lands foul. As Hobbs returns to the plate, he sees his bat lying there . . . in pieces. It shattered on that last swing.

This is the critical moment in a man's life, when all he has counted on comes crashing down, when his golden bat breaks into pieces. His investments fail; his company lets him go; the church fires him; he is leveled by an illness; his wife walks out; his daughter turns up pregnant. What is he to do? Will he stay in the game? Will he shrink back to the dugout? Will he scramble to try to put things back together, as so many men do? The true test of a man, the beginning of his redemption, actually starts when he can no longer rely on what he's used all his life. *The real journey begins when the false self fails.* A moment that seems like an eternity passes as Hobbs stands there, holding the broken pieces, surveying the damage. The bat is beyond repair. Then he says to the bat boy, "Go pick me out a winner, Bobby." He stays in the game and hits a home run to win the series.

God will take away our "bat" as well. He will do something to thwart the false self. Stuart "saved" himself by becoming emotionless. Last year his wife walked out on him. She's had it with his two-dimensional existence; what woman wants to be married to Spock? Alex recently suffered a series of panic attacks that left him almost unable to leave his home. The whole macho construct fell to the ground. At first, nobody could believe it; Alex couldn't believe it. He was invincible, the strongest guy you ever met. But it was all built as a defense against the wound. Our loss doesn't necessarily have to be something so dramatic. A man may simply awaken one day to find himself lost, lost as Dante described himself: "In the middle of the road of my life, I awoke in a dark wood, where the true way was wholly lost." That was the turning point in my life.

I went to Washington, D.C., as a young man to try to make something of myself, to prove something, establish credibility. The damnable thing about it was, I succeeded. My giftedness worked against me by coming through for me. I was recognized and rewarded. But the whole experience felt like an act of survival — not something flowing out of a deep center, but something I had to prove, overcome, grasp. As Manning said of his own impostor, "I studied hard, scored excellent grades, won a scholarship in high school, and was stalked every waking moment by the terror of abandonment and the sense that nobody was there for me." At the end of two years I woke one morning and realized I hated my life.

> How many helps thou giv'st to those
>   who would learn!
> To some sore pain, to others a sinking
>   heart;
> To some a weariness worse than any
>   smart;
> To some a haunting, fearing, blind
>   concern;
> Madness to some; to some the
>   shaking dart

Of hideous death still following as
they turn;
To some a hunger that will not
depart.

To some thou giv'st a deep unrest —
a scorn
Of all they are or see upon the earth;
A gaze, at dusky night and clearing
morn.
As on a land of emptiness and dearth;
To some a bitter sorrow; to some the
sting
Of love misprized — of sick aban-
doning;
To some a frozen heart, oh, worse
than anything!

The messengers of Satan think to mar,
But make — driving the soul from
false to real —
To thee, the reconciler, the one real,
In whom alone the *would be* and the *is*
are met.
(George MacDonald, *Diary of an
Old Soul*)

This is a very dangerous moment, when
God seems set against everything that has
meant life to us. Satan spies his opportunity,

and leaps to accuse God in our hearts. *You see,* he says, *God is angry with you. He's disappointed in you. If he loved you he would make things smoother. He's not out for your best, you know.* The Enemy always tempts us back toward control, to recover and rebuild the false self. We must remember that it is out of love that God thwarts our impostor. As Hebrews reminds us, it is the son whom God disciplines, therefore do not lose heart (12:5–6).

God thwarts us to save us. We think it will destroy us, but the opposite is true — we must be saved from what really will destroy us. If we would walk with him in our journey of masculine initiation we must walk away from the false self — set it down, give it up willingly. It feels crazy; it feels immensely vulnerable. Brad has stopped looking for the group. Stuart has begun to open up his heart to emotion, to relationship, to all that he buried so long ago. Alex stopped "eating glass," stopped the whole macho thing to face what he had never faced inside. I gave up perfectionism, left Washington, and went looking for my heart. We simply accept the invitation to leave all that we've relied on and venture out with God. We can choose to do it ourselves, or we can wait for God to bring it all down.

If you have no clue as to what your false

self may be, then a starting point would be to ask those you live with and work with, "What is my effect on you? What am I like to live with (or work with)? What *don't* you feel free to bring up with me?" If you never, ever say a word in a meeting because you fear you might say something stupid, well then, it's time to speak up. If all you ever do is dominate a meeting because your sense of worth comes from being in charge, then you need to shut up for a while. If you've run to sports because you feel best about yourself there, then it's probably time to give it a rest and stay home with your family. If you never play any game with other men, then it's time you go down to the gym with the guys and play some hoops. In other words, you face your fears head-on. Drop the fig leaf; come out from hiding. For how long? Longer than you want to; long enough to raise the deeper issues, let the wound surface from beneath it all.

Losing the false self is painful; though it's a mask, it's one we've worn for years and losing it can feel like losing a close friend. Underneath the mask is all the hurt and fear we've been running from, hiding from. To let it come to the surface can shake us like an earthquake. Brad felt as if he was going to die; you may too. Or you may feel like Andy

Gullahorn, who wrote the song "Steel Bars" from *Old Hat* (© 1997 by Andy Gullahorn):

> So this is how it feels at the rock bottom of despair
> When the house I built comes crashing down
> And this is how it feels when I know the man that I say I am
> Is not the man that I am when no one's around

But this is not the end of the road; it's the trailhead. What you are journeying toward is freedom, healing, and authenticity. Listen to the next part of Andy's song:

> This is how it feels to come alive again
> And start fighting back to gain control
> And this is how it feels to let freedom in
> And break the chains that enslave my soul

WALKING AWAY FROM THE WOMAN

As we walk away from the false self, we will feel vulnerable and exposed. We will be sorely tempted to turn to our comforters for some relief, those places that we've found solace and rest. Because so many of us turned to the woman for our sense of masculinity, we must walk away from her as well. *I do not mean you leave your wife.* I mean you stop looking to her to validate you, stop trying to make her come through for you, stop trying to get your answer from her. For some men, this may mean disappointing her. If you've been a passive man, tiptoeing around your wife for years, never doing anything to rock the boat, then it's time to rock it. Stand up to her; get her mad at you. For those of you violent men (including achievers), it means *you stop abusing her.* You release her as the object of your anger because you release her as the one who was supposed to make you a man. Repentance for a driven man means you become *kind.* Both types are still going to the woman. Repentance depends on which way you've approached her.

But I have counseled many young men to break up with the woman they were *dating* because they had made her their life. She was the sun of his universe, around which he orbited. A man needs a much bigger orbit than a woman. He needs a mission, a life purpose, and he needs to know his name. Only then is he fit for a woman, for only then does he have something to invite her into. A friend tells me that in the Masai tribe in Africa, a young man cannot court a woman until he has killed a lion. That's their way of saying, until he has been initiated. I have seen far too many young men commit a kind of emotional promiscuity with a young woman. He will pursue her, not to offer his strength but to drink from her beauty, to be affirmed by her and feel like a man. They will share deep, intimate conversations. But he will not commit; he is *unable* to commit. This is very unfair to the young lady. After a year of this sort of relationship a dear friend said, "I never felt secure in what I meant to him."

When we feel the pull toward the golden-haired woman, we must recognize that something deeper is at play. As Bly says,

What does it mean when a man falls in love with a radiant face across the room? It may mean that he has some soul work to do. His soul is the issue. Instead of pursuing the woman and trying to get her alone . . . he needs to go alone himself, perhaps to a mountain cabin, for three months, write poetry, canoe down a river, and dream. That would save some women a lot of trouble. (*Iron John*)

Again, this is not permission to divorce. A man who has married a woman has made her a solemn pledge; he can never heal his wound by delivering another to the one he promised to love. Sometimes she will leave him; that is another story. Too many men run after her, begging her not to go. If she has to go, it is probably because you have some soul work to do. What I am saying is that the masculine journey always takes a man *away* from the woman, in order that he may come back to her with his question answered. A man does not go to a woman to get his strength; he goes to her to *offer* it. You do not need the woman for you to become a great man, and as a great man you do not need the woman. As Augustine said, "Let my soul praise you for all these beauties, but let it not attach itself to them by the trap of love," the trap of addiction because we've taken our soul to her for validation.

But there is an even deeper issue than our question. What else is it we are seeking from the Woman with the Golden Hair? What is that ache we are trying to assuage with her? Mercy, comfort, beauty, ecstasy — in a word, *God.* I'm serious. What we are looking for is God.

There was a time when Adam drank deeply from the source of all Love. He —

our first father and archetype — lived in an unbroken communion with the most captivating, beautiful, and intoxicating Source of life in the universe. Adam had God. True, it was not good for man to be alone, and God in his humility gave us Eve, allowed us to need her as well. But something happened at the Fall; something *shifted*. Eve took the place of God in a man's life. Let me explain.

Adam was not deceived by the serpent. Did you know that? Paul makes it clear in 1 Timothy 2:14 — Adam did not fall because he was deceived. His sin was different; in some ways, it was more serious in that he did it with open eyes. We do not know how long it lasted, but there was a moment in Eden when Eve was fallen and Adam was not; she had eaten, but he yet had a choice. I believe something took place in his heart that went like this: I have lost my *ezer kenegdo*, my soul mate, the most vital companion I've known. I do not know what life will be like, but I know I cannot live without her.

Adam chose Eve over God.

If you think I exaggerate, simply look around. Look at all the art, poetry, music, drama devoted to the beautiful woman. Listen to the language men use to describe her. Watch the powerful obsession at work. What else can this be but *worship?* Men come into the world without the God who was our deepest joy, our ecstasy. Aching for we know not what, we meet Eve's daughters and we are history. She is the closest thing we've ever encountered, the pinnacle of creation, the very embodiment of God's beauty and mystery and tenderness and allure. And what goes out to her is not just our longing for Eve, but our longing for God as well. A man without his true love, his life, his God, will find another. What better substitute than Eve's daughters? Nothing else in creation even comes close.

To a young man who had never been without a girlfriend since the eighth grade, I gave the advice that he should break up, call off all dating for one year. From the look on his face you'd have thought I told him to cut off his arm . . . or something worse. Do you see what is at work here? Notice that the struggle with pornography or masturbation is most difficult when you are lonely, or beat up, or longing for comfort in some way. This will become more intense as you get closer to your wound. The longing for the ache to go away, and the pull toward other comforters can seem overwhelming. I've watched it in many men. I know it in myself. But if this is the water you are truly thirsty for, then why do you remain thirsty after you've had a drink? It's the wrong well.

We must reverse Adam's choice; we must choose God over Eve. We must take our ache to him. For only in God will we find the healing of our wound.

Chapter Seven

HEALING THE WOUND

Desperado, why don't you come to your senses
You been out ridin' fences for so long now
O you're a hard one, but I know
That you got your reasons . . .
You better let somebody love you
Before it's too late.

— THE EAGLES
"Desperado"
(© 1973 by Glenn Fry
and Don Henley)

The task of healing is to respect oneself as a crea-
ture, no more and no less.
— WENDELL BERRY

The deepest desire of our hearts is for union with
God. God created us for union with himself: This
is the original purpose of our lives.
— BRENNAN MANNING

I think I've given a wrong impression of my life with my sons. Rock climbing, canoeing, wrestling, our quest for danger and destruction — you might get the impression we're a sort of military academy of the backwoods or one of those militia cults. So let me tell you of my favorite event of the day. It comes late in the evening, at bedtime, after the boys have brushed their teeth and we've said our family prayers. As I'm tucking them in, one of my boys will ask, "Dad, can we snuggle tonight?" Snuggle time is when I'll cuddle up next to them on a bed that's really not big enough for both of us — and that's the point, to get very close — and there in the dark we'll just sort of talk. Usually we start laughing and then we have to whisper because the others will ask us to "keep it down in there." Sometimes it breaks into tickling, other times it's a chance for them to ask some serious questions about life. But whatever happens, what matters most is what's going on beneath all that: intimacy, closeness, connection.

Yes, my boys want me to guide them into adventure, and they love to test their strength against mine. But all of that takes place in the context of an intimate bond of love that is far deeper than words can express. What they want more than anything, what I love to offer them more than anything, is soul-to-soul oneness. As Tom Wolfe said,

> The deepest search in life, it seemed to me, the thing that in one way or another was central to all living was man's search to find a father, not merely the father of his flesh, not merely the lost father of his youth, but the image of a strength and wisdom external to his need and superior to his hunger, to which the belief and power of his own life could be united. ("The Story of a Novel")

THE SOURCE OF REAL STRENGTH

Guys are unanimously embarrassed by their emptiness and woundedness; it is for most of us a tremendous source of shame, as I've said. But it need not be. From the very beginning, back before the Fall and the assault, ours was meant to be a desperately dependent existence. It's like a tree and its branches, explains Christ. You are the branches, I am the trunk. From me you draw your life; that's how it was meant to be. In fact, he goes on to say, "Apart from me you can do nothing" (John 15:5). He's not berating us or mocking us or even saying it with a sigh, all the while thinking, *I wish they'd pull it together and stop needing me so much.* Not at all. We are *made* to depend on God; we are made for union with him and nothing about us works right without it. As C. S. Lewis wrote, "A car is made to run on gasoline, and it would not run properly on anything else. Now God designed the human machine to run on himself. He himself is the fuel our spirits were designed to burn, or the food our spirits were designed to feed on. There is no other."

This is where our sin and our culture have come together to keep us in bondage and brokenness, to prevent the healing of our wound. Our sin is that stubborn part inside that wants, above all else, to be independent. There's a part of us fiercely committed to living in a way where we do not have to depend on anyone — especially God. Then culture comes along with figures like John Wayne and James Bond and all those other "real men," and the one thing they have in common is that they are *loners*, they don't need anyone. We come to believe deep in our hearts that needing anyone for anything is a sort of weakness, a handicap. This is why a man never, ever stops to ask for directions. I am notorious for this. I know how to get there; I'll find my own way, thank you very much. Only when I am fully and finally and completely lost will I pull over and get some help, and I'll feel like a wimp for doing it.

Jesus knew nothing of that. The Man who never flinched to take on hypocrites and get in their face, the One who drove "a hundred men wi' a bundle o' cords swung free," the Master of wind and sea, lived in a desperate dependence on his Father. "I assure you, the Son can do nothing by himself. He does only what he sees the Father doing"; "I live by the power of the living Father who sent me"; "The words I say are not my own, but my Father who lives in me does his work through me." This isn't a source of embarrassment to Christ; quite the opposite. He brags about his relationship with his Father. He's happy to tell anyone who will listen, "The Father and I are one" (John 5:19; 6:57; 14:10; 10:30 NLT).

Why is this important? Because so many men I know live with a deep misunderstanding of Christianity. They look at it as a "second chance" to get their act together. They've been forgiven, now they see it as their job to get with the program. They're trying to finish the marathon with a broken leg. But follow this closely now: You'll recall that masculinity is an essence that is passed from father to son. That is a picture, as so many things in life are, of a deeper reality. The *true* essence of strength is passed to us from God *through our union with him.* Notice what a deep and vital part of King David's life this is. Remembering that he is a man's man, a warrior for sure, listen to how he describes his relationship to God in the Psalms:

I love you, O LORD, my strength. (18:1)

But you, O LORD, be not far off;
O my Strength, come quickly to help me.
(22:19)

O my Strength, I watch for you;
you, O God, are my fortress, my
loving God. (59:9)

I dare say that David could take on John Wayne or James Bond any day; yet this true man is unashamed to admit his desperate dependence on God. We know we are meant to embody strength, we know we are not what we were meant to be, and so we feel our brokenness as a source of shame. As we spoke of his wound recently, and how he needed to enter into it for healing, Dave protested. "I don't even want to go there. It all feels so true." Men are typically quite harsh with the broken places within them. Many report feeling as though there is a boy inside, and they despise that about themselves. *Quit being such a baby,* they order themselves. But that is not how God feels. He is furious about what's happened to you. "It would be better to be thrown into the sea with a large millstone tied around the neck than to face the punishment in store for harming one of these little ones" (Luke 17:2 NLT). Think of how you would feel if the wounds you were given, the blows dealt to you, were dealt to a boy you loved — your son, perhaps. Would you shame him for it? Would you feel scorn that he couldn't rise above it all? No. You'd feel compassion. As Gerard Manley Hopkins wrote,

> My own heart let me more have pity
>   on; let
> Me live to my sad self hereafter kind.

In the movie *Good Will Hunting,* there is a beautiful picture of what can happen when a man realizes he has "owned" his wound, and discovers he doesn't have to. Will Hunting (played by Matt Damon) is a brilliant young man, a genius, who works as a janitor at MIT and lives in a rough part of town. No one knows about his gift, because he hides it behind a false self of "tough kid from the wrong side of the tracks." He's a fighter (a violent man). That false self was born out of a father-wound; his original father he does not know, and the man who was his foster father would come home drunk and beat Will mercilessly. After he's arrested for getting into a brawl for the umpteenth time, Will is ordered by the court to see a psychologist, Sean (played by Robin Williams). They form a bond; for the first time in Will's life, an older man cares about him deeply. His initiation has begun. Toward the end of one of their last sessions, Sean and Will are talking about the beatings he endured, now recorded in his case file.

WILL: So, uh . . . you know, what is it, like "Will has an attachment disorder," is it all that stuff? "Fear of abandonment"? Is that why I broke up with Skyler [his girlfriend]?

SEAN: I didn't know you had.

WILL: I did.

SEAN: You wanna talk about it?

WILL: (Staring at the floor) No.

SEAN: Hey, Will . . . I don't know a lot, but you see this (holding his

	file) . . . This is not your fault.
WILL:	(Dismisses him)Yeah, I know that.
SEAN:	Look at me, son. It's not your fault.
WILL:	I know.
SEAN:	It's not your fault.
WILL:	(Beginning to grow defensive) I know.
SEAN:	No, no, you don't. It's not your fault.
WILL:	(Really defensive) I know.
SEAN:	It's not your fault.
WILL:	(Trying to end the conversation) All right.
SEAN:	It's not your fault . . . it's not your fault.
WILL:	(Anger) Don't [mess] with me, Sean, not you.
SEAN:	It's not your fault . . . it's not your fault . . . it's not your fault.
WILL:	(Collapses into his arms, weeping) I'm so sorry. I'm so sorry.

It is no shame that you need healing; it is no shame to look to another for strength; it is no shame that you feel young and afraid inside. It's not your fault.

ENTERING THE WOUND

Frederick Buechner's father committed suicide when he was ten. He left a note, to his mother: "I adore and love you, and am no good . . . Give Freddie my watch. Give Jaime my pearl pin. I give you all my love," and then he sat in the garage while the running car filled it with carbon monoxide. It happened on a Saturday morning in the fall. He was to have taken Frederick and his brother to a football game that day. Instead, he took himself forever from their lives. What is a ten-year-old boy to do with such an event?

A child takes life as it comes because he has no other way of taking it. The world had come to an end that Saturday morning, but each time we had moved to another place, I had seen a world come to an end, and there had always been another world to replace it. When somebody you love dies, Mark Twain said, it is like when your house burns down; it isn't for years that you realize the full extent of your loss. For me it was longer than for most, if indeed I have realized it fully even yet, and in the meantime the loss came to get buried so deep in me that after a time I scarcely ever took it out to look at it at all, let alone speak of it. (*The Sacred Journey*)

That is the way we are with our wound, especially men. We bury it deep and never take it out again. But take it out we must, or better, enter into it. I entered my wound through the surprising door of my anger. After we moved to Colorado, about eleven years ago, I found myself snapping at my boys for silly things. A spilled glass of milk would elicit a burst of rage. *Whoa, John, I* thought, *there are things going on inside, you'd better have a look under the hood.* As I explored my anger with the help of my dear friend Brent, I realized I was so furious about feeling all alone in a world that constantly demanded more of me than I felt able to give. Something in me felt young — like a ten-year-old boy in a man's world but without a man's ability to come through. There was much fear beneath the surface; fear that I would fail, fear that I would be found out, and finally, fear that I was ultimately on my own. *Where did all this fear come from?* I wondered. *Why do I feel so alone in the world . . . and so young inside? Why does something in my heart feel orphaned?*

My answer came through several movies. As I've written about in other places, I was blindsided by *A River Runs Through It* because through its beautiful retelling of boys who never really had their father except during their fishing trips, and how in the end they lost even that. I realized I had lost my father, and like Buechner the loss got buried so deep in me that after a time I scarcely ever took it out. I was pierced by *A Perfect World* because I saw there just how much a boy's father means to him and how I longed for that intimacy with a source of strength who loved me and could tell me my name. I so identified with Will Hunting because I, too, was a fighter who saw myself as up against the rest of the world and I had also accepted my wound and never grieved it. I thought it was my fault.

In some ways God had to sneak up on me through those stories because I wasn't willing to just skip happily down the path to my heart's deepest pain. We fight this part of the journey. The whole false self, our "lifestyle," is an elaborate defense against entering our wounded heart. It is a chosen blindness. "Our false self stubbornly blinds each of us to the light and the truth of our own emptiness and hollowness," says Manning. There are readers who even now have no idea what their wound is, or even what false self arose from it. Ah, how convenient that blindness is. Blissful ignorance. But a wound unfelt is a wound unhealed. We must go in. The door may be your anger; it may be rejection that you've experienced, perhaps from a girl; it may be failure, or the loss of the golden bat and the way God is thwarting your false self. It may be a simple prayer: Jesus, take me into my wound.

"Behold," he says, "I stand at the door and knock."

HEALING THE WOUND

If you wanted to learn how to heal the blind and you thought that following Christ around and watching how he did it would make things clear, you'd wind up pretty frustrated. He never does it the same way twice. He spits on one guy; for another, he spits on the ground and makes mud and puts that on his eyes. To a third he simply speaks, a fourth he touches, and a fifth he kicks out a demon. There are no formulas with God. The way in which God heals our wound is a deeply personal process. He is a person and he insists on working personally. For some, it comes in a moment of divine touch. For others, it takes place over time and through the help of another, maybe several others. As Agnes

Sanford says, "There are in many of us wounds so deep that only the mediation of someone else to whom we may 'bare our grief' can heal us."

So much healing took place in my life simply through my friendship with Brent. We were partners, but far more than that, we were friends. We spent hours together fly-fishing, backpacking, hanging out in pubs. Just spending time with a man I truly respected, a real man who loved and respected me — nothing heals quite like that. At first I feared that I was fooling him, that he'd see through it any day and drop me. But he didn't, and what happened instead was validation. My heart knew that if a man I *know* is a man thinks I'm one, too, well then, maybe I am one after all. Remember — masculinity is bestowed by masculinity. But there have been other significant ways in which God has worked — times of healing prayer, times of grieving the wound and forgiving my father. Most of all, times of deep communion with God. The point is this: Healing never happens outside of intimacy with Christ. The healing of our wound flows out of our union with him.

But there are some common themes that I share with you as you seek the restoration of your heart. The first step seems so simple it's almost hard to believe we overlook it, never ask for it, and when we do, we sometimes struggle for days just to get the words out.

It begins with surrender. As Lewis says, "Until you have given yourself to him you will not have a real self." We return the branch to its trunk; we yield our lives to the One who is our Life. And then *we invite Jesus into the wound;* we ask him to come and meet us there, to enter into the broken and unhealed places of our heart. When the Bible tells us that Christ came to "redeem mankind" it offers a whole lot more than forgiveness. To simply forgive a broken man is like telling someone running a marathon, "It's okay that you've broken your leg. I won't hold that against you. Now finish the race." That is cruel, to leave him disabled that way. No, there is much more to our redemption. The core of Christ's mission is foretold in Isaiah 61:

> The Spirit of the Sovereign LORD is
>   on me,
> because the LORD has anointed me
> to preach good news to the poor.
> He has sent me to bind up the bro-
>   kenhearted,
> to proclaim freedom for the captives

and release for the prisoners. (v, 1)

The Messiah will come, he says, to bind up and heal, to release and set free. What? *Your heart.* Christ comes to restore and release you, your soul, the true you. This is *the* central passage in the entire Bible about Jesus, the one he chooses to quote about himself when he steps into the spotlight in Luke 4 and announces his arrival. So take him at his word — ask him in to heal all the broken places within you and unite them into one whole and healed heart. Ask him to release you from all bondage and captivity, as he promised to do. As MacDonald prayed, "Gather my broken fragments to a whole . . . Let mine be a merry, all-receiving heart, but make it a whole, with light in every part." But you can't do this at a distance; you can't ask Christ to come into your wound while you remain far from it. You have to go there with him.

That is why we must grieve the wound. It was not your fault and it did matter. Oh what a milestone day that was for me when I simply allowed myself to say that the loss of my father *mattered.* The tears that flowed were the first I'd ever granted my wound, and they were deeply healing. All those years of sucking it up melted away in my grief. It is so important for us to grieve our wound; it is the only honest thing to do. For in grieving we admit the truth — that we were hurt by someone we loved, that we lost something very dear, and it hurt us very much. Tears are healing. They help to open and cleanse the wound. As Augustine wrote in his *Confessions*, "The tears . . . streamed down, and I let them flow as freely as they would, making of them a pillow for my heart. On them it rested." Grief is a form of validation; it says the wound *mattered*.

We let God love us; we let him get real close to us. I know, it seems painfully obvious, but I'm telling you few men are ever so vulnerable as to simply let themselves be loved by God. After Brad lost his plan for redemption, I asked him, "Brad, why don't you just let God love you?" He squirmed in his chair. "I have such a hard time with that, just being loved. It feels so naked. I'd rather be in control, be admired for what I bring to the group." Later he wrote this in a letter to me:

> After it all came crashing down, I was overwhelmed by sadness and grief. The pain is incredible. In the midst of that God asked me, "Brad, will you let me love you?" I know what he is asking. I

feel anxious that I need to go e-mail all these schools and secure a future. But I'm tired of running away. I want to come home. I flipped through my Bible and came to John 15, "Just as the Father has loved you, I have also loved you, abide in my love." The battle is very intense. At times it is all clear. At others it is a fog. Right now all I can do is cling to Jesus as best I know how and not run from all that is in my heart.

Abiding in the love of God is our only hope, the only true home for our hearts. It's not that we mentally acknowledge that God loves us. It's that we let our hearts come home to him, and stay in his love. MacDonald says it this way:

When our hearts turn to him, that is opening the door to him . . . then he comes in, not by our thought only, not in our idea only, but he comes himself, and of his own will. Thus the Lord, the Spirit, becomes the soul of our souls . . . Then indeed we *are;* then indeed we have life; the life of Jesus has . . . become life in us . . . we are one with God forever and ever. (*The Heart of George Mac-Donald*)

Or as St. John of the Cross echoes, "O how gently and how lovingly dost thou lie awake in the depth and centre of my soul, where thou in secret and in silence alone, as its sole Lord, abidest, not only as in Thine own house or in Thine own chamber, but also as within my own bosom, in close and intimate union" (*Living Flame of Love*). This deep intimate union with Jesus and with his Father is the source of all our healing and all our strength. It is, as Leanne Payne says, "the central and unique truth of Christianity." After a retreat in which I laid out the masculine journey to a small group of men, I received this E-mail:

> My father never left, he just never had time for me or words of encouragement. He has spent his entire life making himself the center of attention. For the first time I understand why I am highly driven, why I never let anyone get close to me — including my wife — and why I am an impostor to most people. I broke down and cried. I feel the presence of God in my heart like I have never felt him before . . . the beginning of a new heart.

Time has come for us to forgive our fathers. Paul warns us that unforgiveness and bitterness can wreck our lives and the lives of others (Eph. 4:31; Heb. 12:15). I am sorry to think of all the years my wife endured the anger and bitterness that I redirected at her from my father. As someone has said, forgiveness is setting a prisoner free and then discovering the prisoner was you. I found some help in Bly's experience of forgiving his own father, when he said, "I began to think of him not as someone who had deprived me of love or attention or companionship, but as someone who himself had been deprived, by his father and his mother and by the culture." My father had his own wound that no one ever offered to heal. His father was an alcoholic, too, for a time, and there were some hard years for my dad as a young man just as there were for me.

Now you must understand: Forgiveness is a choice. It is not a feeling, but an act of the will. As Neil Anderson has written, "Don't wait to forgive until you feel like forgiving; you will never get there. Feelings take time to heal after the choice to forgive is made." We allow God to bring the hurt up from our past, for "if your forgiveness doesn't visit the emotional core of your life, it will be incomplete." We acknowledge that it hurt, that it mattered, and we choose to extend forgiveness to our father. This is *not* saying, "It didn't really matter"; it is *not* saying, "I probably deserved part of it anyway." Forgiveness says, "It was wrong, it mattered, and I release you."

And then we ask God to father us, and to tell us our true name.

GOD'S NAME FOR US

I noticed a few years ago, a ways into my own masculine journey, that I related well to Jesus and to "God" but not to God as *Father*. It's not hard to figure out why. Father has been a source of pain and disappointment to me . . . to many of us. Then I read this in Mac-Donald:

> In my own childhood and boyhood my father was the refuge from all the ills of life, even sharp pain itself. Therefore I say to son or daughter who has no pleasure in the name *Father*, "You must interpret the word by all that you have missed in life. All that human tenderness can give or desire in the nearness and readiness of love, all and infinitely more must be true of the perfect Father — of the maker of fatherhood." (*The Heart of George MacDonald*)

The gift was perfectly timed, for I knew it was time to allow God to father me. (All along the process of my initiation, God has provided words like that, messages, people, gifts to open the next leg of the journey.) Masculinity is passed from father to son, and then from Father to son. Adam, Abraham, Jacob, David, Jesus — they all learned who they were out of their intimacy with God, with the Father. After all, who can give a man this, his own name? God alone. For no one but God sees what the man is. This is usually thought of with a sense of guilt — yes, *God sees me . . . and what he sees is my sin.* That's wrong on two counts.

First off, your sin has been dealt with. Your Father has removed it from you "as far as the east is from the west" (Ps. 103:12). Your sins have been washed away (1 Cor. 6:11). When God looks at you he does not see your sin. He has not one condemning thought toward you (Rom. 8:1). But that's not all. You have a new heart. That's the promise of the new covenant: "I will give you a new heart and put a new spirit in you; I will remove from you your heart of stone and give you a heart of flesh. And I will put my Spirit in you and move you to follow my decrees and be careful to keep my laws"

(Ezek. 36:26–27). There's a reason that it's called good news.

Too many Christians today are living back in the old covenant. They've had Jeremiah 17:9 drilled into them and they walk around believing *my heart is deceitfully wicked*. Not anymore it's not. Read the rest of the book. In Jeremiah 31:33, God announces the cure for all that: "I will put my law in their minds and write it on their hearts. I will be their God, and they will be my people." I will give you a new heart. That's why Paul says in Romans 2:29, "No, a man is a Jew if he is one inwardly; and circumcision is circumcision of the heart, by the Spirit." Sin is not the deepest thing about you. You have a new heart. Did you hear me? Your heart is *good*.

What God sees when he sees you is the *real* you, the true you, the man he had in mind when he made you. How else could he give you the white stone with your true name on it? I've brought you along in Dave's story — how his father dealt him the wound of "mama's boy," how he sought his sense of masculinity through women, how he embraced his wound and its message as final and true. We sat together one day in my office, his life pretty well detailed and unpacked before us, as if we had unpacked trunk of secrets and laid them all out to the light of day. What else was there to say? "You've only got one hope, Dave . . . that your dad was wrong about you."

You must ask God what he thinks of you, and you must stay with the question until you have an answer. The battle will get fierce here. This is the *last* thing the Evil One wants you to know. He will play the ventriloquist; he'll whisper to you as if he were the voice of God. Remember, he's the accuser of the brethren (Rev. 12:10). After I saw *Gladiator*, I so longed to be a man like Maximus. He reminded me of Henry V, from Shakespeare's play — a courageous, valiant man. Maximus is strong and courageous and he fights so well; yet his heart is given over to eternity. He yearns for heaven but stays to fight so that others might be free. I wept at the end, pierced by a longing to be like him. Satan was all over that, telling me that no, I was really Commodus — the conniving wretch who plays the villain in the movie. What made that blow so hard to shake is the fact that I once was Commodus; I was a selfish, conniving man who manipulated everything for my own benefit. That was a long time ago, but the accusation stung.

I left for a trip to England where I did four

conferences in five days. It was a brutal trip and I was under a great deal of spiritual attack. What a relief it was to slump into my seat and catch my plane home. Tired to the bone, spent and beat up, I needed to hear words from my Father. So I began to pour my heart out to him in my journal.

What of me, dear Lord? Are you pleased? What did you see? I am sorry that I have to ask, wishing I knew without asking. Fear, I suppose, makes me doubt. Still, I yearn to hear from you — a word, or image, a name or even just a glance from you.

This is what I heard:

You are Henry V after Agincourt . . . the man in the arena, whose face is covered with blood and sweat and dust, who strove valiantly . . . a great warrior . . . yes, even Maximus.

And then

You are my friend.

I cannot tell you how much those word mean to me. In fact, I'm embarrassed to tel them to you; they seem arrogant. But I share them in hopes that they will help you find your own. They are words of life, words that heal my wound and shatter the Enemy's accusations. I am grateful for them; deeply grateful. Oh, what wonderful stories I could tell here of how many times God has spoken to me and to other men since we've been asking the question. My friend Aaron went to a park near our home and found a place of solitude. There he waited for the Father's voice. What he first heard was this: "True masculinity is spiritual." Aaron has for so long felt that spirituality was feminine; it put him in a terrible bind because he is a very spiritual man, and yet longs to be a real man. God spoke exactly what he needed to hear — masculinity is spiritual. Then he heard, "True spirituality is good." And then, "You are a man. You are a man. You are a man."

It's a battle to get to this place, and once words like these have been spoken the Enemy rushes in to steal them. Remember how he assaulted Christ in the wilderness, right on the heels of hearing words from his Father. Another friend and I were talking about these stories and many more like them. He sort of sighed and said, "Yes, I remember a time in church when I heard God say to me, 'You're doing great. I am proud of you, right where you are.' But I could not believe it. It just doesn't seem true." That is why we always rest on propositional truth. We stand on what Scripture says about us. We are forgiven. Our heart is good. The Father's voice is *never* condemning. From that place we ask God to speak personally to us, to break the power of the lie that was delivered with our wound.

He knows your name.

OUT OF OUR WOUND COMES OUR GLORY

I have a favorite painting in my office, a reprint of Charlie Schreyvogel's *My Bunkie.* It's a scene of four cavalry soldiers done in the Western style of Remington. The action is a rescue; one of the riders has apparently been shot off his horse and three men are galloping in to pick him up. In the foreground, the stranded soldier is being swept up onto the back of the horse of his bunk mate (his "bunkie"), while the other two are providing rifle cover. I love this scene because that is what I want to do and be; I want to ride to the rescue of those who have been shot down. But sitting in my office one day, God began to speak to me about the painting and my role in it. *You cannot be the man who rescues, John, until you are the man without a horse, the man who needs rescuing.*

Yes. True strength does not come out of bravado. Until we are broken, our life will be self-centered, self-reliant; our strength will be our own. So long as you think you are really something in and of yourself, what will you need God for? I don't trust a man who hasn't suffered; I don't let a man get close to me who hasn't faced his wound. Think of the posers you know — are they the kind of man you would call at 2:00 A.M., when life is collapsing around you? Not me. I don't want clichés; I want deep, soulful truth, and that only comes when a man has walked the road I've been talking about. As Buechner says,

> To do for yourself the best that you have it in you to do — to grit your teeth and clench your fists in order to survive the world at its harshest and worst — is, by that very act, to be unable to let something be done for you and in you that is more wonderful still. The trouble with steeling yourself against the harshness of reality is that the same steel that secures your life against being destroyed secures your life also against being opened up

and transformed. (*The Sacred Journey*)

Only when we enter our wound will we discover our true glory. As Bly says, "Where a man's wound is, that is where his genius will be." There are two reasons for this. First, because the wound was given in the place of your true strength, as an effort to take you out. Until you go there you are still posing, offering something more shallow and insubstantial. And therefore, second, it is out of your brokenness that you discover what you have to offer the community. The false self is never wholly false. Those gifts we've been using are often quite true about us, but we've used them to hide behind. We thought that the power of our life was in the golden bat, but the power is in *us*. When we begin to offer not merely our gifts but our true selves, that is when we become powerful.

That is when we are ready for battle.

Chapter Eight

A BATTLE TO FIGHT: THE ENEMY

Enemy-occupied territory — that is what this world is.

— C. S. LEWIS

We are but warriors for the working-day;
Our gayness and our gilt are all besmirch'd
With rainy marching in the painful field . . .
But, by the mass, our hearts are in the trim.

— HENRY V

If we would endeavor, like men of courage, to stand in the battle, surely we would feel the favorable assistance of God from Heaven. For he who giveth us occasion to fight, to the end we may get the victory, is ready to succor those that fight manfully, and do trust in his grace.

— THOMAS À KEMPIS

"Dad, are there any castles anymore?" Luke and I were sitting at the breakfast table; actually, he was seated and I was attending his Royal Highness, making him toast with apricot jam. As soon as he asked the question I knew what his young heart was wondering. Are there any great adventures anymore? Are there any great battles? I wanted to explain that indeed there are, but before I could reply he got this gleam in his eye and asked, "And are there any dragons?" O, how deeply this is written into the masculine soul. The boy is a warrior; the boy is his name. A man needs a battle to fight; he needs a place for the warrior in him to come alive and be honed, trained, seasoned. If Bly is right (and I believe he is), that "the early death of a man's warriors keeps the boy in him from growing up," then the opposite is true — if we can reawaken that fierce quality in a man, hook it up to a higher purpose, release the warrior within, then the boy can grow up and become truly masculine.

As I was working on this book a few days ago, Blaine came downstairs and without a word slipped a drawing he had made in front of me. It is a pencil sketch of an angel with broad shoulders and long hair; his wings are sweeping around him as if just unfurled to reveal that he is holding a large two-handed sword like a Scottish claymore. He holds the blade upright, ready for action; his gaze is steady and fierce. Beneath the drawing are the words, written in the hand of a nine-year-old boy, "Every man is a warrior inside. But the choice to fight is his own." And a little child shall lead them. Blaine knows as deeply as he knows anything that every man is a warrior, yet every man must choose to fight. The warrior is not the only role a man must play; there are others we will explore later. But the warrior is crucial in our movement toward any masculine integrity; it is hardwired into every man.

THE WARRIOR HEART

I have in my files a copy of a letter written by Major Sullivan Ballou, a Union officer in the 2nd Rhode Island. He writes to his wife on the eve of the Battle of Bull Run, a battle he senses will be his last. He speaks tenderly to her of his undying love, of "the memories of blissful moments I have spent with you." Ballou mourns the thought that he must give up "the hope of future years, when, God willing, we might still have lived and loved together, and seen our sons grown up to honorable manhood around us." Yet in spite of his love the battle calls and he cannot turn from it. "I have no misgivings about, or lack of confidence in the cause in which I am engaged, and my courage does not halt or falter . . . how great a debt we owe to those who went before us through the blood and sufferings of the Revolution . . . Sarah, my love for you is deathless, it seems to bind me with mighty cables that nothing but Omnipotence could break" and yet a greater cause "comes over me like a strong wind and bears me unresistably on with all these chains to the battle field."

A man must have a battle to fight, a great mission to his life that involves and yet transcends even home and family. He must have a cause to which he is devoted even unto death, for this is written into the fabric of his being. Listen carefully now: *You do.* That is why God created you — to be his intimate *ally,* to join him in the Great Battle. You have a specific place in the line, a mission God made you for. That is why it is so essential to hear from God about your true name, because in that name is the mission of your life. Churchill was called upon to lead the British through the desperate hours of WWII. He said, "I felt as if I were walking with destiny, and that all my past life had been but a preparation for this hour and for this trial." The same is true of you; your whole life has been preparation.

"I'd love to be William Wallace, leading the charge with a big sword in my hand," sighed a friend. "But I feel like I'm the guy back there in the fourth row, with a hoe." That's a lie of the Enemy — that your place is really insignificant, that you aren't really armed for it anyway. In your life you *are* William Wallace — who else could be? There is no other man who can replace you in your life, in the arena you've been called to. If you leave your place in the line, it will remain empty. No one else can be who you are meant to be. You *are* the hero in your story. Not a bit player, not an extra, but the main man. This is the next leg in the initiation journey, when God calls a man forward to the front lines. He wants to develop and release in us the qualities every warrior needs — including a keen awareness of the enemies we will face.

Above all else, a warrior has a *vision,* he has a transcendence to his life, a cause greater than self-preservation. The root of all our woes and our false self was this: We were seeking to save our life and we lost it. Christ calls a man beyond that, "but whoever loses his life for me and for the gospel will save it" (Mark 8:35). Again, this isn't just about being willing to die for Christ; it's much more daily than that. For years all my daily energy was spent trying to beat the trials in my life and arrange for a little pleasure. My weeks were wasted away either striving or indulging. I was a mercenary. A mercenary fights for pay, for his own benefit; his life is devoted to himself. "The quality of a true warrior," says Bly, "is that he is in service to a purpose greater than himself; that is, to a transcendent cause." That is the moving quality in Ballou's letter; that is the secret of the warrior-heart of Jesus.

Second, a warrior is *cunning*. He knows when to fight and when to run; he can sense a trap and never charges blindly ahead; he knows what weapons to carry and how to use them. Whatever specific terrain you are called to — at home, at work, in the realm of the arts or industry or world politics, you will always encounter three enemies: the world, the flesh, and the devil. They make up a sort of unholy trinity. Because they always conspire together it's a bit difficult to talk about them individually; in any battle at least two of them are involved, but usually it's all three. Still, they each have their own personality, so I'll take them one at a time and then try to show how they collude against us. Let's start with the enemy closest at hand.

THE TRAITOR WITHIN

> However strong a castle may be, if a treacherous party resides inside (ready to betray at the first opportunity possible), the castle cannot be kept safe from the enemy. Traitors occupy our own hearts, ready to side with every temptation and to surrender to them all. (John Owen, *Sin and Temptation*)

Ever since that fateful day when Adam gave away the essence of his strength, men have struggled with a part of themselves that is ready at the drop of a hat to do the same. We don't want to speak up unless we know it will go well, and we don't want to move unless we're guaranteed success. What the Scriptures call the flesh, the old man, or the sinful nature, is that part of fallen Adam in every man that always wants the easiest way out. It's much easier to masturbate than to make love to your wife, especially if things are not well between you and initiating sex with her feels risky. It's much easier to go down to the driving range and attack a bucket of balls than it is to face the people at work who are angry at you. It's much easier to clean the garage, organize your files, cut the grass, or work on the car than it is to talk to your teenage daughter.

To put it bluntly, your flesh is a weasel, a poser, and a selfish pig. And your flesh is *not you*. Did you know that? Your flesh is not the real you. When Paul gives us his famous passage on what it's like to struggle with sin (Rom. 7), he tells a story we are all too familiar with:

> I decide to do good, but I don't *really* do it; I decide not to do bad, but then I do it anyway. My decisions, such as they are, don't result in actions. Something has gone wrong deep within me and gets the better of me every time. It happens so regularly that it's predictable. The moment I decide to do good, sin is there to trip me up. I truly delight in God's commands, but it's pretty obvious that not all of me joins in that delight. Parts of me covertly rebel, and just when I least expect it, they take charge. (*The Message*)

Okay, we've all been there many times. But what Paul concludes is just astounding: "I am not really the one doing it; the sin within me is doing it" (Rom. 7:20 NLT). Did you notice the distinction he makes? Paul says, "Hey, I know I struggle with sin. But I also know that *my sin is not me* — this is not my true heart." You are not your sin; sin is no longer the truest thing about the man who has come into union with Jesus. Your heart is good. "I will give you a new heart and put a new spirit in you . . ." (Ezek. 36:26). The Big Lie in the church today is that you are nothing more than "a sinner saved by grace." You are a lot more than that. You are a new creation in Christ. The New Testament calls you a saint, a holy one, a son of God. In the core of your being you are a good man. Yes, there is a war within us, but it is a *civil* war. The battle is not between us and God; no, there is a traitor within who wars against our true heart fighting alongside the Spirit of God in us:

> A new power is in operation. The Spirit of life in Christ, like a strong wind, has magnificently cleared the air, freeing you from a fated lifetime of brutal tyranny at the hands of sin and death . . . Anyone, of course, who has not welcomed this invisible but clearly present God, the Spirit of Christ, won't know what we're talking about. But for you who welcome him, in whom he dwells . . . if the alive-and-

present God who raised Jesus from the dead moves into your life, he'll do the same thing in you that he did in Jesus . . . When God lives and breathes in you (and he does, as surely as he did in Jesus), you are delivered from that dead life. (Rom. 8:2–3, 9–11 *The Message*)

The *real* you is on the side of God against the false self. Knowing this makes all the difference in the world. The man who wants to live valiantly will lose heart quickly if he believes that his heart is nothing but sin. Why fight? The battle feels lost before it even begins. No, your flesh is your *false self* — the poser, manifest in cowardice and self-preservation — and the only way to deal with it is to crucify it. Now follow me very closely here: We are never, ever told to crucify our heart. We are never told to kill the true man within us, never told to get rid of those deep desires for battle and adventure and beauty. We are told to shoot the traitor. How? Choose against him every time you see him raise his ugly head. Walk right into those situations you normally run from. Speak right to the issues you normally remain silent over. If you want to grow in true masculine strength, then you must stop sabotaging yours.

Rich is a deeply passionate young man who is really trying to learn what it means to be a man. A few weeks ago he had plans to go out with some friends. They promised to call him before they left and then come pick him up; they never called. A few days later, when one of them brought it up, Rich said, "Oh, that's okay. It's no big deal." But inside, he was *furious*. That is sabotage. He deliberately chose to push his true strength down and live the false self. Do that enough and you won't believe you have any strength. I've noticed when I deny the anger I am feeling, it turns into fear. If we will not allow what Sam Keen calls "fire in the belly," something weaker will take its place. I had a chance a few years back to tell my boss what I really thought of him; not in sinful anger (there's a difference), not to hurt him but to help him. He actually asked me to, called to see if I was free to chat for a moment. I knew what he was calling for and I ran; I told him I was busy. For days afterward I felt weak; I felt like a poser. I sabotaged my strength by refusing it.

Sabotage also happens when we give our strength away. Taking a bribe, letting yourself be bought off, accepting flattery in exchange for some sort of loyalty, is sabotage.

Refusing to confront an issue because if you keep quiet you'll get a promotion or be made an elder or keep your job corrupts you down deep. Masturbation is sabotage. It is an inherently selfish act that tears you down. I've spoken with many men whose addiction to masturbation has eroded their sense of strength. So does sexual involvement with a woman you are not married to. Carl is another young man whom the ladies seem to find especially attractive. I am astounded what young women will offer when they are famished for the love and affirmation they have never had from their fathers. They will throw themselves at a man to get a taste of being wanted, desired. Carl came to me because his sexual activity was out of control. Dozens upon dozens of women offered themselves to him and each time he gave in he felt weakened; his resolve to resist was less the next time around.

Things began to change for Carl when he saw the whole sexual struggle not so much as sin *but as a battle for his strength.* He wants to be strong, wants it desperately, and that began to fuel his choice to resist. As à Kempis said, "A man must strive long and mightily within himself, before he can learn fully to master himself." Carl and I spent hours praying through every one of those relationships, confessing the sin, breaking the bonds sexual liaisons form between two souls, cleansing his strength, asking God to restore him. He did, and I am grateful to say those days are over for Carl. It wasn't easy, but it was real; he is happily married now.

THE REAL THING

Start choosing to live out your strength and you'll discover that it grows each time. Rich was after some brakes for his car; he called the parts store and they quoted him a price of $50 for the pair. But when he got down there, the guy told him it would be $90. He was taking Rich for a fool and something in Rich was provoked. Normally he would have said "Oh, that's okay. It's no big deal," and paid the higher price; but not this time. He told the guy that the price was $50 and stood his ground. The guy backed down and stopped trying to rip him off. "It felt great," Rich told me later. "I felt that I was finally acting like a man." Now that may seem like a simple story, but this is where you will discover your strength, in the daily details of your life. Begin to taste your true strength and you'll want *more*. Something in the center of your chest feels weighty, substantial.

We must let our strength show up. It

seems so strange, after all this, that a man would not allow his strength to arrive, but many of us are unnerved by our own masculinity. What will happen if we really let it out? In *Healing the Masculine Soul*, Gordon Dalby tells a remarkable story about a man who was plagued by a recurring dream, a nightmare "in which a ferocious lion kept chasing the man until he dropped exhausted and awoke screaming." The man was dismayed; he did not know what the dream meant. Was the lion a symbol of fear? Something in his life overwhelming him? One day the man was guided by his pastor (a friend of Dalby's) to revisit the dream in prayer:

As they prayed, [the pastor] on impulse invited the man to recall the dream, even in all its fear. Hesitantly, the man agreed, and soon reported that indeed, the lion was in sight and headed his way. [The pastor] then instructed the man, "When the lion comes close to you, try not to run away, but instead, stand there and ask him who or what he is, and what he's doing in your life . . . can you try that?" Shifting uneasily in his chair, the man agreed, then reported what was happening: "The lion is snorting and shaking his head, standing right there in front of me . . . I ask him who he is . . . and — Oh! I can't believe what he's saying! He says, 'I'm your courage and your strength. Why are you running away from me?' "

I had a recurring dream similar to this one for many years — especially in adolescence. A great wild stallion was standing on the ridge of a hill; I sensed danger but not an evil danger, just something strong and valiant and greater than me. I tried to sneak away; the stallion always turned in time to see me and came charging down the hill. I would wake just as he was upon me. It seems crazy that a man would sneak away from his strength, fear it to show up, but that is why we sabotage. Our strength is wild and fierce, and we are more than unsettled by what may happen if we let it arrive. One thing we know: Nothing will ever be the same. One client said to me, "I'm afraid I'll do something bad if I let all this show up." No, the opposite is true. You'll do something bad if you *don't*. Remember — a man's addictions are the result of his refusing his strength.

Years ago Brent gave me a piece of advice that changed my life: "Let people feel the weight of who you are," he said, "and let them deal with it." That brings us into the arena of our next enemy.

THE WORLD

What is this enemy that the Scripture calls "the world"? Is it drinking and dancing and smoking? Is it going to the movies or playing cards? That is a shallow and ridiculous approach to holiness. It numbs us to the fact that good and evil are much more serious. The Scriptures never prohibit drinking alcohol, only drunkenness; dancing was a vital part of King David's life; and while there are some very godly movies out there, there are also some very ungodly churches. No, "the world" is not a place or a set of behaviors — it is any system built by our collective sin, all our false selves coming together to reward and destroy each other. Take all those posers out there, put them together in an office or a club or a church, and what you get is what the Scriptures mean by the world.

The world is a carnival of counterfeits — counterfeit battles, counterfeit adventures, counterfeit beauties. Men should think of it as a corruption of their strength. Battle your way to the top, says the world, and you are a man. Why is it then that the men who get there are often the emptiest, most frightened, prideful posers around? They are mercenaries, battling only to build their own kingdoms. There is nothing transcendent about their lives. The same holds true of the adventure addicts; no matter how much you spend, no matter how far you take your hobby, it's still merely that — a hobby. And as for the counterfeit beauties, the world is constantly trying to tell us that the Golden-Haired Woman is out there — go for her.

The world offers a man a false sense of power and a false sense of security. Be brutally honest now — where does your own sense of power come from? Is it how pretty your wife is — or your secretary? Is it how many people attend your church? Is it *knowledge* — that you have an expertise and that makes others come to you, bow to you? Is it your position, degree, or title? A white coat, a Ph.D., a podium, or a paneled office can make a man feel like pretty neat stuff. What happens inside you when I suggest you give it up? Put the book down for a few moments and consider what you would think of yourself if tomorrow you lost everything that the world has rewarded you for. "Without Christ a man must fail miserably," says MacDonald, "or succeed even more miserably." Jesus warns us against anything that gives a false sense of power. When you walk into a company dinner or a church function, he said, take a backseat.

Choose the path of humility; don't be a self-promoter, a glad-hander, a poser. Climb *down* the ladder; have the mail clerk over for dinner; treat your secretary like she's more important than you; look to be the servant of all. *Where am I deriving my sense of strength and power from?* is a good question to ask yourself . . . often.

If you want to know how the world *really* feels about you, just start living out of your true strength. Say what you think, stand up for the underdog, challenge foolish policies. They'll turn on you like sharks. Remember the film *Jerry McGuire*? Jerry is an agent for professional athletes who comes to a sort of personal epiphany about the corruption of his firm. He issues a memo, a vision statement urging a more humane approach to their work. Let's stop treating people like cattle, he says; stop serving the bottom line and really serve our clients. All his buddies cheer him on; when the firm dumps him (as he knew they would) they rush to seize his clients. I've seen this time and time again. A friend of mine confronted his pastor on some false statements the pastor had made to get his position. This shepherd of the flock started circulating rumors that my friend was gay; he tried to ruin his reputation.

The world of posers is shaken by a real

man. They'll do whatever it takes to get you back in line — threaten you, bribe you, seduce you, undermine you. They crucified Jesus. But it didn't work, did it? You must let your strength show up. Remember Christ in the Garden, the sheer force of his presence? Many of us have actually been afraid to let our strength show up because the world doesn't have a place for it. Fine. The world's screwed up. Let people feel the weight of who you are and let them deal with it.

THE DEVIL

My wife and I were driving home the other day from an afternoon out and running a bit late to get to our son's last soccer game of the season. I was in the driver's seat and we were enjoying a lingering conversation about some dreams we have for the future. After several minutes we realized that we were caught in a traffic jam that was going nowhere. Precious moments slipped by as tension mounted in the car. In an effort to be helpful, Stasi suggested an alternate route: "If you take a right here and go up to First Street, we can cut over and take about five minutes off the drive." I was ready to divorce her. I'm serious. In about twenty seconds I was ready for separation. If the judge had been in the car, I'd have signed the papers right there. Good grief — over a comment about my driving? Is that all that was going on in that moment?

I sat at the wheel silent and steaming. On the outside, I looked cool; inside, here is what was happening: *Geez, doesn't she think I know how to get there? I hate it when she does that.* Then another voice says, *She always does that.* And I say (internally — the whole dialogue took place internally, in the blink of an eye), *Yeah, she does . . . she's always saying stuff like that. I hate that about her.* A feeling of accusation and anger and self-righteousness sweeps over me. Then the voice says, *John, this is never going to change,* and I say, *This is never going to change,* and the voice says, *You know, John, there are a lot of women out there who would be deeply grateful to have you as their man,* and I think, *Yeah — there are a lot of women out there . . .* You get the picture. Change the characters and the setting and the very same thing has happened to you. Only, you probably thought the whole thing was your own mess.

The devil no doubt has a place in our theology, but is he a category we even think about in the daily events of our lives? Has it ever crossed your mind that not every thought that crosses your mind comes from you? What I experienced in the midst of traffic that day happens all the time in marriages, in ministries, in any relationship. We are being lied to all the time. Yet we never stop to say, "Wait a minute . . . who else is speaking here? Where are those ideas coming from? Where are those *feelings* coming from?" If you read the saints from every age before the Modern Era — that pride-filled age of reason, science, and technology we all were thoroughly educated in — you'll find that they take the devil very seriously indeed. As Paul says, "We are not unaware of his schemes" (2 Cor. 2:11). But we, the enlightened, have a much more commonsense approach to things. We look for a psychological or physical or even political explanation for every trouble we meet.

Who caused the Chaldeans to steal Job's herds and kill his servants? Satan, clearly (Job 1:12, 17). Yet do we even give him a passing thought when we hear of terrorism today? Who kept that poor woman bent over for eighteen years, the one Jesus healed on the Sabbath? Satan, clearly (Luke 13:16). But do we consider him when we are having a headache that keeps us from praying or reading Scripture? Who moved Ananias and Sapphira to lie to the apostles?

Satan again (Acts 5:3). But do we really see his hand behind a fallout or schism in ministry? Who was behind that brutal assault on your own strength, those wounds you've taken? As William Gurnall said, "It is the image of God reflected in you that so enrages hell; it is this at which the demons hurl their mightiest weapons."

There is a whole lot more going on behind the scenes of our lives than most of us have been led to believe. Take Christmas for example.

BEHIND THE SCENES

Most of you probably have a Nativity scene that you take out over the holidays and place on a mantel or coffee table. Most of these scenes share a regular cast of characters: shepherds, wise men, maybe a few barnyard animals, Joseph, Mary, and, of course, the baby Jesus. Yes, ours has an angel or two and I imagine yours does as well. But that's about as far as the supernatural gets. What is the overall *mood* of the scene? Don't they all have a sort of warm, pastoral atmosphere to them, a quiet, intimate feel like the one you get when you sing *Silent Night* or *Away in a Manger*? And while that's all very true, it is also very *deceiving* because it is not a full picture of what's really going on. For that, you have to turn to Revelation 12:

> A great and wondrous sign appeared in heaven: a woman clothed with the sun, with the moon under her feet and a crown of twelve stars on her head. She was pregnant and cried out in pain as she was about to give birth. Then another sign appeared in heaven: an enormous red dragon with seven heads and ten horns and seven crowns on his heads. His tail swept a third of the stars out of the sky and flung them to the earth. The dragon stood in front of the woman who was about to give birth, so that he might devour her child the moment it was born. She gave birth to a son, a male child, who will rule all the nations with an iron scepter . . . And there was war in heaven. Michael and his angels fought against the dragon, and the dragon and his angels fought back. But he was not strong enough, and they lost their place in heaven. The great dragon was hurled down — that ancient serpent called the devil or Satan, who leads the whole world astray. He was hurled to the earth, and his angels with him. (vv. 1–5, 7–9)

As Philip Yancey says, I have never seen this version of the story on a Christmas card. Yet it is the truer story, the rest of the picture of what was going on that fateful night. Yancey calls the birth of Christ the Great Invasion, "a daring raid by the ruler of the forces of good into the universe's seat of evil." Spiritually speaking, this is no silent night. It is D-Day. "It is almost beyond my comprehension too, and yet I accept that this notion is the key to understanding Christmas and is, in fact, the touchstone of my faith. As a Christian I believe that we live in parallel worlds. One world consists of hills and lakes and barns and politicians and shepherds watching their flocks by night. The other consists of angels and sinister forces" and the whole spiritual realm. The child is born, the woman escapes and the story continues like this:

Then the dragon was enraged at the woman and went off to make war against the rest of her offspring — those who obey God's commandments and hold to the testimony of Jesus. (Rev. 12:17)

Behind the world and the flesh is an even more deadly enemy . . . one we rarely speak of and are even much less ready to resist. Yet this is where we live now — on the front lines of a fierce spiritual war that is to blame for most of the casualties you see around you and most of the assault against you. It's time we prepared ourselves for it. Yes, Luke, there is a dragon. Here is how you slay him.

Chapter Nine

A BATTLE TO FIGHT: THE STRATEGY

She was right that reality can be harsh and that you shut your eyes to it only at your peril because if you do not face up to the enemy in all his dark power, then the enemy will come up from behind some dark day and destroy you while you are facing the other way.

— FREDERICK BUECHNER

Gird your sword upon your side, O mighty one, clothe yourself with splendor and majesty.
In your majesty ride forth victoriously.

— PSALM 45:3–4

As part of Christ's army, you march in the ranks of gallant spirits. Every one of your fellow soldiers is the child of a King. Some, like you, are in the midst of battle, besieged on every side by affliction and temptation. Others, after many assaults, repulses, and rallyings of their faith, are already

240

standing upon the wall of heaven as conquerors. From there they look down and urge you, their comrades on earth, to march up the hill after them. This is their cry: "Fight to the death and the City is your own, as now it is ours!"

— WILLIAM GURNALL

The invasion of France and the end of WWII actually began the night before the Allies hit the beaches at Normandy, when the 82nd and 101st Airborne Divisions were dropped in behind enemy lines to cut off Hitler's reinforcements. If you've seen *The Longest Day* or *Saving Private Ryan*, you remember the dangers those paratroopers were facing. Alone or in small groups, they moved through the dead of night across a country they had never been to in order to fight an enemy they couldn't see or predict. It was a moment of unparalleled bravery . . . and cowardice. For not every trooper played the man that fateful night. Sure, they jumped; but afterward, many hid. One group took cowardice to a new level.

Too many had hunkered down in hedgerows to await the dawn; a few had even gone to sleep. Pvt. Francis Palys of the 506th saw what was perhaps the worst dereliction of duty. He had gathered a squad near Vierville. Hearing "all kinds of noise and singing from a distance," he and his men sneaked up on a farmhouse. In it was a mixed group from both American divisions. The paratroopers had found [liquor] in the cellar . . . and they were drunker than a bunch of hill-

billies on a Saturday night wingding.
Unbelievable. (*D-Day*)

Unbelievable indeed. These men *knew*
they were at war, yet they refused to act like
it. They lived in a dangerous denial — a
denial that not only endangered them but
countless others who depended on them to
do their part. It is a *perfect* picture of the
church in the West when it comes to spiritual warfare. During a recent church staff
meeting, a friend of mine raised the sugges-
tion that some of the difficulties they were
facing might be the work of the Enemy.
"What do you think?" he asked. "Well, I
suppose that sort of thing does happen,"
one of the other pastors replied. "In the
Third World, perhaps, or maybe to thwart a
major crusade. You know . . . places where
cutting-edge ministry is going on."

STAGE ONE: "I'M NOT HERE"

Incredible. What a self-indictment.
"Nothing dangerous is happening here."
Those men have already been taken out because they've swallowed the Enemy's first
line of attack: "I'm not here — this is all just
you." You can't fight a battle you don't
think exists. This is right out of *The Screwtape*

Letters, where Lewis has the old devil instruct his apprentice in this very matter:

> My dear Wormwood, I wonder you should ask me whether it is essential to keep the patient in ignorance of your own existence. That question, at least for the present phase of the struggle, has been answered for us by the High Command. Our policy, for the moment, is to conceal ourselves.

As for those who want to be dangerous (cutting-edge), take a close look at 1 Peter 5:8–9: "Be self-controlled and alert. Your enemy the devil prowls around like a roaring lion looking for someone to devour. Resist him, standing firm in the faith, because you know that your brothers throughout the world are undergoing the same kind of sufferings." What is the Holy Spirit, through Peter, assuming about your life? *That you are under spiritual attack.* This is not a passage about nonbelievers; he's talking about "your brethren." Peter takes it for granted that every believer is under some sort of unseen assault. And what does he insist you do? *Resist* the devil. Fight back, take a stand.

A ministry partnership that some dear friends were central to has just dissolved this week, I am deeply sad to say. They had teamed up with another organization to bring the gospel to cities across the U.S. These conferences are very powerful; in fact, I've never seen anything even close to the impact they have. Through grateful tears, the attendees talk about the healing, the freedom, the release they have experienced. They recover their hearts and are drawn into an intimacy with God most have never, ever experienced before. It's beautiful and awe-inspiring. Now, do you think the Enemy just lets that sort of thing go swimmingly along without any interference whatsoever?

The partnership hit some choppy water, nothing much at all really, nothing unusual to any relationship, yet the other members simply decided to end the coalition and walk away mid-season. Were there personal issues involved? You bet; there always are. But they were minor. It was mostly misunderstanding and injured pride. There was not one word, not one thought as far as I could tell about the Enemy and what he might be doing to break up so strategic an alliance. When I brought up the fact that they would do well to interpret things with open eyes, keeping the attacks of the Evil One in mind, I was dismissed. These good people with good hearts wanted to explain everything on a "human" level and let me tell you — when you ignore the Enemy, he wins. He simply loves to blame everything on us, get us feeling hurt, misunderstood, suspicious, and resentful of one another.

Before an effective military strike can be made, you must take out the opposing army's line of communication. The Evil One does this all the time — in ministries and especially between couples. Marriage is a stunning picture of what God offers his people. Scripture tells us it is a living metaphor, a walking parable, a Rembrandt painting of the gospel. The Enemy knows this, *and he hates it* with every ounce of his malicious heart. He has no intention of just letting that beautiful portrait be lived out before the world with such deep appeal that no one can resist God's offer. So just like in the Garden, Satan comes in to divide and conquer. Often I'll feel this sense of accusation when I'm with my wife. It's hard to describe and it usually isn't put into words, but I just receive this message that *I'm blowing it.* I finally brought this up with Stasi and tears came to her eyes. "You're kidding," she said. "I've been feeling the very same thing. I thought you were disappointed with *me*." Wait a minute, I thought.

If I'm not sending this message and you're not sending this message . . .

Most of all the Enemy will try to jam communications with Headquarters. Commit yourself to prayer every morning for two weeks and just watch what'll happen. You won't want to get up; an important meeting will be called that interferes; you'll catch a cold; or, if you do get to your prayers, your mind will wander to what you'll have for breakfast and how much you should pay for that water heater repair and what color socks would look best with your gray suit. Many, many times I've simply come under a cloak of *confusion* so thick I suddenly find myself wondering why I ever believed in Jesus in the first place. That sweet communion I normally enjoy with God is cut off, gone, vanished like the sun behind a cloud. If you don't know what's up you'll think you really have lost your faith or been abandoned by God or whatever spin the Enemy puts on it. Oswald Chambers warns us, "Sometimes there is nothing to obey, the only thing to do is to maintain a vital connection with Jesus Christ, to see that nothing interferes with that."

Next comes propaganda. Like the infamous Tokyo Rose, the Enemy is constantly broadcasting messages to try to demoralize us. As in my episode during the traffic jam, he is constantly *putting his spin* on things. After all, Scripture calls him the "accuser of our brethren" (Rev. 12:10 NKJV). Think of what goes on — what you hear and feel — when you really blow it. *I'm such an idiot, I always do that, I'll never amount to anything.* Sounds like accusation to me. How about when you're really trying to step forward as a man? I can guarantee you what will happen when I'm going to speak. I was driving to the airport for a trip to the West Coast, to give a talk to men about *Wild at Heart.* All the way there I was under this cloud of heaviness; I was nearly overcome by a deep sense of *John, you're such a poser. You have absolutely nothing to say. Just turn the car around, go home, and tell them you can't make it.* Now in my clearer moments I know it's an attack, but you must understand that all this comes on so subtly it seems true at the time. I nearly gave in and went home.

When Christ is assaulted by the Evil One in the wilderness, the attack is ultimately on his identity. "*If* you are the Son of God," Satan sneers three times, then prove it (Luke 4:1–13). Brad returned from the mission field last year for a sabbatical. After seven years abroad, most of the time without any real companionship, he was pretty beat up; he felt like a failure. He told me that when he woke in the morning he'd "hear" a voice in his thoughts say, *Good morning . . . Loser.* So many men live under a similar accusation. Craig had really been entering into the battle and fighting bravely the past several months. Then he had a nightmare, a very vivid, grisly dream in which he had molested a little girl. He woke up feeling filthy and condemned. That same week I had a dream where I was accused of committing adultery; I really hadn't, but in my dream no one would believe me. Follow this: So long as a man remains no real threat to the Enemy, Satan's line to him is *You're fine.* But after you do take sides, it becomes *Your heart is bad and you know it.*

Finally, he probes the perimeter, looking for a weakness. Here's how this works: Satan will throw a thought or a temptation at us in hopes that we will swallow it. He knows your story, knows what works with you and so the line is tailor-made to your situation. Just this morning in my prayer time it was pride, then worry, then adultery, then greed, then gluttony. If I thought this was all me, my heart, I'd be very discouraged. Knowing that my heart is good allowed me to block it, right then and there. When

Satan probes, make no agreements. If we make an agreement, if something in our heart says, *Yeah, you're right,* then he pours it on. You'll see a beautiful woman and something in you will say, *You want her.* That's the Evil One appealing to the traitor within. If the traitor says, *Yes, I do,* then the lust really begins to take hold. Let that go on for years and you've given him a stronghold. This can make a good man feel so awful because he thinks he's a lustful man when he's not; it's an attack through and through.

Please don't misunderstand me. I'm not blaming everything on the devil. In almost every situation there are human issues involved. Every man has his struggles; every marriage has its rough spots; every ministry has personal conflicts. But those issues are like a campfire that the Enemy throws gasoline all over and turns into a bonfire. The flames leap up into a raging inferno and we are suddenly overwhelmed with what we're feeling. Simple misunderstandings become grounds for divorce. All the while we believe that it's us, we are blowing it, we're to blame, and the Enemy is laughing because we've swallowed the lie "I'm not here, it's just you." We've got to be a lot more cunning than that.

HANGING ON TO THE TRUTH

In any hand-to-hand combat, there's a constant back-and-forth of blows, dodges, blocks, counterattacks, and so forth. That's exactly what is going on in the unseen around us. Only it takes place, initially, at the level of our thoughts. When we are under attack, we've got to hang on to the truth. Dodge the blow, block it with a stubborn refusal, slash back with what is true. This is how Christ answered Satan — he didn't get into an argument with him, try to reason his way out. He simply stood on the truth. He answered with Scripture and we've got to do the same. This will not be easy, especially when all hell is breaking loose around you. It will feel like holding on to a rope while you're being dragged behind a truck, like keeping your balance in a hurricane. Satan doesn't just throw a thought at us; he throws *feelings* too. Walk into a dark house late at night and suddenly fear sweeps over you; or just stand in a grocery line with all those tabloids shouting sex at you and suddenly a sense of corruption is yours.

But this is where your strength is revealed and even increased — through exercise. Stand on what is true and do not let go. Period. The traitor within the castle will try to lower the drawbridge but don't let him. When Proverbs 4:23 tells us to guard our hearts, it's not saying, "Lock them up because they're really criminal to the core"; it's saying, "Defend them like a castle, the seat of your strength you do not want to give away." As à Kempis says, "Yet we must be watchful, especially in the beginning of the temptation; for the enemy is then more easily overcome, if he is not suffered to enter the door of our hearts, but is resisted without the gate at his first knock."

Remember the scene in *Braveheart* where Robert the Bruce's evil father is whispering lies to him about treason and compromise? He says to Robert what the Enemy says to us in a thousand ways: "All men betray; all men lose heart." How does Robert answer? He yells back,

I don't want to lose heart!
I want to believe, like [Wallace] does.
I will never be on the wrong side again.

That is the turning point in his life . . . and in ours. The battle shifts to a new level.

STAGE TWO: INTIMIDATION

Stasi lived under a cloud of depression for many years. We had seen her find some healing through counseling, but still the depression remained. We had addressed the physical aspects that we could through medication, yet it lingered still. *Okay,* I thought to myself, *the Bible tells me that we have a body, a soul, and a spirit. We've addressed the body and soul issues . . . what's left must be spiritual.* Stasi and I began to read a bit on dealing with the Enemy. In the course of our study she came across a passage that referred to different symptoms that sometimes accompany depression; one of them was dizziness. As she read the passage out loud she sounded surprised. "What about it?" I asked. "Well . . . I get dizzy spells a lot." "Really? How often?" "Oh, every day." "Every day??!!" I had been married to Stasi for ten years and she had never even mentioned this to me. The poor woman had simply thought they were normal for everyone since they were normal for her.

"Stasi, I have never had a dizzy spell in my life. I think we're onto something here." We began to pray against the dizziness, taking authority over any attack in the name of Jesus. You know what happened? It got *worse!* The Enemy, once discovered, usually doesn't just roll over and go away without a fight. Notice that sometimes Jesus rebukes a foul spirit "in a stern voice" (see Luke 4:35). In fact, when he encounters the guy who lives out in the Gerasenes tombs, tormented by a legion of spirits, the first rebuke by Jesus doesn't work. He had to get more information, really take them on (Luke 8:26–33). Now if Jesus had to get tough with these guys, don't you suppose we'll have to as well? Stasi and I held our ground, resisting the onslaught "firm in the faith," as Peter says, and you know what? The dizzy spells ended. They are history. She hasn't had one for seven years.

That is the next level of our Enemy's strategy. When we begin to question him, to resist his lies, to see his hand in the "ordinary trials" of our lives, then he steps up the attack; he turns to intimidation and fear. In fact, at some point in the last several pages you've probably begun to feel something like *Do I really want to get into all this superspiritual hocus-pocus? It's kind of creepy anyway.* Satan will try to get you to agree with intimidation *because he fears you.* You are a huge threat to him. He doesn't want you waking up and fighting back because when you do he loses. "Resist the devil," James says, *"and he will flee from you"* (James

4:7, emphasis added). So he's going to try to keep you from taking a stand. He moves from subtle seduction to open assault. The thoughts come crashing in, all sorts of stuff begins to fall apart in your life, your faith seems paper thin.

Why do so many pastors' kids go off the deep end? You think that's a coincidence? So many churches start off with life and vitality only to end in a split, or simply wither away and die. How come? Why did a friend of mine nearly black out when she tried to share her testimony at a meeting? Why are my flights so often thwarted when I'm trying to take the gospel to a city? Why does everything seem to fall apart at work when you're making some advances at home, or vice versa? Because we are at war and the Evil One is trying an old tactic — strike first and maybe the opposition will turn tail and run. He can't win, you know. As Franklin Roosevelt said, "We have nothing to fear but fear itself."

GOD IS WITH US

Be strong and courageous, because you will lead these people to inherit the land I swore to their forefathers to give them. Be strong and very courageous . . . Have

I not commanded you? Be strong and courageous. Do not be terrified; do not be discouraged, for the LORD your God will be with you wherever you go. (Josh. 1:6–7, 9)

Joshua knew what it was to be afraid. For years he had been second in command, Moses' right-hand man. But now it was his turn to lead. The children of Israel weren't just going to waltz in and pick up the promised land like a quart of milk; they were going to have to fight for it. And Moses was not going with them. If Joshua was completely confident about the situation, why would God have had to tell him over and over and over again not to be afraid? In fact, God gives him a special word of encouragement: "As I was with Moses, so I will be with you; I will never leave you nor forsake you" (Josh. 1:5). How was God "with Moses"? As a mighty warrior. Remember the plagues? Remember all those Egyptian soldiers drowned with their horses and chariots out there in the Red Sea? It was after that display of God's strength that the people of Israel sang, "The LORD is a warrior; the LORD is his name" (Ex. 15:3). God fought for Moses and for Israel; then he covenanted to

Joshua to do the same and they took down Jericho and every other enemy.

Jeremiah knew what it meant to have God "with him" as well. "But the Lord is with me like a mighty warrior," he sang. "So my persecutors will stumble and not prevail" (Jer. 20:11). Even Jesus walked in this promise when he battled for us here on earth:

> You know what has happened throughout Judea, beginning in Galilee after the baptism that John preached — how God anointed Jesus of Nazareth with the Holy Spirit and power, and how he went around doing good and healing all who were under the power of the devil, *because God was with him.* (Acts 10:37–38, emphasis added)

How did Jesus win the battle against Satan? God was *with him.* This really opens up the riches of the promise Christ gives us when he pledges "I am with you always, even to the end of the age" and "I will never leave you nor forsake you" (Matt. 28:20; Heb. 13:5 NKJV). That doesn't simply mean that he'll be around, or even that he'll comfort us in our afflictions. It means *he will fight for us,* with us, just as he has fought for his people all through the ages. So long as we walk with Christ, stay in him, we haven't a thing to fear.

Satan is trying to appeal to the traitor's commitment to self-preservation when he uses fear and intimidation. So long as we are back in the old story of saving our skin, looking out for Number One, those tactics will work. We'll shrink back. But the opposite is also true. When a man resolves to become a warrior, when his life is given over to a transcendent cause, then he can't be cowed by the Big Bad Wolf threatening to blow his house down. After Revelation describes that war in heaven between the angels and Satan's downfall to the earth, it tells how the saints overcame him:

> They overcame him
> by the blood of the Lamb
> and by the word of their testimony;
> they did not love their lives so much
> as to shrink from death. (12:11)

The most dangerous man on earth is the man who has reckoned with his own death. All men die; few men ever really *live*. Sure, you can create a safe life for yourself . . . and end your days in a rest home babbling on about some forgotten misfortune. I'd rather go down swinging. Besides, the less we are trying to "save ourselves," the more effective a warrior we will be. Listen to G. K. Chesterton on courage:

> Courage is almost a contradiction in terms. It means a strong desire to live taking the form of a readiness to die. "He that will lose his life, the same shall save it," is not a piece of mysticism for saints and heroes. It is a piece of everyday advice for sailors or mountaineers. It might be printed in an Alpine guide or a drill book. The paradox is the whole principle of courage; even of quite earthly or quite brutal courage. A man cut off by the sea may save his life if he will risk it on the precipice. He can only get away from death by continually stepping within an inch of it. A soldier surrounded by enemies, if he is to cut his way out, needs to combine a strong desire for living with a strange carelessness about dying. He must not merely cling to live, for then he will be a coward, and will not escape. He must not merely wait for death, for then he will be a suicide, and will not escape. He must seek his life in a spirit of furious indifference

to it; he must desire life like water and yet drink death like wine.

STAGE THREE: CUTTING A DEAL

The third level of attack the Evil One employs, after we have resisted deception and intimidation, is simply to try to get us to cut a deal. So many men have been bought off in one way or another. The phone just rang; a friend called to tell me that yet another Christian leader has fallen into sexual immorality. The church wags its head and says, "You see. He just couldn't keep himself clean." That is naive. Do you think that man, a follower of Christ, in his heart of hearts really *wanted* to fall? What man begins his journey wishing, "I think one day, after twenty years of ministry, I'll torpedo the whole thing with an affair"? He was *picked off;* the whole thing was plotted. In his case it was a long and subtle assignment to wear his defenses down not so much through battle as through *boredom.* I knew that man; he had no great cause to fight for, just the monotony of "professional Christian ministry" that he hated but couldn't get out of because he was being so well paid for it. He was set up for a fall. Unless you are aware that that's what it is, you'll be taken out too.

Notice this — when did King David fall? What were the circumstances of his affair with Bathsheba? "In the spring, at the time when kings go off to war, David sent Joab out with the king's men and the whole Israelite army" (2 Sam. 11:1). David was no longer a warrior; he sent others to do his fighting for him. Bored, sated, and fat, he strolls around on the roof of the palace looking for something to amuse him. The Evil One points out Bathsheba and the rest is history — which, as we all know, repeats itself. William Gurnall warns us,

Persisting to the end will be the burr under your saddle — the thorn in your flesh — when the road ahead seems endless and your soul begs an early discharge. It weighs down every other difficulty of your calling. We have known many who have joined the army of Christ and like being a soldier for a battle or two, but have soon had enough and ended up deserting. They impulsively enlist for Christian duties . . . and are just as easily persuaded to lay it down. Like the new moon, they shine a little in the first part of the evening, but go down before the night is over. (*The Christian in Full Armor*)

THE WEAPONS OF WAR

Against the flesh, the traitor within, a warrior uses discipline. We have a two-dimensional version of this now, which we call a "quiet time." But most men have a hard time sustaining any sort of devotional life because it has no vital connection to recovering and protecting their strength; it feels about as important as flossing. But if you saw your life as a great battle and you *knew* you needed time with God for your very survival, you would do it. Maybe not perfectly — nobody ever does and that's not the point anyway — but you would have a reason to seek him. We give a half-hearted attempt at the spiritual disciplines when the only reason we have is that we "ought" to. But we'll find a way to make it work when we are convinced we're history if we don't.

Time with God each day is not about academic study or getting through a certain amount of Scripture or any of that. It's about connecting with God. We've got to keep those lines of communication open, so use whatever helps. Sometimes I'll listen to music; other times I'll read Scripture or a passage from a book; often I will journal; maybe I'll go for a run; then there are days when all I need is silence and solitude and the rising sun. The point is simply to do *whatever brings me back to my heart and the heart of God*. God has spared me many times from an ambush I had no idea was coming; he warned me in my time with him in the early morning about something that was going to happen that day. Just the other day it was a passage from a book about forgiveness. I sensed he was saying something to me personally. *Lord, am I unforgiving? No,* he said. About an hour later I received a very painful phone call — a betrayal. *Oh, you were telling me to be ready to forgive, weren't you? Yes.*

The discipline, by the way, is never the point. The whole point of a "devotional life" is *connecting with God*. This is our primary antidote to the counterfeits the world holds out to us. If you do not have God and have him deeply, you will turn to other lovers. As Maurice Roberts says,

Ecstasy and delight are essential to the believer's soul and they promote sanctification. We are not meant to live without spiritual exhilaration . . . The believer is in spiritual danger if he allows himself to go for any length of time without tasting the love of Christ . . . When Christ ceases to fill the heart with satisfaction, our souls will go in silent search of other lovers. (*The Thought of God*)

A man will devote long hours to his finances when he has a goal of an early retirement; he'll endure rigorous training when he aims to run a 10k or even a marathon. The ability to discipline himself is there, but dormant for many of us. "When a warrior is in service, however, to a True King — that is, to a transcendent cause," says Bly, "he does well, and his body becomes a hardworking servant, which he requires to endure cold, heat, pain, wounds, scarring, hunger, lack of sleep, hardship of all kinds, do what is necessary."

Against the Evil One we wear the armor of God. That God has provided weapons of war for us sure makes a lot more sense if our days are like a scene from *Saving Private Ryan*. How many Christians have read over those passages about the shield of faith and the helmet of salvation and never really known what to do with them. *What lovely poetic imagery; I wonder what it means.* It means that God has given you armor and you'd better put it on. Every day. This equipment is really there, in the spiritual, unseen realm. We don't see it, but the angels and our enemies do. Start by simply praying through the passage in Ephesians as if suiting up for the arena:

"Therefore put on the full armor of God, so that when the day of evil comes, you may be able to stand your ground, and after you have done everything, to stand. Stand firm then, with the belt of truth buckled around your waist . . ." *Lord, I put on the belt of truth. I choose a lifestyle of honesty and integrity. Show me the truths I so desperately need today. Expose the lies I'm not even aware that I'm believing.* ". . . with the breastplate of righteousness in place . . ." *And yes, Lord, I wear your righteousness today against all condemnation and corruption. Fit me with your holiness and purity — defend me from all assaults against my heart.* ". . . and with your feet fitted with the readiness that comes from the gospel of peace . . ." *I do choose to live for the gospel at any moment. Show me where the larger story is unfolding and keep me from being so lax that I think the most important thing today is the soap operas of this world.*

"In addition to all this, take up the shield of faith, with which you can extinguish all the flaming arrows of the evil one . . ." *Jesus, I lift against every lie and every assault the confidence that you are good, and that you have good in store for me. Nothing is coming today that can overcome me because you are with me.* ". . . Take the helmet of salvation . . ." *Thank you, Lord, for my salvation. I receive it in a new and fresh way from you and I declare that nothing can separate me now from the love of Christ and the place I shall ever have in your kingdom.* ". . . and the sword of the Spirit, which is the word of God . . ." *Holy Spirit, show me specifically today the truths of the Word of God that I will need to counter the assaults and the snares of the Enemy. Bring them to mind throughout the day.* ". . . And pray in the Spirit on all occasions with all kinds of prayers and requests. With this in mind, be alert and always keep on praying for all the saints." *Finally, Holy Spirit, I agree to walk in step with you in everything — in all prayer as my spirit communes with you throughout the day.* (6:13–18)

And we walk in the authority of Christ. Do not attack in anger, do not swagger forth in pride. You will get nailed. I love the scene in *The Mask of Zorro* when the old master swordsman saves his young apprentice — who at that moment has had too much to drink — from rushing upon his enemy. "You would have fought bravely," he says, "and died quickly." All authority in heaven and on earth has been given to Jesus Christ (Matt. 28:18). He tells us this before he gives us the Great Commission, the command to advance his kingdom. Why? We've never made the connection. The reason is, if you are going to serve the True King you're going to need his authority. We dare not take on any angel, let alone a fallen one, in our own strength. That is why Christ extends his authority to us, "and you have been given fullness in Christ, who is the head over every power and authority" (Col. 2:10). Rebuke the Enemy in your own name and he laughs; command him in the name of Christ and he flees.

One more thing: Don't even think about going into battle alone. Don't even try to take the masculine journey without at least one man by your side. Yes, there are times a man must face the battle alone, in the wee hours of the morn, and fight with all he's got. But don't make that a lifestyle of isolation. This may be our weakest point, as David Smith points out in *The Friendless American Male*: "One serious problem is the friendless condition of the average American male. Men find it hard to accept that they need the fellowship of other men." Thanks to the men's movement the church understands now that a man needs other men, but what we've offered is another two-dimensional solution: "Accountability" groups or partners. Ugh. That sounds so old covenant: "You're really a fool and you're just waiting to rush into sin, so we'd better post a guard by you to keep you in line."

We don't need accountability groups; we need fellow warriors, someone to fight alongside, someone to watch our back. A young man just stopped me on the street to say, "I feel surrounded by enemies and I'm all alone." The whole crisis in masculinity today has come because we no longer have a warrior culture, a place for men to learn to fight like men. We don't need a meeting of Really Nice Guys; we need a gathering of Really Dangerous Men. *That's* what we need. I think of Henry V at Agincourt. His army has been reduced to a small band of tired and weary men; many of them are wounded. They are outnumbered five to one. But Henry rallies his troops to his side when he reminds them that they are not mercenaries, but a "band of brothers."

We few, we happy few, we band of
    brothers;
For he to-day that sheds his blood
    with me
Shall be my brother . . .
And gentlemen in England, now a-
    bed
Shall think themselves accursed they
    were not here;
And hold their manhoods cheap
    whiles any speaks
That fought with us.

Yes, we need men to whom we can bare our souls. But it isn't going to happen with a group of guys you don't trust, who really aren't willing to go to battle with you. It's a long-standing truth that there is never a more devoted group of men than those who have fought alongside one another, the men of your squadron, the guys in your foxhole. It will never be a large group, but we don't need a large group. We need a band of brothers willing to "shed their blood" with us.

HONOR WOUNDS

A warning before we leave this chapter: You will be wounded. Just because this battle is spiritual doesn't mean it's not real; it is, and the wounds a man can take are in some ways more ugly than those that come in a firefight. To lose a leg is nothing compared to losing heart; to be crippled by shrapnel need not destroy your soul, but to be crippled by shame and guilt may. You will be wounded by the Enemy. He knows the wounds of your past, and he will try to wound you again in the same place. But these wounds are different; these are honor-wounds. As Rick Joyner says, "It is an honor to be wounded in the service of the Lord."

Blaine was showing me his scars the other night at the dinner table. "This one is where Samuel threw a rock and hit me in the forehead. And this one is from the Tetons when I fell into that sharp log. I can't remember what this one was from; oh, here's a good one — this one is from when I fell into the pond while chasing Luke. This one is a really old one when I burned my leg on the stove camping." He's proud of his scars; they are badges of honor to a boy . . . and to a man. We have no equivalent now for a Purple Heart of spiritual warfare, but we will. One of the noblest moments that await us will come at the Wedding Feast of the Lamb. Our Lord will rise and begin to call those forward who were wounded in battle for his name's sake and they will be honored, their courage rewarded. I think of Henry V's line to his men,

> He that outlives this day, and comes
>   safe home,
> Will stand a tip-toe when the day is
>   named,
> And rouse him at the name of
>   Crispian . . .
> Then will he strip his sleeve and show
>   his scars,
> And say, "These wounds I had on
>   Crispin's day."
> Old men forget; yet all shall be forgot,
> But he'll remember with advantages
> What feats he did that day; then shall
>   our names . . .
> Be in their flowing cups freshly
>   remember'd.

"The kingdom of heaven suffers violence," said Jesus, "and violent men take it by force" (Matt, 11: 12 NASB). Is that a good thing or a bad thing? Hopefully by now you see the deep and holy goodness of masculine aggression and that will help you understand what Christ is saying. Contrast it with this: "The kingdom of heaven is open to passive, wimpy men who enter it by lying on the couch watching TV." If you are going to live in God's kingdom, Jesus says, it's going to take every ounce of passion and forcefulness you've got. Things are going to get fierce; that's why you were given a fierce heart. I love the image of this verse given to us by John Bunyan in *Pilgrim's Progress*:

Then the Interpreter took [Christian] and led him up toward the door of the palace; and behold, at the door stood a great company of men, as desirous to go in, but [dared] not. There also sat a man at a little distance from the door, at a tableside, with a book and his inkhorn before him, to take the names of them that should enter therein; he saw also that in the doorway stood many men in armor to keep it, being resolved to do the men that would enter what hurt and mischief they could. Now was Christian somewhat in amaze. At last, when every man [fell] back for fear of the armed men, Christian saw a man of a very stout countenance come up to the man that sat there to write, saying, "Set down my name, sir," the which when he had done, he saw the man draw his sword, and put a helmet upon his head, and rush toward the door upon the armed men, who laid upon him with deadly force; but the man, not at all discouraged, fell to cutting and hacking most fiercely. So after he had received and given many wounds to those that attempted to keep him out, he cut his way through them all, and pressed forward into the palace.

Chapter Ten

A BEAUTY TO RESCUE

Beauty is not only a terrible thing, it is also a mysterious thing. There God and the Devil strive for mastery, and the battleground is the heart of men.

— FYODOR DOSTOYEVSKY

You'll be glad every night
That you treated her right.

— GEORGE THOROGOOD
"Treat Her Right"
by Roy Head
and Gene Kurtz

Cowboy take me away
Closer to heaven and closer to you.

— DIXIE CHICKS
"Cowboy Take Me Away"
(© 1999 by Martie Seidel
and Marcus Hummon)

Once upon a time (as the story goes) there was a beautiful maiden, an absolute enchantress. She might be the daughter of a king or a common servant girl, but we know she is a princess at heart. She is young with a youth that seems eternal. Her flowing hair, her deep eyes, her luscious lips, her sculpted figure — she makes the rose blush for shame; the sun is pale compared to her light. Her heart is golden, her love as true as an arrow. But this lovely maiden is unattainable, the prisoner of an evil power who holds her captive in a dark tower. Only a champion may win her; only the most valiant, daring, and brave warrior has a chance of setting her free. Against all hope he comes; with cunning and raw courage he lays siege to the tower and the sinister one who holds her. Much blood is shed on both sides; three times the knight is thrown back, but three times he rises again. Eventually the sorcerer is defeated; the dragon falls, the giant is slain. The maiden is his; through his valor he has won her heart. On horseback they ride off to his cottage by a stream in the woods for a rendezvous that gives passion and romance new meaning.

Why is this story so deep in our psyche? Every little girl knows the fable without ever being told. She dreams one day her prince will come. Little boys rehearse their part with wooden swords and cardboard shields. And one day the boy, now a young man, realizes that he wants to be the one to win the beauty. Fairy tales, literature, music, and movies all borrow from this mythic theme. Sleeping Beauty, Cinderella, Helen of Troy, Romeo and Juliet, Antony and Cleopatra, Arthur and Guinevere, Tristan and Isolde. From ancient fables to the latest blockbuster, the theme of a strong man coming to rescue a beautiful woman is universal to human nature. It is written in our hearts, one of the core desires of every man and every woman.

I met Stasi in high school, but it wasn't until late in college that our romance began. Up till that point we were simply friends. When one of us came home for the weekend, we'd give the other a call just to "hang out" — see a movie, go to a party. Then one summer night something shifted. I dropped by to see Stasi; she came sauntering down the hall barefoot, wearing a pair of blue jeans and a white blouse with lace around the collar and the top buttons undone. The sun had lightened her hair and darkened her skin and how is it I never realized she was the beautiful maiden before? We kissed that night, and though I'd kissed a few girls in my time I had never tasted a kiss like that. Needless to say, I was history. Our friendship had turned to love without my really knowing how or why, only that I wanted to be with this woman for the rest of my life. As far as Stasi was concerned, I was her knight.

Why is it that ten years later I wondered if I even wanted to be married to her anymore? Divorce was looking like a pretty decent option for the both of us. So many couples wake one day to find they no longer love each other. Why do most of us get lost somewhere between "once upon a time" and "happily ever after"? Most passionate romances seem to end with evenings in front of the TV. Why does the dream seem so unattainable, fading from view even as we discover it for ourselves? Our culture has grown cynical about the fable. Don Henley says, "We've been poisoned by these fairy tales." There are dozens of books out to refute the myth, books like *Beyond Cinderella* and *The Death of Cinderella*.

No, we have not been poisoned by fairy tales and they are not merely "myths." Far from it. The truth is, we have not taken them seriously enough. As Roland Hein says, "Myths are stories which confront us with something transcendent and eternal." In the case of our fair maiden, we have overlooked two very crucial aspects to that myth. On the one hand, none of us ever really believed the sorcerer was real. We thought we could have the maiden without a fight. Honestly, most of us guys thought our biggest battle was asking her out. And second, we have not understood the tower and its relation to her wound; the damsel is in distress. If masculinity has come under assault, femininity has been brutalized. Eve is the crown of creation, remember? She embodies the exquisite beauty and the exotic mystery of God in a way that nothing else in all creation even comes close to. And so she is the special target of the Evil One; he turns his most vicious malice against her. If he can destroy her or keep her captive, he can ruin the story.

EVE'S WOUND

Every woman can tell you about her wound; some came with violence, others came with neglect. Just as every little boy is asking one question, every little girl is, as well. But her question isn't so much about her strength. No, the deep cry of a little girl's heart is *am I lovely?* Every woman needs to know that she is exquisite and exotic and *chosen*. This is core to her identity, the way she bears the image of God. *Will you pursue me? Do you delight in me? Will you fight for me?* And like every little boy, she has taken a wound as well. The wound strikes right at the core of her heart of beauty and leaves a devastating message with it: *No. You're not beautiful and no one will really fight for you.* Like your wound, hers almost always comes at the hand of her father.

A little girl looks to her father to know if she is lovely. The power he has to cripple or to bless is just as significant to her as it is to his son. If he's a violent man he may defile her verbally or sexually. The stories I've heard from women who have been abused would tear your heart out. Janet was molested by her father when she was three; around the age of seven he showed her brothers how to do it. The assault continued until she moved away to college. What is a violated woman to think about her beauty? Am I lovely? The message is, *No . . . you are dirty. Anything attractive about you is dark and evil.* The assault continues as she grows up, through violent men and passive men. She may be stalked; she may be ignored. Either way, her heart is violated and the message is driven farther in: *you are not desired, you will not be protected, no one will fight for you.* The tower is built brick by brick, and when she's a grown woman it can be a fortress.

If her father is passive, a little girl will suffer a silent abandonment. Stasi remembers playing hide-and-seek in her house as a girl of five or six. She'd find a perfect place to crawl into, full of excited anticipation of the coming pursuit. Snuggled up in a closet, she would wait for someone to find her. No one ever did; not even after she was missing for an hour. That picture became the defining image of her life. No one noticed; no one pursued. The youngest in her family, Stasi just seemed to get lost in the shuffle. Her dad traveled a lot, and when he was home he spent most of his time in front of the TV. An older brother and sister were trouble in their teens; Stasi got the message, "Just don't be a problem; we've already got too much to handle." So she hid some more — hid her desires, hid her dreams, hid her heart. Sometimes she would pretend to be sick just to get a drop or two of attention.

Like so many unloved young women, Stasi turned to boys to try to hear what she never heard from her father. Her high school boyfriend betrayed her on prom night, told her he had been using her, that he really loved someone else. The man she dated in college became verbally abusive.

But when a woman never hears she's worth fighting for, she comes to believe that's the sort of treatment she deserves. It's a form of attention, in a twisted way; maybe it's better than nothing. Then we fell in love on that magical summer night. But Stasi married a frightened, driven man who had an affair with his work because he wouldn't risk engaging a woman he sensed he wasn't enough for. I wasn't mean; I wasn't evil. I was nice. And let me tell you, a hesitant man is the last thing in the world a woman needs. She needs a lover and a warrior, not a Really Nice Guy. Her worst fear was realized — I will never really be loved, never really be fought for. And so she hid some more.

Years into our marriage I found myself blindsided by it all. Where is the beauty I once saw? What happened to the woman I fell in love with? I didn't really expect an answer to my question; it was more a shout of rage than a desperate plea. But Jesus answered me anyway. *She's still in there, but she's captive. Are you willing to go in after her?* I realized that I had — like so many men — married for safety. I married a woman I thought would never challenge me as a man. Stasi adored me; what more did I need to do? I wanted to look like the knight, but I didn't want to bleed like one. I was deeply mistaken about the whole arrangement. I didn't know about the tower, or the dragon, or what my strength was for. The number one problem between men and their women is that we men, when asked to truly fight for her . . . hesitate. We are still seeking to save ourselves; we have forgotten the deep pleasure of spilling our life for another.

OFFERING OUR STRENGTH

> There are three things that are too
>   amazing for me,
> four that I do not understand:
> the way of an eagle in the sky,
> the way of a snake on a rock,
> the way of a ship on the high seas,
> and the way of a man with a maiden.
>   (Prov. 30:18–19)

Agur son of Jakeh is onto something here. There is something mythic in the way a man is with a woman. Our sexuality offers a parable of amazing depth when it comes to being masculine and feminine. The man comes to offer his strength and the woman invites the man into herself, an act that requires courage and vulnerability and selflessness for both of them. Notice first that if the man will not rise to the occasion, nothing will happen. He must move; his strength must swell before he can enter her. But neither will the love consummate unless the woman opens herself in stunning vulnerability. When both are living as they were meant to live, the man enters his woman and offers her his strength. He *spills himself there*, in her, for her; she draws him in, embraces and envelops him. When all is over he is spent; but ah, what a sweet death it is.

And that is how life is created. The beauty of a woman arouses a man to play the man; the strength of a man, offered tenderly to his woman, allows her to be beautiful; it brings life to her and to many. This is far, far more than sex and orgasm. It is a reality that extends to every aspect of our lives. When a man withholds himself from his woman, he leaves her without the life only he can bring. This is never more true than how a man offers — or does not offer — his words. Life and death are in the power of the tongue says Proverbs (18:21). She is made for and craves words from him. I just went upstairs to get a glass of water from the kitchen; Stasi was in there baking Christmas cookies. The place was a mess; to be honest, so was she, covered with flour and wearing a pair of old slippers. But there was something in her eye, something soft and tender, and I said to her, "You look pretty." The tension in her shoulders gave way; something twinkled in her spirit; she sighed and smiled. "Thank you," she said, almost shyly.

If the man refuses to offer himself, then his wife will remain empty and barren. A violent man destroys with his words; a silent man starves his wife. "She's wilting," a friend confessed to me about his new bride. "If she's wilting then you're withholding something," I said. Actually, it was several things — his words, his touch, but mostly his *delight*. There are so many other ways this plays out in life. A man who leaves his wife with the children and the bills to go and find another, easier life has denied them his strength. He has sacrificed them when he should have sacrificed his strength *for* them. What makes Maximus or William Wallace so heroic is simply this: They are willing to die to set others free.

This sort of heroism is what we see in the life of Joseph, the husband of Mary and the stepfather to Jesus Christ. I don't think we've fully appreciated what he did for them. Mary, an engaged young woman, almost a girl, turns up pregnant with a pretty wild story: "I'm carrying God's child." The situation is scandalous. What is Joseph to think; what is he to feel? Hurt, confused, betrayed no doubt. But he's a good man; he will not have her stoned, he will simply "divorce her quietly" (Matt. 1:19).

An angel comes to him in a dream (which shows you what it sometimes takes to get a good man to do the right thing) to convince him that Mary is telling the truth and he is to follow through with the marriage. This is going to cost him. Do you know what he's going to endure if he marries a woman the whole community thinks is an adulteress? He will be shunned by his business associates and most of his clients; he will certainly lose his standing in society and perhaps even his place in the synagogue. To see the pain he's in for, notice the insult that crowds will later use against Jesus. "Isn't this Joseph and Mary's son?" they say with a sneer and a nudge and a wink. In other words, we know who you are — the bastard child of that slut and her foolish carpenter. Joseph will pay big-time for this move. Does he withhold? No, he offers Mary his strength; he steps right between her and all of that mess and takes it on the chin. He spends himself for her.

"They will be called oaks of righteousness" (Isa. 61:3). There, under the shadow of a man's strength, a woman finds rest.

The masculine journey takes a man away from the woman *so that he might return to her.* He goes to find his strength; he returns to offer it. He tears down the walls of the tower that has held her with his words and with his actions. He speaks to her heart's deepest question in a thousand ways. *Yes, you are lovely. Yes, there is one who will fight for you.* But because most men have not yet fought the battle, most women are still in the tower.

USING HER

Most men want the maiden without any sort of cost to themselves. They want all the joys of the beauty without any of the woes of the battle. This is the sinister nature of pornography — enjoying the woman at her expense. Pornography is what happens when a man insists on being energized by a woman; he *uses* her to get a feeling that he is a man. It is a false strength, as I've said, because it depends on an outside source rather than emanating from deep within his center. And it is the paragon of selfishness. He offers nothing and takes everything. We are warned about this sort of man in the story of Judah and Tamar, a story that if it weren't in the Bible you would have thought I drew straight from a television miniseries.

Judah is the fourth son born to Jacob. You might remember him as the one who came up with the idea to sell his brother Joseph into slavery. Judah has three sons himself. When the eldest becomes a man, Judah finds a wife for him named Tamar. For reasons not fully explained to us, their marriage is short-lived. "But Er, Judah's firstborn, was wicked in the LORD's sight; so the LORD put him to death" (Gen. 38:7). Judah gives his second son to Tamar, as was the law and custom of that time. It is Onan's responsibility to raise up children in his brother's name; but he refuses to do it. He is a proud and self-centered man who angers the Lord, "so he put him to death also" (38:10). You're beginning to get the idea here: selfish men, a woman wronged, and the Lord is mad.

Judah has one son left — Shelah. The boy is the last of his strength and Judah has no intention of spending it on Tamar's behalf. He lies to Tamar, telling her to go back home and when Shelah is old enough he'll give him to her as her husband. He does not. What follows is hard to believe, especially when you consider that Tamar is a righteous woman. She disguises herself as a prostitute and sits by the road Judah is known to use. He has sex with her (uses her), but is unable to pay. Tamar takes his seal and cord and staff as a pledge. Later, word gets out that Tamar is pregnant; Judah is filled with what he insists is righteous indignation. He demands that she be burned to death, at which point Tamar produces the witness against him. "See if you recognize whose seal and cord and staff these are." Judah is nailed. He more than recognizes them — he realizes what he's been doing all along. "She is more righteous than I, since I wouldn't give her to my son Shelah" (38:25–26).

A sobering story of what happens when men selfishly refuse to spend their strength on behalf of the woman. But the same thing happens in all sorts of other ways. Pretty women endure this abuse all the time. They are pursued, but not really; they are wanted, but only superficially. They learn to offer their bodies but never, ever their souls. Most men, you see, marry for safety; they choose a woman who will make them feel like a man but never really challenge them to be one. A young man whom I admire is wrestling between the woman he is dating and one he knew but could not capture years ago. Rachel, the woman he is currently dating, is asking a lot of him; truth be told, he feels in way over his head. Julie, the woman he did not pursue, seems more idyllic; in his imagination she would be the perfect mate. Life with Rachel is tumultuous; life with Julie seems calm and tranquil. "You want the Bahamas," I said. "Rachel is the North Atlantic. Which one requires a true man?" In a brilliant twist of plot, God turns our scheme for safety on us, requiring us to play the man.

Why don't men offer what they have to their women? Because we know down in our guts that it won't be enough. There is an emptiness to Eve after the Fall, and no matter how much you pour into her she will never be filled. This is where so many men falter. Either they refuse to give what they can, or they keep pouring and pouring into her and all the while feel like a failure because she is still needing more. "There are three things that are never satisfied," warns Agur son of Jakeh, "four things that never say, 'Enough!': the grave, the barren womb, land, which is never satisfied with water, and fire, which never says, 'Enough!'" The barrenness of Eve you can never hope to fill. She needs God more than she needs you, just as you need him more than you need her.

So what do you do? Offer what you have.

"I'm afraid it won't work," a client said to me when I suggested he move back toward his wife. "She's given up on me coming through for her," he confessed, "and that's good." "No it's not," I said. "That's awful." He was headed to a family reunion back east and I suggested he bring his wife with him, make it a vacation for the two of them. "You need to move toward her." "What if it doesn't work?" he asked. So many men are asking the same question. Work for what? Validate you as a man? Resurrect her heart in a day? Do you see now that you can't bring your question to Eve? No matter how good a man you are you can never be enough. If she's the report card on your strength then you'll ultimately get an F. But that's not why you love her — to get a good grade. You love her because that's what you are made to do; that's what a real man does.

EVE TO ADAM

My friend Jan says that a woman who is living out her true design will be "valiant, vulnerable, and scandalous." That's a far cry from the "church ladies" we hold up as models of Christian femininity, those busy and tired and rigid women who have reduced their hearts to a few mild desires and pretend everything is going just great. Compare their femininity with that of the women named in the genealogy of Jesus. In a list that is nearly all men, Matthew mentions four women: Tamar, Rahab, Ruth, and "Uriah's wife" (1:3, 5–6). That Bathsheba goes unnamed tells you of God's disappointment with her, and of his delight in these three whom he takes a notable exception to name in an otherwise all-male cast. Tamar, Rahab and Ruth . . . whoa; this will open up new horizons of "biblical femininity" for you.

Tamar we now know. Rahab is in the "hall of fame of faith" in Hebrews 11 for committing treason. That's right — she hid the spies who were coming in to scope out Jericho before battle. I've never heard a woman's group study Tamar or Rahab. But what about Ruth? She's often held up as a model at women's studies and retreats — but not in the way God holds her up. The book of Ruth is devoted to one question: How does a good woman help her man to play the man? The answer: She seduces him. She uses all she has as a woman to arouse him to be a man. Ruth, as you'll remember, is the daughter-in-law of a Jewish woman named Naomi. Both women have lost their husbands and are in a pretty bad way; they have no man looking out for them, their financial status is below the poverty line, and they are vulnerable in many other ways as well. Things begin to look up when Ruth catches the eye of a wealthy single man named Boaz. Boaz is a good man, this we know. He offers her some protection and some food. But Boaz is not giving Ruth what she really needs — a ring.

So what does Ruth do? She seduces him. Here's the scene: The men have been working dawn till dusk to bring in the barley harvest; they've just finished and now it's party time. Ruth takes a bubble bath and puts on a knockout dress; then she waits for the right moment. That moment happens to be late in the evening after Boaz has had a little too much to drink: "When Boaz had finished eating and drinking and was in good spirits . . ." (Ruth 3:7). "Good spirits" is in there for the more conservative readers. The man is drunk, which is evident from what he does next: pass out. ". . . He went over to lie down at the far end of the grain pile" (3:7). What happens next is simply scandalous; the verse continues, "Ruth approached quietly, uncovered his feet and lay down."

There is no possible reading of this passage that is "safe" or "nice." This is seduction pure and simple — and God holds it up for all women to follow when he not only gives Ruth her own book in the Bible but also names her in the genealogy. Yes, there are folks that'll try to tell you that it's perfectly common for a beautiful single woman "in that culture" to approach a single man (who's had too much to drink) in the middle of the night with no one else around (the far side of the grain pile) and tuck herself under the covers. They're the same folks who'll tell you that the Song of Solomon is nothing more than a "theological metaphor referring to Christ and his bride." Ask 'em what they do with passages like "Your stature is like that of the palm, and your breasts like clusters of fruit. I said 'I will climb the palm tree; I will take hold of its fruit' " (Song 7:7–8). That's a Bible study, right?

No, I do not think Ruth and Boaz had sex that night; I do not think anything inappropriate happened at all. But this is no fellowship potluck, either. I'm telling you that the church has really crippled women when it tells them that their beauty is vain and they are at their feminine best when they are "serving others." A woman is at her best when she is being a woman. Boaz needs a little help getting going and Ruth has some options. She can badger him: *All you do is work, work, work. Why won't you stand up and be a man?* She can whine about it: *Boaz, pleeease hurry up and marry me.* She can emasculate him: *I thought you were a real man; I guess I was wrong.* Or she can use all she is as a woman to get him to use all he's got as a man. She can arouse, inspire, energize . . . seduce him. Ask your man what he'd prefer.

IT IS A BATTLE

Will you fight for her? That's the question Jesus asked me many years ago, right before our tenth anniversary, right at the time I was wondering what had happened to the woman I married. *You're on the fence, John,* he said. *Get in or get out.* I knew what he was saying — stop being a nice guy and act like a warrior. Play the man. I brought flowers, took her to dinner, and began to move back toward her in my heart. But I knew there was more. That night, before we went to bed, I prayed for Stasi in a way I'd never prayed for her before. Out loud, before all the heavenly hosts, I stepped between her and the forces of darkness that had been coming against her. Honestly, I didn't really know what I was doing, only that I needed to take on the dragon. All hell broke loose. Everything we've learned about spiritual warfare began that night. And you know what happened? Stasi got free; the tower of her depression gave way as I began to truly fight for her.

And it's not just once, but again and again over time. That's where the myth really stumps us. Some men are willing to go in once, twice, even three times. But a warrior is in this for good. Oswald Chambers asks, "God spilt the life of his son that the world might be saved; are we prepared to spill out our lives?" Daniel is in the midst of a very hard, very unpromising battle for his wife. It's been years now without much progress and without much hope. Sitting in a restaurant the other night, tears in his eyes, this is what he said to me: "I'm not going anywhere. This is my place in the battle. This is the hill that I will die on." He has reached a point that we all must come to, sooner or later, when it's no longer about winning or losing. His wife may respond and she may not. That's really no longer the issue. The question is simply this: What kind of man do you want to be? Maximus? Wallace? Or Judah? A young pilot in the RAF wrote just before he went down in 1940, "The universe is so vast and so ageless that the life of one man can only be justified by the measure of his sacrifice."

As I write this chapter, Stasi and I have

just returned from a friend's wedding. It was the best nuptials either of us have ever been to; a wonderful, romantic, holy affair. The groom was young and strong and valiant; the bride was seductively beautiful. Which is what made it so excruciating for me. Oh to start over again, to do it all over the right way, marry as a young man knowing what I know now. I could have loved Stasi so much better; she could have loved me so much better as well. We've learned every lesson the hard way over our eighteen years. Any wisdom contained in these pages was paid for . . . dearly. On top of that Stasi and I were in a difficult place over the weekend; that was the campfire. Satan saw his opportunity and turned it into a bonfire *without even one word between us*. By the time we got to the reception, I didn't want to dance with her. I didn't even want to be in the same room. All the hurt and disappointment of the years — hers and mine — seemed to be the only thing that was ever true about our marriage.

It wasn't until later that I heard Stasi's side of the script, but here is how the two fit together. Stasi: *He's disappointed in me. No wonder why. Look at all these beautiful women. I feel fat and ugly.* Me: *I'm so tired of battling for our marriage. How I wish we could start over. It wouldn't be that hard, you know. There are other options. Look at all these beautiful women.* On and on it came, like a wave overwhelming the shore. Sitting at the table with a group of our friends, I felt I was going to suffocate; I had to get out of there, get some fresh air. Truth be told, when I left the reception I had no intention of going back. Either I'd wind up in a bar somewhere or back in our room watching TV. Thankfully, I found a small library off to the side of the reception hall; alone in that sanctuary I wrestled with all I was feeling for what seemed like an hour. (It was probably twenty minutes.) I grabbed a book but could not read; I tried to pray but did not want to. Finally, some words began to arise from my heart:

> *Jesus, come and rescue me. I know what's going on, I know this is assault. But right now it all feels so true. Jesus, deliver me. Get me out from under this waterfall. Speak to me, rescue my heart before I do something stupid. Deliver me, Lord.*

Slowly, almost imperceptibly, the wave began to lift. My thoughts and emotions quieted down to a more normal size. Clarity was returning. The campfire was just a campfire again. *Jesus, you know the pain and disappointment in my heart. What would you have me do?* (The bar was no longer an option, but I was still planning to just go straight to my room for the rest of the night.) *I want you to go back in there and ask your wife to dance.* I knew he was right; I knew that somewhere down deep inside that's what my true heart would want to do. But the desire still seemed so far away. I lingered for five more minutes, hoping he had another option for me. He remained silent, but the assault was over and the bonfire was only embers. Once more I knew the man I wanted to be.

I went back to the reception and asked Stasi to dance; for the next two hours we had one of the best evenings we've had in a long time. We nearly lost to the Evil One; instead, it will go down as a memory we'll share with our friends for a long, long time.

CLOSE

Stasi has given me a number of wonderful presents over the years, but last Christmas was unforgettable. We'd finished with the feeding frenzy the boys call unwrapping presents. Stasi slipped out of the room with the words, "Close your eyes . . . I have a surprise for you." After a good deal of rustling and whispers, she told me I could look. Before me was a long rectangular box on the family room floor. "Open it," she said. I removed the bow and lifted the lid. Inside was a full-size claymore, a Scottish broadsword exactly like the one used by William Wallace. I had been looking for one for several months, but Stasi did not know that. It was not on my Christmas list. She had done this out of the vision of her own heart, as a way of thanking me for fighting for her.

Here is what her note read:

Because you are a Braveheart, fighting for the hearts of so many people . . . and especially for mine. Thanks to you I know a freedom I never thought was possible. Merry Christmas.

Chapter Eleven

AN ADVENTURE
TO LIVE

Dark and cold we may be, but this
Is no winter now. The frozen misery
Of centuries breaks, cracks, begins to move;
The thunder is the thunder of the floes,
The thaw, the flood, the upstart Spring
Thank God our time is now when wrong
Comes up to face us everywhere,
Never to leave us till we take
The longest stride of soul men ever took.
> — CHRISTOPHER FRY

The place where God calls you is the place where
your deep gladness and the world's deep hunger
meet.
> — FREDERICK BUECHNER

There is a river that winds its way through southern Oregon, running down from the Cascades to the coast, which has also wound its way through my childhood, carving a path in the canyons of my memory. As a young boy I spent many summer days on the Rogue, fishing and swimming and picking blackberries; but mostly, fishing. I loved the name given to the river by French trappers; the river Scoundrel. It gave a mischievous benediction to my adventures there — I was a rogue on the Rogue. Those golden days of boyhood are some of my most cherished memories and so last summer I took Stasi and the boys there, to share with them a river and a season from my life. The lower part of the Rogue runs through some hot and dry country in the summer months, especially in late July, and we were looking forward to kayaking as an excuse to get really wet and find a little adventure of our own.

There is a rock that juts out over that river somewhere between Morrison's Lodge and the Foster Bar. The canyon narrows there and the Rogue deepens and pauses for a moment in its rush to the sea. High rock walls rise on either side, and on the north — the side only boaters can reach — is Jumping Rock. Cliff jumping is one of our family favorites, especially when it's hot and dry and the jump is high enough so that it takes your breath away as you plunge beneath the warmer water at the top, down to where it's dark and cold, so cold that it sends you gasping back for the surface and the sun. Jumping Rock is perched above the river at about the height of a two-story house plus some, tall enough that you can slowly count to five before you hit the water (it's barely a two count from the high dive at your local pool). There's a faculty built into the human brain that makes every cliff seem twice the height when you're looking down from the top and everything in you says, *Don't even think about it.*

So you don't think about it, you just hurl yourself off out into the middle of the canyon, and then you free-fall for what feels like enough time to recite the Gettysburg Address and all your senses are on maximum alert as you plunge into the cold water. When you come back up the crowd is cheering and something in you is also cheering because *you did it.* We all jumped that day, first me, then Stasi, Blaine, Sam, and even Luke. Then some big hulking guy who was going to back down once he saw what the view was like from above, but he had to jump because Luke did it and he couldn't live with himself knowing he'd cowered while a six-year-old boy hurled himself off. After that first jump you have to do it again, partly because you can't believe you did it and partly because the fear has given way to the thrill of such freedom. We let the sun heat us up again and then . . . bombs away.

I want to live my whole life like that. I want to love with much more abandon and stop waiting for others to love me first. I want to hurl myself into a creative work worthy of God. I want to charge the fields at Banockburn, follow Peter as he followed Christ out onto the sea, pray from my heart's true *desire*. As the poet George Chapman has said,

> Give me a spirit that on this life's
> rough sea
> Loves to have his sails fill'd with a
> lusty wind
> Even till his sail-yards tremble, his
> masts crack,
> And his rapt ship runs on her side so
> low
> That she drinks water, and her keel
> ploughs air.

Life is not a problem to be solved; it is an adventure to be lived. That's the nature of it and has been since the beginning when God set the dangerous stage for this high-stakes drama and called the whole wild enterprise *good*. He rigged the world in such a way that it only works when we embrace *risk* as the theme of our lives, which is to say, only when we live by faith. A man just won't be happy until he's got adventure in his work, in his love and in his spiritual life.

ASKING THE RIGHT QUESTION

Several years ago I was thumbing through the introduction of a book when I ran across a sentence that changed my life. God is intimately personal with us and he speaks in ways that are peculiar to our own quirky hearts — not just through the Bible, but through the whole of creation. To Stasi he speaks through movies. To Craig he speaks through rock and roll (he called me the other day after listening to "Running Through the Jungle" to say he was fired up to go study the Bible). God's word to me comes in many ways — through sunsets and friends and films and music and wilderness and books. But he's got an especially humorous thing going with me and books. I'll be browsing through a secondhand book shop when out of a thousand volumes one will say, "Pick me up" — just like Augustine in his *Confessions*. *Tolle legge* — take up and read. Like a master fly fisherman God cast his fly to this cruising trout. In the introduction to the book that I rose to this day, the author (Gil Bailie) shares a piece of advice given to him some years back by a spiritual mentor:

Don't ask yourself what the world needs. Ask yourself what makes you come alive, and go do that, because what the world needs is people who have come alive.

I was struck dumb. It could have been Balaam's donkey, for all I was concerned. Suddenly my life up till that point made sense in a sickening sort of way; I realized I was living a script written for me by someone else. All my life I had been asking the world to tell me what to do with myself. This is different from seeking counsel or advice; what I wanted was freedom from responsibility and especially freedom from risk. I wanted someone else to tell me who to be. Thank God it didn't work. The scripts they handed me I simply could not bring myself to play for very long. Like Saul's armor, they never fit. Can a world of posers tell you to do anything but pose yourself? As Buechner says, we are in constant danger of being not actors in the drama of our lives but reactors, "to go where the world takes us, to drift with whatever current happens to be running the strongest." Reading the counsel given to Bailie I knew it was God speaking to me. It was an invitation to come out of Ur. I set the volume down without turning another page and walked out of that bookstore to find a life worth living.

I applied to graduate school and got accepted. That program would turn out to be far more than a career move; out of the transformation that took place there I became a writer, counselor, and speaker. The whole trajectory of my life changed and with it the lives of many, many other people. But I almost didn't go. You see, when I applied to school I hadn't a nickel to pay for it. I was married with three children and a mortgage, and that's the season when most men completely abandon their dreams and back down from jumping off anything. The risk just seems too great. On top of it all, I received a call about that time from a firm back in Washington, D.C., offering me a plum job at an incredible salary. I would be in a prestigious company, flying in some very powerful circles, making great money. God was thickening the plot, testing my resolve. Down one road was my dream and desire, which I had no means to pay for, and an absolutely uncertain future after that; down the other was a comfortable step up the ladder of success, a very obvious next career move and the total loss of my soul.

I went to the mountains for the weekend to sort things out. Life makes more sense standing alone by a lake at high elevation with a fly rod in hand. The tentacles of the world and my false self seemed to give way as I climbed up into the Holy Cross Wilderness. On the second day God began to speak. *John, you can take that job if you want to. It's not a sin. But it'll kill you and you know it.* He was right; it had False Self written all over it. *If you want to follow Me,* he continued, *I'm heading that way.* I knew exactly what he meant — "that way" headed into wilderness, frontier. The following week three phone calls came in amazing succession. The first was from the Washington firm; I told them I was not their man, to call somebody else. As I hung up the phone my false self was screaming *what are you doing?!* The next day the phone rang again; it was my wife, telling me that the university had called wanting to know where my first tuition installment was. On the third day a call came from a longtime friend who had been praying for me and my decision. "We think you ought to go to school," he said. "And we want to pay your way."

> Two roads diverged in a wood and I,
> I took the one less traveled by.
> And that has made all the difference.

WHAT ARE YOU WAITING FOR?

Where would we be today if Abraham had carefully weighed the pros and cons of God's invitation and decided that he'd rather hang on to his medical benefits, three weeks paid vacation and retirement plan in Ur? What would have happened if Moses had listened to his mother's advice to "never play with matches" and lived a careful, cautious life steering clear of all burning bushes? You wouldn't have the gospel if Paul had concluded that the life of a Pharisee, while not everything a man dreams for, was at least predictable and certainly more stable than following a voice he heard on the Damascus road. After all, people hear voices all the time and who really knows whether it's God or just one's imagination. Where would we be if Jesus was not fierce and wild and romantic to the core? Come to think of it, we wouldn't *be* at all if God hadn't taken that enormous risk of us in the first place.

Most men spend the energy of their lives trying to eliminate risk, or squeezing it down to a more manageable size. Their children hear "no" far more than they hear "yes"; their employees feel chained up and their wives are equally bound. If it works, if a man succeeds in securing his life against all risk, he'll wind up in a cocoon of self-protection and wonder all the while why he's suffocating. If it doesn't work, he curses God, redoubles his efforts and his blood pressure. When you look at the structure of the false self men tend to create, it always revolves around two themes: seizing upon some sort of competence and rejecting anything that cannot be controlled. As David Whyte says, "The price of our vitality is the sum of all our fears."

For murdering his brother, God sentences Cain to the life of a restless wanderer; five verses later Cain is building a city (Gen. 4:12, 17). That sort of commitment — the refusal to trust God and the reach for control — runs deep in every man. Whyte talks about the difference between the false self's desire "to have power *over* experience, to control all events and consequences, and the soul's wish to have power *through* experience, *no matter what that may be*." You literally sacrifice your soul and your true power when you insist on controlling things, like the guy Jesus talked about who thought he finally pulled it all off, built himself some really nice barns and died the same night. "What will it profit a man if he gains the whole world, and loses his own soul?" (Mark 8:36 NKJV). You can lose your soul, by the way, long before you die.

Canadian biologist Farley Mowat had a dream of studying wolves in their native habitat, out in the wilds of Alaska. The book *Never Cry Wolf* is based on that lonely research expedition. In the film version Mowat's character is a bookworm named Tyler who has never so much as been camping. He hires a crazy old Alaskan bush pilot named Rosie Little to get him and all his equipment into the remote Blackstone Valley in the dead of winter. Flying in Little's single-engine Cessna over some of the most beautiful, rugged, and dangerous wilderness in the world, Little pries Tyler for the secret to his mission:

LITTLE: Tell me, Tyler . . . what's in the valley of the Blackstone? What is it? Manganese? (Silence) Can't be oil. Is it gold?

TYLER:	It's kind of hard to say.
LITTLE:	You're a smart man, Tyler . . . you keep your own counsel. We're all of us prospectors up here, right, Tyler? Scratchin' for that . . . that one crack in the ground . . . and never have to scratch again. (After a pause) I'll let you in on a little secret, Tyler. The gold's not in the ground. The gold is not anywhere up here. The real gold is south at 60, sittin' in living rooms, facing the boob tube bored to death. Bored to death, Tyler.

Suddenly the plane's engine coughs a few times, sputters, gasps . . . and then simply cuts out. The only sound is the wind over the wings.

LITTLE:	(Groans) Oh, Lord.
TYLER:	(Panicked) What's wrong?
LITTLE:	Take the stick.

Little hands over control of the powerless

plane to Tyler (who has never flown a plane in his life) and starts frantically rummaging around in an old toolbox between the seats. Unable to find what he's looking for, Little explodes. Screaming, he empties the toolbox all over the plane. Then just as abruptly he stops, calmly rubbing his face with his hands.

TYLER: (Still panicked and trying to fly the plane) What's wrong?

LITTLE: Boredom, Tyler. Boredom . . . that's what's wrong. How do you beat boredom, Tyler? Adventure. ADVENTURE, Tyler!

Little then kicks the door of the plane open and nearly disappears outside, banging on something — a frozen fuel line perhaps. The engine kicks back in just as they are about to fly into the side of a mountain. Little grabs the stick and pulls them into a steep ascent, barely missing the ridge and then easing off into a long, majestic valley below.

Rosie Little may be a madman, but he's also a genius. He knows the secret to a man's heart, the cure for what ails him. Too many men forsake their dreams because they aren't willing to risk, or fear they aren't up to the challenge, or are never told that those desires deep in their heart are *good*. But the soul of a man, the real gold Little refers to, isn't made for controlling things; he's made for adventure. Something in us remembers, however faintly, that when God set man on the earth he gave us an incredible mission — a charter to explore, build, conquer, and care for all creation. It was a blank page waiting to be written; a clean canvas waiting to be painted. Well, sir, God never revoked that charter. It's still there, waiting for a man to seize it.

If you had permission to do what you really want to do, what would you do? Don't ask *how*, that will cut your desire off at the knees. *How* is never the right question; *how* is a faithless question. It means "unless I can see my way clearly I won't believe it, won't venture forth." When the angel told Zechariah that his ancient wife would bear him a son named John, Zechariah asked how and was struck dumb for it. *How* is God's department. He is asking you *what*. What is written in your heart? What makes you come alive? If you could do what you've always wanted to do, what would it be? You see, a man's calling is written on his true heart, and he discovers it when he enters the frontier of his deep desires. To paraphrase Bailie, don't ask yourself what the world needs, ask yourself what makes you come alive because what the world needs are *men* who have come alive.

The invitation in the book shop, I must note, was given to me some years into my Christian life when the transformation of my character was at a point that I could hear it without running off and doing something stupid. I've met men who've used advice like it as permission to leave their wife and run off with their secretary. They are *deceived* about what it is they really want, what they are made for. There is a design God has woven into the fabric of this world, and if we violate it we cannot hope to find life. Because our hearts have strayed so far from home, he's given us the Law as a sort of handrail to help us back from the precipice. But the goal of Christian discipleship is the transformed heart; we move from a boy who needs the Law to the man who is able to live by the Spirit of the law. "My counsel is this: Live freely, animated and motivated by God's Spirit. Then you won't feed the compulsions of selfishness . . . Legalism is helpless in bringing this about; it only gets in the way" (Gal. 5:16, 23 *The Message*).

A man's life becomes an adventure, the whole thing takes on a transcendent purpose when he releases control in exchange for the recovery of the dreams in his heart. Sometimes those dreams are buried deep and it takes some unearthing to get to them. We pay attention to our desire. Often the clues are in our past, in those moments when we found ourselves loving what we were doing. The details and circumstances change as we grow, but the themes remain the same. Dale was the neighborhood ring leader as a boy; in college, he was captain of the tennis team. What makes him come alive is when he is leading men. For Charles it was art; he was always drawing as a child. In high school, what he loved best was ceramics class. He gave up painting after college and finally came alive again when at age fifty-one he got it back.

To recover his heart's desire a man needs to get away from the noise and distraction of his daily life for time with his own soul. He needs to head into the wilderness, to silence and solitude. Alone with himself, he allows whatever is there to come to the surface. Sometimes it is grief for so much lost time. There, beneath the grief, are desires long forsaken. Sometimes it even starts with temptation, when a man thinks that what will really make him come alive is something unholy. At that point he should ask himself, "What is the desire *beneath* this desire? What is it I'm wanting that I think I'll find there?" However the desire begins to surface, we pick up that trail when we allow a cry to rise from the depths of our soul, a cry, as Whyte says, "for a kind of forgotten courage, one difficult to hear, demanding not a raise, but another life."

> I have studied many times
> The marble which was chiseled for
>   me —
> A boat with a furled sail at rest in a
>   harbor.
> In truth it pictures not my destination
> But my life.
> For love was offered me, and I shrank
>   from its disillusionment;
> Sorrow knocked at my door, but I
>   was afraid
> Ambition called to me, but I dreaded
>   the chances.
> Yet all the while I hungered for
>   meaning in my life
> And now I know that we must lift the
>   sail
> And catch the winds of destiny
> Wherever they drive the boat.

To put meaning in one's life may end
   in madness,
But life without meaning is the tor-
   ture
Of restlessness and vague desire —
   It is a boat longing for the sea and
   yet afraid.

(EDGAR LEE MASTERS)

INTO THE UNKNOWN

"The spiritual life cannot be made sub-urban," said Howard Macey. "It is always frontier and we who live in it must accept and even rejoice that it remains untamed." The greatest obstacle to realizing our dreams is the false self's hatred of mystery. That's a problem, you see, because *mystery is essential to adventure*. More than that, mystery is the heart of the universe and the God who made it. The most important aspects of any man's world — his relationship with his God and with the people in his life, his calling, the spiritual battles he'll face — every one of them is fraught with mystery. But that is not a bad thing; it is a joyful, rich part of reality and essential to our soul's thirst for adven-ture. As Oswald Chambers says,

Naturally, we are inclined to be so mathematical and calculating that we look upon uncertainty as a bad thing . . . Certainty is the mark of the common-sense life; gracious uncertainty is the mark of the spiritual life. To be certain of God means that we are uncertain in all our ways, we do not know what a day may bring forth. This is generally said with a sigh of sadness; it should rather be an expression of breathless expectation. (*My Utmost for His Highest*)

There are no formulas with God. Period. So there are no formulas for the man who follows him. God is a Person, not a doctrine. He operates not like a system — not even a theological system — but with all the originality of a truly free and alive person. "The realm of God is dangerous," says Archbishop Anthony Bloom. "You must enter into it and not just seek information about it. Take Joshua and the Battle of Jericho. The Israelites are staged to make their first military strike into the promised land and there's a lot hanging on this moment — the morale of the troops, their confidence in Joshua, not to mention their reputation that will precede them to every other enemy that awaits. This is their D-Day, so to speak, and word is going to get around. How does God get the whole thing off to a good start? He has them march around the city blowing trumpets for a week; on the seventh day he has them do it seven times and then give a big holler. It works marvelously, of course. And you know what? It never happens again. Israel never uses that tactic again.

There's Gideon and his army reduced from thirty-two thousand to three-hundred. What's their plan of attack? Torches and water pots. It also works splendidly and it also never happens again. You recall Jesus healing the blind — he never does it the same way twice. I hope you're getting the idea because the church has really been taken in by the world on this one. The Modern Era hated mystery; we desperately wanted a means of controlling our own lives and we seemed to find the ultimate Tower of Babel in the scientific method. Don't get me wrong — science has given us many wonderful advances in sanitation, medicine, transportation. But we've tried to use those methods to tame the wildness of the spiritual frontier. We take the latest marketing methods, the newest business management fad, and we apply it to ministry. The problem with modern Christianity's obsession with principles is that it removes any real conversation with God. Find the principle, apply the principle — what do you need God for? So Oswald Chambers warns us, "Never make a principle out of your experience; let God be as original with other people as he is with you.

Originality and creativity are essential to personhood and to masculine strength. The adventure begins and our *real* strength is released when we no longer rely on formulas. God is an immensely creative Person and he wants his sons to live that way too. There is a great picture of this in *Raiders of the Lost Ark*, of all places. Of course Indiana Jones is a swashbuckling hero who can handle ancient history, beautiful women, and a forty-five with ease. But the real test of the man comes when all his resources have failed. He's finally found the famous ark, but the Germans have stolen it from him and loaded it onto a truck. They're about to drive off with his dreams under heavy Nazi military protection. Jones and his two companions are watching helplessly as victory slips through their fingers. But Indiana is not finished; oh no, the game has just begun. He says to his friends:

JONES: Get back to Cairo. Get us
     some transport to England

	. . . boat, plane, anything. Meet me at Omars. Be ready for me. I'm going after that truck.
SAULACH:	How?
JONES:	I don't know I'm making this up as I go.

When it comes to living and loving, what's required is a willingness to jump in with both feet and be creative as you go. Here's but one example: A few years ago I got home from a trip on a Sunday afternoon and found the boys playing out on the front yard. It was a cold November day, too cold to be outside, and so I asked them what was up. "Mom kicked us out." Knowing there's often good reason when Stasi banishes them I pressed for a confession, but they maintained their innocence. So, I headed for the door to get the other side of the story. "I wouldn't go in there if I were you, Dad," Sam warned. "She's in a bad mood." I knew exactly what he was describing. The house was shut; inside all was dark and quiet.

Now, let me ask the men reading this: What was everything inside me telling me to do? *Run away. Don't even think about going in. Stay outside.* And you know what? I could have stayed outside and looked like a great dad, playing catch with my sons. But I am tired of being that man; I have run for years. Too many times I've played the coward and I'm sick of it. I opened the door, went inside, climbed the stairs, walked into our bedroom, sat down on the bed and asked my wife the most terrifying question any man ever asks his woman: "What's wrong?" After that it's all mystery. A woman doesn't want to be related to with formulas, and she certainly doesn't want to be treated like a project that has answers to it. She doesn't want to be solved; she wants to be *known*. Mason is absolutely right when he calls marriage the "Wild Frontier."

The same holds true for the spiritual battles that we face. After the Allies landed in France, they encountered something no one had planned or prepared them for: hedgerows. Enclosing every field from the sea to Verdun was a wall of earth, shrubs, and trees. Aerial photographs revealed the existence of the hedgerows, but the Allies assumed they were like the ones found across England, which are two feet high. The Norman hedgerows were ten feet high and impenetrable, a veritable fortress. If the Allies used the solitary gateways into each field, they were mowed down by German machine gunners. If they tried to drive their tanks up and over, the underbelly was exposed to antitank weapons. They had to improvise. American farmboys rigged all sorts of contraptions on the front of the Sherman tanks, which allowed them to punch holes for explosives or break right through the hedgerows. Grease monkeys from the states rebuilt damaged tanks over night. As one captain said,

> I began to realize something about the American Army I had never thought possible before. Although it is highly regimented and bureaucratic under garrison conditions, when the Army gets in the field, it relaxes and the individual initiative comes forward and does what has to be done. This type of flexibility was one of the great strengths of the American Army in World War II. (*Citizen Soldiers*)

It was truly Yankee ingenuity that won the war. This is where we are now — in the midst of battle without the training we really need, and there are few men around to show us how to do it. We are going to have to figure a lot of this out for ourselves. We know how to attend church; we've been taught not to swear or drink or smoke. We know how to be nice. But we don't really know how to fight, and we're going to have to learn as we go. That is where our strength will be crystallized, deepened, and *revealed.* A man is never more a man than when he embraces an adventure beyond his control, or when he walks into a battle he isn't sure of winning. As Antonio Machado wrote,

> Mankind owns four things
> That are no good at sea —
> Rudder, anchor, oars,
> And the fear of going down.

FROM FORMULA TO RELATIONSHIP

I'm not suggesting that the Christian life is chaotic or that a real man is flagrantly irresponsible. The poser who squanders his paycheck at the racetrack or the slot machines is not a man; he's a fool. The sluggard who quits his job and makes his wife go to work so he can stay home to practice his golf swing, thinking he'll make the pro tour, is "worse than an unbeliever" (1 Tim. 5:8). What I *am* saying is that our false self demands a formula before he'll engage; he wants a guarantee of success, and mister, you aren't going to get one. So there comes a time in a man's life when he's got to break away from all that and head off into the unknown with God. This is a vital part of our journey and if we balk here, the journey ends.

Before the moment of Adam's greatest trial God provided no step-by-step plan, gave no formula for how he was to handle the whole mess. That was not abandonment; that was the way God *honored* Adam. *You are a man, you don't need Me to hold you by the hand through this. You have what it takes.* What God *did* offer Adam was friendship. He wasn't left alone to face life; he walked with God in the cool of the day and there they talked about love and marriage and creativity, what lessons he was learning and what adventures were to come. This is what God is offering to us as well. As Chambers says,

> There comes the baffling call of God in our lives also. The call of God can never be stated explicitly; it is implicit. The call of God is like the call of the sea, no one hears it but the one who has the nature of the sea in him. It cannot be stated definitely what the call of God is to, *because his call is to be in comradeship with himself* for his own purposes, and the test is to believe that God knows what he is after.

(*My Utmost for His Highest*, emphasis added)

The only way to live in this adventure — with all its danger and unpredictability and immensely high stakes — is in an ongoing, intimate relationship with God. The control we so desperately crave is an illusion. Far better to give it up in exchange for God's offer of companionship, set aside stale formulas so that we might enter into an informal friendship. Abraham knew this; Moses did as well. Read through the first several chapters of Exodus — it's filled with a give-and-take between Moses and God. "Then the Lord said to Moses," "then Moses said to the Lord." The two act like they know each other, like they really are intimate allies. David — a man after God's own heart — also walked and warred and loved his way through life in a conversational intimacy with God.

When the Philistines heard that David had been anointed king over Israel, they went up in full force to search for him, but David heard about it and went down to the stronghold. Now the Philistines had come and spread out in the Valley of Rephaim; so David inquired of the

LORD, "Shall I go and attack the Philistines? Will you hand them over to me?" The LORD answered him, "Go, for I will surely hand the Philistines over to you." So David went to Baal Perazim, and there he defeated them . . . Once more the Philistines came up and spread out in the Valley of Rephaim; so David inquired of the LORD, and he answered, "Do not go straight up, but circle around behind them and attack them in front of the balsam trees. As soon as you hear the sound of marching in the tops of the balsam trees, move quickly, because that will mean the LORD has gone out in front of you to strike the Philistine army." So David did as the LORD commanded him, and he struck down the Philistines all the way from Gibeon to Gezer. (2 Sam. 5:17–20, 22–25)

Here again there is no rigid formula for David; it changes as he goes, relying on the counsel of God. This is the way every comrade and close companion of God lives. Jesus said, "I no longer call you servants, because a servant does not know his master's business. Instead, I have called you friends, for everything that I learned from my father I have made known to you" (John

15:15). God calls you his friend. He wants to talk to you — personally, frequently. As Dallas Willard writes, "The ideal for divine guidance is . . . a conversational relationship with God: the sort of relationship suited to friends who are mature personalities in a shared enterprise." Our whole journey into authentic masculinity centers around those cool-of-the-day talks with God. Simple questions change hassles to adventures; the events of our lives become opportunities for initiation. "What are you teaching me here, God? What are you asking me to do . . . or to let go of? What in my heart are you speaking to?"

FURTHER UP AND FURTHER IN

For years now I have wanted to climb one of the great peaks — Denali, perhaps, and after that maybe even Everest. Something calls to my heart every time I see a photo or read an account of another attempt. The allure of the wild places we have left haunts me, but there's also the desire for a challenge that requires everything I've got. Yes, even danger; maybe especially danger. Some people think I'm crazy, and I know that this dream may never be realized in my lifetime, but that does not discourage me; there is something symbolic about the desire and I cannot let it go. This is quite crucial for us to understand. We have desires in our hearts that are core to who and what we are; they are almost mythic in their meaning, waking in us something transcendent and eternal. But we can be mistaken about how those desires will be lived out. The way in which God fulfills a desire may be different from what first awakened it.

In the past year or so I've made a number of decisions that make no sense unless there is a God and I am his friend. I left my corporate job and struck out on my own, following a dream I've long feared. I've picked up the shattered pieces of a vision I lost when my best friend and partner Brent was killed in a climbing accident. What feels most crazy of all, I've opened my self to friendship again and a new partner, and we're heading out where Brent and I left off. The battle has been intense; a steep ascent that's taking everything I've got. The stakes I'm playing at now are immense — financially, sure, but more so spiritually, relationally. It's requiring a concentration of body, soul, and spirit I've never before endured.

What is perhaps the hardest part is the misunderstanding I live with from others on a daily basis. Sometimes the winds howl around me; other times I fear I'll fall. The other day I was feeling way out on the end of my rope, cutting a path across a sheer face of risk. Out of my heart rose a question. *What are we doing, God?*

We're climbing Everest.

Chapter Twelve

WRITING THE NEXT CHAPTER

I am sometimes almost terrified at the scope of the demands made upon me, at the perfection of the self-abandonment required of me; yet outside of such absoluteness can be no salvation.
— GEORGE MACDONALD

Freedom is useless if we don't exercise it as characters making choices . . . We are free to change the stories by which we live. Because we are genuine characters, and not mere puppets, we can choose our defining stories. We can do so because we actively participate in the creation of our stories. We are co-authors as well as characters. Few things are as encouraging as the realization that things can be different and that we have a role in making them so.
— DANIEL TAYLOR

Obey God in the thing he shows you, and in-

stantly the next thing is opened up. God will never reveal more truth about himself until you have obeyed what you know already . . . This chapter brings out the delight of real friendship with God.

— OSWALD CHAMBERS

At once they left their nets and followed him.
— MATTHEW 4:20

Now, reader, it is your turn to write — venture forth with God. Remember, don't ask yourself what the world needs . . .

ABOUT THE AUTHOR

John Eldredge is an author, counselor, and lecturer. For twelve years he was a writer and speaker for Focus on the Family, most recently serving on the faculty of the Focus on the Family Institute. Now John is director of Ransomed Heart™ Ministries, a teaching, counseling, and discipling fellowship devoted to helping people recover and live from their deep heart. John lives in Colorado Springs with his wife, Stasi, and their three sons. He loves living in Colorado so he can pursue his other passions, including fly fishing, mountain climbing, and exploring the waters of the West in his canoe.

To learn more about John's seminars, audio tapes, and other resources for the heart, visit his Web site at: www.ransomedheart.com or write to:

Ransomed Heart™ Ministries
P.O. Box 51065
Colorado Springs, CO 80949-1065

Or

www.sacredromance .com